BERTOLT BRECHT
COLLECTED PLAYS

Volume 6

BERTOLT

Bertolt Brecht: Plays, Poetry, & Prose

Edited by

Ralph Manheim and John Willett

Wolfgang Sauerlander, Associate Editor

BRECHT

COLLECTED PLAYS

VOLUME 6

The Good Person of Szechwan

Puntila and Matti, His Hired Man

The Resistible Rise of Arturo Ui

Dansen

How Much Is Your Iron?

Practice Pieces for Actors

VINTAGE BOOKS, *A Division of Random House, New York*

VINTAGE BOOKS EDITION, February 1976
First Edition

Copyright © 1976 by Stefan S. Brecht

Library of Congress Cataloging in Publication Data

Brecht, Bertolt, 1898–1956.   Collected plays.

   (His Plays, poetry, & prose)
Translations from the German.
CONTENTS: v. 1. Baal. Drums in the night. In the jungle of cities. The life
of Edward II of England. The wedding. The beggar, or the dead dog.
He drives out a devil. Lux in tenebris. The catch. [etc.]

I. Manheim, Ralph, ed.   II. Willett, John, ed.
PT2603.R397A29   1971   832'.9'12   71–113718
ISBN 0-394-71670-1 (v. 1)
     0-394-71350-8 (v. 6)

Manufactured in the United States of America

ACKNOWLEDGMENTS

Copyright in the original plays as follows:

The Good Person of Szechwan: The first publication of the original work was in 1948 in an English version by Eric and Maja Bentley. Copyright © 1947 by Eric Bentley and Maja Bentley; renewed in 1975 by Stefan S. Brecht. The first publication in German entitled *Der gute Mensch von Sezuan*. Copyright © 1953 by Suhrkamp Verlag.

Puntila and Matti, His Hired Man: The original work in German entitled *Herr Puntila und sein Knecht Matti* by Bertolt Brecht. Copyright © 1950 by Suhrkamp Verlag vorm. S. Fischer.

The Resistible Rise of Arturo Ui: The original work in German entitled *Der aufhaltsame Aufstieg des Arturo Ui* by Bertolt Brecht. Copyright © 1957 by Suhrkamp Verlag.

Dansen: The original work in German entitled *Dansen* by Bertolt Brecht. Copyright © 1966 by Stefan S. Brecht.

How Much Is Your Iron?: The original work in German entitled *Was kostet das Eisen* by Bertolt Brecht. Copyright © 1966 by Stefan S. Brecht.

Practice Pieces for Actors: The original work in German entitled *Anhang Übungsstücke für Schauspieler* by Bertolt Brecht. Copyright © 1951 by Suhrkamp Verlag Berlin.

These works were translated from *Gesammelte Werke* (Werkausgabe Edition Suhrkamp), a collection of the above works with new material and revisions. Copyright © 1967 by Suhrkamp Verlag.

Contents

Introduction

The Finnish Plays 1940–41

1

When Brecht arrived in Finland on April 17, 1940, those "dark times" which had set in for him in the late 1930s were just about at their blackest. Eight days earlier Hitler's troops had moved into Denmark and begun the invasion of Norway. Some three weeks later the main Blitzkrieg in the West began; by mid-summer France was defeated, Italy had come into the war and all armed resistance to the Nazis on the European mainland had come to a stop. Finland itself, crowded with refugees from the highly disillusioning Soviet-Finnish war of the previous winter and beset by shortages of all kinds, was in an uneasy state of peace which started with the Treaty of Moscow just over a month earlier and was to last until the German invasion of Russia in June 1941. By good luck or good management this just—and only just—covered the period of Brecht's stay in the country.

The family did not bring much with them, having left books, furniture and many of Brecht's typescripts behind them in Sweden, though they reckoned that it would be too dangerous to remain there themselves. Finland they expected to be a mere staging-post on the journey to the United States, where Erwin Piscator had arranged for Brecht to be invited to teach at his newly formed Dramatic Workshop in the New School for Social Research. The invitation was sent off in April, together with the news that Brecht had been put on the quota of permitted immigrants; early in May, accordingly, Helene

Weigel booked their passages on a ship sailing from the northern Finnish port of Petsamo on August 5: the "little door" of his poem "1940." Two reasons were to block this plan: first the taking-over of Petsamo by the Germans after the end of their Norwegian campaign, and secondly (perhaps more vitally for Brecht) the problem of an American visa for Margarete Steffin, the principal collaborator of Brecht's Scandinavian years, whose inclusion with his own family he regarded as personally and professionally essential. So they settled down to wait, at first in a hotel near Helsinki station, then for the next two months in a small apartment in the suburb of Töölö. They had never been quite so isolated before.

Before getting to America Brecht wanted to complete his three major unfinished projects: the Julius Caesar novel, the *Messingkauf Dialogues* and *The Good Person of Szechwan*. At the same time he was still concerned with *Mother Courage,* even though the actual writing had been finished the previous November; he hoped to see it performed, if not in Stockholm then perhaps in Helsinki. The novel seems simply to have lapsed; after completing rather more than half of it before leaving Sweden he spoke of finishing it off but in the end never attempted to do so. The *Messingkauf* preoccupied him rather more, and he did write the four appendices to it, as well as repeatedly returning to its themes in his journal; none the less the dialogues themselves now struck him as dated. But he and Margarete Steffin got down quite soon to concentrated work on *The Good Person of Szechwan*, so that by June 20 this play that had taken him so long had been "in the main" finished. Its long history is outlined in our notes, but the key to Brecht's problems with it lies probably in his feeling that he must write something more uncompromisingly epic after the "opportunism" of *Galileo*, and that "no concessions need be made" when writing for the desk drawer, i.e., with so little hope of performance.

His first systematic attack on this play, launched in the spring of 1939 but mainly carried out that summer, had run into the sand around the time of the German invasion of Poland which opened the Second World War. It thus overlapped the writing of the two rather trivial one-act plays which are also included in this volume, and preceded the group of practice scenes which he wrote in the winter of 1939–40 for the Stockholm acting school directed by Naima Wifstrand where Helene Weigel was then teaching. Here, and even more so in Helsinki, the dark winters were bad for work, and for much of the early part of 1940 Brecht suffered from influenza, so that the Szechwan play was left on one side. As the notes will show, it was conceived from an early stage as a "parable" play—the first play for which Brecht used this term—and may well have been intended as a vehicle for Helene Weigel, to whom he dedicated it. (Later all such dedications were to disappear from his works.) In Finland the main spell of writing seems to have carried on smoothly enough from where he had left off the previous September, without leading to any major changes in the scheme as then outlined in his "Press Report" (pp. 362–65). Up to about August, therefore, there were no Shen Teh and Shui Ta, but the much less euphonious Li Gung and Lao Go, while the whole musical, poetical element was only to be introduced later, when he and Margarete Steffin gave the play its final overhaul after her serious illness (she was tubercular) of the following winter.

Not long after Brecht's arrival in Helsinki he was introduced by an Anglo-Finnish friend, Mary Pekkala, to the fifty-four-year-old author Hella Wuolijoki. This remarkable woman, whose friendship was to be crucial for his whole Finnish experience, was an Esthonian by birth who had briefly been married to a Finnish social-democratic politician early in the century, had then made a great deal of money in timber at the end of the First World War and bought the 1,200-acre Marlebäck estate in the province of Tavasthus north of Helsinki, which she was farming. A former chairman of Suomen Nafta, her sympathies were none the less Communist, and at the beginning of July she lent the Brechts a house on the estate and for the next three months saw a great deal of them. The result was a quite radical transformation in Brecht's work. To begin with, inspired in part by August Oehler's edition of the Greek epigrams, which his son gave him to read, his poetry became much more condensed, with a new emphasis on concrete objects; the results can be seen in the so-called "Steffin Collection" which he put together that winter at the time of his friend's illness. At the same time his view of his earlier writings was altering; he could now look back at his first book of poems *Die Hauspostille* and judge its peculiar blend of anarchic desperation and real force; he could reconsider the *Messingkauf* in terms that foreshadow the *Short Organum* of eight years later, yet find that to read it was "like having a cloud of dust blown into my face." Three factors were at work together here: the desperate situation consequent on the fall of France, leaving a class-ridden England wide open to invasion; the stories which Hella Wuolijoki often told about Finnish peasant life; and above all the pervasive beauty of the surroundings and the Finnish summer climate, which give Brecht's writings at this precarious juncture a quality of simple natural enjoyment that they had scarcely had since he left Augsburg in the early 1920s, but from now on never quite lost.

"It is understandable that these people should love their landscape . . ." he noted a few days after arriving at Marlebäck:

> its waters teeming with fish, its forests with their fine trees and their scents of birches and berries. the huge summers, bursting in overnight after endless winters, an intense heat following the intense cold. and just as daytime disappears in winter, so does nighttime in summer. then the air is so strong and tastes so good as almost to sate one. and the music that fills this clear sky! there is nearly always a wind, and thanks to the great variety of plants which it strikes—grasses, wheat, undergrowth, and forests—a gentle harmony arises, now getting louder now dying away, which one hardly notices but which is always there.

And again, at the end of July:

> marvellous, the stories wuolijoki tells, about the people on the estate, in the forests where she used to own big sawmills, in the heroic period. she looks wise and lovely as she tells of the tricks of simple people and the stupidity of the upper crust, shaking with perpetual laughter, and now and again looking at you through cunningly screwed-up eyes as she accompanies the various personages' remarks by epic, fluid movements of her lovely fat hands as though beating time

to some music nobody else can hear. (loose-wristed, she beats a horizontal figure of eight).

Brecht and Margarete Steffin had a plan to transcribe these stories and make a collection of them, but, as the latter noted after a few frustrating attempts,

> If one takes down HW's stories in shorthand and then sees them in black and white it is remarkable how they lose their sparkle. Much of their charm is due to the repetitions and the lively play of her features, also to the beautiful way in which her gestures accompany them. When written down they probably need to be reduced to a tenth of their length.

These were to a great extent the raw materials which now went into *Puntila*, the only true comedy ever written by Brecht, and a work which must have come as an entirely unexpected bonus from his Finnish stay.

By July 30 he was feeling "totally incapable of working at a play." *Szechwan* still needed the final touches, and till he had given them he felt that he could not go back to the Caesar novel. Though so far Hella Wuolijoki had evidently not tried to draw Brecht into her own work, during August she talked to him about her plan for a play about Snellman, one of the founders of Finnish nationalism, and this led him to realize that however they might agree about people and politics her ideas of the stage were a long way behind his. The previous year the Finnish Dramatists' League, with ministerial backing, had announced a competition for a "popular play" to be submitted by the end of the coming October. Wuolijoki had already begun work on a play on the Puntila theme, which she had used some years earlier for an unsuccessful film treatment (as described in our notes). Now she showed it to Brecht and suggested that they should collaborate on a script for the competition. From that point, starting in earnest on August 27, Brecht took over, larding the dialogue, however, with some of the stories which Margarete Steffin had been trying to transcribe (whence the prefatory note on pp. 403–04) and imbuing it with the atmosphere of Marlebäck and its region as he himself saw them. The big house of the estate, painted white and built in the early nineteenth century "with two rows of eight big windows apiece" and a huge stone cowshed nearby; the bath-hut or sauna down by the river; even the pleasure felt when relieving oneself out of doors at three o'clock in the morning: all these things, vividly described by Brecht in his journal, were now absorbed into the play. The result, only three weeks later, was "a fat little calf of a play. it contains more landscape than any other of my plays except perhaps BAAL." Hella Wuolijoki, who now saw the result for the first time, was clearly taken aback by the flatness of the epic technique and perhaps not wholly in accord with the picture given of her homeland, which she could have wished jollier. None the less, closer study made her a good deal more enthusiastic about it, so that she went on to make the Finnish version. This was duly sent in and, not surprisingly, won no kind of a prize.

It must have been the master-man relationship in *Puntila*, with the master as the Sancho Panza of the two, that prompted Brecht just at this time to turn to Diderot's somewhat Sterne-like novel *Jacques le Fataliste*, whose ironical dialogue form helped to inspire his next work. This was the *Flüchtlingsgespräche*, or *Dialogues between Exiles*, in which a physicist called Ziffel, a slightly unworldly Marxist who is partly a self-portrait, holds desultory, sardonic conversations in the Helsinki station restaurant with the free-thinking worker Kalle about a wide cross-section of German, anti-Nazi, and general European problems of the time. His tone of voice was carried straight over from the play, particularly from Matti's part, and beyond that is traceable, as Brecht himself recognized, to Hašek's *Schweik*, a book that was among the most influential of all his models. It is characteristic, however, of Brecht's concern with proper names (Elisabeth Hauptmann once called him a "name fetishist") that he should have transferred Matti's original name of Kalle to the very similar working-class skeptic in the new work. In effect this Schweikian Kalle now stepped across from the play into what Brecht termed "the old Ziffel plan," conceived originally as the memoirs of a single man with interspersed short stories. He began work on the new dialogues very soon after giving *Puntila* to Hella Wuolijoki to read, though he first spent a week or two trying to make an adaptation of Yamamoto Yuzo's Japanese play *Chink Okichi*, whose rights she had secured. This he sketched out in ten or eleven scenes under the new title *Die Judith von Shimoda*, but thereafter apparently abandoned.

By now the Brechts' hostess had decided to sell Marlebäck in view of the increasing difficulties of running the estate, and on October 7 they moved back to another small apartment in Helsinki. Here the bulk of the work on the *Flüchtlingsgespräche* appears to have been done (it was not intended for the stage, and will therefore be included among Brecht's prose). At the beginning of December *Mother Courage*, on whose songs he had meantime been working with the composer Simon Parmet, was under consideration by the Helsinki Swedish Theater, but nothing materialized, apparently because of the growing Nazi presence in Finland, while his plans received another setback when a further visa application for Margarete Steffin, this time to Mexico, was refused just as she fell ill. He was then toying with the idea of a play for children based on the life of Confucius, a highly formalized work (to judge from the one completed scene) somewhat reminiscent of the *Lehrstücke*, which they started working on early in the new year. This was interrupted (and perhaps finally torpedoed) by the revision of *The Good Person of Szechwan*, which at last took place towards the end of January. The visa situation was still extremely unclear, since even apart from the Steffin problem the family's U.S. visas had not yet arrived, while their Mexican visas needed to be used soon if they were to be sure of them. None the less, once this long-drawn-out play could be retyped and sent out (inter alia to Kurt Weill in New York), Brecht's mind seems once again to have turned to America. He read Mordecai Gorelik's new book *New Theatres for Old*, which he had in some measure helped to inspire, together with some of the American criticisms of it. And "reflecting on the american theater," he noted on March 10,

i was again struck by the idea i once had in new york, of writing a gangster play that would recall certain events familiar to us all. (the gangster play we know.)

—this last phrase being in English, a language in which he would increasingly have to think.

The Resistible Rise of Arturo Ui, as this project became, was as quickly written as *Puntila* and underwent far fewer changes. Within three weeks it was effectively there, apparently without any of the elaborate plans and preparations common to Brecht's stage works; it was as if, at this critical point both in history and in his own fortunes, he was suddenly writing for fun. This was to be the last of those works which he wrote about his old mythical America (starting with the "cold Chicago" of *In the Jungle of Cities*), and into it he poured his and his family's extensive knowledge of gangster movies and lore, together with his accumulated mockery of the Nazis who threatened his life, and a spontaneous sense of parody which he turned against the elevated style of the Elizabethan drama in general, against Richard III's courtship scene, and against the quite unrelated garden scene from *Faust I* (which can be found echoed respectively in scenes 13 and 12 of the new play). From the formal point of view too, it was interesting as an attempt to add speed to the generally lethargic epic structure; there is no reason, he noted, why epic works should not condense time just as well as enlarge it. Far more than *The Good Person of Szechwan* it was written with performance in mind, and that, to Brecht, was part of the enjoyment of writing it. Thereafter, he noted in the middle of April, he felt like writing "something totally unperformable": *Ui part II*, "Spain/Munich/Poland/France."

Of course he did not write this. Nor did he follow up his other new ideas: for a Cassandra play and for another morality in the line of *The Good Person*, to be called *The Weakness of the Flesh*. He began to catch himself evading difficult questions, putting them off until he should have reached the United States; at the same time the indifference surrounding him suggested that "with every announcement of a Hitler victory I lose significance as a writer"; more practically, perhaps,

> my two means of production, cigars and (english) detective stories are running short and will have to be rationed.

None the less his luck was turning. First he heard from Zurich on April 22 that the première of *Mother Courage* there had been a great success; then on May 2 the U.S. visas for the family at last came through (according to Helene Weigel, the consul in Helsinki had insisted on a certificate of good standing from the German authorities, which some unknown official in Berlin had miraculously sent); finally on the 12th Margarete Steffin had been allowed a tourist visa to visit the U.S. That same night Hella Wuolijoki and other Finnish friends gave them a farewell dinner in a Helsinki restaurant, and the following day they left for Leningrad and the long trip via Siberia to the American West Coast. One of Brecht's last acts before going was to make a contract with his hostess by which her version of *Puntila*, which named them as co-authors, could be licensed by her (and if necessary altered) for performance in the Scandinavian countries. Brecht in turn could dispose of it anywhere else.

2

Still expecting to go to work with Piscator at the New School, Brecht had already sent his friend the script of *Galileo* and tried to interest him in *Fear and Misery of the Third Reich*. A month before leaving Helsinki he wrote that

> i was incredibly isolated here, and under such conditions it is infinitely difficult to do literary work—all the same i managed to complete one or two things which i hope to be able to bring you in person.

Though in the event he decided not to go on to New York, once his ship had landed in San Pedro that July, but to settle in California instead, it was still Piscator first and foremost who he hoped would put on performances of the "one or two things." Oddly enough they seem to have excluded *Puntila*, which Brecht to all outward appearances quite forgot about during his six years in the United States. But he gave Piscator

both *Arturo Ui* and *The Good Person of Szechwan,* and the
director did indeed set loyally to work to do what he could
with them. Though Brecht told him that the former would in
his view be the "easier to perform," it seems to have been the
latter which interested him the more, and he recommended it
to the Theater Guild for eventual New York production. His
enthusiasm was somewhat damped, however, when he heard
that Brecht had been showing the play to Elisabeth Bergner
in Los Angeles, and the project seems to have stopped there.
Later, in June 1942, Brecht's friend Alexander Granach tried
to interest Anna May Wong, the Hollywood Chinese actress
who had played Klabund's *Chalk Circle* in London, and there
was again talk of a possible production on Broadway. Not long
afterwards, the Zurich Schauspielhaus accepted it, and it was
there that the eventual première took place on February 4,
1943.

In the late summer of 1941, while Piscator's Theater Guild
project was still a possibility, he also came near to setting up
a production of *Arturo Ui.* According to H. R. Hays, Piscator
and Hanns Eisler came out together to see him, with a great
air of urgency, and pressed him to make an immediate translation of the play for a production that was to be financed by
the trade unions. By September 23 Hays had done this, as
yet seemingly without contract or payment. Brecht, who had
been asking Piscator whether he should try to interest Oscar
Homolka (in Hollywood) in playing the lead, now failed to
tie up the arrangements with Hays or even to maintain touch
with Piscator; for reasons outlined in volume 7 (prime among
them being Margarete Steffin's death on the journey through
Russia) he was at that time in a state of considerable disorienta-
tion. In any case the production fell through. Meanwhile, however, Kurt Weill had been fascinated by the script of *The
Good Person of Szechwan,* and when Brecht eventually came
to New York in February 1943 (having left California four days
after the Zurich première) Weill told him that he too, after
his first great Broadway success with *Lady in the Dark,* would
like to arrange a Broadway production of the Brecht work.
The immediate result was the revised and in many ways quite
radically changed version of the play, which Brecht sketched

out before leaving for Santa Monica and intensive work on their joint *Schweyk* project. The full script, which exists only in one copy and has never been performed or published, must have been written there later the same summer, probably in collaboration with Ruth Berlau, who is named by Brecht as working with him on this play but seems to have been little involved with the original Finnish version.

This new version of the play is discussed, for the first time, in our detailed notes. Probably it was the one which Brecht gave Christopher Isherwood to read that September in the hope that he might agree to make the translation; the result being only "a few polite compliments." It does not, however, seem to have been quite the script that Weill wanted, since the agreement which the two men drew up that winter provided for a "semi-opera," a term which the composer was in the habit of using for his *Der Silbersee* of 1933 (a work with musical "numbers" like *The Threepenny Opera*, but of a less jazzy kind). Brecht wrote to Weill that he had no wish to be "a mere librettist," and appears to have delayed the actual signing of the agreement; none the less he agreed that Weill should nominate an American "lyric" writer, and told him that

> our renewed collaboration, which has been great fun for me, leads me to think that we are not going to differ about anything all that widely.

According to David Drew, the lyric writer Weill had in mind was Langston Hughes, with whom he was later to work on the musical version of *Street Scene*, and he continued trying to interest Broadway in the project until the following September. Even when he died six years later, a *Szechwan* "opera" was still on the list of works which he wanted to write, though Brecht by then was already back in Berlin. As it turned out the first production of the play in the U.S. was given at Hamline University, St. Paul, in March 1948, some five months after Brecht had left. It used the 1941 version, which he had given Eric Bentley to translate some time before, and since then, though directors and translators have made their own adaptations, no other Brecht text has been seen.

3

Curiously enough the only one of these plays which Brecht ever directed himself was the one which he had bothered least about while in the United States. This was of course *Puntila*, whose production by his faithful supporters at the Zurich Schauspielhaus was decided around the same time, spring 1948, Brecht having gone to that city immediately on his return to Europe. The play had not been staged in Scandinavia, the Finns having joined in the German invasion of Russia while the Brechts were still at sea somewhere between Vladivostok and the Los Angeles harbor of San Pedro. Hella Wuolijoki had been sentenced to lifelong imprisonment in 1943, then released the following year, and had now become a Popular Front deputy and the director of Finnish Radio. Nominally the play was to be directed by the resident director Kurt Hirschfeld, but in fact Brecht had an equal responsibility, even though the conditions of his residence in Switzerland forbade any acknowledgment that he was working there. Puntila was played by Leonard Steckel, formerly one of Piscator's actors in Berlin, who had previously directed the Zurich premières of both *Galileo* and *The Good Person of Szechwan*, also playing the title part in the former. The sets, which seem for Brecht to have been the principal interest of the production, were by Teo Otto, with whom he had worked some two decades earlier on *Die Massnahme*. As usual Brecht made further revisions and cuts in the course of production, as outlined in the notes, none of them however of major importance. Not long after, the Munich publisher Kurt Desch came to Zurich to see him, and signed a contract for the rights to the play. The following year Brecht arranged that in future half the royalties should be paid to Hella Wuolijoki. Whether this was an acknowledgment of joint authorship so much as a form of return for her hospitality and help is open to doubt; certainly he never named her as co-author of the play, nor even as a "collaborator" like Elisabeth Hauptmann or Margarete Steffin.

Back in Berlin he followed up his immense success there with *Mother Courage* by staging *Puntila* once more, this time with Erich Engel as his co-director, in November 1949 as the first production of his newly formed Berliner Ensemble. Essentially this was a revised edition of the Zurich production, with Steckel again as Puntila and the same Emma and Lisu (respectively Therese Giehse and Regine Lutz); Caspar Neher, who had wanted to do the play in Zurich but was regarded as over-committed there, was now responsible for the sets. However, there were some significant changes, of which probably the most important lay in the playing (and makeup) of Puntila himself as a much less genially sympathetic character, the reception of Zuckmayer's *The Devil's General* having perhaps helped to show how dangerously seductive such full-blooded authoritarian personalities can be to the German audience. Matti too, played now by Erwin Geschonneck, had more of the somewhat gloomy skepticism which Brecht had put into the part. To simplify the antagonisms all the bad (i.e., ruling-class) characters except Eva wore masks, the good (their employees) not. The Puntila song was written to introduce and link the scenes; Paul Dessau set it to music (and later, after Brecht's death, was to make an opera version of the whole play). It was all presented as a "popular play by Bertolt Brecht after Hella Wuolijoki's stories," and in 1950 she came for the first time to see it, writing to Brecht subsequently:

. . . and as for what you have made of Puntila, here we would never have known how to put him on the stage . . .

Early in 1952 the production was re-rehearsed and revived, this time with the comic actor Curt Bois as Puntila, a performance which he repeated for the film version some three years later. Some of Brecht's suggestions for the filming are given in the notes. The result, certainly, was not very successful, the love story in particular being hopelessly conventionalized. The director was Alberto Cavalcanti.

Ui and *The Good Person of Szechwan* were not tackled by the Berliner Ensemble until after Brecht's death. Thus it was the Frankfurt-am-Main theater under Harry Buckwitz which first presented the latter in Germany, though Brecht himself attended four days of rehearsal and tried (according to his journal) "to bring some clarity and lightness into the perfor-

mance." Not long before he died his young assistant Benno
Besson staged a pilot production in the East German city
of Rostock, casting Käthe Reichel of the Ensemble as Shen
Teh/Shui Ta; but the full production to which this led could
no longer be supervised by Brecht himself and was not one
of the Ensemble's major triumphs. It was different with *Ui*,
which he had been shy of staging before a German audience
so long as he lived, or even of showing to the younger members
of his own entourage. Again a pilot production was mounted,
this time by his assistant Peter Palitzsch in Stuttgart in West
Germany in 1958, then developed by Palitzsch jointly with
Manfred Wekwerth (whose criticisms of the pilot version can
be found in the notes) into one of the most brilliant of all the
Berliner Ensemble's Brecht productions. As part of the back-
wash of this the play at long last reached the American (and
also the English) stage, though too late, of course, for its moral
to be what Brecht had originally intended. Something of his
own possible aim in presenting it to an eventual German
audience can be seen in the epilogue which he had added to
it, as well as in the two alternative prologues given in the
notes. The success which it had suggests that he rather underestimated both that audience and the play itself, which has a
good deal more force than the circumstances of its writing
might imply.

4

Looking at Brecht's Finnish works as a group it is difficult to
see any common thread other than that between *Puntila* and
the *Flüchtlingsgespräche;* the three plays are too different from
one another. They do not lie in any logical pattern, two of
them indeed being almost unpredictable additions to the main
corpus of his work, windfalls, as it were, of his Finnish stay.
Puntila was stimulated by Hella Wuolijoki and by the competition which she wanted them to enter; in the case of *Ui* the
writing fit seems simply to have seized him; both were so

quickly written as to have a spontaneity and freshness that is relatively rare in his plays. With *The Good Person of Szechwan* there was a total contrast, for few of his works were so laboriously planned and revised, so that although it was brought to completion in Finland the real question is whether the mood of the twelve months which he spent there is in any way detectable in the finished script. Oddly enough it can be argued that the changes made in the play during that period were less helpful than they should have been; certainly the light, steely structure which he had envisaged, the powerful heroine and the dusty, semi-industrialized setting somehow disappeared in favor of something quainter and sweeter, while the financial side of the plot became too complicated to make much sense. Though Brecht himself surely never intended it, the play as a result lends itself too easily to a prettified, sentimental interpretation, particularly when the neutral "Mensch" of the title is rendered "Woman," with its ensuing temptation to play the heroine as that hackneyed figure, the good-hearted prostitute. In the stratified history of this work she was of course already there, as was the memory of Klabund's *Chalk Circle*, but Brecht had done a lot to bury them and it is a pity if they get disinterred.

Both *The Good Person* and *Ui* were described as "parables," and the former's ethical preoccupations were something that had never been quite so strongly emphasized in Brecht's work. They can be seen again in his short-lived *The Weakness of the Flesh* project, which deals with "the man who, in view of the wickedness of the world, aims to become a villain but cannot manage it," and whose message "how much easier and more natural it is to do good rather than evil" was to recur in *The Caucasian Chalk Circle* three years later. Perhaps such concerns can be related to the discussions on Marxist ethics which his journal shows him to have been involved in around the beginning of his Finnish stay, but he does also seem to have been involved in some larger ideological reorientation. Not only were his judgments of Soviet policy prior to the German invasion (notably during the Soviet-Finnish war) extremely critical, but in March 1941 he came to the very important conclusion that he had been wrong to see socialism as a great order, or reordering, of things—"eine grosse Ordnung," as he had often in the past termed it—and that he should henceforward define it as a great process of production, "eine grosse Produktion," using production in the widest sense of human productivity, which it was socialism's job to unshackle. This shift of ground surely reflects his awareness of the order created in the USSR and of that preached by Hitler, as well as the likelihood, under the Nazi-Soviet alliance, of such order becoming a common interest. In both *Mother Courage* and the *Flüchtlingsgespräche* "Ordnung" has become a dirty word.

It is noticeable too that although Brecht remained as hostile as ever to the English class system, and never seems to have applied for any visa to Britain or the Commonwealth, he was reading a good deal of previously unfamiliar English literature —Boswell, Macaulay, Wordsworth, Arnold, and Lytton Strachey all being mentioned in his journal at this time. This made him aware, apparently for the first time, of the great richness of the English literary and indeed educational tradition as against the German, nor was it possible not to relate them in some measure to England's situation as the last country then holding out against Hitler; *Puntila* was actually written as the battle of Britain was being fought, with London in flames. Something of Brecht's thinking on this theme emerges in his reflections on poetry, and the Finnish poems form a crucial group in his oeuvre. But it can hardly have been a coincidence that he should now have written two of the most "English" in feeling of his plays: *Puntila* with its unforced humor, at once dry and warm; *Ui* with its Elizabethan parody and its use of flippancy as a weapon of attack. When he prefaced the *Flüchtlingsgespräche* with an epigraph from P. G. Wodehouse it was in its small way a symbolic gesture.

What struck Brecht himself when he came to take stock of his work shortly before leaving Finland was the absence of common features in his plays of the past three years, from *Fear and Misery of the Third Reich* to *Ui*:

> the plays tend to fly apart like constellations in the new physics, as though here too some kind of dramaturgical core had exploded.

Yet even if the Finnish batch are outwardly quite inconsistent with one another, it is possible to identify the factors—literary, philosophical, military, environmental—which helped shape them, and at least to recognize their effect on the works. It was, then, the unexpected combination of a number of such factors at this time that created the explosion, and Brecht was not far out in feeling that something of the sort must have taken place. Ultimately each of them can be seen as politically grounded, itself a result of the rather larger explosions taking place in the affairs of the world. These larger explosions could not be described directly:

> puntila means hardly anything to me, the war everything; about puntila i can write virtually everything, about the war nothing. i don't mean just "may," but truly "can."
> interesting how remote literature as a practical activity is from the centers where events really decide things.

They were none the less echoed in Brecht's work. Remoteness can be a strength.

THE EDITORS

The Good Person of Szechwan

A Parable Play

Collaborators: R. Berlau, M. Steffin

Translator: Ralph Manheim

CHARACTERS

WANG, a water seller

THE THREE GODS

SHEN TEH/SHUI TA

YANG SUN, an unemployed flier

MRS. YANG, his mother

MRS. SHIN, a widow

A FAMILY OF EIGHT

LIN TO, a carpenter

MRS. MI TZU, the house owner

THE POLICEMAN

THE CARPET DEALER AND HIS
   WIFE

THE OLD PROSTITUTE

SHU FU, the barber

THE PRIEST

THE UNEMPLOYED MAN

THE WAITER

PASSERS-BY IN THE PROLOGUE

Scene: The capital of Szechwan, a half-Europeanized city

Prologue

A Street in the Capital of Szechwan

Evening. Wang the water seller introduces himself to the audience.

WANG I sell water here in the capital of Szechwan. It's hard work. When water is scarce, I must go far to find any. And when it's plentiful, I get nothing for it. Our whole province is plagued by bitter poverty. Everyone says that only the gods can help us. To my delight, a cattle dealer whose business takes him to distant places tells me that some of the highest gods are on the way, and may be expected to visit Szechwan. It seems that heaven is very much alarmed at the many complaints that have been rising up. For three days I have been waiting here at the city gate, especially toward evening, in the hope of being first to welcome them. They would hardly find time for me later on, they are sure to be surrounded by prominent citizens and very much in demand. If only I recognize them! They won't necessarily come together. They may come singly for fear of attracting attention. It can't be those men over there, they are coming home from work. (*He looks at a group of passing workers*) Their shoulders are bowed low from carrying heavy loads. That fellow can't possibly be a god, there's ink on his fingers. At the very most, he works in the office at one of the cement factories. Even those gentlemen (*two gentlemen pass by*) don't strike me as gods, they have a brutal look, as if they were in the habit of beating people, and gods have no need of that. But what about those three? They look entirely different. They are well fed, they show no sign of any occupation, and their shoes are dusty, they must have come from far away. They are the gods. Enlightened Ones, I await your orders! (*He throws himself on the ground*)

THE FIRST GOD (*delighted*)   Are we expected here?

WANG (*gives them water*)   You have been expected for a long time. But only I knew that you were coming.

THE FIRST GOD   We require a lodging for the night. Do you know of one?

WANG   One? Many. The city is at your service, O Enlightened Ones. Where do you wish to stay?

(*The gods exchange significant looks*)

THE FIRST GOD   Try the first house, my son. Begin with the very first.

WANG   I am only afraid of arousing the enmity of the powerful if I single out one of them for the privilege.

THE FIRST GOD   For that very reason we command you: take the first.

WANG   That's Mr. Fo's house over there. Just a moment, please. (*He runs to a house and pounds on the door. It is opened, but it can be seen that he is turned away. He comes back hesitantly*)

WANG   Too bad. Mr. Fo has gone out, and his servants are afraid to take any responsibility in his absence, because he is very strict. Won't he be furious when he finds out whom they have turned away?

THE GODS (*smiling*)   Undoubtedly.

WANG   Just another moment. The next house belongs to the widow Su. She will be beside herself with joy. (*He runs over but apparently is again turned away*) I shall have to inquire over there. She says she has only one small room, and it hasn't been put in order. I'll go straight to Mr. Cheng.

THE SECOND GOD   But a small room is all we need. Say we are coming.

WANG   Even if it hasn't been cleaned? Why, it may be crawling with spiders.

THE SECOND GOD   That doesn't matter. Where there are spiders there won't be many flies.

THE THIRD GOD (*amiably to Wang*) My son, go to Mr. Cheng's house or some other. I must admit that I don't really care for spiders.
(*Wang knocks at a door and is admitted*)

VOICE FROM THE HOUSE Don't bother us with your gods! We have troubles of our own!

WANG (*returns to the gods*) Mr. Cheng is terribly sorry. His house is full of relatives and he doesn't dare to face you, Enlightened Ones. Between you and me, I think there are wicked people among them, whom he doesn't wish you to see. He fears your judgment. That must be it.

THE THIRD GOD Are we so terrifying?

WANG Only to evil men, I suppose. Everyone knows that the province of Kwan has been beset by floods for many years.

THE SECOND GOD Indeed? How so?

WANG No doubt because the people are lacking in piety.

THE SECOND GOD Nonsense. It's because they've let the dam fall apart.

THE FIRST GOD Shhh! (*To Wang*) Have you still hope, my son?

WANG How can you ask? I need only go a little farther and take my pick of rooms. The people are dying to serve you. Unfortunate circumstances, don't you see? I'll be right back. (*He goes away hesitantly and stops, unable to make up his mind*)

THE SECOND GOD What did I tell you?

THE THIRD GOD It may be the circumstances after all.

THE SECOND GOD Circumstances in Shun, circumstances in Kwan, and circumstances in Szechwan. There are no god-fearing people any more, that's the naked truth which you are not willing to face. Our mission has failed, why won't you admit it?

THE FIRST GOD We may find some good people any minute. We can't expect everything to come our way.

THE THIRD GOD The resolution says the world can go on as it is if we find enough good people who succeed in living a life worthy of a human being. The water seller is such a man unless I am very much mistaken. (*He goes over to Wang who is still standing there irresolutely*)

THE SECOND GOD He *is* very much mistaken. When the water
seller gave us a drink from his cup, I saw something. Take
a look at his cup. (*He shows it to the first god*)

THE FIRST GOD It has two bottoms.

THE SECOND GOD A swindler.

THE FIRST GOD All right, that cuts him out. But what does
one corrupted man amount to? We shall find plenty who
meet the conditions. We must find one. For two thousand
years we have been hearing this complaint, that the world
can't go on as it is, that no one can live in it and remain
good. It's high time we discovered someone who manages
to keep our commandments.

THE THIRD GOD (*to Wang*) Is it impossible then to find
lodging?

WANG Not for you. How can you think of such a thing? If
I haven't found one right off, I am to blame for not going
about it the right way.

THE THIRD GOD I can't believe that. (*He turns back to the
others*)

WANG They're beginning to catch on. (*He addresses a gentleman*) Honored sir, forgive me for speaking to you, but three
of the highest gods, of whose impending arrival all Szechwan
has been speaking for years, have indeed arrived and are in
need of a lodging. Don't pass me by. See for yourself. One
glance will convince you. For heaven's sake don't miss this
chance. Such an opportunity doesn't come twice. Invite the
gods to your home before someone else snaps them up.
They're sure to accept.

(*The gentleman has walked away*)

WANG (*turning to another*) Dear sir, you have heard the news.
Would you happen to have a room? It doesn't have to be
palatial. It's the intention that counts.

THE GENTLEMAN How am I to know what sort of gods you've
got there? You never know whom you're taking into your
house. (*He goes into a tobacco shop*)

(*Wang runs back to the three*)

WANG I've found someone who is sure to take you in. (*He
sees his cup standing on the ground, looks toward the gods
in confusion, picks it up and runs back again*)

THE FIRST GOD That doesn't sound encouraging.

WANG (*when the gentleman comes out of the shop*) Well, how about that lodging?

THE GENTLEMAN How do you know I'm not living at an inn myself?

THE FIRST GOD He won't find anything. We can strike Szechwan off the list.

WANG It's three of the chief gods. Definitely. Their statues in the temples look just like them. If you hurry over and invite them, they may accept.

THE GENTLEMAN (*laughing*) I can imagine the kind of scoundrels you're trying to palm off on me. (*Goes out*)

WANG (*grumbling after him*) You swivel-eyed skinflint! Have you no piety? You'll all roast in brimstone for your indifference. It's no skin off the gods' ass. But you'll be sorry. You'll be paying off your guilt down to the fourth generation. You've covered all Szechwan with shame. (*Pause*) There's no one left but Shen Teh, the prostitute. She can never say no. (*He calls "Shen Teh." She looks out the upstairs window*)

WANG They've come and I can't find them a lodging. Can you take them in for the night?

SHEN TEH I don't see how I can, Wang. I'm expecting a gentleman. But how is it possible that you can't find them a lodging?

WANG I can't go into that now. But Szechwan is one enormous sink.

SHEN TEH I'll just have to hide when he comes. Then perhaps he'll go away. He wanted to take me out.

WANG Can we come up in the meantime?

SHEN TEH Yes, but you must speak softly. Can I tell them the truth?

WANG No. They mustn't find out about your profession. We'd better wait down here. But you won't slip out with him?

SHEN TEH I've been having a hard time. If I haven't got the rent money by tomorrow morning, I'll be thrown out.

WANG At a time like this you shouldn't think of money.

SHEN TEH I don't know. Does the stomach stop rumbling on

the emperor's birthday? But never mind, I'll take them in.
(*She is seen putting out the light*)

THE FIRST GOD   It's hopeless if you ask me.
(*They go up to Wang*)

WANG (*frightened when he sees them standing behind him*)
I've found you a lodging. (*He wipes the sweat off his face*)

THE GODS   Really? Then let's be going.

WANG   There's no hurry. Take your time. The room is being
put in order.

THE THIRD GOD   Very well, we'll sit here and wait.

WANG   But there's so much traffic here. Let's go over there.

THE SECOND GOD   We like to watch the people. That's what
we came for.

WANG   Yes, but this draft.

THE SECOND GOD   Never mind that, we're hardened.

WANG   Maybe you'd like me to show you Szechwan by night?
We could take a little stroll.

THE THIRD GOD   We've done enough walking for today. (*Smiling*) But if you'd rather have us go somewhere else you
need only say so.
(*They walk toward the rear*)

THE THIRD GOD   Does this place suit you?
(*They sit down on a stoop. Wang sits on the ground a little
to one side*)

WANG (*taking the bull by the horns*)   You will be staying
with a young lady who lives by herself. There's no one
better in all Szechwan.

THE THIRD GOD   That's splendid.

WANG (*to the audience*)   When I picked up my cup a moment
ago, they looked at me so strangely. Can they have noticed
something? I'm afraid to look them in the eye.

THE THIRD GOD   You seem exhausted.

WANG   A little. From running.

THE FIRST GOD   Do the people here have a hard life?

WANG   The good ones.

THE FIRST GOD (*gravely*)   You too?

WANG   I know what you mean. I'm not good. But I have a
hard time of it, too.

(*Meanwhile the gentleman has appeared outside Shen Teh's*

house and has whistled several times. Wang has started with alarm each time)

THE THIRD GOD (*softly to Wang*) I believe he has gone away now.

WANG (*in confusion*) So he has.

(*He stands up and runs out into the square, leaving his carrying pole behind. But meanwhile the following has happened: The gentleman has gone away and Shen Teh, after stepping quietly through the door and calling "Wang" in a soft voice, has gone down the street. Then Wang calls softly "Shen Teh" and obtains no answer*)

WANG She's let me down. She's gone off after her rent money, and I have no lodging for the Enlightened Ones. They are tired and waiting. I can't go back to them again and say: "Nothing has come of it." My own hideaway, a culvert, is out of the question. And surely the gods would not wish to stay with a man whose dishonest business methods they have detected. I won't go back, not for anything in the world. But my carrying pole is there. What can I do? I don't dare to go and get it. I'll leave the city and hide from them somewhere, since, much as I revere them, I have been unable to help them. (*He rushes away*)

(*No sooner has he gone than Shen Teh comes back, looks on the other side of the street and sees the gods*)

SHEN TEH Are you the Enlightened Ones? My name is Shen Teh. I shall be pleased if you consent to stay in my room.

THE THIRD GOD But where has the water seller gone?

SHEN TEH I must have missed him.

THE FIRST GOD He must have thought you were not coming and been afraid to face us.

THE THIRD GOD (*picks up the carrying pole*) We'll leave it with you. He needs it.

(*Led by Shen Teh, they enter the house*)

(*It grows dark, then light again. In the dawn the gods step out the door, led by Shen Teh, who lights the way with a lamp. They take their leave*)

THE FIRST GOD Dear Shen Teh, we thank you for your hospitality. We shall not forget that it was you who took us in. Give the water seller his pole and tell him that we thank him too, for showing us someone who was good.

SHEN TEH   I am not good. I must make a confession: when Wang asked me to provide you with lodging, I hesitated.

THE FIRST GOD   Hesitation makes no difference as long as you overcome it. You have given us more than a night's lodging. Many, including some of us gods, were beginning to doubt whether there were any good people left. The main purpose of our journey was to find out if this were so. Now that we have found one good soul, we can go our way with a light heart. Good-bye.

SHEN TEH   Wait, Enlightened Ones, I am not at all sure that I am good. I should like to be, but how am I to pay my rent? I may as well admit it: I sell myself in order to live, but even so I can't make ends meet, for many others are obliged to do the same. I am willing to do anything, but who is not? Of course I should be glad to keep the commandments, to honor my father and mother, and tell the truth. I should be overjoyed not to covet my neighbor's house, and delighted to keep faith with a husband. Nor should I wish to take advantage of anyone, or to rob the helpless. But what am I to do? Even by breaking a commandment or two, I scarcely get by.

THE FIRST GOD   All those misgivings, Shen Teh, are merely the doubts of a good person.

THE THIRD GOD   Good-bye, Shen Teh. Give the water seller my warmest greetings. He has been a good friend to us.

THE SECOND GOD   I'm afraid it hasn't done him much good.

THE THIRD GOD   The best of luck.

THE FIRST GOD   Most of all, be good, Shen Teh. Good-bye. (*They turn to go. They are already waving good-bye*)

SHEN TEH (*anxiously*)   But I'm not sure of myself, Enlightened Ones. How can I be good when everything is so expensive?

THE SECOND GOD   Unfortunately there's nothing we can do about that. We can't meddle in questions of economics.

THE THIRD GOD   Wait! Just a moment. If she were a little better off, she might stand more of a chance.

THE SECOND GOD We can't give her anything. We couldn't answer for it up there.

THE FIRST GOD Why not?

(*They put their heads together and engage in an animated discussion*)

THE FIRST GOD (*to Shen Teh, with embarrassment*) We have heard that you haven't been able to get the money for your rent. We are not poor. It goes without saying that we will pay for our night's lodging. Here. (*He gives her money*) But don't tell anybody we have paid. It might be misinterpreted.

THE SECOND GOD Very much so.

THE THIRD GOD It shouldn't be, it's quite permissible. There's no reason why we shouldn't pay for our lodging. There wasn't one word to the contrary in the resolution. Good-bye. (*The gods go out quickly*)

1

A Small Tobacco Shop

The shop is not yet fully furnished and not yet open for business.

SHEN TEH (*to the audience*) It is now three days since the gods went away. They said they wished to pay me for their night's lodging. And when I looked to see what they had given me, I saw that it was more than a thousand silver dollars.—I have bought a tobacco shop with the money. Yesterday I moved in, and I hope I shall now be able to do a great deal of good. There's Mrs. Shin, for instance, the former owner of the shop. Yesterday she came and asked me for rice for her children. And there she is again, crossing the square with her bowl.

(*Enter Mrs. Shin. The women bow to one another*)

SHEN TEH How do you do, Mrs. Shin.

MRS. SHIN   How do you do, Miss Shen Teh. How do you like your new home?

SHEN TEH   Very well. Have the children spent a good night?

MRS. SHIN   Hm, in a strange house, if you can call that hovel a house. The smallest has begun to cough.

SHEN TEH   That's bad.

MRS. SHIN   You don't know what bad means, you're doing all right. Never mind, you'll learn a thing or two in this dump. The neighborhood is a slum.

SHEN TEH   But the workers from the cement factory come here at noon, don't they? That's what you told me.

MRS. SHIN   But aside from them nobody ever buys anything. Not even the neighbors.

SHEN TEH   You didn't tell me that when you sold me the shop.

MRS. SHIN   Don't start finding fault. First you rob me and my children of our home, then you call it a dump in the slums. This is too much. (*She weeps*)

SHEN TEH (*quickly*)   Let me get you the rice.

MRS. SHIN   I also wanted to ask you to lend me some money.

SHEN TEH (*pouring the rice into the bowl*)   I can't do that. I haven't sold anything yet.

MRS. SHIN   But I need it. What do you expect me to live on? You've taken everything I owned. And now you're cutting my throat. I'll leave my children on your doorstep, you bloodsucker! (*She snatches the bowl from Shen Teh's hands*)

SHEN TEH   Don't lose your temper. You'll spill your rice. (*Enter an elderly couple and a shabbily dressed man*)

THE WIFE   Oh, my dear Shen Teh, we've heard that you're doing so well. Why, you've set yourself up in business. Imagine, we have no place to go. Our tobacco shop has failed. We were wondering if we mightn't stay with you for just one night. You know my nephew, don't you? He's come too, he never leaves us.

THE NEPHEW (*looking around*)   Nice shop you've got here.

MRS. SHIN   Who are they in God's name?

SHEN TEH   When I came here from the country, they were my first landlords. (*To the audience*) When what little money I had was gone, they put me out in the street. They must be afraid I'll turn them down. They are poor.

They have no shelter.
They have no friends.
They need someone.
How can I say no?
(*Amiably to the new arrivals*) Welcome. I shall be glad to put you up. Unfortunately I have only a small room behind the shop.

THE HUSBAND   That will do. Don't worry.

THE WIFE (*while Shen Teh brings in tea*)   We'll sit back here, so as not to be in your way. You must have chosen a tobacco shop because you remembered your first home. We'll be able to give you some pointers. As a matter of fact, that's why we've come.

MRS. SHIN (*sardonically*)   Let's hope a few customers come too.

THE WIFE   Could that be a dig at us?

THE HUSBAND   Shh. Here comes a customer now.
(*A ragged man enters*)

THE RAGGED MAN   I beg your pardon. I'm unemployed.
(*Mrs. Shin laughs*)

SHEN TEH   What can I do for you?

THE UNEMPLOYED MAN   I heard you were opening tomorrow. I thought to myself sometimes goods are damaged in unpacking. Have you a cigarette to spare?

THE WIFE   Of all the nerve, begging for tobacco. If at least it were bread!

THE UNEMPLOYED MAN   Bread is expensive. A few puffs from a cigarette and I'm a new man. I'm all in.

SHEN TEH (*giving him cigarettes*)   It's important to be a new man. I'll consider you my first customer, you'll bring me luck.
(*The unemployed man quickly lights up a cigarette, inhales and goes out coughing*)

THE WIFE   Was that wise, my dear Shen Teh?

MRS. SHIN   If you start off like that, you won't keep your shop for three days.

THE HUSBAND   I bet he had money in his pocket.

SHEN TEH   But he said he had nothing.

THE NEPHEW   How do you know he wasn't lying?

SHEN TEH (*angrily*)   How do I know he *was* lying?

THE WIFE (*shaking her head*)   She can't say no. You're too good, Shen Teh. If you want to hold on to your shop, you'll have to turn people down now and then.

THE HUSBAND   Say it doesn't belong to you. Say it belongs to a relative who demands a strict accounting. Can't you do that?

MRS. SHIN   She could do that if she didn't always have to play the Lady Bountiful.

SHEN TEH (*laughing*)   Grumble away. I'll change my mind about the room and take back the rice.

THE WIFE (*horrified*)   Is the rice yours too?

SHEN TEH (*to the audience*)
They are wicked.
They are no one's friend.
They grudge even a bowl of rice.
They need everything for themselves.
Who can find fault with them?
(*Enter a little man*)

MRS. SHIN (*seeing him, leaves in a hurry*)   I'll look in tomorrow. (*Goes out*)

THE LITTLE MAN (*calls after her*)   Hey, Mrs. Shin. You're the one I wanted to see.

THE WIFE   Does she come here regularly? Has she some claim on you?

SHEN TEH   She has no claim, but she's hungry. That matters more.

THE LITTLE MAN   She knows why she's clearing out. Are you the new owner? I see you've started stocking the shelves. But those stands don't belong to you. Not unless you pay for them. That old tramp who was sitting here never paid for them. (*To the others*) I'm the carpenter, you see.

SHEN TEH   I thought they were included in the furnishings I paid for.

THE CARPENTER   It's all a put-up job. Naturally you're in cahoots with this Mrs. Shin. I want my hundred silver dollars, or my name isn't Lin To.

SHEN TEH   How can I give them to you? I have no money left.

THE CARPENTER In that case I'll have you auctioned off. On the spot. If you don't pay up this minute, I'll have you auctioned off.

THE HUSBAND (*prompting Shen Teh*) Cousin!

SHEN TEH Couldn't I pay you next month?

THE CARPENTER (*screaming*) No!

SHEN TEH Don't be so hard, Mr. Lin To. I can't meet everyone's demands at once. (*To the audience*)

A little indulgence and your strength redoubles.

See how the cart horse stops by a tuft of grass.

Look away for a moment, he'll pull better.

Have a little patience in June, the tree

Will sag beneath its load of peaches when August comes.

How shall we live together without patience?

A slight postponement

Makes the most distant goals attainable.

(*To the carpenter*) Won't you be patient just for a short while, Mr. Lin To?

THE CARPENTER Who's going to be patient with me and my family? (*He pulls one of the stands away from the wall as though to take it away with him*) Pay up, or I'll take the stands away.

THE WIFE My dear Shen Teh, why don't you turn the whole matter over to your cousin? (*To the carpenter*) Make a note of your claim and Miss Shen Teh's cousin will pay it.

THE CARPENTER Cousin! I know these cousins.

THE NEPHEW Stop laughing like a fool. I know him personally.

THE HUSBAND He's as sharp as a razor.

THE CARPENTER Very well. He'll get my bill. (*He tips the stand over, sits down on it, and writes out his bill*)

THE WIFE He'll tear the shirt off your back for his wretched boards if nobody stops him. Never recognize a claim, warranted or not, or before you know it you'll be up to your ears in claims, warranted or not. Throw a piece of meat in your garbage pail, and all the mongrels in the neighborhood will be at each other's throats in your back yard. What are law courts for?

SHEN TEH The courts won't support him if his work doesn't.

He's done his work, he doesn't want to go off empty-handed. He has his family. It's too bad that I can't pay him. What will the gods say?

THE HUSBAND   You did your bit by taking us in, that's more than enough.

(*Enter a limping man and a pregnant woman*)

THE LIMPING MAN (*to the couple*)   Ah, so there you are. Fine relatives you are. Leaving us standing on the corner!

THE WIFE (*embarrassed, to Shen Teh*)   This is my brother Wung and my sister-in-law. (*To the two of them*) Stop complaining. Sit down over there and don't get in our old friend Miss Shen Teh's way. (*To Shen Teh*) I believe we shall have to take them both in, my sister-in-law is four months gone. What do you think?

SHEN TEH   You are welcome.

THE WIFE   Say thank you. There are cups back there. (*To Shen Teh*) They had no place to go. It's a good thing you've got this shop.

SHEN TEH (*laughing, to the audience as she brings tea*)   Yes, it's a good thing I've got it.

(*Enter Mrs. Mi Tzu, the house owner, with a sheet of paper in her hand*)

MRS. MI TZU   Miss Shen Teh, I am Mrs. Mi Tzu, the house owner. I hope we shall get along. This is a lease. (*While Shen Teh reads the lease*) Ah, ladies and gentlemen, isn't there something beautiful about the opening of a small business? (*She looks around*) There are still a few empty spaces on the shelves, but you'll manage. I presume you can give me a few references?

SHEN TEH   Is that necessary?

MRS. MI TZU   But I have no idea who you are.

THE HUSBAND   Perhaps we can vouch for Miss Shen Teh? We've known her ever since she came to the city, we'd trust her with our last dollar.

MRS. MI TZU   And who are you?

THE HUSBAND   I'm Ma Fu, the tobacconist.

MRS. MI TZU   Where's your shop?

THE HUSBAND   At the moment I have no shop. I've just sold it, you see.

MRS. MI TZU   I see. (*To Shen Teh*) And you have no one else who can supply me with information about you?

THE WIFE (*prompting*)   Cousin. Cousin.

MRS. MI TZU   You must have someone who can assure me that I'm taking the right kind of person into my house. This is a respectable house, my dear. Otherwise I can't give you a lease.

SHEN TEH (*slowly, with downcast eyes*)   I have a cousin.

MRS. MI TZU   Oh, you have a cousin? In town? Then we can go straight over to see him. What is he?

SHEN TEH   He doesn't live here, he lives in another city.

THE WIFE   In Shung, isn't that what you said?

SHEN TEH   Mr. . . . Shui Ta. In Shung.

THE HUSBAND   Why, I know him. A tall, lean man.

THE NEPHEW (*to the carpenter*)   I take it you've had dealings with Miss Shen Teh's cousin too. About the shelves.

THE CARPENTER (*grumpily*)   I'm just making out his bill. Here it is! (*He hands it over*) I'll be back tomorrow morning. (*Goes out*)

THE NEPHEW (*calling after him, eying Mrs. Mi Tzu*)   Don't worry. Her cousin will pay.

MRS. MI TZU (*with a probing look at Shen Teh*)   I shall be very glad to meet him. Good evening, miss. (*Goes out*)

THE WIFE (*after a pause*)   Now it will all come out. Rest assured, she'll know all about you by tomorrow morning.

THE SISTER-IN-LAW (*in an undertone to the nephew*)   This won't last very long.

(*Enter an old man led by a boy*)

THE BOY (*motioning toward the rear*)   Here they are.

THE WIFE   Hello, grandpa. (*To Shen Teh*) The dear old man. He must have been worried about us. And the little fellow, hasn't he grown? He eats like an ostrich. Who else have you got with you?

THE HUSBAND (*looking out*)   Only your niece.

THE WIFE (*to Shen Teh*)   A young relative from the country. I hope we're not too many for you. There weren't so many of us when you lived with us, were there? Yes, more and more of us kept coming. The worse things got, the more of us there were. And the more of us there were, the worse things got. But now we'd better lock the door, or there won't be any peace. (*She locks the door and all sit down*) We mustn't get in your way in the shop, that's the main thing. Because if we do, how will you keep the kettle boiling? This is how we figured: in the daytime the young ones will go out, only grandpa and my sister-in-law will stay home, and maybe me. The others will only look in once or twice in the course of the day. Right? Light that lamp over there and make yourselves at home.

THE NEPHEW (*facetiously*)   If only her cousin doesn't turn up tonight, the imposing Mr. Shui Ta!

(*The sister-in-law laughs*)

THE BROTHER (*reaching for a cigarette*)   One more or less won't make any difference, will it?

THE HUSBAND   Of course not.

(*All take cigarettes. The brother hands around a jug of wine*)

THE NEPHEW   Her cousin will pay.

THE GRANDFATHER (*gravely, to Shen Teh*)   Good evening. (*Shen Teh, confused at the belated greeting, bows. In one hand she has the carpenter's bill, in the other the lease*)

THE WIFE   Couldn't you people sing something to entertain our hostess?

THE NEPHEW   Grandpa can begin.

(*They sing the* "Song of the Smoke")

THE GRANDFATHER

Once I thought intelligence was sure to aid me
I was quite an optimist when younger
Now I realize it never paid me:
How can our intelligence compete with hunger?
    Therefore I said: Drop it!
    Like smoke twisting gray
    Into ever colder coldness you
    Will blow away.

THE HUSBAND

Since the conscientious man gets strictly nowhere
I adopted crookedness instead

But the crooked path made going slower
There just is no way for us to get ahead.
　　Likewise I say: Drop it!
　　Like smoke twisting gray
　　Into ever colder coldness you
　　Will blow away.

THE NIECE
　　Old folks, so they say, find little fun in hoping.
　　They need time and time begins to press.
　　To the young, I'm told, the gates are open
　　Yet they open, so I'm told, on nothingness.
　　　　And I too say: Drop it!
　　　　Like smoke twisting gray
　　　　Into ever colder coldness you
　　　　Will blow away.

THE NEPHEW   Where did you get the wine?

THE SISTER-IN-LAW   He pawned the bale of tobacco.

THE HUSBAND   What? The tobacco was all we had left. We never touched it, not even to get a place to sleep. You stinker!

THE BROTHER   Are you calling me a stinker because my wife is dying of the cold? You've been drinking it yourself. Give me that jug!

(*They fight. The stands topple over*)

SHEN TEH (*implores them*)   Oh, be careful of the shop, don't break everything. It's a gift of the gods. Take what there is, but don't destroy it.

THE WIFE (*skeptically*)   This shop isn't as big as I thought. Maybe we shouldn't have told auntie and the others. If they come along, it's going to be terribly crowded.

THE SISTER-IN-LAW   And our hostess isn't so friendly any more.

(*Voices are heard from outside. Knocking at the door*)

CRIES   Open up!—It's us!

THE WIFE   Is it you, auntie? What will we do now?

SHEN TEH   Oh, my beautiful shop! Oh, my hopes! Hardly opened and it's not a shop any more. (*To the audience*)
The lifeboat that could save us

Is drawn into the depths.
Too many drowning hands
Clutch at it avidly.
CRIES (*from outside*)   Open up!

Interlude

Under a Bridge

The water seller sits huddled by the river.

WANG (*looking around*)   All quiet. For four days now I've
been hiding. They won't find me, I'm keeping my eyes open.
I purposely went in the same direction as they. On the second day they crossed the bridge. I heard their steps above
me. By now they must be far away. I'm safe.
(*He lies back and falls asleep. Music. The embankment becomes transparent and the gods appear*)

WANG (*holds his arm before his face as though to ward off a
blow*)   Don't say it. I know. I went from house to house
and I didn't find anyone willing to take you in. Now you
know. Now go your way.

THE FIRST GOD   Ah, but you did find someone. When you had
gone, she came. She took us in for the night, she watched
over our sleep, and she lighted the way for us in the morning
when we left. It was you who told us she was good. And she
was good.

WANG   Then it was Shen Teh who took you in?

THE THIRD GOD   Of course.

WANG   And I, man of little faith, I ran away. Only because I
thought: she won't come. She won't come because she's
poor.

THE GODS
O weak man.
Well-meaning but weak man!

Where there is affliction, he thinks, there is no goodness.
Where there is danger, he thinks, there is no courage.
O weakness, that sees no good anywhere.
O hasty judgment! O unreflecting despair!

WANG   I am very much ashamed, Enlightened Ones.

THE FIRST GOD   And now, water seller, do us a favor: hurry back to the capital and keep an eye on Shen Teh, so as to keep us informed. She is doing well now. She seems to have received money with which to buy a small shop that will allow her to follow the promptings of her gentle heart. Show an interest in her goodness, for no one can be good for long unless goodness is demanded of him. We for our part will go our way, we will search and find other good people resembling our good person of Szechwan. That will put a stop to the rumor that our earth is no longer a fit place for good people to live in.

(*They vanish*)

2

The Tobacco Shop

People sleeping all about. The lamp is still burning. Knocking at the door.

THE WIFE (*sits up, groggy with sleep*)   Shen Teh! Somebody's knocking. Where can she be?

THE NEPHEW   She must be out getting breakfast. Her cousin foots the bill.

(*The wife laughs and shuffles to the door. Enter a young gentleman, and behind him the carpenter*)

THE YOUNG GENTLEMAN   I am her cousin.

THE WIFE (*in utter amazement*)   What are you?

THE YOUNG GENTLEMAN   My name is Shui Ta.

THE GUESTS (*shaking each other awake*) Her cousin!—But that was a joke. She hasn't got any cousin!—But somebody's here who says he *is* her cousin.—Incredible, at this time of day!

THE NEPHEW If you are our hostess' cousin, sir, get us some breakfast and be quick about it.

SHUI TA (*putting out the lamp*) The first customers will be here soon. Kindly get dressed immediately so I can open my shop.

THE HUSBAND Your shop? I thought it was our friend Shen Teh's shop. (*Shui Ta shakes his head*) What, it's not her shop?

THE SISTER-IN-LAW So she's put one over on us. Where is she, anyway?

SHUI TA She has been detained. She sends word that now I'm here she can do no more for you.

THE WIFE (*shaken*) And we thought she was so good.

THE NEPHEW Don't believe him. Look for her.

THE HUSBAND Exactly. (*He organizes them*) You and you and you and you, comb the whole town for her. We'll stay here with grandpa to hold the fort. Meanwhile the kid can be getting us something to eat. (*To the boy*) You see that pastry shop on the corner? Slip in and stuff your shirt full.

THE SISTER-IN-LAW Take a few of those little yellow cakes too.

THE HUSBAND But be careful the baker doesn't catch you. And steer clear of the policeman.

(*The boy nods and goes out. The others finish dressing*)

SHUI TA Won't cake-stealing be bad for the reputation of this shop that has given you shelter?

THE NEPHEW Don't worry about him. We'll find her soon enough. She'll tell him where to get off.

(*The nephew, the brother, the sister-in-law, and the niece go out*)

THE SISTER-IN-LAW (*on her way out*) Leave us some breakfast.

SHUI TA (*calmly*) You won't find her. My cousin regrets of course that she is unable to observe the laws of hospitality forever. Unfortunately there are too many of you. This is a tobacco shop and it's Miss Shen Teh's livelihood.

THE HUSBAND   Our Shen Teh could never have brought herself to say such a thing.

SHUI TA   You may be right. (*To the carpenter*) The trouble is there's so much poverty in this city that no one person can hope to relieve it. Sad to say, nothing has changed in the eleven centuries since a poet wrote:
The governor, when asked what would be needed
To help the sufferers from cold in this city, replied:
A blanket ten thousand feet long
That would simply cover all the slums.
(*He starts straightening out the shop*)

THE CARPENTER   I see that you've undertaken to put your cousin's affairs in order. There's a small debt for shelves, she's acknowledged it before witnesses. A hundred silver dollars.

SHUI TA (*taking the bill out of his pocket, not unfriendly*) Don't you think a hundred silver dollars is rather too much?

THE CARPENTER   No. Nor can I make it any less. I have a wife and children to feed.

SHUI TA (*hard*)   How many children?

THE CARPENTER   Four.

SHUI TA   In that case I offer you twenty silver dollars.
(*The husband laughs*)

THE CARPENTER   Are you crazy? These stands are walnut.

SHUI TA   In that case take them away.

THE CARPENTER   What do you mean?

SHUI TA   They're too expensive for me. I request you to take your walnut stands away.

THE WIFE   That's telling him. (*She too laughs*)

THE CARPENTER (*unsure of himself*)   Send for Miss Shen Teh. She seems to be a better sort than you.

SHUI TA   Definitely. She's ruined.

THE CARPENTER (*resolutely picks up a stand and carries it to the door*)   You can pile your merchandise on the floor. It's all the same to me.

SHUI TA (*to the husband*)   Help him.

THE HUSBAND (*also takes a stand and carries it grinning to the door*)   All right. Out with the stands!

THE CARPENTER   You dog! Do you want my family to starve?

SHUI TA   I repeat my offer: twenty silver dollars, because I'd rather not pile my merchandise on the floor.

THE CARPENTER   One hundred.

(*Shui Ta looks indifferently out the window. The husband prepares to carry the stand out the door*)

THE CARPENTER   At least don't smash it on the door frame, you idiot. (*In despair*) But they were made to measure. They fit into this space, they won't fit anywhere else. These boards are no good to anybody, sir.

SHUI TA   Exactly. That's why I'm offering only twenty silver dollars. Because these boards are no good to anybody.

(*The wife squeals with delight*)

THE CARPENTER (*suddenly weary*)   It's too much for me. Keep the shelves and pay what you like.

SHUI TA   Twenty silver dollars.

(*He lays two large coins on the table. The carpenter takes them*)

THE HUSBAND (*carrying the stands back*)   Enough for a lot of boards that aren't any good to anybody.

THE CARPENTER   Yes, maybe enough to get drunk on. (*Out*)

THE HUSBAND   That takes care of him!

THE WIFE (*wiping away tears of laughter*)   "They're walnut!" —"Take them away!"—"A hundred silver dollars! I have four children!"—"In that case I'll pay twenty!"—"But they're no good to anybody!"—"Exactly! Twenty silver dollars!" That's the way to treat such people!

SHUI TA   Yes. (*Gravely*) Quick now, get out.

THE HUSBAND   *We* should get out?

SHUI TA   Yes, you. You're thieves and parasites. If you go quickly and waste no time arguing, nothing will happen to you.

THE HUSBAND   Better not answer. No use shouting on an empty stomach. Where can that boy be?

SHUI TA   Yes, where is the boy? I told you before that I don't want him in my shop with stolen cake. (*Suddenly shouting*) I repeat: Get out!

(*They remain seated*)

SHUI TA (*again calm*)   As you wish.

(*He goes to the door and bows deeply to someone outside. A policeman appears in the doorway*)

SHUI TA I presume I am addressing the police officer in charge of this district?

THE POLICEMAN Yes, Mr. . . .

SHUI TA Shui Ta. (*They exchange smiles*) Nice weather we're having!

THE POLICEMAN A trifle warm perhaps.

SHUI TA Perhaps a trifle warm.

THE HUSBAND (*in an undertone to his wife*) If he chews the fat until the kid gets back, we're done for. (*He tries to motion secretly to Shui Ta*)

SHUI TA (*ignoring him*) There's a difference between judging the weather in a cool shop and out on the dusty street.

THE POLICEMAN A big difference.

THE WIFE (*to the husband*) Don't worry. The kid will stay away if he sees the policeman standing in the doorway.

SHUI TA Do come in. It's really cooler in here. My cousin and I have opened a shop. I wish to tell you that we attach the utmost importance to being on good terms with the authorities.

THE POLICEMAN (*stepping in*) You're very kind, Mr. Shui Ta. Yes, it really is cool in here.

THE HUSBAND (*in an undertone*) He's asked him in on purpose. Now the boy won't see him.

SHUI TA Guests! Acquaintances of my cousin, so I'm told. They're passing through. (*Bows are exchanged*) We were just saying good-bye.

THE HUSBAND (*in a hoarse voice*) Well, we'll be going now.

SHUI TA I shall tell my cousin that you thank her for putting you up but hadn't time to wait for her.

(*Noise from the street. Cries of "Stop, thief!"*)

THE POLICEMAN What's that?

(*The boy appears in the doorway. Cakes and cookies are falling out of his shirt. The wife motions desperately to him to leave. He turns and starts to go*)

THE POLICEMAN You stay put! (*He grabs him*) Where did you get those cakes?

THE BOY Over there.

THE POLICEMAN Oh! Stolen, eh?

THE WIFE We didn't know. He did it on his own hook. You little no-good!

THE POLICEMAN Mr. Shui Ta, can you explain?
(*Shui Ta is silent*)

THE POLICEMAN Aha! I'm taking you all to the precinct.

SHUI TA I'm really dismayed that such a thing should have happened in my shop.

THE WIFE He was watching when the boy went out.

SHUI TA I can assure you, officer, that I should hardly have asked you in if I had wished to conceal a robbery.

THE POLICEMAN That stands to reason. So you'll surely understand, Mr. Shui Ta, that it's my duty to take these people into custody. (*Shui Ta bows*) Get going! (*He drives them out*)

THE GRANDFATHER (*solemnly from the doorway*) Good morning.

(*All go out except for Shui Ta. He continues to clean up. Enter Mrs. Mi Tzu*)

MRS. MI TZU So you're the cousin I've heard about. What does this mean, the police leading people out of my building? What makes your cousin think she can start a lodging house here? That's what happens when you take people in who only yesterday were living in a flophouse and begging millet cakes from the baker on the corner. You see, I know what's what.

SHUI TA Yes, I see. They've been telling you bad things about my cousin. They've told you she committed the crime of being hungry. She was notoriously poor. Her reputation couldn't have been any worse: she was down and out.

MRS. MI TZU She was a common ordinary . . .

SHUI TA Pauper. Don't be afraid to say the hard word.

MRS. MI TZU No sentimentality, if you please. I'm talking about her way of life, not her income. I presume she had a certain income or she wouldn't have taken this shop. An elderly gentleman or two must have helped. How else would one get a shop? This is a respectable house, sir. The tenants don't pay rent to live under the same roof with a person of her kind. Certainly not. (*Pause*) I'm not inhuman, but I've got my obligations.

SHUI TA (*coldly*) Mrs. Mi Tzu, I'm busy. Just tell me how much it will cost us to live in this respectable house.

MRS. MI TZU You've got a cool head on you, I'll hand you that.

SHUI TA (*taking the lease out of the drawer*) The rent is very high. I gather from the lease that it's payable by the month.

MRS. MI TZU (*quickly*) But not for people like your cousin.

SHUI TA What does that mean?

MRS. MI TZU It means that people like your cousin must pay six months' rent in advance: two hundred silver dollars.

SHUI TA Two hundred silver dollars! That's outrageous. How do you expect me to raise such a sum? I can't expect a large turnover. My only hope is that the girls who sew bags in the cement factory smoke a great deal, because I hear their work is exhausting. But they're badly paid.

MRS. MI TZU You should have thought of that before.

SHUI TA Mrs. Mi Tzu, have mercy! It's true, my cousin made the unpardonable mistake of sheltering a few unfortunates. But she can learn. I'll see to it that she learns. On the other hand, how can you find a better tenant than one who knows the gutter because that's where she's come from. She'll work her fingers to the bone to pay the rent punctually, she'll do everything in her power, make every sacrifice, sell everything, shrink back from nothing, and with all that she'll be still as a mouse, as quiet as a fly, and submit to you in every way sooner than go back down. Such a tenant is worth her weight in gold.

MRS. MI TZU Two hundred silver dollars in advance, or back she goes on the street where she came from.

(*Enter the policeman*)

THE POLICEMAN I don't wish to disturb you, Mr. Shui Ta.

MRS. MI TZU The police seem to be taking an unusual interest in this shop.

THE POLICEMAN You mustn't get the wrong impression, Mrs. Mi Tzu. Mr. Shui Ta has done us a service and I've only come to thank him in the name of the police.

MRS. MI TZU Well, that's no business of mine. I hope, Mr.

Shui Ta, that my proposition will meet with your cousin's approval. I like to be on good terms with my tenants. Good morning, gentlemen. (*Goes out*)

SHUI TA   Good morning, Mrs. Mi Tzu.

THE POLICEMAN   Are you having trouble with Mrs. Mi Tzu?

SHUI TA   She's demanding the rent in advance because my cousin doesn't strike her as respectable.

THE POLICEMAN   And you haven't got the money? (*Shui Ta is silent*) But a man like you, Mr. Shui Ta, must be able to get credit?

SHUI TA   Perhaps. But how is someone like Shen Teh to find credit?

THE POLICEMAN   Then you're not staying here?

SHUI TA   No. And I won't be coming back. I was only able to give her a hand on my way through. I was only able to prevent the worst. Soon she'll be left to her own resources. I can't help wondering what will happen then.

THE POLICEMAN   Mr. Shui Ta, I'm sorry you are having difficulties with the rent. I must admit that at first we looked on this shop with mixed feelings, but the resolute stand you took just now showed us the kind of man you are. We of the police are quick to find out which people are to be regarded as pillars of law and order.

SHUI TA (*bitterly*)   Officer, to save this shop which my cousin regards as a gift of the gods, I'm prepared to do anything the law permits. But hardness and duplicity are helpful only in our dealings with those below us in the social scale, for the dividing lines are cleverly drawn. I am in the position of the man who had just got rid of the rats in his cellar, when the whole river flowed in. (*After a short pause*) Do you smoke?

THE POLICEMAN (*putting two cigars in his pocket*)   All of us down at the precinct would be sorry to lose you, Mr. Shui Ta. But you must try to understand how Mrs. Mi Tzu feels about it. Shen Teh, we may as well face it, lived by selling herself to men. You may argue: what was she to do? How, for instance, was she to pay her rent? But the fact remains: it's not respectable. Why? In the first place, love shouldn't be for sale, for then it becomes mercenary love. In the second place, it's not respectable with someone who pays you, but only with someone you love. In the third place, it shouldn't be for a handful of rice, but for love. I know what you're going to say: what's the use of moralizing after the milk is spilt? What is she to do? She has to raise six months' rent. You've got me there, Mr. Shui Ta, I just don't know. (*He thinks hard*) Mr. Shui Ta, I've got it! Find her a husband!

(*Enter a little old woman*)

THE OLD WOMAN A good cheap cigar for my husband. You see, tomorrow is our fortieth wedding anniversary and we're having a little celebration.

SHUI TA (*politely*) Forty years and still celebrating!

THE OLD WOMAN As far as our means permit. We own the carpet shop across the street. I hope we'll be good neighbors, people should be, the times are hard.

SHUI TA (*offering several boxes*) Words as old as they are true, I'm afraid.

THE POLICEMAN Mr. Shui Ta, we need capital. Well, I suggest a marriage.

SHUI TA (*apologetically to the old woman*) I'm afraid I've been molesting the officer with my private troubles.

THE POLICEMAN We haven't got the six months' rent. All right, we marry a little money.

SHUI TA That won't be so easy.

THE POLICEMAN Why not? She's a good match. She has a small, promising business. (*To the old woman*) What do you think?

THE OLD WOMAN (*hesitantly*) Well . . .

THE POLICEMAN An ad in the paper.

THE OLD WOMAN (*doubtfully*) If the young lady agrees . . .

THE POLICEMAN Why wouldn't she? I'll write it out for you. One good turn deserves another. Don't imagine the authorities are without feeling for the struggling small businessman. You give us a hand and we write out your matrimonial advertisement for you. Hahaha! (*He busily pulls out his notebook, licks his pencil stump and starts writing*)

SHUI TA (*slowly*) Not a bad idea.

THE POLICEMAN "What . . . respectable . . . gentleman with a small capital . . . widower considered . . . desires marriage

. . . into promising tobacco shop?" And then we add: "Attractive appearance."—How's that?

SHUI TA   If you don't think it's an exaggeration.

THE OLD WOMAN (*amiably*)   Not at all. I've seen her.

(*The policeman tears the leaf out of his notebook and hands it to Shui Ta*)

SHUI TA   I am horrified to see how much luck is needed to keep from being crushed! How many brilliant ideas! How many good friends! (*To the policeman*) For all my determination I was at my wits' end over the rent. And then you came and helped me with a piece of good advice. I'm really beginning to see a ray of hope.

3

Evening in the Park

A young man in ragged clothes is watching a plane which seems to be describing a high arc over the park. He takes a rope out of his pocket and looks around for something. As he starts toward a large willow tree, two prostitutes come along. One is old, the other is the niece from the family of eight.

THE YOUNG ONE   Good evening, young man. Coming home with me, sweetie?

SUN   I might, ladies, if you'll buy me something to eat.

THE OLD ONE   Are you crazy? (*To the young one*) Come along, dearie. He's a waste of time. It's the unemployed flier.

THE YOUNG ONE   But there won't be anyone in the park now, it's going to rain.

THE OLD ONE   You never know.

(*They go on. Sun, looking around, takes out his rope and tosses it over a willow limb. But then he is disturbed again. The two prostitutes come back quickly. They do not see him*)

THE YOUNG ONE   It's going to pour in a minute.

(*Shen Teh comes strolling along*)

THE OLD ONE   Look, there she comes, the monster. She ruined you and your whole family.

THE YOUNG ONE   She didn't do it. It was her cousin. She took us in, and then she offered to pay for the cakes. I've got nothing against her.

THE OLD ONE   I have. (*Aloud*) Ah, here comes our fancy friend with the moneybags. She has a shop, but does that prevent her from trying to take our customers away?

SHEN TEH   No need to bite my head off. I'm on my way to the teahouse by the pond.

THE YOUNG ONE   Is it true you're going to marry a widower with three children?

SHEN TEH   Yes, I'm meeting him there.

SUN (*impatiently*)   Why don't you tarts get a move on? Can't I have any peace around here?

THE OLD ONE   Shut your trap!

(*The two prostitutes go out*)

SUN (*calling after them*)   Scavengers! (*To the audience*) Even in a remote spot like this they never get tired of fishing for victims, even in the bushes, even in the rain they hunt desperately for customers.

SHEN TEH (*angrily*)   Why are you so mean to them? (*Sees the rope*) Oh!

SUN   What are you gaping at?

SHEN TEH   What's the rope for?

SUN   Run along, sister. Run along. I've got no money, nothing, not a red cent. And if I had one, I wouldn't buy you, I'd buy a last cup of water.

(*It starts raining*)

SHEN TEH   What's the rope for? You mustn't.

SUN   Is it any of your business? Beat it.

SHEN TEH   It's raining.

SUN   Don't try to stand under my tree.

SHEN TEH (*standing motionless in the rain*)   No.

SUN   Forget it, sister, it won't get you anywhere. You can't do business with me. Anyway you're too ugly. Bowlegs.

SHEN TEH   That's not true.

SUN   Don't show them. All right, to hell with it, come in under the tree as long as it's raining.

(*She goes slowly over and sits down under the tree*)

SHEN TEH   Why do you want to do that?

SUN   You want to know? All right, I'll tell you, just to get rid of you. (*Pause*) Do you know what a flier is?

SHEN TEH   Yes, I saw some fliers in a teahouse once.

SUN   No, you didn't. Maybe some stupid windbags in flying helmets, clods with no ear for an engine or feeling for a plane. They only get into a crate by bribing the hangar boss. Say to one of them: drop your crate through the clouds from a height of 2,000 feet, then pick her up again with a flick of the stick, and he'll say: "It's not in my contract." Anybody who can't land his crate as gently as if it were his own behind, is no flier but a damn fool. I'm a flier. But I'm the biggest damn fool of all, because I read all the books on flying in school in Peking. But there was one page in the book that I didn't read, the one that said no fliers were needed any more. So now I'm a flier without a plane, a mail pilot without any mail. But you wouldn't understand.

SHEN TEH   I think I understand.

SUN   No, when I say, you can't understand, it means you can't understand.

SHEN TEH   (*half laughing, half crying*)   When we were little, we had a crane with a broken wing. He was friendly and put up with our tricks and strutted after us screaming that we shouldn't run too fast. But in the spring and fall, when the big flocks came flying over our village, he got awfully restless and I understood very well.

SUN   Don't cry.

SHEN TEH   No.

SUN   It's bad for your complexion.

SHEN TEH   I've stopped.

(*She wipes away the tears with her sleeve. Leaning against the tree, he reaches for her face, without looking toward her*)

SUN   You can't even wipe your face properly. (*He wipes it with a handkerchief. Pause*) If you must sit here to keep me from hanging myself, say something at least.

SHEN TEH   I don't know anything to say.

SUN   Tell me the truth, sister, why do you want to cut me down?

SHEN TEH   It frightens me. I'm sure you were only going to do it because it's such a gloomy evening. (*To the audience*)
In our country
There should be no gloomy evenings
Or great bridges over the rivers
Even the hour between night and morning
And the whole long winter season too are dangerous.
For what with the misery
A trifle is enough
To make people throw
Away their unbearable lives.

SUN   Tell me about yourself.

SHEN TEH   What is there to tell? I have a small shop.

SUN (*ironically*)   Oh, so you don't walk the streets, you've got a shop!

SHEN TEH (*firmly*)   I have a shop, but I used to walk the streets.

SUN   And this shop, I suppose, was a gift of the gods?

SHEN TEH   Yes.

SUN   One fine evening they stood there and said: Here's money for you.

SHEN TEH (*laughing softly*)   One morning.

SUN   You're not much of an entertainer.

SHEN TEH (*after a pause*)   I can play the zither a little and imitate people. (*She speaks in a deep voice, imitating a dignified gentleman*) "Good Lord, I must have forgotten my pocketbook!" But then I got the shop. The first thing I did was to give away my zither. I said to myself, now I can be a deadhead, and it won't matter.
I'm rich, I said to myself.
I walk alone. I sleep alone.
For a whole year, I said to myself
I'll have nothing to do with a man.

SUN   But now you're going to marry one? The one in the tea-house by the pond.
(*Shen Teh is silent*)

SUN   Come to think of it, what do you know about love?

SHEN TEH   Everything.

SUN   Nothing, sister. Or did you enjoy it?

SHEN TEH   No.

SUN (*strokes her face, but without turning toward her*)   Do you enjoy this?

SHEN TEH   Yes.

SUN   Easy to please, aren't you? What a town!

SHEN TEH   Haven't you any friends?

SUN   Plenty, but none who want to hear that I'm still out of a job. They make a face as if someone were complaining because there's water in the ocean. What about you? Have you got a friend?

SHEN TEH (*hesitantly*)   A cousin.

SUN   Don't trust him around the corner.

SHEN TEH   He's only been here once. Now he's gone away and he'll never come back again. But why do you talk as if everything were so hopeless? They say that to speak without hope is to speak without kindness.

SUN   Keep on talking! A voice is always a voice.

SHEN TEH (*eagerly*)   There are still friendly people in spite of all the misery. Once when I was little, I fell down with a load of brushwood. An old man helped me up and even gave me a penny. I've often remembered that. Especially people who haven't got much to eat are glad to share it. Maybe people just like to show their mettle, and what better way is there of showing it than to be friendly? Meanness is just a kind of clumsiness. When someone sings a song or makes a machine or plants rice, he's actually being friendly. You're friendly too.

SUN   It doesn't seem to take much, the way you look at it.

SHEN TEH   Yes. And now I've felt a raindrop.

SUN   Where?

SHEN TEH   Between my eyes.

SUN   More to the left or more to the right?

SHEN TEH   More to the left.

SUN   Good. (*After a while, sleepily*) And you're through with men?

SHEN TEH (*smiling*)   But I'm not bowlegged.

SUN   Maybe not.

SHEN TEH   Certainly not.

SUN (*leaning wearily against the tree*)   But I haven't eaten in two days or had anything to drink since yesterday, so I couldn't love you, sister, even if I wanted to.

SHEN TEH   It's nice in the rain.

(*Wang the water seller appears. He sings the* "Song of the Water Seller in the Rain")

WANG

Peddling water is my business
Hills and dales I go exploring
For a pint or two of liquid.
I come back and here it's pouring.
I stand shouting: Buy my water!
And no one buys it
And nobody's thirsty
They grin and despise it.
(Buy water, you devils!)

Oh, if I could stop this deluge!
Just last night I dreamt that seven
Years went by without a rainfall
Rubbed my hands, gave thanks to heaven!
How they shouted: Give me water
As they reached their hands out for my bucket!
And the measure of their doses
Hinged on how I liked their noses.
(They panted, the devils!)

(*Laughing*)
Weeds and grasses, drink your fill now
While the rain-soaked clouds are breaking
Lying back with mouths wide open
You can have it for the taking.
I stand shouting: Buy my water!
And no one buys it
And nobody's thirsty
They grin and despise it.
(Buy water, you devils!)

(*The rain has stopped. Shen Teh sees Wang and runs toward him*)

SHEN TEH   Oh, Wang, you're back again! I've got your carrying pole.

WANG   Many thanks for keeping it! How are you, Shen Teh?

SHEN TEH   Very well. I've met a very brave, intelligent man. And I'd like to buy a cup of your water.

WANG   Just tilt your head back and open your mouth, you'll have all the water you want. That willow tree is still dripping.

SHEN TEH

But I want your water, Wang
That you've carried so far
That has made you tired
That's hard to sell because it's raining.
I need it for that young man.
He's a flier. A flier
Is braver than other people. With the clouds for company
Braving the tempest
He flies through the skies bringing
Friends in distant countries
The friendly mail.
(*She pays and runs back to Sun with the cup. Laughing, she calls out to Wang*) He's fallen asleep. Despair and the rain and me have tired him out.

Interlude

Wang's Night Lodging in a Culvert

The water seller is asleep. Music. The culvert becomes transparent and the gods appear to the sleeper.

WANG (*beaming*)   I've seen her, Enlightened Ones! She's the same as ever!

THE FIRST GOD   We are very pleased.

WANG   She's in love. She showed me her lover. She's really getting along fine.

THE FIRST GOD   We are glad to hear it. Let us hope that will fortify her in her striving to do good.

WANG   It will! She does as many good deeds as she can.

THE FIRST GOD   What kind of good deeds? Tell us about them, my dear Wang!

WANG   She has a friendly word for everyone.

THE FIRST GOD (*eagerly*)   Yes? Go on!

WANG   Seldom does anyone leave her little shop without tobacco just because he has no money.

THE FIRST GOD   Not bad. Anything else?

WANG   She lodged a family of eight!

THE FIRST GOD (*triumphantly to the second*)   A family of eight! (*To Wang*) And something more perhaps?

WANG   Even though it was raining, she bought a cup of my water.

THE FIRST GOD   Yes, yes, of course. Modest good deeds. They were to be expected.

WANG   But they run into money. A small shop doesn't bring in very much.

THE FIRST GOD   Of course not. But a clever gardener can do wonders with a small patch of ground.

WANG   That's exactly what she does. Every morning she hands out rice; I assure you it uses up more than half her earnings.

THE FIRST GOD (*slightly disappointed*)   I suppose it does. Not bad for a beginning.

WANG   Remember, these are hard times. Once she had to call in a cousin to help her when her shop was in difficulties.
No sooner was there a place sheltered from the wind
Than the ruffled birds of the whole wintry sky
Came flying, fighting
For room and the hungry fox bit through
The thin wall and the one-legged wolf
Tumbled the little rice bowl over.
In short, her affairs were too much for her to handle by herself. But everyone agrees that she's a good girl. Already so

much good flows from her shop that she's known far and wide as "The Angel of the Slums." Whatever Lin To the carpenter may say!

THE FIRST GOD   What's that? Does Lin To the carpenter speak badly of her?

WANG   Oh, he only says that the stands in her shop weren't fully paid for.

THE SECOND GOD   What's that you say? A carpenter wasn't paid? In Shen Teh's shop? How could she let such a thing happen?

WANG   I suppose she didn't have the money.

THE SECOND GOD   That makes no difference. Debts are debts. The slightest suggestion of irregularity must be avoided. The commandments must be fulfilled both in letter and spirit.

WANG   But it was only her cousin, Enlightened One, not she herself.

THE SECOND GOD   Then her cousin must never cross her threshold again.

WANG (*dejectedly*)   I understand, Enlightened One. In Shen Teh's defense let me point out that her cousin is looked upon as a most estimable businessman. Even the police respect him.

THE FIRST GOD   Well, we will not condemn the cousin without a hearing. I admit that I know nothing about business. Perhaps we ought to find out what is customary in such matters. And anyway, business! Is it really necessary? Everybody's doing business. Were the Seven Good Kings in business? Did Kung the Righteous sell fish? What has business to do with an upright, honorable life?

THE SECOND GOD (*very much disgruntled*)   In any case it must never happen again.

(*He turns to go. The two other gods also turn*)

THE THIRD GOD (*last in line, with embarrassment*)   Forgive the rather harsh tone we have taken today. We are very tired, and we haven't been getting enough sleep. Those lodgings! The rich give us the warmest recommendations to the poor, but the poor haven't room enough.

THE GODS (*grumbling as they move off*)   Weak, even she, the best of them!—Nothing conclusive!—Pitiful, pitiful! The heart's in the right place, but the result is negligible! At least she could . . .

(*They can no longer be heard*)

WANG (*calls after them*) Don't be unmerciful, Enlightened Ones. Don't ask too much for a beginning!

4

The Square outside Shen Teh's Shop

A barber shop, a carpet shop, and Shen Teh's tobacco shop. It is morning. Outside Shen Teh's shop two remnants of the family of eight are waiting: the grandfather and the sister-in-law. Also the unemployed man and Mrs. Shin.

THE SISTER-IN-LAW She didn't come home last night.

MRS. SHIN Incredible behavior! At last her horrid cousin leaves, she condescends to hand out a little of her extra rice now and then, and one two three she starts staying out all night, running around God knows where!

(*Loud voices are heard from the barber shop. Out staggers Wang, followed by the fat barber, Mr. Shu Fu, brandishing a heavy curling iron*)

MR. SHU FU I'll teach you to molest my customers with your stinking water. Take your cup and clear out!

(*Wang reaches for the cup that Mr. Shu Fu is holding out to him. Mr. Shu Fu strikes him on the hand with the curling iron. Wang screams*)

MR. SHU FU There! Let that be a lesson to you! (*He goes puffing back into his shop*)

THE UNEMPLOYED MAN (*picks up the cup and hands it to Wang*) You can have the law on him for hitting you.

WANG My hand is done for.

THE UNEMPLOYED MAN Any bones broken?

WANG   I can't move it.

THE UNEMPLOYED MAN   Sit down and pour some water on it.
(*Wang sits down*)

MRS. SHIN   At least the water won't cost you anything.

THE SISTER-IN-LAW   Eight o'clock, and you can't even find a
rag in this place. She's got to go gallivanting around. Disgraceful!

MRS. SHIN (*gloomily*)   She's forgotten us!

(*Down the street comes Shen Teh, carrying a pot of rice*)

SHEN TEH (*to the audience*)   I'd never seen the city in the
early morning. At this time of day I was always lying with
my filthy blanket over my head, afraid to wake up. Today
I've been out among the newsboys, the men who scrub the
streets, and the ox carts bringing in fresh vegetables from
the country. I've come a long way from Sun's neighborhood, but with every step I feel more light-hearted. I've
always heard that you walk on air when you're in love, but
the best part of it is that you walk on the ground, on asphalt.
Let me tell you: in the morning the blocks of buildings are
like heaps of rubble with lights lighting up inside, and the
sky is pink and still transparent, because there's no dust. Let
me tell you: you're missing a good deal if you're not in love
and you don't see your city at the hour when it gets out of
bed like a sober old craftsman filling his lungs with fresh air
and reaching for his tools, as the poets say. (*To those waiting*) Good morning! Here's your rice! (*She dishes it out,
then sees Wang*) Good morning, Wang. I'm giddy today.
On my way I looked at myself in every shop window and
now I feel like buying myself a shawl. (*After brief hesitation*) I'd so much like to look beautiful. (*She quickly enters
the carpet shop*)

MR. SHU FU (*who has reappeared in his doorway, to the audience*)   I am overwhelmed to see how beautiful Miss Shen
Teh, the owner of the tobacco shop across the street, looks
today; I'd never noticed her before. I've been looking at her
for three minutes and I think I'm already in love with her.
How incredibly charming she is! (*To Wang*) Get out of
here, you ruffian! (*He goes back into his barber shop*)

(*Shen Teh and a very old couple, the carpet dealer and his wife, come out of the carpet shop. Shen Teh is carrying a shawl, the carpet dealer is holding a mirror*)

THE OLD WOMAN   It's very pretty and not expensive, because there's a tiny little hole in it.

SHEN TEH (*looking at the shawl on the old woman's arm*)   The green one is nice too.

THE OLD WOMAN (*smiling*)   But unfortunately it's not slightly damaged.

SHEN TEH   Yes, that's too bad. I can't afford to be extravagant. My shop doesn't take in very much and I have big expenses.

THE OLD WOMAN   For charity. Don't do so much. When you're starting out, every bowl of rice counts.

SHEN TEH (*trying on the shawl with the hole in it*)   That can't be helped, but now I feel frivolous. Is the color becoming to me?

THE OLD WOMAN   You'd better ask a man.

SHEN TEH (*turning to the old man*)   Is it becoming to me?

THE OLD MAN   Why don't you ask . . .

SHEN TEH (*very politely*)   No, I'm asking you.

THE OLD MAN (*just as politely*)   The shawl is becoming to you. But wear the dull side out.
   (*Shen Teh pays*)

THE OLD WOMAN   If he doesn't like it on you, you can always exchange it. (*Draws her aside*) Has he any money?

SHEN TEH (*laughing*)   Goodness, no!

THE OLD WOMAN   Then how on earth will you pay the six months' rent?

SHEN TEH   The rent! I'd completely forgotten!

THE OLD WOMAN   Just as I thought. And next Monday is the first. I have an idea. You know, once we had come to know you, my husband and I had our doubts about that matrimonial advertisement. We decided to help you out if necessary. We've saved a little money, we can lend you the two hundred silver dollars. If you like, you can pledge your stock of tobacco as security. But of course there needn't be anything between us in writing.

SHEN TEH   Would you really lend money to anyone so scatterbrained?

THE OLD WOMAN   Frankly, we might think twice before lend-

ing it to your cousin, who is anything but scatterbrained, but
we'll gladly lend it to you.

THE OLD MAN (*coming up to them*)   Then it's settled?

SHEN TEH   I wish the gods could have heard your wife just
now, Mr. Deng. They are looking for good people who are
also happy. If you can help me when love has got me into
difficulties, you must be happy.

(*The old people exchange smiles*)

THE OLD MAN   Here is the money.

(*He hands her an envelope. Shen Teh takes it and bows.
The old people bow too. They go back into their shop*)

SHEN TEH (*to Wang, holding up her envelope*)   This is the
six months' rent. Isn't it a miracle? And what do you think
of my shawl, Wang?

WANG   Did you buy it for the man I saw in the park?

(*Shen Teh nods*)

MRS. SHIN   You might take a look at his broken hand instead
of bothering him with your shady goings-on.

SHEN TEH (*horrified*)   What's wrong with your hand?

MRS. SHIN   The barber smashed it with his curling iron right
here before our eyes.

SHEN TEH (*aghast at her thoughtlessness*)   And I didn't notice!
You must go straight to the doctor or your hand will get
stiff and you won't be able to work properly any more. That
would be dreadful. Come, get up! Hurry!

THE UNEMPLOYED MAN   It's not the doctor he should see, it's
the judge! The barber is rich, he can collect damages.

WANG   Do you think there's any chance?

MRS. SHIN   If it's really broken. But is it?

WANG   I think so. It's all swollen. Would I get a life pension?

MRS. SHIN   You'd need witnesses.

WANG   But you all saw it! You can all testify.

(*He looks around. The unemployed man, the grandfather,
and the sister-in-law are sitting against the wall, eating. No
one looks up*)

SHEN TEH (*to Mrs. Shin*)   But you saw it yourself!

MRS. SHIN   I don't want any truck with the police.

SHEN TEH (*to the sister-in-law*)   Then you!

THE SISTER-IN-LAW   Me? I wasn't looking.

MRS. SHIN   Of course you were looking! I saw you looking. You're just afraid because the barber's so influential.

SHEN TEH (*to the grandfather*)   I'm sure *you* will testify.

THE SISTER-IN-LAW   They won't accept his testimony. He's gaga.

SHEN TEH (*to the unemployed man*)   It could mean a life pension.

THE UNEMPLOYED MAN   They've put me on the books twice for begging. My testimony would only hurt him.

SHEN TEH (*incredulously*)   Then not one of you is willing to tell the plain truth? His hand was broken in broad daylight, you were all looking on, and none of you is willing to speak? (*Angrily*)
Oh, you wretched people!
Your brother suffers violence and you shut your eyes.
The injured man cries aloud and you say nothing?
The violent man goes about selecting his victim
And you say: he won't touch us for we show no displeasure.
What a city this is, what people you are!
When an injustice is done in a city, there must be an uproar.
Where there is no uproar, it would be better for the city
To perish in flames before the night falls.
Wang, if no one who saw it will be your witness, I will be your witness and say that I saw it.

MRS. SHIN   That will be perjury.

WANG   I don't know if I can let you do that. But perhaps I'll have to. (*Looking anxiously at his hand*) Do you think it's swollen enough? It seems to me the swelling has gone down.

THE UNEMPLOYED MAN (*reassuring him*)   No, it certainly hasn't gone down.

WANG   Are you sure? Why yes, I'd say it's even swollen a little more. Maybe my wrist is broken after all. I'd better go straight to the judge. (*Holding his hand gingerly, his eyes glued to it, he runs off*)
(*Mrs. Shin runs into the barber shop*)

THE UNEMPLOYED MAN   She's gone to the barber's to butter him up.

THE SISTER-IN-LAW   We can't change the world.

SHEN TEH (*discouraged*)   I didn't mean to scold you. It's just that I'm horrified. No, I did mean to scold you. Get out of my sight.

(*The unemployed man, the sister-in-law, and the grandfather go out, eating and grumbling*)

SHEN TEH (*to the audience*)

They don't respond any more. Wherever you put them
They stay put, and when you send them away
They go quickly.
Nothing moves them any longer. Only
The smell of food makes them look up.

(*An old woman runs in. It is Mrs. Yang, Sun's mother*)

MRS. YANG (*breathlessly*)   Are you Miss Shen Teh? My son has told me everything. I am Mrs. Yang, Sun's mother. Just imagine, he's been offered a flying job. This morning, just a little while ago, a letter came from Peking. From an airport superintendent.

SHEN TEH   You mean he'll be able to fly again? Oh, Mrs. Yang!

MRS. YANG   But it costs so much money: five hundred silver dollars.

SHEN TEH   That's a good deal, but we can't let money stand in his way. After all, I've got the shop.

MRS. YANG   If you could only do something!

SHEN TEH (*throwing her arms around her*)   I'd be glad to help him!

MRS. YANG   You'd be giving an able young man a chance!

SHEN TEH   They have no right to prevent a person from being useful. (*After a pause*) The trouble is that I won't get enough for the shop, and these two hundred silver dollars are only a loan. You can take them, though. I'll sell my stock of tobacco and pay them back out of that. (*She gives her the old couple's money*)

MRS. YANG   Oh, Miss Shen Teh, a friend in need is a friend indeed. The people here in town were all calling him the dead flier, because they thought he had as much chance as a corpse of flying again.

SHEN TEH   But we still need three hundred silver dollars to get him the job. We must put our heads together, Mrs. Yang. (*Slowly*) I know someone who might help me. Someone who has already given me good advice. I didn't want to call

him back, because he's such a hard, crafty man. This must really be the last time. But obviously a flier must fly.
(*A distant sound of airplane engines*)

MRS. YANG   If the man you speak of could only get the money! Look, that's the morning mail plane on its way to Peking.

SHEN TEH (*with determination*)   Wave, Mrs. Yang! I'm sure the flier can see us. (*She waves her shawl*) You wave too!

MRS. YANG (*waving*)   Do you know the flier?

SHEN TEH   No. I know someone who's going to fly. Yes, the man without hope will fly, Mrs. Yang. One man at least will rise above all this misery, one man at least will rise above us all! (*To the audience*)

Yang Sun, my beloved, with the clouds for company
Braving the tempest
Flying through the skies, bringing
Friends in distant countries
The friendly mail.

Interlude

In Front of the Curtain

Shen Teh enters carrying the mask and clothes of Shui Ta, and sings "The Song of the Defenselessness of the Gods and the Good People."

In our country
A useful man needs luck. Only
If he has influential helpers
Can he make himself useful.
The good
Cannot help themselves and the gods are powerless.
　　So why can't the gods have bazookas and gunboats
　　Dreadnoughts and machine-guns, bombers and mortars
　　To shatter the wicked and succor the good folk?
　　What's good for the good can't hurt the immortals!

(She puts on Shui Ta's clothes and takes a few steps in his manner)

The good
Cannot stay good for long in our country.
Where plates are empty, the diners are soon at each other's
    throats.
Ah, the divine commandments
Are little help against penury.
    So why can't the gods come down in the markets
    And hand out their bounty to each and his brother
    And let us, once hunger and thirst have been sated
    Be friendly and kindly toward one another?

(She puts on Shui Ta's mask and continues to sing in his voice)

Merely to get your dinner
Requires the ruthlessness of an empire builder.
Without trampling on twelve others
No one can help a wretched man.
    So why can't the gods decide in the heavens
    To make the world good for the good people in it?
    Why can't they come down with tanks and with cannon
    Make merciless war upon evil and win it?

5

The Tobacco Shop

Shui Ta sits behind the counter reading the paper. He pays no attention to Mrs. Shin who talks as she is scrubbing the floor.

MRS. SHIN   A small shop like this is quickly ruined, take it
from me, when certain rumors start going around the neigh-

borhood. It's high time a respectable man like you did something about this shady affair between the young lady and that Yang Sun over in Yellow Street. Don't forget that only yesterday Mr. Shu Fu, the barber next door, who owns twelve houses and has only one wife and an old one at that, intimated in my hearing that he took a flattering interest in the young lady. He has already made inquiries about her financial situation. That shows genuine affection, if you ask me. (*Obtaining no answer, she finally goes out with her bucket*)

SUN's VOICE (*from outside*) Is this Miss Shen Teh's shop?

MRS. SHIN's VOICE Yes, this is it. But her cousin's here today. (*Shui Ta runs to the mirror with the light steps of Shen Teh and is about to arrange his hair when he sees his mistake in the mirror. He turns away with a soft laugh. Enter Yang Sun. Behind him Mrs. Shin, full of curiosity. She goes past him to the back room*)

SUN I am Yang Sun. (*Shui Ta bows*) Is Shen Teh here?

SHUI TA No, she's not here.

SUN I presume you know how it is between us. (*He starts giving the shop the once-over*) An honest-to-goodness shop! I always thought she'd made it up. (*He looks with satisfaction into the little boxes and porcelain pots*) Man, I'm going to fly again! (*He takes a cigar and Shui Ta gives him a light*) Do you think we can squeeze another three hundred silver dollars out of the shop?

SHUI TA May I ask: do you intend to sell it immediately?

SUN Have we got the three hundred in cash? (*Shui Ta shakes his head*) It was decent of her to fork over the two hundred right away. But without the three hundred they won't get me anywhere.

SHUI TA Perhaps she was a little hasty in offering you the money. It may cost her her shop. They say that haste is the wind that blew the house down.

SUN I need the money in a hurry or not at all. And that girl isn't the kind that holds back when it comes to giving something. Just between us men, she hasn't held anything back so far.

SHUI TA I see.

SUN   Which is all to her credit.

SHUI TA   May I ask what the five hundred silver dollars would be used for?

SUN   Certainly. I can see you're sizing me up. The superintendent of the Peking airport, an old friend of mine from flying school, can get me the job if I cough up five hundred silver dollars.

SHUI TA   Isn't that a lot of money to be asking?

SUN   No. He's got to pin a charge of negligence on a pilot who's as conscientious as they come because he's got a big family. See what I mean? That's in confidence, see, no need for Shen Teh to know about it.

SHUI TA   Perhaps not. But tell me this: won't that superintendent sell you out in a few weeks' time?

SUN   Not me. He won't catch me being negligent. I've been out of a job too long.

SHUI TA (*nods*)   The hungry dog pulls the cart home quicker. (*He studies Sun for a time*) That's a big responsibility. Mr. Yang Sun, you are asking my cousin to abandon her few possessions and all her friends in this town, and to put herself entirely in your hands. I presume you intend to marry Shen Teh?

SUN   I'd be willing to.

SHUI TA   But wouldn't it be a pity to let the shop go for a song? We won't get much for it if we have to sell in a hurry. The two hundred silver dollars you've got there would pay the rent for the next six months. Wouldn't it tempt you to keep up the tobacco shop?

SUN   Me? You want people to see Yang Sun the flier, standing behind a counter: "Do you desire a strong cigar or a mild one, honored sir?" That's no business for a Yang Sun, not in this day and age.

SHUI TA   And is flying a good business, may I ask?

SUN (*taking a letter out of his pocket*)   I'm getting two hundred and fifty silver dollars a month, mister! Here's the letter, see for yourself. See the stamp and the postmark? Peking.

SHUI TA   Two hundred and fifty silver dollars. That's a good deal.

SUN   Did you think I was going to fly for nothing?

SHUI TA   It seems to be a good job. Mr. Yang Sun, my cousin has asked me to help you obtain this flier's job that means so much to you. From my cousin's point of view I can see no valid reason why she shouldn't follow the promptings of her heart. She is fully entitled to her share in the joys of love. I am prepared to liquidate everything here. Here comes Mrs. Mi Tzu, the owner of the house; I wanted to ask her for advice.

MRS. MI TZU (*enters*)   Good morning, Mr. Shui Ta. I suppose it's about the rent that's due the day after tomorrow.

SHUI TA   Mrs. Mi Tzu, circumstances have arisen that make it very doubtful whether my cousin will keep the shop. She is planning to be married and her future husband, (*he introduces Yang Sun*) Mr. Yang Sun, is taking her to Peking to start a new life. If I am offered enough money for my tobacco, I shall sell.

MRS. MI TZU   How much do you need?

SUN   Three hundred on the line.

SHUI TA (*quickly*)   No, five hundred.

MRS. MI TZU (*to Sun*)   Maybe I can help you out. (*To Shui Ta*) How much did the tobacco cost you?

SHUI TA   My cousin originally paid a thousand silver dollars for it, and very little of it has been sold.

MRS. MI TZU   A thousand silver dollars! She was swindled of course. I'll make you an offer. I'll give you three hundred silver dollars for the whole shop if you move out the day after tomorrow.

SUN   Will do. That's it, old man!

SHUI TA   It's too little.

SUN   It's enough.

SHUI TA   I need at least five hundred.

SUN   What for?

SHUI TA   Excuse me, I'll have to talk this over with my cousin's fiancé. (*Aside to Sun*) The whole stock of tobacco is pledged to two old people as security for the two hundred silver dollars that you were given yesterday.

SUN (*hesitantly*)   Is there anything in writing?

SHUI TA   No.

SUN (*to Mrs. Mi Tzu after a short pause*)   We can make out with three hundred.

MRS. MI TZU   But I must be sure there are no outstanding claims against the shop.

SUN   Tell her.

SHUI TA   There are no outstanding claims.

SUN   When can we have the three hundred?

MRS. MI TZU   The day after tomorrow. Think it over. If you wait a month or so, you'll get a better price. I'm willing to pay three hundred, but only because this seems to be a case of young love and I like to do my part. (*Goes out*)

SUN (*calling after her*)   It's a deal. All the little pots and sacks and boxes, we'll let the whole thing go for three hundred, and no more headaches. (*To Shui Ta*) Maybe in the next two days somebody'll make us a better offer. Then we could even pay back the two hundred.

SHUI TA   Not in such a short time. We won't get one silver dollar more than Mi Tzu's three hundred. I trust you have money for two tickets and enough to tide you over?

SUN   Of course.

SHUI TA   How much?

SUN   Anyway, I'll get it even if I have to steal it.

SHUI TA   Oh! So that's more money to be raised?

SUN   Don't go into a tizzy, old man. I'll get to Peking all right.

SHUI TA   But it must be expensive for two.

SUN   Two? I'm leaving the girl here. In the beginning she'd only get in the way.

SHUI TA   I see.

SUN   Why do you look at me as if I were a leaky oil can? I'm only trying to make the best of things.

SHUI TA   And what do you expect my cousin to live on?

SUN   Can't you do something for her?

SHUI TA   I'll try. (*Pause*) I wish you'd return the two hundred silver dollars, Mr. Yang Sun, and leave them here until you're able to show me two tickets to Peking.

SUN   And I, dear brother-in-law, wish you'd mind your own business.

SHUI TA   Miss Shen Teh . . .

SUN   Let me worry about her.

SHUI TA   . . . may not want to sell her shop when she finds out . . .

SUN   Never mind, that won't stop her.

SHUI TA   And you're not afraid of my opposition?

SUN   Come off it!

SHUI TA   You seem to forget that she's human and has a certain amount of sense.

SUN (*amused*)   It always hands me a laugh the way some people think they can make the females in their family listen to sensible arguments. Haven't you ever heard of the power of love or the itching of the flesh? You're going to appeal to her reason? She hasn't got any reason. On the other hand, she's been stepped on all her life, the poor little thing. If I put my hand on her shoulder and say: "Come with me," she'll hear bells, she won't know her own mother any more.

SHUI TA (*with difficulty*)   Mr. Yang Sun!

SUN   Mr. . . . whatever your name is!

SHUI TA   My cousin is attached to you because . . .

SUN   Let's say because I've got my hand on her bosom. Put that in your pipe and smoke it. (*He takes another cigar, then puts a few in his pocket, and finally puts the box under his arm*) You won't be going to her with nothing to offer: I said I'd marry her and I stick to it. She'll bring the three hundred or you will, one or the other! (*Goes out*)

MRS. SHIN (*sticks her head out of the back room*)   Not very prepossessing, is he? And all Yellow Street knows he's got that girl where he wants her.

SHUI TA (*crying out*)   The shop is gone! He's not in love! This is ruin! I'm lost! (*He runs around like a captive animal, repeating over and over "The shop is gone!" Then suddenly he stops still and speaks to Mrs. Shin*) Mrs. Shin, you grew up in the gutter and so did I. Are we irresponsible? No. Do we lack the brutality that's needed? No. I'm ready to take you by the neck and shake you until you cough up the money you've stolen from me, you know that. These are dreadful times, this city is hell, and yet we claw our way up the smooth wall. Then one of us is overtaken by disaster:

he's in love. That does it, he's lost. One moment of weakness and you're done for. How can we get rid of all our weaknesses, especially the most fatal of all, love? It's an impossible weakness. It's too expensive. Tell me, do you call it living to be always on your guard? What kind of a world are we living in?

Caresses turn to strangling.

A sigh of love becomes a cry of terror.

Why are those vultures circling?

A girl is going to a rendezvous.

MRS. SHIN I think I'd better get the barber. You must speak to the barber. He's an upstanding man. He's the right man for your cousin. (*Receiving no answer, she dashes off*)

(*Shui Ta starts running around again until Mr. Shu Fu appears, followed by Mrs. Shin, who, however, withdraws at a sign from Mr. Shu Fu*)

SHUI TA (*hurries toward him*) Dear sir, I know by hearsay that you have shown a certain interest in my cousin. Permit me to set aside the rules of etiquette, which call for reserve: The young lady is in great danger.

MR. SHU FU Oh!

SHUI TA Only a few hours ago my cousin was the owner of a shop, now she is little more than a beggar. Mr. Shu Fu, this shop is ruined.

MR. SHU FU Mr. Shui Ta, Miss Shen Teh's charm resides not in the solvency of her shop but in the goodness of her heart. The name they have for the young lady here in the neighborhood tells the whole story: The Angel of the Slums.

SHUI TA Dear sir, in a single day her goodness cost my cousin two hundred silver dollars. This sort of thing has got to be stopped.

MR. SHU FU Permit me to differ: her goodness must be given free rein. It is the young lady's nature to do good. Why worry about her feeding four people as, to my profound emotion, I have seen her doing every morning? Why shouldn't she feed four hundred? I hear, for example, that she has been racking her brains for a way to shelter a few homeless people. My houses behind the cattle yard are empty. They stand at her disposal. And so forth and so on. Such are the ideas that have come to me in the last few days. May I hope, Mr. Shui Ta, that Miss Shen Teh will lend an ear to them?

SHUI TA   Mr. Shu Fu, she will lend an admiring ear to such noble thoughts.

(*Enter Wang with the policeman. Mr. Shu Fu turns around and studies the shelves*)

WANG   Is Miss Shen Teh here?

SHUI TA   No.

WANG   I am Wang, the water seller. You must be Mr. Shui Ta?

SHUI TA   So I am. Good morning, Wang.

WANG   I am a friend of Shen Teh.

SHUI TA   I know that you are one of her oldest friends.

WANG (*to the policeman*)   Do you see? (*To Shui Ta*) I've come on account of my hand.

THE POLICEMAN   No question about it, it's in bad shape.

SHUI TA (*quickly*)   I see, you need a sling.

(*He brings a shawl from the back room and tosses it to Wang*)

WANG   But this is her new shawl.

SHUI TA   She doesn't need it any more.

WANG   But she bought it to please a certain person.

SHUI TA   The way things have turned out, that is no longer necessary.

WANG (*makes a sling from the shawl*)   She is my only witness.

THE POLICEMAN   Your cousin allegedly saw the barber Shu Fu strike the water seller with his curling iron. Do you know anything about it?

SHUI TA   All I know is that my cousin herself was not present when the trifling incident took place.

WANG   That is a misunderstanding. Wait until Shen Teh comes in, it will all be cleared up. Shen Teh will testify. Where is she?

SHUI TA (*gravely*)   Mr. Wang, you call yourself my cousin's friend. My cousin has dreadful worries right now. She has been shamefully exploited by any number of people. From now on she can't afford the slightest weakness. I feel sure you wouldn't want her to ruin herself completely by telling anything other than the truth in your case.

WANG (*confused*)   But she advised me to go to the judge.

SHUI TA   Was the judge supposed to cure your hand?

THE POLICEMAN   No. He was supposed to make the barber pay up.

(*Mr. Shu Fu turns around*)

SHUI TA   Mr. Wang, it's a principle with me never to interfere in disputes between my friends.

(*Shui Ta bows to Mr. Shu Fu, who returns the bow*)

WANG (*taking off the sling and putting it down, sadly*)   I understand.

THE POLICEMAN   I guess that lets me out. You tried your game on the wrong party, an honest man. Better be a little more careful with your complaints next time, friend. If Mr. Shu Fu doesn't put mercy before justice, you can still end up in the clink for slander. Get going now!

(*Both go out*)

SHUI TA   Please forgive the incident.

MR. SHU FU   It is forgiven. (*With urgency*) And the affair with that "certain person" (*he points at the shawl*) is really over? Really and truly?

SHUI TA   Completely. She has seen through him. Of course it will take her some time to get over it.

MR. SHU FU   We shall be kind and considerate.

SHUI TA   Her wounds are fresh.

MR. SHU FU   She will go to the country.

SHUI TA   For a few weeks. But before she goes she will be glad to talk things over with someone she can trust.

MR. SHU FU   Over a small supper, in a small but excellent restaurant.

SHUI TA   All very discreet. I shall hasten to notify my cousin. She will be reasonable. She's dreadfully upset over her shop, which she regards as a gift from the gods. Be so kind as to wait a few minutes. (*Goes out into the back room*)

MRS. SHIN (*poking her head in*)   Are congratulations in order?

MR. SHU FU   Yes, indeed. Mrs. Shin, kindly tell Miss Shen Teh's protégés before nightfall that I am putting them up in my houses behind the cattle yard.

(*She grins and nods*)

MR. SHU FU (*standing up, to the audience*)   What do you think of me, ladies and gentlemen? Could anyone do more? Could anyone be more unselfish? More sensitive? More farsighted? A little supper! How crude, people would ordinarily think, how gross! But no such thing will happen, certainly not. No contact, not even apparently by accident while passing the salt. There will be an exchange of ideas. Two souls will find one another over the flowers on the table, white chrysanthemums I should think. (*He makes a note of it*) No, there will be no exploiting of an unfortunate situation, no taking advantage of a disillusionment. Help and understanding will be offered, but almost in silence. They will be acknowledged by no more than a glance, but perhaps there will be added meaning in that glance.

MRS. SHIN   Then everything is going as you wished, Mr. Shu Fu?

MR. SHU FU   Oh, quite as I wished. I predict that there will be changes in this neighborhood. A certain individual has been given his walking papers, and certain designs against this shop are going to be nipped in the bud. Certain people who have the audacity to sully the reputation of the most virtuous girl in this city will have me to deal with from now on. What do you know of this Yang Sun?

MRS. SHIN   He's the filthiest, laziest . . .

MR. SHU FU   He is nothing. He doesn't exist. There is no such person, Mrs. Shin.

(*Enter Sun*)

SUN   What's going on around here?

MRS. SHIN   Mr. Shu Fu, would you like me to call Mr. Shui Ta? He wouldn't want to have strangers hanging around the shop.

MR. SHU FU   Miss Shen Teh is having an important conference with Mr. Shui Ta, that must not be interrupted.

SUN   What? She's here? I didn't see her come in. What kind of a conference? I've got to be in on that.

MR. SHU FU (*stops him from going into the back room*)   You'll just have to wait, sir. I believe I know who you are. I wish you to know that Miss Shen Teh and I are about to announce our engagement.

SUN   What?

MRS. SHIN   That surprises you, doesn't it?

(*Sun wrestles with the barber in an attempt to get into the back room. Out steps Shen Teh*)

MR. SHU FU   I beg your pardon, dear Shen Teh. Perhaps you will explain what . . .

SUN   What's going on, Shen Teh? Are you out of your mind?

SHEN TEH (*breathlessly*)   Sun, my cousin and Mr. Shu Fu have agreed that I should listen to Mr. Shu Fu's ideas about how to help the people in this neighborhood. (*Pause*) My cousin is opposed to our relationship.

SUN   And you agree?

SHEN TEH   Yes. (*Pause*)

SUN   Did they tell you I was a bad man?

(*Shen Teh is silent*)

SUN   Because maybe I am, Shen Teh. And that's why I need you. I'm a low character. No money, no manners. But I'm not going to take this lying down. They're ruining your life, Shen Teh. (*He goes over to her. In a muffled voice*) Just look at him! Haven't you any eyes in your head? (*Laying his hand on her shoulder*) Poor little thing, what are they trying to push you into now? A practical marriage? If it hadn't been for me they'd have dragged you off to the slaughter. Just tell me: if I hadn't come along, wouldn't you have gone off with him?

SHEN TEH   Yes.

SUN   A man you don't love!

SHEN TEH   Yes.

SUN   Have you forgotten everything? The rain?

SHEN TEH   No.

SUN   How you cut me down, how you bought me a glass of water, how you promised me money so I could fly again.

SHEN TEH (*trembling*)   What do you want?

SUN   I want you to come away with me.

SHEN TEH   Mr. Shu Fu, forgive me, I'm going away with Sun.

SUN   We love each other, you see. (*He leads her to the door*) Where have you got the key to the shop? (*He takes it out of her pocket and gives it to Mrs. Shin*) Put it on the doorstep when you're through. Come, Shen Teh.

MR. SHU FU   But this is abduction! (*Shouts into the back room*) Mr. Shui Ta!

SUN   Tell him to stop shouting around here.

SHEN TEH   Please don't call my cousin, Mr. Shu Fu. He doesn't
see eye to eye with me, I know that. But he's not right, I can
feel it. (*To the audience*)
I want to go with the man I love.
I don't want to reckon the cost.
I don't want to think about whether it's right.
I don't want to know whether he loves me.
I want to go with the man I love.

SUN   That's the way it goes.

(*Both go out*)

Interlude

In Front of the Curtain

*Shen Teh in wedding dress on the way to her wedding, turns
to the audience.*

SHEN TEH   I've had a dreadful experience. As I stepped out the
door, happy and full of expectation, the carpet dealer's old
wife was standing in the street. Trembling, she told me that
her husband had fallen ill from excitement and worry over
the money they loaned me. She thought the best thing would
be for me to give them back the money right away. Of
course I promised. She was very much relieved, she tearfully
gave me her best wishes and begged my forgiveness for not
fully trusting my cousin, or, she was sorry to say, Sun. When
she had gone, I was so horrified at myself that I had to sit
down on the doorstep. In a surge of feeling I had thrown
myself into Sun's arms again. I couldn't resist his voice or
his caresses. The bad things he had said to Shui Ta were no
lesson to Shen Teh. As I was sinking into his arms, I thought:
the gods wanted me to be good to myself, too.
To let none be destroyed, not even oneself
To bring happiness to all, including oneself

Is good.

How could I simply forget those two good old people? Like a small hurricane blowing toward Peking, Sun just swept away my shop and all my friends with it. But he isn't bad, and he loves me. As long as I am near him, he will do no evil. What a man says to other men means nothing. He wants to impress them, to make them think he's big and strong and so very hard-boiled. When I tell him the two old people can't pay their taxes, he'll understand. He'll go to work in the cement factory sooner than owe his flying career to a disgraceful action. Of course flying is a great passion with him. Will I be strong enough to awaken the good in him? Now, on my way to the wedding, I am teetering between joy and fear. (*She goes out quickly*)

6

Private Room in a Cheap Restaurant in the Slums

A waiter is pouring wine for the wedding guests. Around Shen Teh stand the grandfather, the sister-in-law, the niece, Mrs. Shin, and the unemployed man. A priest stands alone in the corner. Front stage, Sun is talking with his mother, Mrs. Yang. He is wearing a dinner jacket.

SUN   Bad news, mama. She just told me, as if butter wouldn't melt in her mouth, that she can't sell the shop for me. Some people are raising a claim; it seems they loaned her the two hundred silver dollars she gave you. Though her cousin says there's nothing in writing.

MRS. YANG   What did you tell her? Naturally you can't marry her.

SUN   There's no point in discussing such things with her, she's too pigheaded. I sent for her cousin.

MRS. YANG   But he wants to marry her off to the barber.

SUN   I've punctured that marriage. The barber didn't know what hit him. It won't take her cousin long to realize that the shop is done for if I don't pay back the two hundred, because the creditors will attach it, but that my job is gone too if I don't get the additional three hundred.

MRS. YANG   I'll watch for him outside. Now go to your bride, Sun.

SHEN TEH (*to the audience as she pours wine*)   I wasn't mistaken in him. He didn't show the slightest sign of disappointment. Despite the hard blow it must be to him to give up flying, he's perfectly cheerful. I love him very dearly. (*She motions Sun to come over to her*) Sun, you haven't drunk with the bride yet.

SUN   What should we drink to?

SHEN TEH   To the future.

(*They drink*)

SUN   When the bridegroom's dinner jacket won't be rented any more.

SHEN TEH   But the bride's dress will still be exposed to the rain now and then.

SUN   To everything we wish for!

SHEN TEH   May it soon come true!

MRS. YANG (*on her way out, to Mrs. Shin*)   I'm delighted with my son. I've always told him he could get any girl he wanted. Why, he's a trained pilot and mechanic. And what does he say to me now? I'm marrying for love, mama, he says. Money isn't everything. It's a love match. (*To the sister-in-law*) It was bound to happen sooner or later, wasn't it? But it's hard on a mother, very hard. (*Calling back to the priest*) Don't make it too short. If you take as long with the ceremony as you did haggling over your fee, it will be just right. (*To Shen Teh*) We shall have to wait a little while, my dear. One of our dearest guests hasn't come yet. (*To all*) Forgive us, please. (*Goes out*)

THE SISTER-IN-LAW   Patience comes easy as long as the wine holds out.

(*They sit down*)

THE UNEMPLOYED MAN   We're not missing anything.

SUN (*loudly and jocosely in front of the guests*)   Before we're married, I'd better give you a little test. It doesn't seem unnecessary when people marry so quickly. (*To the guests*) You see, I don't know yet what kind of a wife I'm getting. That worries me. For instance, can you make five cups of tea out of three tea leaves?

SHEN TEH   No.

SUN   Then I won't get any tea. Can you sleep on a straw tick the size of that book the priest is reading?

SHEN TEH   Two together?

SUN   Alone.

SHEN TEH   In that case, no.

SUN   I'm horrified to see what kind of a wife I'm getting.

(*All laugh. Behind Shen Teh, Mrs. Yang steps into the doorway. She shrugs her shoulders as a sign to Sun that the expected guest is not to be seen*)

MRS. YANG (*to the priest, who shows her his watch*)   Don't be in such a hurry. It can't be more than a few minutes. They're all drinking and smoking, nobody's in a hurry. (*She sits down with the guests*)

SHEN TEH   But shouldn't we talk it over and decide how to straighten things out?

MRS. YANG   Please, please, not a word about business today. It injects such a common note into a celebration, don't you think?

(*The doorbell rings. All look toward the door but no one enters*)

SHEN TEH   Who is your mother waiting for, Sun?

SUN   It's to be a surprise for you. By the way, what's your cousin Shui Ta doing? We get along fine. He's got a head on his shoulders. Why don't you say something?

SHEN TEH   I don't know. I don't want to think about him.

SUN   Why not?

SHEN TEH   Because I don't like you to get along with him. If you love me, you can't love him.

SUN   In that case, the three gremlins can take him: the breakdown gremlin, the fog gremlin, and the out-of-gas gremlin. Drink, stubborn! (*He makes her drink*)

THE SISTER-IN-LAW (*to Mrs. Shin*) There's something fishy around here.

MRS. SHIN What did you expect?

THE PRIEST (*steps resolutely up to Mrs. Yang, watch in hand*) I must be going, Mrs. Yang. I've got another wedding, and a funeral tomorrow morning.

MRS. YANG Do you think all this delay amuses me? We were hoping one jug of wine would be enough. And now look how it's dwindling. (*Aloud to Shen Teh*) I can't understand why your cousin should keep us waiting like this!

SHEN TEH My cousin?

MRS. YANG But my dear, that's who we're waiting for. I'm old-fashioned enough to feel that such a close relative of the bride ought to attend her wedding.

SHEN TEH Oh, Sun, is it on account of the three hundred silver dollars?

SUN (*without looking at her*) You've heard why it is. She's old-fashioned. And I'm considerate. We'll just wait another fifteen minutes, and if he hasn't come by then it means the three gremlins have got him and we'll go ahead.

MRS. YANG I'm sure you all know that my son is getting a job as a mail pilot. I'm very glad. You've got to make good money these days.

THE SISTER-IN-LAW I hear it's in Peking. Is that right?

MRS. YANG Yes, in Peking.

SHEN TEH Sun, you'd better tell your mother it's all up with Peking.

SUN Your cousin will tell her if he feels the same way as you. Between you and me, I don't.

SHEN TEH (*horrified*) Sun!

SUN How I hate this Szechwan! What a town! Do you know what the people all look like when I half-close my eyes? Like horses. They crane their necks in alarm: what's that thundering overhead? What, they won't be needed any more? What, their time is up? They can bite each other to death in their city of horses! All I want is to get out of here!

SHEN TEH But I promised the old couple to give them their money back.

SUN You've told me that. And if you're that stupid, it's a good thing your cousin is coming. Drink and leave business to us. We'll take care of it.

SHEN TEH (*aghast*)   But my cousin can't come.

SUN   What do you mean?

SHEN TEH   He's gone.

SUN   And how do you picture our future? Just tell me that.

SHEN TEH   I thought, you still have the two hundred silver dollars. We can give them back tomorrow and keep the tobacco that's worth much more, and sell it together outside the cement factory because we can't pay the rent.

SUN   Forget it! Forget it this minute, sister! You want me to stand out in the street peddling tobacco to the cement workers, me, Yang Sun, the flier. I'd sooner run through the two hundred in one night, I'd sooner throw them in the river! And your cousin knows me. It was all settled that he'd bring the three hundred to the wedding.

SHEN TEH   My cousin can't come.

SUN   And I thought he couldn't stay away.

SHEN TEH   He can't be where I am.

SUN   How mysterious!

SHEN TEH   Sun, you've got to realize that he's no friend of yours. I'm the one who loves you. My cousin Shui Ta doesn't love anybody. He's a friend to me, but not to any of my friends. He agreed to let you have the old people's money because he was thinking of the pilot's job in Peking. But he won't bring the three hundred silver dollars to the wedding.

SUN   Why not?

SHEN TEH (*looking him straight in the eye*)   He says you bought only one ticket to Peking.

SUN   Yes, that was yesterday, but look what I've got to show him today. (*He half-pulls two slips of paper out of his breast pocket*) No need for the old lady to see. It's two tickets to Peking, for me and for you. Do you still think your cousin objects to our marriage?

SHEN TEH   No. It's a good job. And my shop is gone.

SUN   I sold our furniture on your account.

SHEN TEH   Don't say any more! Don't show me the tickets! I'm too much afraid that I might go off with you. But, Sun,

I can't give you the three hundred silver dollars. What would become of the two old people?

SUN   And what about me? (*Pause*) Better drink. Or are you the cautious type? I can't stomach a cautious woman. When I drink, I'm flying again. And if you drink, maybe, maybe you'll understand me.

SHEN TEH   Don't think I don't understand you. I know you want to fly and I can't help you.

SUN   "Here's a plane, sweetheart, but it's only got one wing!"

SHEN TEH   Sun, there's no honorable way of our getting the job in Peking. That's why I need the two hundred silver dollars you got from me. Give them to me immediately, Sun!

SUN   "Give them to me immediately, Sun!" What are you talking about anyway? Are you my wife or not? Because you're selling me out, you know that, don't you? Luckily, and luckily for you too, it doesn't depend on you any more. It's all settled.

MRS. YANG (*icily*)   Sun, are you sure the bride's cousin is coming? Staying away like this, it almost looks as if he had some objection to this marriage.

SUN   Where did you get that idea, mama? Him and me are like this. I'll open the door wide so he won't have any trouble finding us when he comes running in to be best man to his friend Sun. (*He goes to the door and kicks it open. Then he comes back, staggering a little because he has had too much to drink, and sits down again beside Shen Teh*) We'll wait. Your cousin's got more sense than you. Love, he says wisely, is an indispensable part of life. And what's more, he knows what it would mean to you: no more shop and no husband either!

(*They wait*)

MRS. YANG   At last!

(*Steps are heard. All look toward the door. But the steps pass by*)

MRS. SHIN   There's going to be a scandal. I can feel it, I can smell it. The bride is waiting to be married, but the groom is waiting for her honorable cousin.

SUN   Her honorable cousin is taking his time.

SHEN TEH (*softly*)   Oh, Sun!

SUN   God, to be sitting here with the tickets in my pocket and a little fool that can't count. I can see the day coming when you'll send the police after me to collect your two hundred silver dollars.

SHEN TEH (*to the audience*)   He is wicked and he wants me to be wicked too. Here I am, I love him, and he is waiting for my cousin. But around me the defenseless are sitting: the old woman with the sick husband, the poor who wait at the door in the morning for rice, and an unknown man from Peking who is worried about his job. They all trust me and that protects me.

SUN (*staring at the glass jug in which the wine is almost gone*)   The glass jug is our clock. We are poor people, and when the guests have drunk up the wine, the clock has run down forever.

(*Footsteps are heard again and Mrs. Yang motions him to be still*)

THE WAITER (*enters*)   Do you wish to order another jug of wine, Mrs. Yang?

MRS. YANG   No, I think we've had enough. Wine only overheats one, don't you think?

MRS. SHIN   Besides, it must be expensive.

MRS. YANG   Drinking always makes me perspire.

THE WAITER   In that case, may I ask you to pay the check?

MRS. YANG (*ignoring him*)   Ladies and gentlemen, please be patient a little longer, our relative must be on his way. (*To the waiter*) Don't interrupt the party.

THE WAITER   I can't let you leave without paying the check.

MRS. YANG   But everyone knows me here!

THE WAITER   Exactly.

MRS. YANG   Disgraceful, these waiters nowadays! What do you think, Sun?

THE PRIEST   A very good day to you all. (*Goes out ponderously*)

MRS. YANG (*in despair*)   Just keep your seats. The priest will be back in a few minutes.

SUN   Forget it, mama. Ladies and gentlemen, now that the priest has gone, we can't detain you any longer.

THE SISTER-IN-LAW   Come, grandpa!

THE GRANDFATHER (*solemnly drains his glass*)   To the bride!

THE NIECE (*to Shen Teh*) Don't mind him. He means to be friendly. He's fond of you.

MRS. SHIN A big flop, if you ask me!

(*All the guests leave*)

SHEN TEH Should I go too, Sun?

SUN No, you wait. (*He pulls her bride's veil so that it slants*) Isn't this your wedding? I'm going to wait, and the old lady will wait too. She at least wants to see her eagle in the clouds. I'm almost beginning to think it will be St. Neverkin's Day before she steps out the door and sees his plane thundering over the house. (*Addressing the empty chairs, as though the guests were still there*) Ladies and gentlemen, what's happened to the conversation? Don't you like it here? The wedding has only been postponed a little on account of the important relative we're expecting, and because the bride doesn't know what love is. To entertain you, I, the bridegroom, will sing you a song. (*He sings* "The Song of St. Neverkin's Day")

There's a song that they tell of among the poor folk
Of this world that's so grim and gray
When the poor woman's son will ascend the king's throne
And that day is Saint Neverkin's Day.
On Saint Neverkin's Day
He'll sit on the king's golden throne.

And on that famous day a man's goodness will pay
And his wickedness cost him his life.
Then desert and reward will sit down at one board
As cozy as husband and wife.
On Saint Neverkin's Day
As congenial as husband and wife.

And the grass will look down on the singing blue sky
And the pebbles will wander upstream.
Every man will be good, without work there'll be food
Life on earth will become a sweet dream.
On Saint Neverkin's Day
Life on earth will become a sweet dream.

On Saint Neverkin's Day I shall fly my own plane
And you will sit down with the best
And my unemployed friends will find jobs without end
And you, poor old woman, will rest.
  On Saint Neverkin's Day
  Poor woman, you will rest.

And because we can't wait one minute more
All this will come into sight
Not when the day has half passed away
But long before morning light
  On Saint Neverkin's Day
  Long before morning light.

MRS. YANG   He won't come.
  (*The three sit there, two of them looking toward the door*)

Interlude

Wang's Night Lodging

Again the gods appear to the water seller in a dream. He has fallen asleep over a large book. Music.

WANG   It's good you have come, Enlightened Ones! Allow me a question that troubles me deeply. In the tumbledown hut of a priest who has gone away to become a worker in the cement factory, I found a book, and in it I discovered a strange passage. I should like to read it to you. Here it is. (*With his left hand he leafs through an imaginary book placed over the book he has in his lap. He lifts up the imaginary book and reads from it while the real book remains in his lap*) "In Sung there is a place known as Thorny Grove. Catalpas, cypresses, and mulberry trees grow there. Now the trees that are one or two spans around are chopped down by people who need stakes for their dog cages. Those that are three or four feet around are chopped down by the rich and distinguished families that require boards for their coffins. Those that are seven or eight feet around are chopped down by the people who need beams for their luxurious homes. Thus none of them attains its full measure of years, all are destroyed in mid-growth by saw and ax. That is the penalty for usefulness."

THE THIRD GOD   But then the most useless would be the best.

WANG   No, the most fortunate. The worst is the most fortunate.

THE FIRST GOD   What people will write!

THE SECOND GOD   Why does this parable move you so deeply, water seller?

WANG   Because of Shen Teh, Enlightened One! She has come to grief in love because she obeys the commandments of charity. Perhaps she is really too good for this world, Enlightened Ones!

THE FIRST GOD   Nonsense! You poor weak wretch! You seem to be half-devoured by lice and doubt.

WANG   Assuredly, Enlightened One! Forgive me! I only thought you might intervene.

THE FIRST GOD   Impossible. Our friend here (*he points to the third god, who has a black eye*) intervened in a quarrel only yesterday. You see the result.

WANG   But her cousin had to be called again. He is an uncommonly clever man, as I've learned by bitter experience, yet even he could do nothing. Her shop seems to be lost.

THE THIRD GOD (*alarmed*)   Perhaps we ought to help her after all?

THE FIRST GOD   It is my opinion that she must help herself.

THE SECOND GOD (*severely*)   A bad situation is an opportunity to prove oneself. Suffering purifies!

THE FIRST GOD   We are putting all our hopes in her.

THE THIRD GOD   Our search isn't doing very well. Here and there we find good beginnings, admirable intentions, plenty of lofty principles, but all that doesn't add up to true goodness. When we do find someone who is halfway good, he isn't living a life worthy of a human being. (*Confidentially*) The nights are getting worse and worse. You can tell where we've been spending them by the straw on our clothes.

WANG   Just one thing. Couldn't you at least . . .

THE GODS   We can do nothing.—We are only observers. We
are convinced that our good person will find her way on
this dark earth.—Her strength will increase with her burden.
—Just wait, water seller. You'll see that this will have a
happy . . .
(*The gods' shapes have become paler and paler, their voices
fainter and fainter. They disappear, and the voices cease*)

7

Yard behind Shen Teh's Shop

*Some household goods on a cart. Shen Teh and Mrs. Shin are
taking down washing from the line.*

MRS. SHIN   I can't see why you're not fighting tooth and nail
for your shop.

SHEN TEH   How can I? I haven't even got the rent. I have to
give the old people back their two hundred silver dollars
today, but since I've given them to someone else, I'll have to
sell my tobacco to Mrs. Mi Tzu.

MRS. SHIN   Then everything's gone! No husband, no tobacco,
no place to rest your head. That's what comes of trying to
go the rest of us one better. What are you going to live on
now?

SHEN TEH   I don't know. Perhaps I can earn a little sorting
tobacco.

MRS. SHIN   How did Mr. Shui Ta's pants get here? He must
have gone off naked.

SHEN TEH   He's got another pair.

MRS. SHIN   I thought you said he'd gone for good? Why
would he leave his pants behind?

SHEN TEH   Maybe he doesn't need them any more.

MRS. SHIN   Then we needn't pack them?

SHEN TEH   No.

(*Mr. Shu Fu bursts in*)

MR. SHU FU   Don't tell me. I know all about it. You've sacri-
ficed your happiness to prevent two old people who trusted
you from being ruined. It's not for nothing that this malig-
nant, distrustful neighborhood calls you the "Angel of the
Slums." Your honorable fiancé couldn't rise to your moral
stature, so you left him. And now you're closing this shop,
this little haven of refuge for so many. I can't bear the sight.
Morning after morning I've stood at the door of my shop,
watching you dish out rice to your little group of paupers.
Can that be gone forever? Is goodness to perish? Oh, if only
you'd let me help you in your good work! No, don't say a
word. I want no assurances, no promise to accept my help!
But here (*he pulls out a checkbook and signs a check which
he lays on the cart*) I'm giving you a blank check, you can
write in any sum you like. And now I leave you, happy and
serene, asking nothing in return, on my tiptoes, reverently,
without a thought for myself. (*Goes out*)

MRS. SHIN   (*examines the check*)   You're saved. People like you
are lucky. You always find a sucker. But now be quick.
Write in a thousand silver dollars and I'll run to the bank
with it before he comes to his senses.

SHEN TEH   Put the washbasket on the cart. I can pay you for
the washing without the check.

MRS. SHIN   What? You're not going to accept the check?
That's a crime. Is it only because you think you'd have to
marry him? That would be plain madness. His kind want to
be led by the nose. It gives them real pleasure. Are you still
hanging on to that flier when everybody on Yellow Street
and around here too knows how badly he's treated you?

SHEN TEH   It's all the fault of poverty. (*To the audience*)

At night I saw him puffing up his cheeks in his sleep: his face
    was evil.

And in the morning I held his coat up to the light and saw
    the wall through it.

When I saw his crafty smile, I was afraid, but

When I saw the holes in his shoes, I loved him very much.

MRS. SHIN   So you still defend him? I've never seen anything so idiotic. (*Angrily*) It will be a relief to me when we get you out of the neighborhood.

SHEN TEH (*staggers as she takes down the washing*)   I feel a little dizzy.

MRS. SHIN (*takes the washing from her*)   Do you often feel dizzy when you stretch or bend down? If only it's not a little stranger! (*Laughs*) He certainly fixed you. If that's how it is, you can forget about your big check! It wasn't meant for this kind of thing. (*She goes to the rear with a basket*)

(*Shen Teh stands motionless, looking after her. Then she looks down at her body and feels it; a great joy is seen in her face*)

SHEN TEH (*softly*)   Oh joy! A little man is coming to life inside me. Nothing can be seen yet. But he's already there. The world is expecting him in secret. In the cities they are already saying: Someone is on his way—a man to be reckoned with. (*She presents her little son to the audience*) A flier!
Salute a new conqueror
Of unknown mountains and inaccessible countries! One
Who will carry the mail from man to man
Across pathless deserts!
(*She begins to walk back and forth, leading her little son by the hand*) Come, my son, look at the world. This is a tree. Bow to it, say good day. (*She shows him how to bow*) Good, now you know each other. Listen, here comes the water seller. A friend. Give him your hand. Don't be afraid. "A glass of fresh water, please, for my son. It's hot today." (*She gives him the glass*) Oh, the policeman. We'd better steer clear of him. We might pick a few cherries over there, in that orchard belonging to the rich Mr. Feh Pung. But we mustn't let anyone see us. Come, poor fatherless child. You too want cherries. Quiet, son, quiet! (*They advance cautiously, peering around*) No, this way, the bushes will hide us. No, don't go barging straight ahead, that won't do in a case like this. (*He seems to be tugging her along, she resists*) We'll have to watch our step. (*She suddenly gives in*) All

right, if you must . . . (*She lifts him up*) Can you reach the cherries? Stuff them in your mouth, that's a good place for them. (*She herself eats one that he puts in her mouth*) Tastes good. Oh my! The policeman. Time to run. (*They flee*) Here's the street. Easy now, walk slowly, so as not to attract attention. As if we hadn't done a thing . . . (*She sings, walking along with the child*)

Once there was a juicy plum
That attacked a harmless bum.
But the man was very quick
Bit the plum right in the neck.

(*Wang the water seller has entered, leading a child by the hand. He watches Shen Teh with amazement*)

SHEN TEH (*as Wang coughs*)   Oh, Wang! How are you?

WANG   Shen Teh, I heard you were having trouble, that you even have to sell your shop to pay your debts. But now I've found this homeless child. He was running around in the cattle yard. He seems to belong to Lin To the carpenter, who lost his shop a few weeks ago and has been drinking ever since. His children are starving. What can we do about them?

SHEN TEH (*takes the child from him*)   Come, little man! (*To the audience*)

Hey, you people. Someone is asking for shelter.
A citizen of tomorrow is asking you for a today!
His friend, the conqueror whom you know
Vouches for him.

(*To Wang*) He can perfectly well live in Mr. Shu Fu's shacks. Where I may be going, too. I'm expecting a child myself. But don't tell anyone, or Yang Sun will hear of it, and he won't want us. Go find Mr. Lin To in the lower city and tell him to come here.

WANG   Many thanks, Shen Teh. I knew you would think of something. (*To the child*) You see, goodness always knows a way. I'll go quickly and bring your father. (*He starts off*)

SHEN TEH   Oh, Wang, I've just remembered. What about your hand? I wanted to testify for you, but my cousin . . .

WANG   Don't worry about my hand. See, I've already learned to manage without my right hand. I hardly miss it. (*He shows her how he can manage his carrying pole without his right hand*) See how I do it?

SHEN TEH But you mustn't let it get stiff. Take this cart, sell everything, take the money and go to the doctor. I'm so ashamed to have failed you. And what you must think of me for accepting the barber's shacks!

WANG The homeless will be able to live there now, and you yourself. That's more important than my hand. I'll go get the carpenter. (*Goes*)

SHEN TEH (*calls after him*) Promise you'll go to the doctor with me.

(*Mrs. Shin has come back, motioning to her all the while*)

SHEN TEH What's the matter?

MRS. SHIN Are you crazy, giving away the cart with everything you own? What do you care about his hand? If the barber finds out, he'll throw you out of the only lodging you're likely to find. You haven't paid me for the washing yet.

SHEN TEH Why are you so mean? (*To the audience*)
Isn't it exhausting
To trample your fellows? The veins in your temples
Are swollen with the strain of your greed.
Candidly held out
A hand gives and receives with equal ease.
Greedy clutching strains it. Oh
How tempting it is to be generous. How pleasant
It is to be friendly. A kindly word
Slips out like a sigh of well-being.
(*Mrs. Shin goes out angrily*)

SHEN TEH (*to the child*) Sit here and wait for your father.
(*The child sits down on the ground*)
(*Enter the elderly couple who called on Shen Teh the day she opened her shop. Husband and wife are carrying large bales*)

THE WIFE Are you alone, Shen Teh?
(*When Shen Teh nods, she calls in her nephew who is also carrying a bale*)

THE WIFE Where's your cousin?

SHEN TEH He has gone away.

THE WIFE   Is he coming back?

SHEN TEH   No. I'm giving up the shop.

THE WIFE   We know that. That's why we've come. Here we have a few bales of leaf tobacco that someone owed us. Would you kindly take them to your new home along with your own belongings? We still have no place to put them, and carrying them through the streets we attract too much attention. I don't see how you can refuse us a favor after the rough deal we got in your shop.

SHEN TEH   I'll gladly do you the favor.

THE HUSBAND   And if anyone asks you whom the bales belong to, you can say they belong to you.

SHEN TEH   Who is likely to ask me?

THE WIFE (*giving her a sharp look*)   The police, for instance. They've got it in for us, they want to ruin us. Where do you want us to put the bales?

SHEN TEH   Come to think of it, I shouldn't like to do anything right now that might send me to jail.

THE WIFE   That's just like you. It's all the same to you if we lose these few wretched bales of tobacco, all we've been able to save in the world.

(*Shen Teh is obstinately silent*)

THE HUSBAND   Don't you see that with this tobacco we could start manufacturing in a small way. It would give us a start.

SHEN TEH   All right, I'll keep the bales for you. We'll put them in the back room for now.

(*She goes in with them. The child looks after her. Then, looking timidly around, he goes to the garbage can, fishes around in it and begins to eat. Shen Teh and the three come back*)

THE WIFE   You realize that we're putting ourselves completely in your hands?

SHEN TEH   Yes. (*She notices the child and freezes with horror*)

THE HUSBAND   We'll come to see you the day after tomorrow in Mr. Shu Fu's houses.

SHEN TEH   You must go now, I'm not feeling well. (*She pushes them out. They go*) He's hungry. He's fishing in the garbage pail.

(*She lifts up the child and expresses her horror at the fate*) *of poor children, showing the audience the child's dirty mouth. She proclaims her own determination not to treat her own child so coldheartedly*)

O son, O flier. What kind of world
Will you be born into? Will they leave
You too to fish in garbage? Look at
That filthy mouth! (*She displays the child*) Is this
A way to treat your fellow creatures? Have you
No compassion with the fruit
Of your wombs? No pity
For yourselves, you unfortunates? Then I
Will fight for my own at least, even if I have to
Turn tiger. Yes, now
That I've seen this, I will break
With them all and never rest
Until I have saved my son, at least my son.
What I have learned in the gutter, my school
Of brutality and guile, shall
Serve you now, my son. To you
I will be good, a tiger and wild beast
To all others if necessary. And
It is necessary.

(*She goes inside to turn herself into her cousin. On the way out*) I've got to do it again, for the last time, I hope. (*She has taken Shui Ta's pants along*)

(*Mrs. Shin comes back and looks after her with curiosity. Enter the sister-in-law and the grandfather*)

THE SISTER-IN-LAW   The shop's closed. All her stuff is in the yard. This is the end.

MRS. SHIN   That's what comes of being irresponsible, sensual, and selfish. And where's she headed? Downhill. To Mr. Shu Fu's shacks with the rest of you.

THE SISTER-IN-LAW   She's in for a surprise. We've come to complain. Damp rat holes with rotten floors! The barber only let us have them because the soap he had stored there was getting mouldy. "I've got lodgings for you, what do you say to that?" It's disgraceful, that's what we say.

(*Enter the unemployed man*)

THE UNEMPLOYED MAN   Is it true that Shen Teh is leaving?

THE SISTER-IN-LAW Yes, she wanted to slip away behind our backs.

MRS. SHIN She's ashamed because she's ruined.

THE UNEMPLOYED MAN (*excitedly*) She's got to send for her cousin! Tell her, all of you, to send for her cousin! He's the only one who can do anything.

THE SISTER-IN-LAW That's the truth. He's awfully stingy, but at least he'll save her shop, and then she'll help us.

THE UNEMPLOYED MAN I wasn't thinking of us, I was thinking of her. But it's true, he should be sent for on our account too.

(*Enter Wang with the carpenter. He is leading two children by the hand*)

THE CARPENTER I really can't thank you enough. (*To the others*) We're getting a place to live.

MRS. SHIN Where?

THE CARPENTER In Mr. Shu Fu's houses. And it was little Feng who swung it! Ah, there you are! "Here's someone asking for shelter!" That's what Miss Shen Teh said, so I'm told, and, one two three, she found us a place. Thank your little brother, you two! (*The carpenter and his children bow merrily to the child*)

THE CARPENTER Our thanks, petitioner for lodging!

(*Shui Ta has come out of the house*)

SHUI TA May I ask what you are all doing here?

THE UNEMPLOYED MAN Mr. Shui Ta!

WANG How do you do, Mr. Shui Ta. I didn't know you were back. You know Lin To the carpenter. Miss Shen Teh has promised him a place in Mr. Shu Fu's houses.

SHUI TA Mr. Shu Fu's houses are not available.

THE CARPENTER Then we can't live there?

SHUI TA No. They are going to serve another purpose.

THE SISTER-IN-LAW Does that mean we have to move out?

SHUI TA I'm afraid so.

THE SISTER-IN-LAW But where are we all to go?

SHUI TA (*shrugging his shoulders*) Miss Shen Teh, who has left town, gave me to understand that she has no intention of abandoning you. But from now on all this must be managed more sensibly. No more food will be distributed free of charge. Instead, everyone will be given an opportunity to improve his condition by honorable labor. Miss Shen Teh has decided to give you all work. None of you who follow me now to Mr. Shu Fu's houses will regret it.

THE SISTER-IN-LAW Does that mean we're all supposed to work for Shen Teh?

SHUI TA Yes, you will cut tobacco. There are three bales in the back room. Go get them!

THE SISTER-IN-LAW Don't forget that we had a shop of our own. We prefer to work for ourselves. We've got our own tobacco.

SHUI TA (*to the unemployed man and the carpenter*) Perhaps you would like to work for Shen Teh, since you have no tobacco of your own?

(*The carpenter and the unemployed man go glumly into the house. Enter Mrs. Mi Tzu*)

MRS. MI TZU Well, Mr. Shui Ta, how about that sale? Here are three hundred silver dollars.

SHUI TA Mrs. Mi Tzu, I have decided not to sell but to sign the lease.

MRS. MI TZU What? You don't need the money for the flier any more?

SHUI TA No.

MRS. MI TZU Can you pay the rent?

SHUI TA (*takes the barber's check from the cart and fills it out*) I have a check here for ten thousand silver dollars, signed by Mr. Shu Fu, who takes an interest in my cousin. See for yourself, Mrs. Mi Tzu. Before six this afternoon you will have your two hundred silver dollars for the next six months' rent. And now, Mrs. Mi Tzu, allow me to get on with my work. I'm very busy today and must beg you to excuse me.

MRS. MI TZU Oh, so Mr. Shu Fu has stepped into the flier's shoes! Ten thousand silver dollars! All the same, I'm amazed at the fickleness and frivolity of young girls nowadays, Mr. Shui Ta. (*Goes*)

(*The carpenter and the unemployed man bring in the bales*)

THE CARPENTER I'm damned if I know why I should carry your bales.

SHUI TA   I know, and that is sufficient. Your son here has a healthy appetite. He wants to eat, Mr. Lin To.

THE SISTER-IN-LAW (*sees the bales*)   Has my brother-in-law been here?

MRS. SHIN   Yes.

THE SISTER-IN-LAW   I thought so. I know those bales. That's our tobacco.

SHUI TA   I wouldn't say that so loud. It's my tobacco, as you can see from the fact that it was in my back room. But if you have any doubts, we can go to the police and clear up your doubts. Shall we?

THE SISTER-IN-LAW (*malignantly*)   No.

SHUI TA   It seems you have no tobacco of your own after all. Under these circumstances perhaps you will accept the helping hand that Miss Shen Teh is holding out to you? Now will you kindly show me the way to Mr. Shu Fu's houses? (*Taking the carpenter's youngest child by the hand, Shui Ta goes out, followed by the carpenter, his other children, the sister-in-law, the grandfather, and the unemployed man. The sister-in-law, the carpenter, and the unemployed man carry the bales*)

WANG   He's a bad man, but Shen Teh is good.

MRS. SHIN   I don't get it. There's a pair of pants missing from the clothesline, and her cousin is wearing them. That must mean something. I wish I knew what.

(*Enter the two old people*)

THE OLD WOMAN   Isn't Miss Shen Teh here?

MRS. SHIN (*tersely*)   Gone.

THE OLD WOMAN   That's strange. She was going to bring us something.

WANG (*looking sorrowfully at his hand*)   She was going to help me too. My hand is getting stiff. I'm sure she'll be back soon. Her cousin never stays long.

MRS. SHIN   That's a fact, isn't it?

Interlude

Wang's Night Lodging

Music. In a dream the water seller imparts his apprehensions to the gods. The gods are still engaged in their long wanderings. They seem tired. Pausing briefly, they look back at the water seller over their shoulders.

WANG Before you appeared and woke me, O Enlightened Ones, I was dreaming. I saw my dear sister Shen Teh in great distress, plodding through the rushes by the river, in the place where the suicides are found. She was staggering strangely and her head was bent as though she were carrying something soft but heavy, which pressed her down into the mud. When I cried out to her, she called back that she had to carry the bundle of precepts to the other shore without getting them wet, for water would wash away the letters. Actually I saw nothing on her shoulders. But I remembered to my horror that you gods once lectured her about the cardinal virtues to reward her for taking you in when you were—oh, the shame of it!—at a loss for a night lodging. I feel sure you understand my concern for her.

THE THIRD GOD What do you propose?

WANG A slight relaxation of the precepts, O Enlightened Ones. A slight alleviation of the burden, O Merciful Ones, in view of the hard times.

THE THIRD GOD For instance, Wang, for instance?

WANG For instance, that only benevolence should be required instead of love, or . . .

THE THIRD GOD But you poor soul, that's even harder!

WANG Or fairness instead of justice.

THE THIRD GOD But that means more work!

WANG Then plain decency instead of honor!

THE THIRD GOD But that's even more, you man of doubt!
(*They go wearily on their way*)

8

Shui Ta's Tobacco Factory

Shui Ta has set up a small tobacco factory in Mr. Shu Fu's shacks. Several families, mostly women and children, sit huddled behind bars, terribly crowded. Among them are the sister-in-law, the grandfather, the former carpenter, and his children.

(*Enter, in front of them, Mrs. Yang, followed by her son Sun*)

MRS. YANG (*to the audience*) I must tell you how my son, thanks to the wisdom and severity of the universally respected Mr. Shui Ta, has been transformed from a depraved young man into a useful citizen. As the whole neighborhood knows, Mr. Shui Ta has opened a small but already thriving tobacco factory near the cattle yard. Three months ago I had occasion to drop in on him with my son. He made me wait a short while but then he received me.

(*Shui Ta comes out of the factory and approaches Mrs. Yang*)

SHUI TA What can I do for you, Mrs. Yang?

MRS. YANG Mr. Shui Ta, I should like to put in a plea for my son. The police came to see us this morning and told us that you, in the name of Miss Shen Teh, had registered a complaint against him for breach of promise and the fraudulent acquisition of two hundred silver dollars.

SHUI TA Quite so, Mrs. Yang.

MRS. YANG Mr. Shui Ta, for the gods' sake, can't you for once put mercy before justice? The money is gone. He squandered it in two days when the pilot's job fell through. I know he's no good. He's sold my furniture and was going off to Peking without his old mother. (*She weeps*) Miss Shen Teh used to think the world of him.

SHUI TA　What have you got to say for yourself, Mr. Yang Sun?

SUN (*gloomily*)　The money's gone.

SHUI TA　Mrs. Yang, in view of the weakness which my cousin for some unfathomable reason had for your depraved son, I am willing to give him another chance. She told me she thought honest work might improve his character. He can have a job in my factory. The two hundred silver dollars will be deducted in installments from his wages.

SUN　Then it's factory or clink?

SHUI TA　It's up to you.

SUN　I don't suppose I could speak to Shen Teh?

SHUI TA　No.

SUN　Where do I work?

MRS. YANG　A thousand thanks, Mr. Shui Ta! You are infinitely kind and the gods will reward you. (*To Sun*) You have strayed from the narrow path. Try to become a better man by honest work until you can look your mother in the eye again.

(*Sun follows Shui Ta into the factory. Mrs. Yang returns front stage*)

MRS. YANG (*to the audience*)　The first weeks were hard on Sun. The work didn't appeal to him. He had little opportunity to distinguish himself. It wasn't until the third week that a slight incident helped him out. He and Lin To, the former carpenter, were carrying bales of tobacco.

(*Sun and Lin To, the former carpenter, are each carrying two bales of tobacco*)

THE FORMER CARPENTER (*halts with a groan and sinks down on one of the bales*)　I'm all in. I'm too old for this kind of work.

SUN (*also sits down*)　Why don't you tell them what they can do with their bales?

THE FORMER CARPENTER　What would we live on? Just to scrape along, I've had to put the kids to work. If only Miss Shen Teh were here to see it. She was good.

SUN   They come worse. If the circumstances hadn't been so miserable, we'd have hit it off very nicely. I wonder where she is. We'd better be moving. He usually turns up about this time.

(*They stand up*)

SUN (*sees Shui Ta coming*)   Give me one of your bales, you cripple! (*Sun picks up one of Lin To's bales in addition to his own*)

THE FORMER CARPENTER   Many thanks. If she were here, helping an old man like this would put you in her good books. Oh dear!

(*Enter Shui Ta*)

MRS. YANG (*to the audience*)   And naturally Mr. Shui Ta has an eye for a good worker who is willing to bestir himself. And he steps in.

SHUI TA   Hey, you two! What's going on? Why are you carrying only one bale?

THE FORMER CARPENTER   I'm a little tired today, Mr. Shui Ta, and Yang Sun was kind enough . . .

SHUI TA   Just go back and take three bales, my friend. If Yang Sun can do it, so can you. Yang Sun has his heart in his work. You haven't.

MRS. YANG (*to the audience, while the former carpenter gets two more bales*)   Of course Mr. Shui Ta didn't say a word to Sun, but he knew what was what. And next Saturday at the pay desk . . .

(*A table is set up and Shui Ta comes in with a pouch of money. Standing beside the foreman—the former unemployed man— he hands out the pay. Sun steps up to the table*)

THE FOREMAN   Yang Sun—six silver dollars.

SUN   I beg your pardon, but it can't be more than five. Exactly five silver dollars. (*He takes the list that the foreman is holding*) See, here it says six days, that's a mistake, I was absent one day, I had to go to court. The pay may be lousy, but (*hypocritically*) I won't take money I haven't earned!

THE FOREMAN   All right, five silver dollars! (*To Shui Ta*) An unusual case, Mr. Shui Ta!

SHUI TA   How can the pay sheet say six days when it was only five?

THE FOREMAN   I must have made a mistake, Mr. Shui Ta. (*To Sun, coldly*) It won't happen again.

SHUI TA (*motions Sun aside*)   I noticed the other day that you're a strong man with the firm's interest at heart. Today I see that you are also honest. Does the foreman often make mistakes to the firm's disadvantage?

SUN   He has friends among the workers, they regard him as one of their own.

SHUI TA   I understand. One good turn deserves another. Do you want a bonus?

SUN   No. But I should like to point out that I am also intelligent. I've had a pretty good education, you see. The foreman means well by the men, but with his lack of education he doesn't understand what the firm needs. Give me a week's trial, Mr. Shui Ta, and I believe I can demonstrate that my intelligence is worth more to the firm than sheer brawn.

MRS. YANG (*to the audience*)   Those were bold words, but that evening I said to my Sun: "You're a flier. Show that you can also rise off the ground where you are now. Fly, my eagle!" And true enough, it's amazing what great things education and intelligence can accomplish. How can anyone hope to get ahead without them? My son performed real miracles in Mr. Shui Ta's factory!

(*Sun stands firmly planted behind the workers. They are passing a basket of leaf tobacco over their heads*)

SUN   Hey, you! That's no way to work! I want to see that basket move! (*To a child*) Why don't you sit on the floor, then you won't be in anybody's way. And you could be doing some pressing in between, yes, I mean you! You lazy bastards, what do you think we pay you for? Come on with that basket! Damn it! Put grandpa over there, he can shred with the kids! We've had enough loafing around here! And now everybody in cadence! (*He claps out the time and the basket moves faster*)

MRS. YANG (*to the audience*)   And no amount of hostility or abuse on the part of ignorant persons—he came in for plenty of that—deterred my son from doing his duty.

(*One of the workers strikes up the* "Song of the Eighth Elephant." *The others join in the chorus*)

Elephants seven had Mr. Chin
Plus an eighth, an early riser.
Seven were wild and the eighth was tame
Number eight was the supervisor.
    Step lively!
    This wood is Mr. Chin's.
    You've got to clear it, root and branch
    Before the night begins.

Elephants seven cleared the wood
And on top of the eighth rode the master.
Lazy number eight spied from early to late
To make sure that the others worked faster.
    Dig harder!
    This wood is Mr. Chin's
    You've got to clear it, root and branch
    Before the night begins!

Elephants seven were thoroughly sick
Of uprooting little and big trees.
Old Chin in his heaven frowned down on the seven
To the eighth he fed barrels of chick peas.
    How come, sir?
    This wood is Mr. Chin's
    You've got to clear it, root and branch
    Before the night begins.

Elephants seven had all lost their tusks.
Number eight had two tusks strong and flashing.
The eighth he rushed toward them and ruthlessly gored them
While the master sat up there laughing.
    Keep digging!
    This wood is Mr. Chin's
    You've got to clear it, root and branch
    Before the night begins.

(Shui Ta has sauntered forward, smoking a cigar. Yang Sun has laughingly joined in the chorus of the third verse and speeded up the rhythm of the last verse by clapping his hands)

MRS. YANG (*to the audience*)   We really owe Mr. Shui Ta a debt of thanks. He seldom interfered, but with wisdom and discipline he brought out all the good that was in Sun! He didn't make all sorts of fantastic promises like his widely praised cousin, but forced him to do honest work. Today Sun is a different man from what he was three months ago. I'm sure you'll agree. As the ancients said: "The superior man is like a bell; if you strike it, it rings, if you don't strike it, it doesn't ring."

9

Shen Teh's Tobacco Shop

The shop has been transformed into an office with easy chairs and fine carpets. It is raining. Shui Ta, grown fat, is showing the old couple from the carpet shop to the door. Mrs. Shin looks on in amusement. She is wearing conspicuously new clothes.

SHUI TA   I'm sorry, I can't say when she'll be back.
THE OLD WOMAN   Today we received a letter enclosing the two hundred silver dollars we once loaned her. There was no return address. But the letter must be from Shen Teh. We'd like to write her. What is her address?
SHUI TA   I'm sorry, I don't know that either.
THE OLD MAN   Come on, let's go.
THE OLD WOMAN   She's bound to come back sooner or later. (*Shui Ta bows. Worried and uncertain, the two old people leave*)
MRS. SHIN   They got their money back too late. Now they've lost their shop because they couldn't pay their taxes.
SHUI TA   Why didn't they come to me?
MRS. SHIN   People don't like to come to you. At first they

must have been waiting for Shen Teh to come back, because they had nothing in writing. Then at the critical moment the old man fell ill, and his wife was at his bedside day and night.

SHUI TA (*is feeling sick and has to sit down*)   It's another dizzy spell.

MRS. SHIN (*bustling around him*)   You're six months gone. Excitement isn't good for you. It's lucky you have me. Everyone needs a helping hand. Don't worry, I'll be with you when your time comes. (*She laughs*)

SHUI TA (*feebly*)   Can I count on it, Mrs. Shin?

MRS. SHIN   Of course you can. It will cost you a little, of course. Loosen your collar, you'll feel better.

SHUI TA (*pitifully*)   It's all for the baby, Mrs. Shin.

MRS. SHIN   All for the baby.

SHUI TA   But I'm filling out too fast. People must notice.

MRS. SHIN   They think it comes from prosperity.

SHUI TA   And what's to become of the child?

MRS. SHIN   You ask me that three times a day. He will be put out to nurse. The best place money can afford.

SHUI TA   Yes. (*Anxiously*) And he must never see Shui Ta.

MRS. SHIN   Never. Only Shen Teh.

SHUI TA   But the rumors in the neighborhood. The water seller and his gossip. Everyone's watching the shop.

MRS. SHIN   As long as the barber doesn't find out, there's no harm done. Take a sip of water.

(*Enter Sun in a fashionable suit with a businessman's briefcase. He is surprised to see Shui Ta in Mrs. Shin's arms*)

SUN   Am I disturbing you?

SHUI TA (*stands up with difficulty and staggers to the door*) See you tomorrow, Mrs. Shin.

(*Mrs. Shin puts on her gloves and goes out smiling*)

SUN   Gloves! Where does she get them and what for? Is she milking you by any chance? (*When Shui Ta does not answer*) Is it possible that even you are amenable to tender feelings? Hard to believe. (*He takes a paper from his briefcase*) Anyway you haven't been in good shape lately, you're not the same. Moody. Undecided. Are you sick? It's bad for business. Here's another gripe from the police. They want to close the factory. They say the most they can tolerate is twice the legal number of people to a room. You've got to do something, Mr. Shui Ta!

(*Shui Ta looks at him absently for a moment. Then he goes to the back room and returns with a paper bag. From it he takes a new derby hat which he throws on the desk*)

SHUI TA   The firm wishes its employees to be properly dressed.

SUN   You mean you bought it for me?

SHUI TA (*with indifference*)   Try it on.

(*With a look of astonishment Sun puts it on. Shui Ta studies the effect and tries to set the hat at a suitable angle*)

SUN   I'm much obliged, but don't try to change the subject. You've got to see the barber today and discuss the new plan.

SHUI TA   The barber's conditions are unacceptable.

SUN   I wish you'd finally tell me what these conditions are.

SHUI TA (*evasively*)   The shacks are good enough.

SUN   Yes, good enough for the scum that work there, but not good enough for the tobacco. Too damp. Before our next meeting, I'm going to have a talk with Mrs. Mi Tzu about her premises. If we get them, we can fire all those beggars, wrecks, and cripples. They're no good. If I tickle Mrs. Mi Tzu's fat knees over a cup of tea, we'll get the place for half the price.

SHUI TA (*sharply*)   You will do nothing of the kind. In the interest of the firm, I expect your conduct to be at all times crisp, businesslike, and impersonal.

SUN   Why are you so irritable? The nasty rumors in the neighborhood?

SHUI TA   I am not concerned with rumors.

SUN   Then it must be the rain. Rain always makes you so irritable and melancholy. I wish I knew why.

WANG'S VOICE (*from outside*)

Peddling water is my business
Hills and dales I go exploring
For a pint or two of liquid.
I come back and here it's pouring.
I stand shouting: Buy my water!
And no one buys it

And nobody's thirsty
They grin and despise it.

SUN There comes that damned water seller. He's going to start agitating again.

WANG'S VOICE (*from outside*) Isn't there any goodness left in this city? Not even here where the good Shen Teh used to live? Where is she, who bought a cup of water from me even though it was raining, many months ago, in the joy of her heart? Where is she now? Has no one seen her? Has no one had news of her? She went into this house one evening and never came out again.

SUN Shouldn't I stop his mouth for good? What business is it of his where she is? Come to think of it, I bet your only reason for not telling is that you don't want me to find out.

WANG (*enters*) Mr. Shui Ta, I ask you again when Shen Teh is coming back. Six months have passed since she went away. (*When Shui Ta is silent*) Meanwhile many things have happened that could never have happened if she had been here. (*When Shui Ta is still silent*) Mr. Shui Ta, there's a rumor in the neighborhood that something must have happened to Shen Teh. We, her friends, are very worried. Would you kindly tell us her address?

SHUI TA I'm afraid I have no time right now, Mr. Wang. Come back next week.

WANG (*excitedly*) People have noticed that in the last few days the rice she used to give the needy has been put outside the door again.

SHUI TA And what do they infer from that?

WANG That Shen Teh never went away at all.

SHUI TA And what else? (*When Wang is silent*) In that case I will give you my answer. It is final. If you are Shen Teh's friend, Mr. Wang, stop asking where she is. That is my advice.

WANG Fine advice! Mr. Shui Ta, before she disappeared, Shen Teh told me she was pregnant.

SUN What?

SHUI TA (*quickly*) That's a lie!

WANG (*very earnestly to Shui Ta*) Mr. Shui Ta, don't imagine that Shen Teh's friends will ever stop asking about her. A good person isn't easily forgotten. There aren't many. (*Out*) (*Shui Ta stares after him. Then he goes quickly into the back room*)

SUN (*to the audience*)   Shen Teh pregnant! I'm going mad! I've been doublecrossed! She must have told her cousin, and naturally that bastard shipped her out on the double. "Pack your bags and clear out before the child's father gets wind of it!" It's a crime against nature. It's inhuman. I've got a son! A Yang's coming up! And what happens? The girl disappears, and I'm left here slaving! (*He flies into a rage*) He soft-soaps me with a hat! (*He stamps on it*) Criminal! Thief! Kidnapper! And the girl without a protector! (*Sobs are heard from the back room. He stands still*) Wasn't that somebody crying? Who can it be? It's stopped. Who can be crying in the back room? Shui Ta, the hard-boiled bastard, certainly isn't crying. Who can it be? And the rice outside the door in the morning—what does it mean? Is the girl here after all? Is he hiding her? Who else could be crying in there? Wouldn't that be something! If she's pregnant, I've got to find her at all costs!

(*Shui Ta returns from the back room. He goes to the door and looks out into the rain*)

SUN   All right, where is she?

SHUI TA (*raises his hand and listens*)   One moment! It's nine o'clock. But you can't hear anything today. It's raining too hard.

SUN (*ironically*)   What are you listening for?

SHUI TA   The mail plane.

SUN   Very funny.

SHUI TA   I once heard you wanted to fly. Have you dropped that idea?

SUN   I have no complaint about my present job, if that's what you mean. I can do without night work, you know. Flying the mail is night work. I've got kind of attached to this firm. It's my former fiancée's firm after all, even if she has gone away. She has gone away, hasn't she?

SHUI TA   Why do you ask?

SUN   Maybe because I'm not entirely indifferent to her affairs.

SHUI TA My cousin might be interested to hear that.

SUN In any case I'm sufficiently concerned over her affairs that I wouldn't keep my hands folded if I discovered, for instance, that she was being deprived of her freedom.

SHUI TA By whom?

SUN By you.

(*Pause*)

SHUI TA What would you do?

SUN I might want to reconsider my position in the firm.

SHUI TA Oh! And suppose the firm—myself, that is—offered you a suitable position, could it count on your dropping your inquiries about your former fiancée?

SUN Possibly.

SHUI TA And how do you picture your new position in the firm?

SUN Full control. I picture throwing you out, for instance.

SHUI TA And what if the firm threw you out instead?

SUN I'd probably come back, but not alone.

SHUI TA Not alone?

SUN With the police.

SHUI TA With the police. And suppose the police didn't find anyone here?

SUN I presume they'd look in the back room! Mr. Shui Ta, my longing for the lady of my heart is irresistible. I feel that if I ever want to hold her in my arms again I've got to do something. (*Calmly*) She's pregnant, she needs a man. I'll talk it over with the water seller. (*He goes*)

(*Shui Ta stands motionless, looking after him. Then he goes quickly into the back room. He comes back with an armful of Shen Teh's belongings, underwear, dresses, toilet articles. He looks at length at the shawl that Shen Teh had bought from the carpet sellers. Then he packs it all up into a bundle, which he hides under the desk when he hears sounds. Enter Mrs. Mi Tzu and Mr. Shu Fu. They greet Shui Ta, put down their umbrellas and take off their galoshes*)

MRS. MI TZU It's coming on fall, Mr. Shui Ta.

MR. SHU FU A sad time of year!

MRS. MI TZU And where is your charming manager? That wicked lady killer! Of course you wouldn't know that side of him. Still, he knows how to combine his charm with his professional duties, so you only stand to gain by it.

SHUI TA (*bowing*)   Won't you be seated?

(*They sit down and start smoking*)

SHUI TA   My friends, an unforeseen event, which may have certain consequences, obliges me to hasten the negotiations I have recently initiated concerning the future of my business. Mr. Shu Fu, my factory is in difficulties.

MR. SHU FU   It always is.

SHUI TA   But now the police have threatened in so many words to close it unless I can show that I am negotiating for new premises. Mr. Shu Fu, the factory is the sole remaining possession of my cousin, in whom you have always taken so much interest.

MR. SHU FU   Mr. Shui Ta, I feel a profound reluctance to discuss your constantly expanding projects. I suggest a little supper with your cousin, you bring up your financial difficulties. I offer your cousin houses for the homeless, you set up a factory in them. I hand her a check, you cash it. Your cousin disappears! You ask for 100,000 silver dollars and tell me my houses aren't big enough. Where is your cousin, sir?

SHUI TA   Don't worry, Mr. Shu Fu. I am now in a position to inform you that she will be back soon.

MR. SHU FU   Soon? When? I've been hearing that "soon" for several weeks.

SHUI TA   I haven't asked you to sign anything. I have only asked if you would take a friendly interest in my project if my cousin came back.

MR. SHU FU   I have told you a thousand times that I will discuss nothing further with you, but am prepared to discuss anything whatsoever with your cousin. You, however, seem bent on impeding such a discussion.

SHUI TA   No longer.

MR. SHU FU   When will it take place?

SHUI TA (*uncertainly*)   In three months.

MR. SHU FU (*with annoyance*)   Then I will give you my signature in three months.

SHUI TA   But preparations must be made.

MR. SHU FU   You can make all the preparations, Shui Ta, if you are sure this time that your cousin is really coming back.

SHUI TA   Mrs. Mi Tzu, are you for your part prepared to certify to the police that I can have your workshops?

MRS. MI TZU   Certainly, if you will let me have your manager. You've known for weeks that this was my condition. (*To Mr. Shu Fu*) The young man has such a fine business head, and I need someone to administer my property.

SHUI TA   But you must realize that I can't let Mr. Yang Sun go just now with all these difficulties and the uncertain state of my health. I've always been willing to let you have him, but . . .

MRS. MI TZU   There's always a "but."
    (*Pause*)

SHUI TA   Very well, he will report to your office tomorrow.

MR. SHU FU   I am very glad you have finally brought yourself to this decision, Shui Ta. If Miss Shen Teh should really come back, the young man's presence here would be most undesirable. As we all know, he had a very unwholesome influence on her in the past.

SHUI TA (*bowing*)   Unquestionably. Do please forgive my long hesitation, so unworthy of a businessman, in these two matters concerning my cousin and Mr. Yang Sun. They were once very fond of each other.

MRS. MI TZU   You are forgiven.

SHUI TA (*looking toward the door*)   My friends, let us conclude our discussion. Gathered on these premises, formerly the small and shabby shop where the poor people of the neighborhood bought our good Shen Teh's tobacco, we, her friends, resolve to establish twelve fine branch stores, where Shen Teh's good tobacco will be sold in the future. I am told that the people now call me the tobacco king of Szechwan. In reality, I have carried on this business solely in the interest of my cousin. It will belong to her and her children and grandchildren.

(*From outside come the sounds of a crowd. Enter Sun, Wang, and the policeman*)

THE POLICEMAN   Mr. Shui Ta, I regret to say that the angry

mood prevailing in this neighborhood obliges me to follow up information communicated by a member of your own firm, to the effect that you have unlawfully sequestered your cousin Miss Shen Teh.

SHUI TA   That is not true.

THE POLICEMAN   Mr. Yang Sun, here present, declares that he heard the sound of someone crying in the room behind your office and that it can only have been a woman.

MRS. MI TZU   That is ridiculous. Mr. Shu Fu and myself, two respected citizens of this city, whose word the police can scarcely doubt, are prepared to testify that no one has been crying around here. We have been quietly smoking our cigars.

THE POLICEMAN   I regret to say that my orders are to inspect the room in question.

(*Shui Ta opens the door. The policeman bows and goes to the threshold. He looks in, then turns around with a smile*)

THE POLICEMAN   It's true, there's no one.

SUN (*who has joined him*)   But somebody *was* crying! (*His eyes light on the bundle that Shui Ta had shoved under the desk. He pounces on it*) This wasn't here before! (*He opens it, revealing Shen Teh's clothes, etc.*)

WANG   Those are Shen Teh's things. (*He runs to the door and calls out*) They've found her clothes!

THE POLICEMAN (*taking possession of the things*)   You say your cousin has gone away. A bundle of effects belonging to her is found under your desk. Where can the girl be reached, Mr. Shui Ta?

SHUI TA   I don't know her address.

THE POLICEMAN   That is most unfortunate.

CRIES FROM THE CROWD   Shen Teh's clothes have been found!— The tobacco king has murdered the girl and done away with the body.

THE POLICEMAN   Mr. Shui Ta, I must request you to follow me to headquarters.

SHUI TA (*bowing to Mrs. Mi Tzu and Mr. Shu Fu*)   My dear friends, I must ask your forgiveness for this disgraceful incident. But there are still judges in Szechwan. I am certain that all this will soon be cleared up. (*He goes out ahead of the policeman*)

WANG A terrible crime has been committed!

SUN (*in consternation*) But someone *was* crying!

Interlude

Wang's Night Lodging

Music. For the last time the gods appear to the water seller in a dream. They are greatly changed. After their long wanderings, exhaustion and all manner of bitter experiences have left their mark. One has had his hat knocked off, one has left his leg in a fox trap, and all three are barefoot.

WANG At last you appear! Dreadful things are happening in Shen Teh's tobacco shop, Enlightened Ones! Shen Teh went away again, months ago! Her cousin has taken everything! He was arrested today. They say he murdered her to gain possession of her shop. But I don't believe it, because she appeared to me in a dream and said her cousin was keeping her a prisoner. O, Enlightened Ones, you must come back at once and find her.

THE FIRST GOD This is abominable. Our whole search has been a failure. We found few good people, and those we found were not living lives worthy of human beings. We had already decided to settle for Shen Teh.

THE SECOND GOD If she is still good.

WANG Good she is, but she has disappeared.

THE FIRST GOD Then all is lost.

THE SECOND GOD Watch your dignity.

THE FIRST GOD What good is dignity now? We shall have to resign if she isn't located. Look at the world we've found: nothing but misery, baseness, and ungodliness. Even the landscape has turned against us. Beautiful trees are beheaded by cables; beyond the mountains we see great clouds of smoke and hear the thunder of cannon, and nowhere a good person who is able to make his way.

THE THIRD GOD   Ah, water seller, our commandments seem to be fatal! I'm afraid all the moral precepts we have drawn up will have to be crossed out. People have trouble enough saving their bare lives. Good intentions bring them to the edge of the abyss, good deeds topple them into it. (*To the other two gods*) You'll have to admit the world is not fit to live in!

THE FIRST GOD (*violently*)   No, it's mankind that's worthless.

THE THIRD GOD   Because the world is too cold!

THE SECOND GOD   Because men are too weak!

THE FIRST GOD   A little dignity, my friends! Brothers, we must not despair. After all, we have found one human being who is good and has not become wicked but only disappeared. We must hasten to find her. One is enough. Didn't we say that everything could be made right again if only one person were found who could stand up against this world, only one? (*They quickly vanish*)

10

Courtroom

In groups: Mr. Shu Fu and Mrs. Mi Tzu. Sun and his mother. Wang, the former carpenter, the unemployed man, the sister-in-law, the grandfather, the young prostitute (the niece), the two old people. Mrs. Shin. The policeman.

THE OLD MAN   He's too powerful.

WANG   He's planning to open twelve new shops.

THE FORMER CARPENTER   How can the judge hand down a fair verdict when the defendant's friends, Shu Fu the barber and Mrs. Mi Tzu the property owner, are his friends too?

THE SISTER-IN-LAW   Last night, Mrs. Shin was seen taking a fat goose to the judge's kitchen in behalf of Mr. Shui Ta. The grease was dripping through the basket.

THE OLD WOMAN (*to Wang*) Our poor Shen Teh will never be found again.

WANG Only the gods can uncover the truth.

THE POLICEMAN Silence! The court!

(*Enter the three gods in judges' robes. As they pass front stage to their seats, they can be heard whispering*)

THE THIRD GOD It's sure to come out. The certificates were so clumsily forged.

THE SECOND GOD The judge's sudden attack of stomach trouble is bound to arouse suspicion.

THE FIRST GOD I wouldn't think so, he ate half a goose.

MRS. SHIN Look! New judges!

WANG And very good ones!

(*The third god, who is last in line hears him, turns around, and smiles at him. The gods sit down. The first god strikes the desk with his gavel. The policeman brings in Shui Ta, who is received with catcalls but strides along with an imperious air*)

THE POLICEMAN Brace yourself. Justice Fu Yi Cheng isn't here. But the new judges also look very benevolent.

(*Shui Ta sees the gods and falls into a faint*)

THE YOUNG PROSTITUTE What's this? The tobacco king has fainted.

THE SISTER-IN-LAW Yes, at the sight of the new judges!

WANG He seems to know them! I don't understand.

THE FIRST GOD (*opens the proceedings*) Are you Shui Ta, the tobacco wholesaler?

SHUI TA (*very faintly*) Yes.

THE FIRST GOD You are accused of doing away with your cousin Miss Shen Teh in order to take over her business. Do you plead guilty?

SHUI TA No.

THE FIRST GOD (*thumbing through papers*) First witness. The precinct police officer will tell the court what he knows about the characters of the accused and his cousin.

THE POLICEMAN (*steps forward*) Miss Shen Teh was a young lady who wished to be nice to everyone, who lived and let live, as they say. Mr. Shui Ta, on the other hand, is a man of principles. The young lady's generosity sometimes compelled him to take stern measures. Unlike the young lady, however, he was always on the side of the law, your honors. His cousin had trustingly taken a certain group of people into her house —he showed them up for a gang of thieves. In another instance he prevented Miss Shen Teh at the last moment from committing sheer perjury. Mr. Shui Ta is known to me as a respectable and law-abiding citizen.

THE FIRST GOD   Is there anyone else present who wishes to testify that the accused is not the sort of man who would commit the crime imputed to him?

(*Mr. Shu Fu and Mrs. Mi Tzu step forward*)

THE POLICEMAN (*whispers to the gods*)   Mr. Shu Fu, a highly influential citizen!

MR. SHU FU   In our city Mr. Shui Ta enjoys the reputation of an upstanding businessman. He is vice-president of the chamber of commerce and his name has been suggested for district justice of the peace.

WANG (*interrupting*)   By you! You're in cahoots with him!

THE POLICEMAN (*whispering*)   An undesirable!

MRS. MI TZU   As president of the United District Charities, I wish to bring it to the attention of the court that Mr. Shui Ta is not only preparing to lodge a large number of persons in the best possible quarters, light, airy rooms in his tobacco factory, but also contributes regularly to our home for the disabled.

THE POLICEMAN (*whispering*)   Mrs. Mi Tzu, a close friend of Justice Fu Yi Cheng!

THE FIRST GOD   Yes, yes, but now we must see whether anyone has something less favorable to say of the accused.

(*Wang, the former carpenter, the old couple, the unemployed man, the sister-in-law, and the young prostitute step forward*)

THE POLICEMAN   The scum of the neighborhood!

THE FIRST GOD   Well, what do you know of Shui Ta's general behavior?

CRIES (*intermingled*)   He ruined us!—He blackmailed me!—

He made us do wicked things!—Exploited the helpless!—Lied!—Swindled!—Committed murder!

THE FIRST GOD   Accused, what have you to say for yourself?

SHUI TA   I have done nothing but save my cousin's bare livelihood, your honors! I came only when she was in danger of losing her little shop. I had to come three times. I never wanted to stay. The last time the circumstances obliged me to. I have had nothing but trouble the whole time. Everybody loved my cousin and I had to do the dirty work. That's why they hate me.

THE SISTER-IN-LAW   You can say that again! Take our case, for instance, your honors! (*To Shui Ta*) I won't say anything about the bales of tobacco.

SHUI TA   Why not? Why not?

THE SISTER-IN-LAW (*to the gods*)   Shen Teh put us up, and he had us arrested.

SHUI TA   You stole cakes!

THE SISTER-IN-LAW   Now he's pretending to care about the baker's cakes! He only wanted the shop for himself!

SHUI TA   The shop wasn't a flophouse, you selfish beasts!

THE SISTER-IN-LAW   But we had no place to go!

SHUI TA   There were too many of you!

WANG   And these people? (*He points to the old couple*) Are they selfish too?

THE OLD MAN   We put our savings into Shen Teh's business. Why did you cheat us out of our shop?

SHUI TA   Because my cousin wanted to help a flier fly. I had to find the money.

WANG   That may be what she wanted, but you wanted that well-paid job in Peking. The shop wasn't good enough for you.

SHUI TA   The rent was too high!

MRS. SHIN   I can vouch for that.

SHUI TA   And my cousin had no head for business.

MRS. SHIN   For that too. Besides, she was in love with the flier.

SHUI TA   Isn't she entitled to be in love?

WANG   Of course she is! So why did you try to make her marry a man she didn't love, the barber here?

SHUI TA   The man she loved was a scoundrel.

WANG   Him? (*He points to Sun*)

SUN (*jumps up*)   And because he was a scoundrel, you took him into your office!

SHUI TA   To help you! To help you improve!

THE SISTER-IN-LAW   And turn him into a slave driver!

WANG   And when you'd finished improving him, didn't you sell him to this woman? (*He points to Mrs. Mi Tzu*) She's been telling the whole neighborhood.

SHUI TA   Because she wouldn't let me have her workshops unless he tickled her knees!

MRS. MI TZU   That's a lie! Not another word about my workshops! I wash my hands of you, you murderer! (*She flounces out with offended dignity*)

SUN (*firmly*)   Your honors, I feel obliged to put in a word for him!

THE SISTER-IN-LAW   Naturally you feel obliged. He's your boss.

THE UNEMPLOYED MAN   He's the worst slave driver that's ever been seen. He's depraved.

SUN   Your honors, whatever the accused may have made of me, he is not a murderer. A few minutes before he was arrested, I heard Shen Teh's voice coming from the room behind the shop!

THE FIRST GOD (*eagerly*)   Then she was alive? Tell us exactly what you heard!

SUN (*triumphantly*)   Sobs, your honors, sobs!

THE THIRD GOD   And you knew who it was?

SUN   Positive. Wouldn't I recognize her voice?

MR. SHU FU   I should think so. You made her cry often enough!

SUN   I made her happy too. But then he decided (*pointing to Shui Ta*) to sell her to you.

SHUI TA (*to Sun*)   Because you didn't love her!

WANG   No. For the money!

SHUI TA   But what was the money needed for, your honors? (*To Sun*) You wanted her to abandon all her friends, but the barber offered his houses and his money to help her help the poor. To enable her to do good I had to promise her to the barber.

WANG   Why didn't you let her do good when the big check was made out? Why did you push Shen Teh's friends into your stinking sweatshop, that tobacco factory of yours, tobacco king?

SHUI TA   It was for the child.

THE FORMER CARPENTER   What about my children? What have you done to my children?

(*Shui Ta is silent*)

WANG   Now you have nothing to say! The gods gave Shen Teh her shop as a little spring of goodness. She always wanted to do good, and you always came and prevented her.

SHUI TA (*beside himself*)   Because if I hadn't, the spring would have dried up, you idiot.

MRS. SHIN   That is true, your honors.

WANG   What good is a spring you can't draw anything out of?

SHUI TA   Good deeds bring ruin.

WANG (*savagely*)   And evil deeds bring prosperity, is that it? What have you done with the good Shen Teh, you evil man? How many good people are there anyway, Enlightened Ones? She was good! When that man over there broke my hand, she wanted to testify for me. And now I am testifying for her. She was good, I swear it. (*He raises his hand to swear*)

THE THIRD GOD   What's wrong with your hand, water seller? It's stiff.

WANG (*points to Shui Ta*)   He's to blame and no one else. She wanted to give me money for the doctor, but then he came. You were her deadly enemy!

SHUI TA   I was her only friend!

ALL   Where is she?

SHUI TA   Gone away.

WANG   Where?

SHUI TA   I won't tell you.

ALL   But why did she have to go away?

SHUI TA (*screaming*)   Because you'd have torn her to pieces! (*A sudden silence*)

SHUI TA (*has slumped on his chair*)   I can't go on. I will explain everything. If the court is cleared and only the judges remain, I will make a confession.

ALL   He's going to confess!—He's as good as convicted!

THE FIRST GOD (*strikes the desk with his gavel*) Clear the court.

(*The policeman clears the court*)

MRS. SHIN (*on her way out, laughing*)   They've got a surprise coming!

SHUI TA   Are they gone? All of them? I can't keep silent any longer. I have recognized you, Enlightened Ones!

THE SECOND GOD   What have you done with our good person of Szechwan?

SHUI TA   Let me confess the awful truth, I am your good person! (*He removes his mask and tears off his outer garments. Shen Teh stands before the judges*)

THE SECOND GOD   Shen Teh!

SHEN TEH   Yes, it is I. Shui Ta and Shen Teh, I am both of them.

Your order long ago
To be good and yet to live
Tore me like lightning into two halves. I
Don't know how it happened: I could not
Be good at once to others and myself.
To help myself and others was too hard for me.
Ah, your world is hard. Too much poverty, too much despair!
The hand that is held out to the wretched
Is soon wrenched off! He who helps the lost
Is himself lost! For who can
Long refuse to be wicked when starvation kills?
Where was I to take all that was needed? Only
From myself! But then I would die. Good intentions
Crushed me to the ground. But when I did wrong
I strode in power and ate good meat!
There must be something wrong with your world. Why
Is wickedness so richly rewarded and why does such hard
    punishment
Await the good? Oh, there was in me
Such eagerness to indulge myself. And I had also
A secret knowledge, for my foster-mother
Washed me in gutter water! That gave me
A sharp eye. Yet pity

Brought me such pain that ferocious rage overcame me
At the sight of misery. Then
I felt a change come over me.
My teeth turned to fangs. A kind word
Was bitter as ashes in my mouth. And yet
I wished to be an angel to the slums. To give
Was a passion with me. A happy face
And I walked on clouds.
Condemn me: all my crimes
Were committed to help my neighbors
To love my beloved and
Save my little son from want.
O gods, for your great projects
I, poor mortal, was too small.

THE FIRST GOD (*with every indication of horror*) Speak no more, unhappy creature! We were so glad to have found you again, and now what are we to think?

SHEN TEH I'm only trying to tell you that I am the wicked man who committed the crimes they have all been telling you about!

THE FIRST GOD The good person of whom all had only good to say!

SHEN TEH No, the bad person too!

THE FIRST GOD A misunderstanding! A few unfortunate incidents! A few heartless neighbors! A little too much zeal!

THE SECOND GOD But how is she to go on living?

THE FIRST GOD She will manage. She is strong and strapping, she can endure a good deal.

THE SECOND GOD But didn't you hear what she said?

THE FIRST GOD (*violently*) Muddled, extremely muddled! What she says is inconceivable, absolutely inconceivable. Are we to admit that our commandments are fatal? Are we to give up our commandments? (*Stubbornly*) Never! Is the world to be changed? How? By whom? No, everything is in order. (*He strikes the desk quickly with his gavel*) And now . . . (*At a sign from him, music rings out; a rosy glow is seen*)
Let us go home. This little world
Has moved us deeply. Its joys and sorrows
Have greatly cheered and grieved us. Yet

Up there beyond the stars we shall be glad
To think of you, Shen Teh, the good person
Who here below bears witness to our spirit
And holds the little lamp in the cold darkness.
Farewell! Good luck!
(*At a sign from him the ceiling opens. A pink cloud descends. On it the three gods rise very slowly*)

SHEN TEH   Oh no, Enlightened Ones! Don't go away! Don't leave me! How am I going to face those two good old people who have lost their shop, and the water seller with his stiff hand? How am I going to defend myself against the barber whom I don't love and Sun whom I do love? And I'm with child, soon my little son will be here, wanting to eat. I can't stay here! (*She looks frantically toward the door through which her tormentors will enter*)

THE FIRST GOD   You'll manage. Just be good and everything will turn out all right!
(*Enter the witnesses. They look with amazement at the judges hovering on their pink cloud*)

WANG   Show your veneration! The gods have appeared among us! Three of the highest gods have come to Szechwan, looking for a good person. They found one, but . . .

THE FIRST GOD   No buts! Here she is!

ALL   Shen Teh!

THE FIRST GOD   She wasn't dead, she was only hidden. She will remain in your midst, a good person!

SHEN TEH   But I need my cousin!

THE FIRST GOD   Not too often!

SHEN TEH   At least once a week!

THE FIRST GOD   Once a month: that will do!

SHEN TEH   Oh, don't go away, Enlightened Ones! I haven't told you everything. I need you terribly!

THE GODS (*sing the* "Trio of the Vanishing Gods on their Cloud")

All too long on earth we've lingered
Swiftly drops the fleeting day:
Shrewdly studied, closely fingered
Precious treasures melt away.

Now the golden flood is dying
While your shadows onward press
Time that we too started flying
Homeward to our nothingness.

SHEN TEH   Help!
THE GODS

The search is over, therefore we
Must really hurry on
So glory be and glory be
To good Shen Teh of Szechwan!

(*As Shen Teh desperately holds out her arms toward them,
they vanish, smiling and waving*)

Epilogue

*One of the players steps before the curtain and, addressing the
audience apologetically, speaks the epilogue.*

Ladies and gentlemen, don't be annoyed
We know this ending leaves you in the void.
A golden legend we set out to tell
But then somehow the ending went to hell.
We're disappointed too, struck with dismay
All questions open though we've closed our play.
Especially since we live by your enjoyment.
Disgruntled spectators mean unemployment.
It's sad but true, the heavens defend us
We're ruined unless you recommend us.
Fear may well have blocked *our* inspiration
But what's *your* answer to the situation?
For love nor money we could find no out:
Refashion man? Or change the world about?
Or turn to different gods? Or don't we need
Any? Our bewilderment is great indeed.

There's only one solution comes to mind:
That you yourselves should ponder till you find
The ways and means and measures tending
To help good people to a happy ending.
Ladies and gentlemen, in you we trust:
The ending must be happy, must, must, must!

Puntila and Matti, His Hired Man

A Folk Play

After the tales and the draft of a play by Hella Wuolijoki

Translator: Ralph Manheim

CHARACTERS

PUNTILA, a landowner
EVA, his daughter
MATTI, his chauffeur
THE WAITER
THE JUDGE
THE ATTACHÉ
THE COW DOCTOR
BOOTLEG EMMA
THE PHARMACIST'S HELPER
THE DAIRYMAID
THE TELEPHONE OPERATOR

A FAT MAN
A WORKER
THE REDHEAD
THE SICKLY-LOOKING WORKER
RED SURKKALA
HIS FOUR CHILDREN
LAINA, the cook
FINA, the chambermaid
THE LAWYER
THE PARSON
THE PARSON'S WIFE
FORESTRY WORKERS

[Proper names of three syllables are accented on the first syllable: Puntila, Kurgela, etc.]

Prologue

Dear audience, it's not an easy fight
Though here and there we seem to glimpse the light.
But laughter too can help to win the day
And that's why we have made a comic play.
The jokes that we tonight present for sale
Will not be measured on a druggist's scale
But more like spuds in hefty sacks.
Sometimes, I won't deny, we use an ax.
This evening we are going to show you all
A certain prehistoric animal
Estatium possessor—in English, squire.
Its food and drink consumption couldn't be higher
And uses it has none. In regions where
This relic still survives in its plush lair
It is a plague. Tonight you'll see this creature
At large in a country blessed by Mother Nature
Which, if you fail to see it in our stage designs
Perhaps you'll piece together from our lines:
Cool lakes, birch forests, summer without night
The clatter of milk pails at the dawn of day
As Finland's villages awaken and the gray
Smoke rises from red-shingled roofs. All this you'll see
We hope, in following Puntila's history.

1

Puntila Finds a Human Being

Back room of the Park Hotel in Tavasthus. Puntila, the judge, the waiter. The judge falls off his chair, drunk.

PUNTILA   Waiter, how long have we been here?

WAITER   Two days, Mr. Puntila.

PUNTILA   (*reproachfully to the judge*) Did you hear that? Only two measly days! And here you are, lying down on the job, claiming to be tired. I'm not asking much of you, just to have a few drinks with me while I talk about myself and how lonely I feel and what I think of the government! But even that seems to be too much of an effort. You all pass out on me, the spirit is willing but the flesh is weak. Where's that doctor who was challenging the whole world only yesterday? The station master was still here to see them carrying him away, and then around seven *he* went under after a heroic struggle, blubbering. The pharmacist was still going strong, but what's become of him now? These men are supposed to be our leading citizens, people will repudiate them in disgust. (*To the sleeping judge*) Have you ever stopped to think of the example you're setting the population of Tavastland, a judge who can't even drop into a tavern without passing out? If I had a hired man who was as lazy about his plowing as you are with your drinking, I'd fire him on the spot. You dog, I'd say, I'll teach you to lie down on the job. See here, Fredrik, you're an educated man, people look up to you for an example. Don't you know what they expect of you? They expect stamina and a sense of responsibility. You weak man! Why can't you pull yourself together and sit up and talk with me? (*To the waiter*) What day is it today?

WAITER   Saturday, Mr. Puntila.

PUNTILA   That's funny. It ought to be Friday.

WAITER   I beg your pardon, but it's Saturday.

PUNTILA   Huh, contradicting! A fine waiter you are! Trying to get rid of your customers by insulting them. Waiter, bring me another aquavit, and listen carefully so you don't get everything mixed up again: one aquavit and one Friday. Have you got that straight?

WAITER   Yes, Mr. Puntila. (*He runs out*)

PUNTILA   (*to the judge*)   Wake up, weakling. Don't leave me alone like this! Capitulating to a couple of bottles of aquavit! It can't be. You've hardly had a smell of the stuff. While I was rowing you across the aquavit, you crawled off into the bottom of the boat, you were afraid to look over the edge, you ought to be ashamed of yourself. Look, I'm stepping out (*he acts it out*), I'm walking on the aquavit. Do I sink? (*He sees Matti, his chauffeur, who has been standing in the doorway for some time*) Who are you?

MATTI   I'm your chauffeur, Mr. Puntila.

PUNTILA   (*suspiciously*)   Who? Repeat that.

MATTI   I'm your chauffeur.

PUNTILA   Anybody can say that. I don't know you.

MATTI   Maybe you've never taken a good look at me. I've only been with you for five weeks.

PUNTILA   And where have you come from now?

MATTI   From out there. I've been sitting in the car for two days, waiting for you.

PUNTILA   What car?

MATTI   Your car. The Studebaker.

PUNTILA   Sounds odd to me. Can you prove it?

MATTI   And let me tell you one thing: I'm not going to wait out there another minute. I've got it up to here. You can't treat a man like that.

PUNTILA   What do you mean: a man? Are you a man? A minute ago you said you were a chauffeur. Ha, I've caught you contradicting yourself. Admit it.

MATTI   You'll see if I'm not a man, Mr. Puntila. Because I'm not going to let you treat me like a dog, waiting out in the road till you deign to come out.

PUNTILA   A minute ago you said you wouldn't stand for it.

MATTI   Exactly. Pay me what's coming to me, 175 marks. I'll pick up my reference later.

PUNTILA   I know that voice. (*He goes around him, examining him like a strange animal*) Your voice sounds perfectly human. Sit down and have an aquavit, we've got to get acquainted.

WAITER (*comes in with a bottle*)   Your aquavit, Mr. Puntila, and today is Friday.

PUNTILA   Good. (*Pointing to Matti*) This is a friend of mine.

WAITER   Yes, it's your chauffeur, Mr. Puntila.

PUNTILA   Oh, so you're a chauffeur. I've always said you meet the most interesting people when you travel. Fill the glasses.

MATTI   I'm curious to know what you're up to now. I don't know if I want to drink your aquavit.

PUNTILA   I see, you're the suspicious type. You've got something there. Never sit down at a table with strangers. Why, if you fall asleep, they might rob you. I'm Puntila, got a big farm in Lammi, I'm an upright citizen. I own 90 cows. It's safe to drink with me, brother.

MATTI   Fine. I'm Matti Altonen and I'm pleased to make your acquaintance. (*He drinks Puntila's health*)

PUNTILA   I have a good heart, and I'm proud of it. One time I picked up a beetle on the road and took him into the woods to keep him from being run over. Yes, sometimes I overdo it. I put him down on a stick and let him crawl. You've got a good heart too, I can see that. I can't stand people who are always thinking about "me, me, me." They ought to be horsewhipped. Some of our farmers are always trying to save on the hired hands' food. If I had my way, my help would live on roast beef. They're human too, and they want something decent to eat, same as me. Why not? Don't you agree?

MATTI   Definitely.

PUNTILA   Did I really make you wait outside? I don't like that, I can't forgive myself. If I do it again, kindly hit me on the head with a monkey wrench. Are you my friend, Matti?

MATTI   No.

PUNTILA   Thank you. I knew it. Look at me, Matti. What do you see?

MATTI   Well, let's see . . . A big clod, stinking drunk.

PUNTILA   That shows how deceptive appearances can be. You've got me all wrong. Matti, I'm a sick man.

MATTI   Very sick.

PUNTILA   That's what I like to hear. Some people don't realize. Seeing me like this, you wouldn't suspect it. (*Gloomily, with a penetrating look at Matti*) I get attacks.

MATTI   You don't mean it.

PUNTILA   It's no joke. They come over me at least once every three months. I wake up, and all of a sudden I'm stone sober. What do you think of that?

MATTI   And you get these attacks regularly?

PUNTILA   Regularly. All the rest of the time I'm perfectly normal, same as you see me now. In perfect control of my mind, master of my senses. And then this attack comes on. First something goes wrong with my eyes. Instead of two forks (*he holds up a fork*), I only see one.

MATTI   (*horrified*)   You mean you're half blind?

PUNTILA   I only see half the world. But that's not the worst of it. When these attacks come over me and I'm absolutely dead sober, I degenerate into an animal. I lose all my inhibitions. Brother, you can't hold the things I do in that state against me. Not if there's an ounce of kindness in you, when you remember that I'm a sick man. (*With horror in his voice*) I'm positively responsible. Do you know what responsible means, brother? A responsible man is a man who's capable of anything. For instance, he loses sight of his own child's welfare, he has no feeling for friendship. A man like that would trample his own dead body. And that's because he's responsible, as the lawyers call it.

MATTI   Don't you do anything about these attacks?

PUNTILA   Brother, I do what I can. Everything that's humanly possible. (*He picks up his glass*) Here, this is my only medicine. I gulp it down without batting an eyelash, and take my word for it, I don't measure it with a baby spoon. There's one thing I can say for myself: I fight these attacks of raving sobriety like a man. But what good does it do? They're always getting the better of me. Take my thoughtless treatment of a fine man like you. Here, help yourself, it's boiled beef. I can't help wondering what stroke of luck brought you to me. How do you account for it?

MATTI   I lost the job I had before. Through no fault of my own.

PUNTILA   How come?

MATTI   I saw ghosts.

PUNTILA   Real ones?

MATTI (*shrugs his shoulders*)   I was working for Mr. Pappmann. Nobody knew why there should be ghosts. There'd never been any before I came. If you ask me, I think it was because of the lousy food. When people's stomachs are weighed down with sludge, they get bad dreams, maybe even nightmares. One thing I can't stand is bad cooking. I was thinking of walking out, but there were no other prospects. I was depressed, so I began telling gloomy stories in the kitchen, and pretty soon the kitchen girls were seeing babies' heads on the fences at night and giving notice. One time a gray ball rolled down off the cow barn, it looked like a head, so when the chief dairymaid heard me talking about it, she puked. And the chambermaid quit after I'd seen a black-looking man roaming around outside the bath-hut about eleven o'clock at night, with his head under his arm and he asked me for a light for his pipe. Mr. Pappmann yelled and screamed at me; he said it was all my fault, I was scaring his help away, and there weren't any ghosts. But when I told him he was mistaken, that for instance when his wife was away at the hospital having her baby I'd seen a white ghost two nights in succession coming out of the chief dairymaid's room and climbing into Mr. Pappmann's window, he couldn't think of anything to say. But he fired me. On my way out I told him I thought the ghosts would calm down if better food were served, because they couldn't stand the smell of meat for instance.

PUNTILA   I see, you only lost your job because they scrimped on food for the help. It's all right with me if you like to eat, as long as you handle my tractor properly and you're not uppity and you give Puntila his due. We've got everything we need, there's plenty of wood in the forest, isn't there? We'll see eye to eye, everybody sees eye to eye with Puntila. (*He sings*) "Why must you sue me, darling mine? In bed we always got on fine." Puntila would be only too happy to chop down birch trees with you and dig the stones out of the fields and drive the tractor. But do they let him? They put a stiff collar on me, it's scraped away two chins already. It doesn't look right for papa to plow; it doesn't look right for papa to tickle the hired girls; it doesn't look right for papa to drink coffee with the help. But now I'm good and sick of it. I'm going to Kurgela and get my daughter engaged to the attaché, and as soon as she's married off I'll sit down to table in my shirtsleeves and there won't be anybody to supervise me. Mrs. Klinckmann will hold her tongue, I'll fuck her and that's that. And I'll raise everybody's wages, because the world is wide, and I'll keep my forest, and there'll be enough for all of you and enough for the master too.

MATTI (*laughs loud and long*)   You're right as rain, but calm down. And now maybe we ought to wake up the judge, but we'd better go easy, or we'll scare him and he'll send us to jail for a hundred years.

PUNTILA   I only want to be sure there's no gulf between us. Say there's no gulf.

MATTI   I take it as an order, Mr. Puntila. No gulf.

PUNTILA   Brother, we have to talk about money.

MATTI   Definitely.

PUNTILA   But it's sordid to talk about money.

MATTI   Then we won't talk about money.

PUNTILA   Wrong again. Why shouldn't we be sordid? Aren't we free men?

MATTI   No.

PUNTILA   See? And being free men, we do what we please. And right now we please to be sordid. Because we've got to squeeze out a dowry for my only child; that's the fact we've got to look in the eye, with cold drunken clarity. I see two possibilities: I could sell one of my forests, or I could sell myself. What do you advise?

MATTI   I wouldn't want to sell myself if I had a forest to sell.

PUNTILA   What, sell the forest? You're a big disappointment to me, brother. Do you know what a forest is? Is a forest just 10,000 cords of wood? Or is it a green enchantment? And you want to sell a green enchantment? For shame!

MATTI   Then do the other.

PUNTILA   You too, Brutus? Can you really want me to sell myself?

MATTI   How can you sell yourself anyway?

PUNTILA   Mrs. Klinckmann.

MATTI   At Kurgela, where we're going now? The attaché's aunt?

PUNTILA   She's got a soft spot for me.

MATTI   And you're thinking of selling her your body? That's terrible.

PUNTILA   Not at all. But what about my freedom? But I think I'll sacrifice myself. What am I anyway?

MATTI   There's something in that.

(*The judge wakes up, looks for a bell that isn't there and rings it*)

JUDGE   Order in the court.

PUNTILA   He thinks he's in court because he's asleep. Brother, that was a knotty question—which is worth more, a forest like my forest or a man like me?—but you've settled it. You're a splendid fellow. There, take my wallet and pay up and put it in your pocket, I'd only lose it. (*Pointing to the judge*) Pick him up and carry him out. I lose everything, I wish I didn't have a thing. That's the best. Money stinks, and don't forget it. That's my dream. Me penniless, and the two of us tramping through our beautiful Finland, or maybe in a pinch we could have a little roadster, anybody'd lend us that much gas, and now and then when we're tired, we'll drop into a little bar like this and have a drink or two in exchange for chopping wood, you could do it with one hand behind your back, brother.

(*They go out, Matti carrying the judge*)

2

Eva

The entrance hall of the manor house in Kurgela. Eva Puntila is eating chocolates while waiting for her father. Eino Silakka, the attaché, appears at the top of the stairs. He is very sleepy.

EVA   Mrs. Klinckmann must be dreadfully upset.

ATTACHÉ   My aunt never stays upset very long. I just phoned again to see what had become of them. It seems that a car with two raving maniacs in it just drove through the village.

EVA   That's them all right. Isn't it lucky? I can always tell when people are talking about my father. Whenever I hear about somebody chasing a hired man with a horsewhip or making some cottager's widow a present of a limousine, I can be sure it was my father.

ATTACHÉ   But this is a different kind of a house, enfin. What disturbs me is the scandal. I may not have a head for figures and how many gallons of milk we can ship to Kaunas, I never touch the stuff, but I know a scandal when I see one. When after his eighth cognac the attaché at the French embassy in London shouted across the table at the Duchess of Catrumple that she was a whore, I instantly predicted a scandal. And I was right. I think they're coming now. Angel, I'm a wee bit tired. Will you forgive me if I retire? (*Out quickly*)

(*An enormous crash. Enter Puntila, the judge and Matti*)

PUNTILA   Here we are. But please, no fuss, don't wake anybody up. We'll just have one last bottle among friends, and then we'll turn in. Are you happy?

EVA   We expected you three days ago.

PUNTILA   We were delayed, but we haven't forgotten a thing. Matti, get the suitcase. I hope you kept it on your lap the way I told you, because if anything's broken we'll die of thirst in this place. We've been speeding, because we thought you'd be waiting.

THE JUDGE   May we congratulate you, Eva?

EVA   Papa, you're so awful. Here I've been sitting all week in a strange house with nothing but an old novel and the attaché and his aunt, dying of boredom.

PUNTILA   We really hurried. I kept telling them we mustn't let the grass grow under our feet. I had certain things to discuss with the attaché about the engagement. When we were held up I consoled myself with the thought that the attaché was here and you had somebody to keep you company. Careful with that suitcase, Matti, don't let anything happen to it. (*With infinite caution he helps Matti with the suitcase*)

JUDGE   You complain of being left alone with the attaché. What's the matter? Have you quarreled?

EVA   Oh, I don't know. One can't exactly quarrel with him.

JUDGE   You know, Puntila, Eva doesn't show much enthusiasm about the whole business. She accuses the attaché of being a man one can't quarrel with. I had a divorce case once where the wife complained that her husband never clouted her when she threw the lamp at him. She felt neglected.

PUNTILA   There! One more happy landing! When Puntila sets his hand to a thing, it prospers. What's the matter? You're not happy. I can sympathize. If you ask me, steer clear of that attaché. He's not a man.

EVA   (*seeing Matti grin*)   I only said I doubted if I could have much of a time alone with the attaché.

PUNTILA   Just what I've been saying. Take Matti here. Any girl would have a good time with him.

EVA   You're impossible, papa. I only said that I wasn't sure. (*To Matti*) Take the suitcase upstairs.

PUNTILA   Wait a minute! We'll be needing a couple of bottles. I want to have a little talk with you to decide whether the attaché suits me. Have you got yourself engaged at least?

EVA   No, I haven't got myself engaged. We didn't talk about anything like that. (*To Matti*) Leave that suitcase closed.

PUNTILA   What? Not engaged? In three days? What on earth did you do? I don't like that in a man. I get engaged in three minutes flat. Bring him down, I'll call in the kitchen maids and show him how much time it takes me to get engaged. Let's have those bottles. The burgundy, no, the liqueur.

EVA   No, you're not drinking any more. (*To Matti*) Take the suitcase up to my room, second on the right.

PUNTILA (*alarmed when Matti picks up the suitcase*)   Why, Eva, that's not nice of you. You can't deny your own father a drink. I promise just to have this one little bottle as quietly as can be, with the cook or the chambermaid and Fredrik, he's thirsty too, don't be inhuman.

EVA   I stayed up just to prevent you from waking the kitchen staff.

PUNTILA   I'm sure Mrs. Klinckmann—where is she anyway?— would be glad to sit up with me for a while. Fredrik is tired anyway, let him go to bed, and I'll have a little talk with the old girl. I was meaning to anyway, we've always had a soft spot for each other.

EVA   I do wish you'd pull yourself together. Mrs. Klinckmann is furious enough with you already for being three days late. I doubt if you'll even lay eyes on her tomorrow.

PUNTILA   I'll go knock on her door and straighten everything out. I know how to handle her. You don't know anything about these things, Eva.

EVA   All I know is that no woman is going to sit with you in that state. (*To Matti*) Now will you kindly take that suitcase upstairs. These three days have been enough for me.

PUNTILA   Eva, won't you listen to reason. If you don't want me to wake Mrs. Klinckmann, get me the little plump one, must be the housekeeper, and I'll have a bit of a chat with her.

EVA   Don't overdo it, papa, unless you want me to carry it upstairs myself and drop it by mistake.

(*Puntila stands transfixed with horror. Matti goes out with the suitcase. Eva follows him*)

PUNTILA (*subdued*)   Imagine a child treating her father like this. (*Appalled, he turns to go.*) Come along Fredrik.

JUDGE   What do you mean to do now, Johannes?

PUNTILA   I'm going away, I don't like it here. My goodness, I hurry, I arrive in the dead of night, and am I welcomed with open arms? Makes me think of the prodigal son. Suppose they'd greeted him with cold reproaches instead of bringing out the fatted calf! I'm getting out of here.

JUDGE   Where to?

PUNTILA   What a question? Haven't you noticed that my own daughter won't give me a drink? She leaves me no choice. I'm going out into the black night to see where I can scare up a bottle or two.

JUDGE   Be reasonable, Puntila. You won't get any liquor at two-thirty A.M. The sale of alcoholic beverages without a doctor's prescription is illegal.

PUNTILA   What, you're abandoning me too? No legal liquor, you say? I'll show you that I can come by legal liquor at any hour of the day or night.

EVA (*reappears at the top of the stairs*)   Papa, take that coat off at once.

PUNTILA   You shut up, Eva, and honor thy father and mother that thy days may be long on earth! What a house! You drop in for a visit and they hang your bowels on the line to dry. And telling me I won't get a woman. You'll see if I get a woman. Tell la Klinckmann I can do without her company. As far as I'm concerned, she's a foolish virgin without any oil in her lamp. And now I'll speed away so fast that the earth will resound and the curves straighten out in terror! (*He goes out*)

EVA (*coming down*)   You! Stop him.

MATTI (*coming down behind her*)   Too late. He's too quick.

JUDGE   I don't think I'll wait up for him. I'm not as young as I used to be, Eva. I don't think he'll come to any harm. He's always lucky. Where's my room? (*Goes upstairs*)

EVA   Third door to the right. (*To Matti*) We'd better stay up to make sure he doesn't start drinking and hobnobbing with the help.

MATTI   That kind of familiarity is bad. One time when I was working in a paper mill, the porter quit because the boss asked him how his son was getting along.

EVA   People are always taking advantage of my father. That's his trouble. He's too good.

MATTI   Yes, it's a lucky thing for us all that he drinks now and then. Because when he drinks he's a good man, he sees white mice and wants to pat them because he's so good.

EVA   That's no way to talk about your employer. I don't like it. And don't take what he said about the attaché too literally. He was only joking, and I don't want you repeating it all over the place.

MATTI   That the attaché isn't a man? What is a man anyway? Some say this, some say that. I was working for a brewer's wife one time. She had a daughter who was so modest she called me into the bath-hut to bring her a bathrobe. And there she was standing, stark naked. "Bring me a bathrobe," she said, "the men always look when I go for a swim."

EVA   I don't quite see what you're driving at.

MATTI   I'm not driving at anything, just talking to pass the time and keep you company. When I'm talking with my employers, I never have any opinions, they don't like the help to have opinions.

EVA   (*after a short pause*)   The attaché is highly respected in the diplomatic corps, he has a brilliant career ahead of him. I want you to know that. He's one of the brightest of the younger men.

MATTI   I see.

EVA   All I meant by what I said before in your hearing was that I hadn't had as good a time as my father seemed to think. But of course it doesn't really matter whether a man is amusing or not.

MATTI   I once knew a man who wasn't the least bit amusing, but that didn't prevent him from making a million in oil and margarine.

EVA   My engagement was arranged long ago. We grew up together. The only trouble is that I seem to be the vivacious type and I get bored easily.

MATTI   So you're beginning to have your doubts?

EVA   I didn't say that. I can't see why you persist in misunderstanding me. You must be tired. Why don't you go to bed?

MATTI   I'm keeping you company.

EVA   There's no need to. I only wanted to make it clear that the attaché is a very intelligent and kindly man who shouldn't be judged by his looks or by what he says or does. He is very attentive to me and anticipates my slightest wish. He would never do anything vulgar or act familiar or make a display of his virility. I have the grestest esteem for him. But maybe you're sleepy?

MATTI   Just go on talking. I concentrate better when I close my eyes.

3

Puntila Becomes Engaged to Four Early-rising Women

Early morning in the village. Small wooden houses. One bears a sign saying "Post Office," another "Veterinary," still another "Pharmacy." In the middle of the square is a telegraph pole. Puntila in his Studebaker has run into the telegraph pole and is cursing at it.

PUNTILA   Clear the road in Tavastland! Out of the way, you low-down telegraph pole, don't get in Puntila's way. Who do you think you are? Do you own a forest, do you own any cows? See! So stand back. When I call the constable and he pulls you in for a Red, you'll be sorry and wish you hadn't. (*He gets out*) It's about time you got out of the way. (*He goes to one of the houses and taps on the window. Bootleg Emma looks out*)

PUNTILA   Good morning, my dear madam. Have you slept well? I come to you for assistance. I'm Puntila, I have a big farm in Lammi, and I'm in deep trouble. I simply must find some legal alcohol for my cows who are desperately sick with scarlet fever. Where in this delightful village does the cow doctor live? Show me where the cow doctor hangs out or I'll knock your lousy shanty down for you.

BOOTLEG EMMA   Gracious! You're in an awful state. Our cow doctor's house is right here. But did I hear you say you needed alcohol? I've got alcohol, good, strong stuff, I make it myself.

PUNTILA   Get thee behind me, woman. How dare you tempt me with your illegal booze? I drink only legal alcohol, anything else would stick in my throat. I'd rather be dead than flout the laws of Finland. I'm a law-abiding citizen. If I want to cut somebody's throat, I do it legally or not at all.

BOOTLEG EMMA   My dear sir, if that's how you feel about it, I hope your legal booze gives you the epizootic.
(*She disappears into her hut. Puntila runs to the veterinary's house and rings. The veterinary looks out*)

PUNTILA   Cow doctor, cow doctor! I've found you at last. I'm Puntila. Big farm in Lammi. I've got ninety cows and all ninety of them are down with scarlet fever. I need some legal alcohol in a hurry.

COW DOCTOR   It seems to me you've come to the wrong place. My advice to you is to calm down and run along.

PUNTILA   Cow doctor, don't disappoint me; you can't really be a cow doctor or you'd know what everybody in all Tavastland gives Puntila when his cows have scarlet fever. Because I'm telling you the truth. If I told you they had the glanders, I'd be lying, but when I tell you it's scarlet fever, it's a delicate hint from one gentleman to another.

COW DOCTOR   And if I don't take the hint?

PUNTILA   Then maybe I'll tell you that Puntila is the roughest customer in all Tavastland. There's even a folksong about it. He has three cow doctors on his conscience already. Now do you catch my meaning, doctor?

COW DOCTOR (*laughing*)   Yes, now I catch your meaning. If you're as big a man as all that, I guess I'll have to give you your prescription. If I could only be sure it's scarlet fever.

PUNTILA   Cow doctor, when they have red spots, and two of them already have black spots, wouldn't you diagnose the disease in its most desperate form? And the headache they must have when they can't sleep and they toss and turn all night and can't think of anything but their sins.

COW DOCTOR   In that case it's my duty to give them relief. (*He throws down the prescription*)

PUNTILA   And send the bill to Puntila Farms in Lammi.

(*Puntila runs to the pharmacy and rings loudly. While he is waiting, Bootleg Emma steps out of her hut*)

BOOTLEG EMMA (*sings while washing bottles*)

One day when the plums had ripened
Came a carriage to our town
Rolling southward in the morning
And a sweet young man stepped down.

(*She goes back into her house. The pharmacist's helper looks out of the window of the pharmacy*)

PHARMACIST'S HELPER   Don't wreck the bell!

PUNTILA   Better to wreck the bell than wait all day. Tum-tiddle-blup. I need a drink for ninety cows, my dear. Oh you sweet little pudding!

PHARMACIST'S HELPER   If you ask me, what you need is a policeman.

PUNTILA   My dear child! A policeman for Puntila of Lammi! One wouldn't be any use, you'd need two. But why the police? I love policemen, they have bigger feet than anybody else and five toes on each foot, because they stand for law and order, and so do I! (*He gives her the prescription*) Here, my little bunny rabbit, here's law and order for you. (*The pharmacist's helper goes in to get the alcohol. While Puntila is waiting, Bootleg Emma comes out of her house again*)

BOOTLEG EMMA (*sings*)

While we girls were busy picking
Plums, he lay down in the lea
Blond his beard, and looking upward
Smiled and saw what he could see.

(*She goes back into the house. The pharmacist's helper brings the alcohol*)

PHARMACIST'S HELPER (*laughs*)   That's a mighty big bottle. I only hope you have plenty of herring to settle your cows' stomachs. (*She gives him the bottle*)

PUNTILA   Glug, glug, glug. Ah, lovely Finnish music, the loveliest in all the world. Good Lord, I almost forgot. Now I've got my liquor, but no girl. And you've got no liquor and no man either. O, beautiful filler of prescriptions, I wish to become engaged to you.

PHARMACIST'S HELPER   Many thanks, Mr. Puntila of Lammi, but I only become engaged in the rightful proper way, with a ring and a sip of wine.

PUNTILA   Suits me, as long as you promise to be my fiancée. But you must become engaged, it's high time. What kind of life have you got? Tell me about yourself, I've got to know all about you if I'm going to be your fiancé.

PHARMACIST'S HELPER   Me? All right, I'll tell you about my life. I spent four years at the university and now the pharmacist pays me less than his cook. I send half my wages to my mother in Tavasthus. She has a weak heart, and I've inherited it. I'm on duty every other night. The pharmacist's wife is jealous because the pharmacist follows me around. The doctor's handwriting is illegible and once I got two prescriptions mixed up, and I'm always burning my dress with the medicines, and laundry is so expensive. I can't find a boyfriend, the police captain and the secretary of the cooperative and the bookseller are all married. I believe my life is sad.

PUNTILA   There you have it. Better stick to Puntila. Here, have a sip.

PHARMACIST'S HELPER   But where's the ring? A sip of wine and a ring, that's the rule.

PUNTILA   Haven't you any curtain rings?

PHARMACIST'S HELPER   Will one be enough?

PUNTILA   No, my dear, not one. A whole bunch. Puntila needs lots of everything. If he only had one girl, he mightn't even notice her. See what I mean?

(*While the pharmacist's helper goes out for a curtain rod, Bootleg Emma comes out of the house again*)

BOOTLEG EMMA (*sings*)

While the plum preserve was cooking
He inspected what was what
Graciously and smilingly
Stuck his thumb in every pot.

(*The pharmacist's helper gives Puntila the rings from the curtain rod*)

PUNTILA (*putting a ring on her finger*)   Come to Puntila Farms a week from Sunday. We're having a big engagement shindig. (*He hurries off. Lisu the dairymaid comes along with her pail*) Hey, little pigeon, wait! I want you. Where are you off to so early in the morning?

DAIRYMAID   To milk the cows.

PUNTILA   What? How can you sit there with nothing but a pail between your legs? Don't you want a man? Is that a life? Tell me about your life, you interest me.

DAIRYMAID   I'll tell you about my life: I get up at half past three and clean the manure out of the barn and brush the cows. Then I milk the cows and then I wash the milk pails with lye that burns my hands. Then I clean out the manure again and drink a cup of coffee, but it's cheap stuff and it stinks. I eat a slice of bread and butter and I take a little nap. In the afternoon I cook myself some potatoes and eat them with gravy, I never see any meat. Once in a while the housekeeper gives me an egg or I find one. Then I sweep out some more manure, brush the cows, milk them and wash the pails. It adds up to thirty gallons a day. For supper I eat bread and milk. They give me two quarts a day, but I have to buy the rest of my food off the farm. They give me every fifth Sunday off, but some nights I go dancing, and when I'm unlucky, I get a baby. I've got two dresses and I've got a bicycle.

PUNTILA   And I've got a big farm and a flour mill and a sawmill, but no wife. What do you say, little pigeon? Here's the ring, take a sip from my bottle, that makes it legal and proper. Come to Puntila Farms a week from Sunday. Is it a deal?

DAIRYMAID   It's a deal.

(*Puntila goes on*)

PUNTILA   Down the village street we go. I wonder who else is up so early. They're irresistible when they come crawling out of their featherbeds. Their eyes are still bright and sinful, and the world is still young. (*He comes to the telephone exchange. Sandra, the telephone operator, is standing there*)

PUNTILA Good morning, bright eyes! You must be the wise woman who knows everything from listening in on the telephone. Good morning!

TELEPHONE OPERATOR Good morning, Mr. Puntila. What brings you here so early in the morning?

PUNTILA I'm courting.

TELEPHONE OPERATOR I've been on the phone half the night, trying to locate you.

PUNTILA You see, you do know everything. And you've really been up half the night, all by yourself? I'm curious to know what kind of life you lead.

TELEPHONE OPERATOR I'll tell you about my life: They pay me fifty marks, but they've kept me at the switchboard for thirty years. I have a little potato patch out in back and that's where I get my potatoes. I buy herring to eat with them, but coffee keeps going up. I know everything that happens in the village and several miles around. You'd be amazed at all the things I know. That's why nobody ever married me. I'm the secretary of the Workers' Club, my father was a shoemaker. Switchboard, boiled potatoes, and knowing everything; that's my life.

PUNTILA In that case you need a change. And right away. Wire the main office and tell them you're marrying Puntila of Lammi. Here's your ring and here's your drink, all legal and proper, and a week from Sunday I'm expecting you at Puntila Farms.

TELEPHONE OPERATOR (*laughing*) I'll be there. I know you're having an engagement celebration for your daughter.

PUNTILA (*to Bootleg Emma*) And you, dear madam, must have heard that I'm getting engaged all around. You'll be with us too, I hope.

BOOTLEG EMMA AND THE PHARMACIST'S HELPER (*sing*)

When we ate the good plum butter
He had long since gone away.
But we never have forgotten
That young man, so light and gay.

PUNTILA And now I'll drive on, around the pond and through the pine trees, and I'll be on time for the fair. Tum-tiddle-blup. Oh, maidens of Tavastland, getting up so early all these years, and all for nothing, until one day Puntila comes along and it pays off. Come hither, come hither, all ye who rise up so early in the morn to light fires and make smoke. Come on your little bare feet; the fresh grass knows your steps and Puntila can hear them.

4

The Hiring Market

Hiring market on the village square in Lammi. Puntila and Matti are looking for hired hands. Atmosphere of a country fair. Music and many voices.

PUNTILA   Bad enough letting me drive away all by myself, but not even waiting up for me, making me pull you out of bed to take you to the fair—I won't forget that in a hurry. It's as bad as the apostles on the Mount of Olives. Shut up, now I know I've got to keep an eye on you. One little drink too many and you take advantage of me for your own personal convenience.

MATTI   Yes, Mr. Puntila.

PUNTILA   I'm not going to quarrel with you, I'm too exhausted, I'm just telling you as a friend, learn to know your place, it's for your own good. Wanting too much will land you in jail. No employer can stomach a servant whose eyes start popping out when he sees what the masters eat. But when a servant contents himself with what he's got, they'll keep him on forever. Why wouldn't they? When you see a servant working his fingers to the bone, you're willing to forget his faults. But when all he wants is time off and roasts as big as toilet seats, he makes you good and sick, and out he goes. Naturally you'd like it the other way round.

MATTI   You're perfectly right, Mr. Puntila. One time I read in the Sunday supplement of the *Helsinki Sanomat* that modesty is a sign of good breeding. A man who's reserved and holds his passions in check will go far. They say that Kotilainen, who owns three paper mills in Viborg, is the soul of modesty. Shouldn't we start looking before they snap up the best men?

PUNTILA   I need powerful men. (*Examining a big man*) This one's not bad, about the right build. I don't like his feet. You'd rather sit around than work, wouldn't you? His arms are no longer than that fellow's, who's shorter, but then his arms are unusually long. (*To the shorter man*) How are you at cutting peat?

A FAT MAN   Can't you see I'm talking business with that man?

PUNTILA   I'm talking business with him too, and I wish you wouldn't butt in.

THE FAT MAN   Who's butting in?

PUNTILA   None of your insolent questions, I won't stand for it. (*To the worker*) I pay half a mark a yard at Puntila Farms. You can report on Monday. What's your name?

THE FAT MAN   This is an outrage. Here I'm telling the man about the living quarters for his family, and you worm your way in. Some people shouldn't even be allowed in the market.

PUNTILA   Oh, so you have a family? I can use them all, your wife can work in the fields. Is she strong? How many children? How old are they?

THE WORKER   Three. Eight, eleven and twelve. The oldest is a girl.

PUNTILA   We can use her in the kitchen. You fit the bill to a T. (*To Matti, loud enough for the fat man to hear*) What do you say to the way people behave nowadays?

MATTI   I'm speechless.

THE WORKER   How about the living quarters?

PUNTILA   You'll live like kings. You can show me your papers in the café, wait for me over there by the wall. (*To Matti*) I'd take that one over there for his build, but his pants are too good, he won't work. Always take a good look at the clothing; too good and they think they're too good to work, too ragged and the character's bad. I can see through a man at a glance, I don't care about his age, your old-timers will carry just as much or more, because they're afraid of being fired. The main thing, in my opinion, is the man himself. It's better if he's not exactly a cripple, but I'm not interested in intelligence, the smart ones spend the whole day figuring out how many hours they've worked. I don't like that, I like to be on friendly terms with my help. I want to take a look at a dairymaid too, remind me. But first find me another man or two, so I can have my choice. But now I've got to make a phone call. (*Goes out into the café*)

MATTI (*speaks to a redhaired worker*) We're looking for a man for Puntila Farms, to cut peat. But I'm only the chauffeur, it isn't up to me, the old man's making a phone call.

THE REDHEAD What's it like at Puntila Farms?

MATTI Not bad. Four quarts of good milk. I'm told they give you potatoes too. The room isn't very big.

THE REDHEAD How far is the schoolhouse? I've got a little girl.

MATTI About an hour's walk.

THE REDHEAD That's nothing in good weather.

MATTI No, it's all right in the summer.

THE REDHEAD (*after a pause*) I wouldn't mind, I haven't found anything much, and the market will be closing soon.

MATTI I'll talk to him. I'll tell him you're a modest man. He likes that, and not a cripple. He'll be easier to get along with after he's through telephoning. Here he comes.

PUNTILA (*coming out of the café in good spirits*) Found anything? I want to take a pig home too, it can run to twelve marks or so, remind me.

MATTI This is a good man here. I remembered what you taught me and I've questioned him. He'll mend his pants as soon as he gets some thread.

PUNTILA Yes, he looks good. Plenty of fire. Have some coffee with us, we'll talk it over.

MATTI But you'd better be sure it's going to work out, Mr. Puntila, because the market will be closing soon, and after that he won't find anything.

PUNTILA Why shouldn't it work out, between friends? I rely on your judgment, Matti, with you I can't go wrong. I know you, I respect you. (*Approaching a sickly-looking man*) Say, what about this man? I like his eyes. I need peat-cutters, but there's farm work too. Come along, we'll talk it over.

MATTI Mr. Puntila, I don't want to interfere, but he won't do. He couldn't take it.

THE SICKLY-LOOKING MAN What do you mean? How do you know I couldn't take it?

MATTI Eleven and a half hours a day in the summer. I just wouldn't want you to be disappointed, Mr. Puntila. You'll only have to fire him when you find out that he can't do the work or when you take a good look at him tomorrow.

PUNTILA Let's get over to the café.

(*The first worker, the redhead, and the sickly-looking man follow him and Matti to the café. They all sit down on a bench outside*)

PUNTILA Hey, bring us some coffee. Before we talk business, there's something I've got to clear up with my friend here. Matti, you must have noticed just now that I was on the verge of one of those attacks I told you about. The way I spoke to you I'd have understood you perfectly if you'd hauled off and socked me. Can you forgive me, Matti? I can't get down to business when I think there's been bad blood between us.

MATTI That's water under the bridge. Let's not talk about it. These men want their contracts, you'd better attend to that first.

PUNTILA (*writes something on a slip of paper for the first worker*) I see how it is, Matti; you reject me. You're trying to punish me, that's why you're so cold and businesslike. (*To the worker*) I'm writing down what we agreed on, about your wife too. I provide milk and flour, and beans in the winter.

MATTI And now his earnest money, the contract isn't valid without it.

PUNTILA Don't rush me. Let me drink my coffee in peace. (*To the waitress*) Another cup, no, bring us the pot and we'll serve ourselves. Say, isn't she the strapping wench? This market makes me sick. When I want to buy horses and cows, I go to the market and think nothing of it. But you're

men, and that shouldn't be, human beings weren't made to
be marketed. Am I right?

THE SICKLY-LOOKING MAN   Dead right.

MATTI   I beg your pardon, Mr. Puntila, you're not right. They
need work and you have work to be done, that's a business
proposition; whether you attend to it in a church or in a
market, it's still a market. And I wish you'd clinch the deal.

PUNTILA   You're angry with me. That's why you won't say
I'm right when it's perfectly obvious. Do you look at *me* to
see if my legs are straight like you were looking into a
horse's mouth?

MATTI   (*laughs*)   No, I take you on faith. (*Indicating the redhead*) He's got a wife, but his little girl is still going to
school.

PUNTILA   Is she cute? There's that fat slob again. Throwing
his weight around. He's the kind that antagonizes the working class, wants everybody to know who's the boss. I bet
you he's an officer in the National Defense Corps and makes
his hired hands drill on Sunday so they'll beat the Russians.
What do you fellows think?

THE REDHEAD   My wife could do the washing. She gets more
done in a morning than most women working all day.

PUNTILA   Matti, I see the waters are still ruffled between us.
Tell the story about the ghosts, it'll give them a laugh.

MATTI   Later. Give them their money. It's getting late. You're
wasting these men's time.

PUNTILA   (*drinking*)   Nothing doing. I refuse to be steam-
rollered into inhuman behavior. I've got to get acquainted
with these men before we tie ourselves up for better or
worse. I've got to tell them what kind of a man I am. Then
they'll know if they can get along with me or not. That's
the question: what kind of a man am I?

MATTI   Mr. Puntila, take it from me, they're not interested.
They want their contracts. My advice to you is to take this
one (*pointing to the redhead*), he may be all right and you're
still in condition to tell. And my advice to you is to try and
find something else. You'll starve trying to cut peat.

PUNTILA   There's Surkkala. What's he doing here?

MATTI   He's looking for a job. Remember, the parson made

you promise to fire him because he's supposed to be a Red.

PUNTILA What, Surkkala? The only intelligent tenant I've got. Give him ten marks earnest money this minute. Tell him to join us; we'll take him back in the Studebaker, we'll tie his bicycle on the bumper, and no more nonsense about his going somewhere else. He's got four children too. What must he think of me? The parson can lick my ass. My house is closed to him from now on, he's inhuman, Surkkala's a first-class worker.

MATTI I'll run over in a minute. There's no hurry, he won't find anything else with his reputation. I only wish you'd settle with these men. If you ask me, you're not serious, you're just having a little fun.

PUNTILA (with a sorrowful smile) Is that what you think of me, Matti? I've given you plenty of opportunity, but you just don't understand me.

THE REDHEAD Wouldn't you kindly make out my contract now? Or I'd better be looking for something else.

PUNTILA Matti, you're scaring them away. You're such a tyrant, forcing me to act against my nature. But I'll convince you yet that Puntila is different. I don't buy human beings in cold blood, I give them a home at Puntila Farms. Am I right?

THE REDHEAD In that case I'd better be going. I need a job. (He goes out)

PUNTILA Stop! Now he's gone. I could have used that man. I don't care about his pants. I look deeper. I don't believe in closing a deal when I've been drinking, not even one little glass. How can you do business when you want to sing because life is beautiful? When I think of our drive home—the best time to see Puntila Farms is at nightfall, because of the birches—what we need is another drink. There, have a drink, make merry with Puntila, that's what I like to see, I don't count the cost when I'm in pleasant company. (He quickly gives each one a mark. To the sickly-looking man) Don't let him scare you away, he's got a grudge against me. You'll do the work all right, I'll give you a light job in the flour mill.

MATTI Then why not give him a contract?

PUNTILA What for? Now that we know each other. I give
you my word that everything's all right. Do you know what
that means, the word of a Tavastland farmer? Mount Hatelma
can crumble, it's not likely, but it's possible, the castle in
Tavasthus can cave in, why not, but the word of a Tavastland farmer stands firm, everybody knows that. Just come
with us.

THE SICKLY-LOOKING MAN Thank you, Mr. Puntila. I'll certainly come.

MATTI You'll cut and run if you have any sense. I've got
nothing against you, Mr. Puntila. I'm only worried about
these men.

PUNTILA (affably) Well spoken, Matti. I knew you wouldn't
bear a grudge. And I value your frankness and concern for
my best interests. But Puntila can afford to throw his interests to the winds, you'll soon find that out. All the same,
Matti, I always want you to tell me what you think. Promise
you will. (To the others) He lost his job in Tammerfors
because one time when this bank president he was working
for was driving he damn near stripped the gears and Matti
told him he should have been a butcher.

MATTI That was stupid of me.

PUNTILA (gravely) I respect you for that kind of stupidity.

MATTI (stands up) Well, let's be going. And what about Surkkala?

PUNTILA Matti, Matti, O man of little faith! Didn't I tell you
we were taking him home with us, because he's a first-class
worker and a man of independent mind? Which reminds me
of that fat slob who was trying to grab these men out from
under my nose. I'm going to give him a piece of my mind.
He's a typical capitalist.

5

Scandal at Puntila Farms

The yard at Puntila Farms. A bath-hut, the interior of which is visible. Forenoon. Over the door leading into the house Laina the cook and Fina the chambermaid are nailing a sign saying "Welcome to the Engagement Celebration!" Puntila and Matti come in through the gate, followed by a few workers, among them Red Surkkala.

LAINA   Welcome home! Miss Eva and His Excellency and His Honor are here already. They're having breakfast.

PUNTILA   Surkkala, the first thing I want to do is apologize to your family. Bring me the children, all four of them. I want them to hear from me in person how sorry I am for all the worry and anxiety they must have gone through.

SURKKALA   There's no need of it, Mr. Puntila.

PUNTILA   (*gravely*)   Oh yes, there is.
    (*Surkkala goes out*)

PUNTILA   These gentlemen will be staying. Bring them some aquavit, Laina, I'm taking them on to work in the forest.

LAINA   I thought you were selling the forest.

PUNTILA   Me? Me sell a forest? My daughter's got her dowry between her legs. Am I right?

MATTI   Maybe we could pay them their earnest money now, Mr. Puntila. Then you won't have it on your mind.

PUNTILA   I'm going to the sauna. Fina, get the gentlemen some aquavit and some coffee for me. (*He goes into the bath-hut*)

THE SICKLY-LOOKING MAN   Do you think he'll sign me up when he comes out?

MATTI   Not if he's sober and takes a good look at you.

THE SICKLY-LOOKING MAN   But when he's drunk, he doesn't write contracts.

MATTI   I warned you not to come out here before you had it down in black and white.

(*Fina brings aquavit and each of the workers takes a glass*)

THE WORKER   What's he like otherwise?

MATTI   Too familiar. It won't make much difference to you, you'll be out in the woods, but he's got me with him in the car, I'm at his mercy, and before I know it he's acting human. I won't be able to take it much longer.

(*Surkkala comes back with his four children. The oldest, a girl, is carrying the baby*)

MATTI (*to Surkkala in an undertone*)   For God's sake get out of here quick. By the time he's had his bath and his coffee, he'll be stone sober, and God help you if he lays eyes on you. My advice is to keep out of his sight for the next two days.

(*Surkkala nods and starts off with the four children*)

PUNTILA (*who has listened while undressing but not heard the last, looks out of the sauna and sees Surkkala and the children*)   I'll be with you in a minute. Matti, come in here, I need you to pour on water. (*To the sickly-looking man*) You can come in too. We'll get acquainted.

(*Matti and the sickly-looking man follow Puntila into the bath-hut. Matti pours water over Puntila. Surkkala slips away quickly with his children*)

PUNTILA   One pail is plenty. I hate water.

MATTI   You'll need another few bucketfuls. Then a cup of coffee, and you'll be fit to welcome your guests.

PUNTILA   I'm fit to welcome them right now. You just want to torture me.

THE SICKLY-LOOKING MAN   I agree. He's had enough. Water doesn't agree with Mr. Puntila.

PUNTILA   You hear that, Matti? There's a man who has some feeling for me. Tell him how I put that fat slob in his place this morning.

(*Fina enters*)

PUNTILA   Here comes our little treasure with the coffee. Is it good and strong? I'd like some liqueur with mine.

MATTI   Why do you think you're drinking coffee? No liqueur.

PUNTILA   I know. You're angry with me for making the men wait. But tell the story about the fat slob. I want Fina to hear it too. (*Tells the story*) There was this disagreeable

pimple-faced fat slob at the hiring market, a regular capitalist, trying to sneak a worker away from me. I told him off,
but when we were ready to leave, there was his buggy right
next to the car. You go on, Matti, I've got to drink my
coffee.

MATTI When he saw Mr. Puntila, he saw red. He took his
whip and gave his horse such a smack that it reared.

PUNTILA If there's one thing I can't abide, it's cruelty to animals.

MATTI Mr. Puntila took the horse by the bridle and calmed
him down and gave the fat slob a piece of his mind. I expected the guy to go for him with his whip, but he didn't
dare because there were too many of us. He mumbled something about some people having no education, he probably
thought we wouldn't hear him, but when Mr. Puntila takes
a real dislike to somebody, he has very sharp ears, and he
had his come-back all ready. "If *you're* so educated, maybe
you've heard that fat people are extremely likely to die of
apoplexy." That's what he said.

PUNTILA Tell them how he got as red as a turkey cock and
was so mad he couldn't think of a clever answer in front of
all those people.

MATTI He got as red as a turkey cock, and Mr. Puntila told
him not to work himself up, it was bad for him with all that
unhealthy fat. And he shouldn't ever get red in the face, it
showed the blood was rushing to his brain, which was bad
on account of his dependents.

PUNTILA You forgot to say that I was talking to you most of
the time, telling you we should go easy on him and not get
him excited. That's what really got his dander up, did you
notice?

MATTI We talked about him as if he wasn't there at all, and
the people laughed harder and harder and he got redder and
redder. Actually that's when he went red as a turkey cock.
Before that he was more like faded brick. He had it coming
to him, why did he have to hit his horse? I once saw a man
get so mad because his train ticket had fallen out of his hat
band where he'd put it for safekeeping, that he stamped on
his hat in front of a whole carful of people.

PUNTILA   You've lost the thread. I also told him that physical exertion, like whipping a horse, for instance, was poison for him. Which was one more reason why he shouldn't mistreat his animals, no, not he.

FINA   Nobody should.

PUNTILA   For that you're entitled to a glass of liqueur, Fina. Go get some.

MATTI   She's got her coffee. You must be feeling better by now, Mr. Puntila.

PUNTILA   I feel worse.

MATTI   I really admired you for punishing that man. You could perfectly well have said: What business is it of mine? Why should I make enemies in the neighborhood?

PUNTILA   (*who is gradually sobering up*) I'm not afraid of having enemies.

MATTI   That's a fact. But how many men can say that? You can. You can send your mares somewhere else.

FINA   Why should he send his mares somewhere else?

MATTI   Well, after it was all over, I heard that this fat slob is the new owner of Summala, and they've got the only stallion for five hundred miles around that's good enough for our mares.

FINA   So it was the new owner of Summala! And you didn't find that out until afterwards?

(*Puntila stands up and goes to the rear of the bath-hut where he pours another pail of water on his head*)

MATTI   We didn't find out afterwards. Mr. Puntila knew it all along. He even yelled at him as a parting shot that his stallion was too beat up for our mares. What were the exact words?

PUNTILA   (*laconically*) Something or other.

MATTI   No, it wasn't something or other. It was something very witty.

FINA   It will be dreadful if we have to send our mares so far.

PUNTILA   (*darkly*) Another cup of coffee. (*It is given him*)

MATTI   I'm told the people of Tavastland are famous for their love of animals. That's why I was so surprised at this fat slob. And something else I found out. He's Mrs. Klinckmann's brother-in-law. I'll bet if Mr. Puntila had known that he'd have treated him even rougher.

(*Puntila looks at him*)

FINA Was the coffee strong enough?

PUNTILA Don't ask stupid questions. You saw me drink it, didn't you? (*To Matti*) Don't sit around, you, do something, shine shoes, wash the car, it must look like a manure cart. Don't argue, and if I catch you spreading malicious gossip, I'll put it in your letter of reference, and don't forget it. (*Comes out gloomily in his bathrobe*)

FINA Why did you let him behave like that with the owner of Summala?

MATTI Am I his guardian angel? I see him doing something fine and generous—and stupid because it's to his own disadvantage—and you want me to prevent him? I couldn't see my way clear. When he's that drunk, he has real fire in him. He'd despise me, and I wouldn't like him to despise me when he's drunk.

PUNTILA (*calls from outside*) Fina.

(*Fina follows him with his clothes*)

PUNTILA (*to Fina*) I've made a decision. Listen carefully, or they'll twist my words around the way they always do. (*Pointing to one of the workers*) I'd have taken that one. He doesn't try to curry favor with me, he just wants to work, but I've changed my mind, I'm not taking any of them. I'm selling the forest, and you can lay the blame on that scoundrel in there, who deliberately kept me in the dark about something I should have known. Which reminds me of something else. (*Calls*) Hey, you. (*Matti steps out of the bath-hut*) Yes, you. Give me your jacket. Yes, your jacket, do you hear? (*Matti gives him his jacket*) I've got you now, you crook. (*Shows him the wallet*) What do I find in your pocket? The first time I laid eyes on you I knew you for a jailbird. Is this my wallet or isn't it?

MATTI Yes, Mr. Puntila.

PUNTILA That does it: ten years in jail; all I need to do is phone the police.

MATTI Yes, Mr. Puntila.

PUNTILA But I won't do you the favor. So you can lounge around in a cell, taking it easy and eating the taxpayers' bread? That would suit you, wouldn't it? Especially at harvest time. It would keep you away from the tractor. But I'll put it in your letter of reference, see?

MATTI Yes, Mr. Puntila.

(*Puntila in a rage starts for the house. Eva is standing in the doorway, with a straw hat over her arm. She has been listening*)

THE SICKLY-LOOKING MAN Want me to come along, Mr. Puntila?

PUNTILA No, I can't use you. The work would be too much for you.

THE SICKLY-LOOKING MAN But the hiring's over now.

PUNTILA You should have thought of that before instead of trying to take advantage of my friendly humor. I never forget the people who try to do that. (*He goes gloomily into the house*)

THE WORKER That's the way they are. They drive you out here in their car, and now we can hike back. Five miles, and no job. That's what happens when you fall for their friendly act.

THE SICKLY-LOOKING MAN I'm going to report him.

MATTI Who to?

(*The embittered workers leave*)

EVA Why don't you stick up for yourself? We all know that he always gives somebody his wallet to pay with when he's drinking.

MATTI He wouldn't understand it if I stuck up for myself. I've noticed that employers don't like to see a man stick up for himself.

EVA Stop being so mealymouthed and humble. I'm not in a joking mood today.

MATTI I know. You're getting engaged to the attaché.

EVA Don't be a brute. The attaché is a very nice man. He's just not the kind one wants to marry.

MATTI Such things happen. A woman can't marry all the nice men in the world or all the attachés, she's got to pick a particular one.

EVA My father leaves it entirely up to me. You heard him, he told me I could even marry you. Only he promised the attaché my hand and he wouldn't want people to say that he's not a man of his word. That's the only reason I'm so nice to him and may even end up taking him.

MATTI That puts you up a tree.

EVA I'm not up a tree if you must use these gross expressions. I really don't know why I discuss such delicate matters with you.

MATTI It's a perfectly human custom to talk things over. It puts us way ahead of the animals. If cows could talk things over, for instance, the slaughterhouse would be on its way out.

EVA What has that got to do with the fact that I probably wouldn't be happy with the attaché? And that I wish he'd break it off, but how am I going to suggest it to him?

MATTI It can't be done with a hint. It'll take a hammer.

EVA What do you mean by that?

MATTI I mean I'll have to attend to it. I am a brute.

EVA How do you suppose you can help me in a delicate situation like this?

MATTI Well, when Mr. Puntila was drunk, he was kind enough to say something about your marrying me. Suppose I took him at his word. And you felt attracted by my brute strength, made you think of Tarzan, and the attaché caught us together and said to himself: hm, running around with a chauffeur, she's not worthy of me.

EVA I can't ask that of you.

MATTI It would only be part of my job, like washing the car. Fifteen minutes is all it would take. We'd only have to show him that we're intimate.

EVA How do you intend to do that?

MATTI I could call you by your first name in his presence.

EVA How, for instance?

MATTI "Eva, your blouse is open at the neck."

EVA (*reaches behind her*) It is not. Oh, that was your act. But that won't bother him. He has too many debts to be that squeamish.

MATTI   Then I could take out my handkerchief, and out comes your stocking with it.

EVA   That's better. But he'd only say you had a secret passion for me and stole it from my room when I wasn't there. (*Pause*) You seem to have a very fertile imagination in these things.

MATTI   I'm doing my best, Miss Eva. I'm trying to think of every suggestive situation we could possibly get into. That way I'm bound to hit on something.

EVA   You can stop that kind of thinking right away.

MATTI   All right, I'll stop.

EVA   What, for instance?

MATTI   If he's so much in debt, we'll just have to come out of the bath-hut together. Nothing less would work, he'd always find some innocent explanation. If I take you in my arms and kiss you, for instance, he can say I assaulted you because I just couldn't resist your beauty. And so on.

EVA   I never know when you're making fun of me and laughing behind my back. With you I can never be sure.

MATTI   Why do you want to be sure? You're not investing money. As your father would say, it's more human to be unsure. That's the way I like to see a woman.

EVA   I can imagine.

MATTI   See? You've got a pretty good imagination too.

EVA   I only said that with you there's no knowing what your intentions really are.

MATTI   Do you know what a dentist's intentions are when you sit down in his chair?

EVA   When you talk like that, I don't think I want to be alone in the bath-hut with you. I'm sure you'd take advantage of the situation.

MATTI   Here we go. Now you're sure again. If you keep on shillyshallying, I'll lose my desire to compromise you, Miss Eva.

EVA   That's fine. The less desire the better. Very well, I agree to your sauna act. I trust you. They'll be through with breakfast soon, and then they're sure to start pacing up and down on the balcony, talking about the engagement. We'd better go in right away.

MATTI   You go ahead, I'll be getting a deck of cards.

EVA   What for?

MATTI   We've got to kill time in the sauna, don't we? (*He goes into the house, she goes slowly toward the sauna. Laina, the cook, comes in with her basket*)

LAINA   Good morning, Miss Eva. I'm going out to pick some cucumbers. Would you like to come along?

EVA   No, I have a slight headache. I think I'll take a bath. (*She goes into the bath-hut. Laina stands there shaking her head. Puntila and the attaché come out of the house, smoking cigars*)

ATTACHÉ   You know, Puntila, I think I'll take Eva down to the Riviera and borrow Baron Vaurien's Rolls Royce. That will be good publicity for Finland and its diplomatic corps. How many presentable women have we anyway in our diplomatic corps?

PUNTILA   (*to Laina*)   Where did my daughter go? She left the house a minute ago.

LAINA   She's in the bath-hut, Mr. Puntila. She had a dreadful headache and wanted to take a bath. (*Goes out*)

PUNTILA   Funny ideas she gets. Who ever heard of taking a bath for a headache?

ATTACHÉ   It is original, but do you know, Puntila, we don't give our Finnish baths their due. I was telling the under-secretary only the other day, when we were discussing ways and means of swinging a foreign loan. We've got to find new ways of publicizing Finnish culture. Why, for instance, aren't there any Finnish baths on Piccadilly?

PUNTILA   What I want to know from you is whether the foreign minister will really come to Puntila Farms for our celebration.

ATTACHÉ   He definitely promised. He's obligated to me because I introduced him to the Lehtinens of the Commercial Bank. He's interested in nickel.

PUNTILA   I want to speak to him.

ATTACHÉ   He has a soft spot for me, everybody says so at the ministry. Listen to what he said to me. These were his very words: "You're a man we can send anywhere. You'll never

do anything indiscreet, you're not interested in politics." He
thinks I make an excellent impression.

PUNTILA   Yes, Eino, I believe you've got plenty of gray matter, I'll be very much surprised if you don't carve out a fine
career for yourself. But don't forget what I said about the
foreign minister coming here. I insist. That will show me
what they think of you.

ATTACHÉ   I'm sure he'll come. I'm lucky. My luck is proverbial
at the ministry. When I lose something, someone always returns it; it never fails.

(*Matti comes in with a towel over his shoulder and goes into
the bath-hut*)

PUNTILA (*to Matti*)   Hey, you. Haven't you got anything better to do? I'd be ashamed to loaf like that, I'd wonder if I
was earning my pay. You're not getting any reference out
of me. You'll rot like a haddock that nobody wants to eat
because it's fallen behind the barrel.

MATTI   Yes, Mr. Puntila.

(*Puntila turns back to the attaché. Matti goes calmly into
the bath-hut. At first Puntila thinks no harm; then suddenly
it occurs to him that Eva must be in there too, and he looks
after Matti in consternation*)

PUNTILA (*to the attaché*)   How have you been getting along
with Eva?

ATTACHÉ   Splendidly. She's a little cool toward me, but that's
her nature. It makes me think of our attitude toward Russia.
In the language of diplomacy, our relations are correct.
Come. I think I'll pick Eva a bunch of white roses.

PUNTILA (*glancing toward the bath-hut, goes out with him*)   I
think that would be a good idea.

MATTI (*in the bath-hut*)   They saw me come in. We're doing
all right.

EVA   I'm surprised my father didn't stop you. Laina told him
I was here.

MATTI   He didn't think fast enough. He must have a terrible
hangover. Anyway we wouldn't want that to happen so
soon, it would spoil everything. The intention to compromise isn't enough. Something's got to have happened.

EVA   I doubt if they'll really see anything wrong. So early in
the day.

MATTI   Don't say that. Love in the morning is a sign of mad
passion. Twenty-one? (*He deals the cards*) I once had a boss
in Viborg who could eat at any time of day. In the middle
of the afternoon, right before coffee time, he'd order a roast
chicken. Eating was a passion with him. He was in the government.

EVA   I fail to see the connection.

MATTI   What do you mean? Some people are really keen on
love. You lead. Do you think they wait for sunset out in the
barn? And it's summer now, everybody's in the mood for it.
But there are too many people around. So we slip into the
bath-hut. Say, it's hot. (*He takes off his jacket*) Why don't
you make yourself comfortable? I won't eat you. How about
a penny a point?

EVA   Aren't you being indecent? I'm not a dairymaid, you
know.

MATTI   What's wrong with dairymaids?

EVA   You have no sense of respect.

MATTI   I've often been told that. Chauffeurs are known to be
an insubordinate lot, with no respect for the better classes.
That's because we hear the better classes talking in the back
seat. I've got twenty-one; what have you got?

EVA   I'm not used to that kind of talk. At the convent school
in Brussels everyone was very refined.

MATTI   I'm not talking about refined and unrefined, I'm talking
about stupidity. Your deal, but cut them first, we wouldn't
want any irregularities.

(*Puntila and the attaché come back. The attaché is carrying
a bunch of roses*)

ATTACHÉ   She's so clever. I say to her: "You'd be perfect if
only you weren't so rich," and she comes right back at me
with: "I rather enjoy being rich!" Ha ha ha! And do you
know, Puntila, Mademoiselle Rothschild is clever too, she
gave me the exact same answer when I met her at the home
of the Baroness Vaurien.

MATTI   You've got to giggle as if I were tickling you. If we don't lay it on thick they'll shamelessly ignore us. (*Eva giggles a little over her cards*) That doesn't sound giggly enough.

ATTACHÉ (*stopping still*)   Isn't that Eva?

PUNTILA   No, of course not. It must be someone else.

MATTI (*still playing cards, in a loud voice*)   You certainly are ticklish!

ATTACHÉ   Listen!

MATTI (*softly*)   Put up a bit of a fight.

PUNTILA   That's the chauffeur in the sauna. I think you'd better take your posies into the house.

EVA (*still playing, aloud*)   No! No!

MATTI   Yes, yes!

ATTACHÉ   Listen to that, Puntila. It really does sound like Eva.

PUNTILA   Don't be insulting, if you please.

MATTI   Call me darling and cut out the vain resistance.

EVA   No, no no! (*In an undertone*) What else should I say?

MATTI   Say: I mustn't. Throw yourself into the part. Sound lascivious!

EVA   You mustn't!

PUNTILA (*roaring*)   Eva!

MATTI   More! More! Mad passion! (*He puts the cards away as they continue to play the love scene*) If he comes in, we'll have to put on a show. It can't be helped.

EVA   No, I couldn't.

MATTI (*kicking over the bench*)   Then go out and face the music, but try to look like a wet poodle.

PUNTILA   Eva!

(*Matti carefully runs his hand through Eva's hair to make her look disheveled and she undoes the top button of her blouse. Then she goes out*)

EVA   Did you call, papa? I was just going to change and go for a swim.

PUNTILA   What's got into you, carrying on like that in the bath-hut? Do you think we're deaf?

ATTACHÉ   Don't lose your temper, Puntila. Why shouldn't Eva be in the bath-hut?

(*Matti comes out and stops behind Eva*)

EVA (*not noticing Matti, somewhat intimidated*) But papa, what do you think you heard? It was nothing.

PUNTILA Hm, you call that nothing. Would you kindly turn around!

MATTI (*affecting embarrassment*) Mr. Puntila, I was only playing twenty-one with the young lady. Here are the cards if you don't believe me. It's all a misunderstanding.

PUNTILA You shut up. You're fired. (*To Eva*) What do you expect Eino to think of you?

ATTACHÉ Oh, never mind, Puntila, if they were playing twenty-one, it was all a misunderstanding. Princess Bibesco once got so excited playing baccarat that she broke a string of pearls. Here, Eva, I've brought you some white roses. (*He gives her the roses*) Come, Puntila, let's play a game of billiards. (*He pulls him away by the sleeve*)

PUNTILA (*angrily*) You'll hear from me later, Eva. And you, if I ever hear you saying one word to my daughter instead of taking your filthy cap off and standing at attention, embarrassed because you haven't washed your ears, shut up, you can pack your rags. You're expected to look up to your employer's daughter as you would to a higher being who has descended to earth. Don't bother me, Eino, do you think I'm going to tolerate such behavior? (*To Matti*) Now repeat, what must you do?

MATTI I must look up to her as I would to a higher being who has descended to earth, Mr. Puntila.

PUNTILA And stand there in wide-eyed wonder that such things exist.

MATTI I stand here in wide-eyed wonder that such things exist, Mr. Puntila.

PUNTILA And turn red as a lobster because you had impure thoughts about women before you were even confirmed, and the sight of such innocence makes you want to sink into the ground. Understand?

MATTI I understand.

(*The attaché pulls Puntila into the house*)

EVA What a flop!

MATTI His debts must be even bigger than we thought.

6

A Conversation about Crayfish

Kitchen at Puntila Farms. Evening. Dance music is heard from outside. Matti is reading the newspaper.

FINA (*enters*)   Miss Eva wishes to speak to you.

MATTI   All right. Just let me finish my coffee.

FINA   You don't have to finish it on account of me. Just to make me think you're not in a hurry. If you ask me, you're getting ideas because Miss Eva talks to you now and then. But why wouldn't she, who else has she got to talk to around here?

MATTI   On an evening like this it's a pleasure to get ideas. You for instance, Fina, if you feel like taking a look at the river with me, I'll forget that Miss Eva wants me.

FINA   I don't think I feel like it.

MATTI (*picks up the newspaper*)   You thinking about that schoolteacher?

FINA   There's nothing between me and the schoolteacher. He was friendly, he wanted to improve my mind, so he loaned me a book.

MATTI   Such an educated man, too bad he's so underpaid. I get 300 marks and a teacher gets 200, but then I've got to know more than he does. If a teacher doesn't know anything, what harm can it do? So the peasants won't learn how to read the paper. In the old days that was backward, but what good does it do anybody to read the papers now? There's nothing in them anyway, on account of the censorship. I'd even go so far as to say that if they abolished schoolteachers altogether, they wouldn't need the censorship. Think of all the money the government would save. But if I break down on the district road, the bosses have to hike home through the mud and they're so drunk they end up in the ditch.

(*Matti motions Fina over to him and she sits down on his lap. The judge and the lawyer enter from the bath-hut, with their towels over their shoulders*)

JUDGE Haven't you got something to drink? Some of that lovely buttermilk we had before?

MATTI Would you like the maid to get it for you?

JUDGE No, just show us where it is.

(*Matti ladles some out for them. Fina goes out*)

LAWYER Excellent.

JUDGE Whenever I'm here at Puntila Farms I have some after my steam bath.

LAWYER Ah, these summer nights in Finland . . .

JUDGE They keep me busy. Paternity suits are a hymn to the Finnish summer night. In the courtroom you can see what a beautiful place a birch forest is. They can't go near the river without getting giddy. I had one woman in court who put the blame on the hay for smelling so strong. Berry picking is unsafe too, and they pay a high price for milking cows. There ought to be a barbed wire fence around every clump of woods by the roadside. The sexes go to the bath-hut separately, because the temptation would be too great, but then they go walking in the fields together. There's just no holding them in the summertime. They climb down off their bicycles, they climb up into haylofts; it happens in the kitchen because it's close and out of doors because there's a cool breeze. Some get babies because the summer's too short and some because the winter's too long.

LAWYER One good thing about it is that older people come in for their share. I'm thinking of the eye-witnesses. They take it all in. They see the couple disappearing into the woods, they see the wooden shoes at the foot of the hayloft ladder. They see a girl coming out of the blueberry patch all flushed and overheated when everybody knows that blueberry picking is normally a cool and restful occupation. And seeing isn't the whole of it, they hear too. The milk cans clank and the beds creak. Their eyes and ears participate, so they get something out of the summer too.

JUDGE (*hearing the bell ring, to Matti*) You'd better go see

what they want. Or would you like us to tell them that you
believe in the eight-hour day?
(*He goes out with the lawyer. Matti sits down again with
his newspaper*)

EVA (*enters, wielding an unbelievably long cigarette holder and
swinging her hips in a seductive way that she has picked up
at the movies*)   I rang for you. Are you still busy?

MATTI   Me, no. My work is over until six in the morning.

EVA   I was wondering if you wouldn't like to row over to the
island with me to catch a few crayfish for the banquet tomorrow.

MATTI   Isn't it getting on toward bedtime?

EVA   I'm not tired. I can't sleep in the summer, I don't know
why. Can you sleep if you go to bed at this hour?

MATTI   Yes.

EVA   I envy you. Then get me the nets. My father wants crayfish. (*She turns on her heel and starts to go, again with the
walk she has seen in the movies*)

MATTI (*changing his mind*)   I think I'll go at that. I'll row you
over.

EVA   You're not too tired?

MATTI   No, I've revived. I feel as fresh as a daisy. But you'll
have to change, you can't wade in that rig.

EVA   The nets are in the harness room. (*Out*)
(*Matti puts on his jacket*)

EVA (*coming back in shorts*)   But you haven't got the nets.

MATTI   We'll catch them with our hands. It's much nicer, I'll
teach you how.

EVA   But it's easier with a net.

MATTI   I was over on the island a few days ago with Laina
and Fina. We caught them with our hands and it was real
nice, you can ask them. I'm quick. What about you? Some
people are all thumbs. The crayfish are quick of course and
the stones are slippery, but it's not dark; hardly any clouds,
I just looked.

EVA (*hesitating*)   I'd rather take the nets, we'll get more.

MATTI   Do we need so many?

EVA   My father only eats what there's a lot of.

MATTI This is getting serious. I thought just a few and we'd talk. It's such a nice night.

EVA Stop saying that everything's nice. Just get the nets.

MATTI Let's not be so serious! Do we want to exterminate the crayfish? A few pocketfuls will do. I know a place that's swarming with them. In five minutes we'll have enough to show.

EVA What do you mean by that? Do you really want to catch crayfish?

MATTI (*after a pause*) Maybe it is a little late. I've got to take the car out at six to meet the attaché at the station. If we wade around on the island until three or four, I won't get very much sleep. Of course I can row you over if you insist. (*Eva turns without a word and goes out. Matti takes his jacket off again and sits down with his paper. Laina comes in from the bath-hut*)

LAINA Fina and the dairymaid sent me to see if you'd like to come down to the pond. They're still batting the breeze.

MATTI I'm tired. I was at the hiring market today, and before that I was down in the bog with the tractor and the cables snapped.

LAINA I'm all worn out from baking. These parties are too much. But I could hardly tear myself away, it's so light out it's a sin to go to bed. (*Looks out the window as she leaves*) Maybe I'll go back down for a while. The groom is going to play the harmonica, I like that. (*She goes out, dead tired but resolute*)

EVA (*enters*) I want you to drive me to the station.

MATTI It will take me five minutes to turn the Studebaker around. I'll wait for you out in front.

EVA Good. I see you don't ask me what I'm going to the station for.

MATTI My guess is that you're taking the eleven-ten to Helsinki.

EVA You don't seem surprised.

MATTI Why should I be? Surprise in a chauffeur doesn't lead to much. It's unimportant and seldom noticed.

EVA I'm going to Brussels for a few weeks to stay with a

friend. You'll have to lend me two hundred marks for my ticket. I don't want to disturb my father. I'll write him about it and of course he'll pay you back.

MATTI (*without much enthusiasm*)   Of course.

EVA   I hope you're not worried about your money. My father may not care whom I get engaged to, but he certainly wouldn't want to be indebted to you.

MATTI (*cautiously*)   I'm not so sure he'd feel he owed it to me under the circumstances.

EVA (*after a pause*)   Pardon me for asking.

MATTI   I don't think your father will be very happy about your running out on your engagement in the middle of the night, with the cakes already in the oven, so to speak. Yes, in an unguarded moment he advised you to marry me, but you shouldn't hold that against him. Your father only wants what's best for you. He's intimated as much to me. When he's drunk, or let's say, when he's had a glass too many, he doesn't know what's best for you, he lets his feelings run away with him. But when he's sober, his wits come back and he buys you an attaché, a good investment. You'll be an ambassador's wife in Paris or Reval, in a position to do what you please if you feel like doing something some nice night, and if you don't feel like it you won't have to.

EVA   So now you're advising me to take the attaché?

MATTI   Miss Eva, you're not in a financial position to displease your father.

EVA   Then you've changed your mind? You're a weathervane.

MATTI   Sure. But people aren't fair about weathervanes. They don't stop to think. A weathervane is firm and strong, it's made of iron. The trouble is that it has no solid underpinning, nothing to hold it steady. Unfortunately, I haven't any underpinning either. (*He rubs thumb and forefinger together*)

EVA   Then, unfortunately, I'd better think twice before taking your advice if your lack of underpinning prevents you from giving me honest advice. It seems to me you've suddenly noticed my father's concern for me because you're afraid to risk the money for my ticket.

MATTI   There's my job to think of, too. I think it's a pretty good one.

EVA   You seem to be quite a materialist, Mr. Altonen. Or as you and your friends would say, you know which side your bread is buttered on. I've never seen anybody show such unabashed concern for his money and his convenience in general. I see that the rich aren't the only people who worry about money.

MATTI   I'm sorry if I've disappointed you. I couldn't help it because you put it to me so directly. If you'd just dropped a hint, left it hanging in mid-air, let me read between the lines so to speak, we wouldn't have had to say a word about money. Money always injects a sour note.

EVA   (*sits down*)   I won't marry the attaché.

MATTI   I've been thinking it over and I don't see why you object to marrying him more than anybody else. They all look pretty much the same to me, and I know them like a book. They have nice manners, they won't throw their boots at you, not even when they're drunk, they're not difficult about money, especially if it's not theirs, and they're able to appreciate a girl like you, same as they can tell one wine from another, because they've learned how.

EVA   I won't have the attaché. I think I'll have you.

MATTI   What do you mean by that?

EVA   My father could give us a sawmill.

MATTI   Give *you* a sawmill, you mean.

EVA   He'd give it to both of us if we get married.

MATTI   I was working on an estate in Karelia one time. The master was a former hired hand. The mistress sent him out fishing when the parson came calling. When she had other company, he'd pull the corks out of the bottles and then he'd sit by the stove playing solitaire. They had big children. They called him by his first name. "Victor, go get our galoshes and don't dawdle." That wouldn't appeal to me, Miss Eva.

EVA   No, you want to be the master. I can imagine how you'd treat your wife.

MATTI   Have you given it much thought?

EVA   Of course not. You seem to think I spend the whole day
thinking about you. Where did you get that idea? Anyway,
I'm sick of hearing you talking about yourself all the time,
what you want and what appeals to you and what you've
heard. I see through your innocent little stories and your
insolence. I don't care for egotists, and I can't bear the sight
of you. There! (*Goes out*)
(*Matti sits down with his newspaper again*)

7

The League of Mr. Puntila's Fiancées

*The yard at Puntila Farms. Sunday morning. On the balcony
Puntila is arguing with Eva while shaving. Church bells are
heard in the distance.*

PUNTILA   You're marrying the attaché and that's that. Or you
won't get a penny from me. I'm responsible for your future.
EVA   The other day you said I shouldn't marry him because
he's not a man. You said I should marry the man I love.
PUNTILA   I say a lot of things when I've had a glass too many.
And I don't like you twisting my words around. And if I
catch you with that chauffeur again, you'll hear from me.
Suppose we'd had strangers here when you came out of the
sauna together. Can you imagine the scandal? (*He suddenly
looks off into the distance and bellows*) Why are the horses
out there in the clover?
VOICE   The groom put them there.
PUNTILA   Get them out of there this minute. (*To Eva*) If I'm
away for one afternoon, everything goes haywire around
here. And why, I ask you, are the horses in the clover? Because the groom is carrying on with the gardener's daughter.
And why has the bull been at that yearling cow when everybody knows it will stunt her growth? Because the dairymaid

is carrying on with the student farmer. So naturally she has no time to see that the bull doesn't mount my heifers, she just gives him the run of the place. It's disgusting. And I'm going to give that gardener girl a piece of my mind. If she didn't spend her time lying around with the groom, I'd have more than a measly two hundred pounds of tomatoes to sell this year. How can she be expected to have the right feeling for my tomatoes? They've always been a gold mine. I won't stand for all these flirtations on my farm, they cost me a pretty penny, do you hear me, and that goes for you and the chauffeur too. I'm not going to let you ruin the farm, that's where I draw the line.

EVA I'm not ruining the farm.

PUNTILA I'm warning you. I won't tolerate a scandal. I'm spending 6,000 marks on your wedding, I've moved heaven and earth to marry you into the best society. It's costing me a forest. Have you any idea what a forest is? And you carry on with every Tom, Dick, and Harry, not to mention a common chauffeur.

(*Matti has come into the yard and stands listening*)

PUNTILA If I've given you a fine education in Brussels, it's not so you should throw yourself at a chauffeur. Keep your distance with the help, if you don't they get fresh and walk over you. Plenty of distance and no familiarities or the result is chaos, and on that score I'm adamant. (*Goes into the house*)

(*The four women from Kurgela appear at the gate. After a brief consultation they take off their head scarfs, put on straw wreaths, and send one of their number ahead. Sandra, the telephone operator, appears in the yard*)

TELEPHONE OPERATOR Good morning. I should like to see Mr. Puntila.

MATTI I don't think he'll see anybody today. He's not feeling very well.

TELEPHONE OPERATOR I imagine he'll see his fiancée.

MATTI You're engaged to him?

TELEPHONE OPERATOR I am under that impression.

PUNTILA'S VOICE And I forbid you to use words like love. It's just another way of saying lechery and disorder and I won't have it, not on my farm. The engagement is set, I've had a pig slaughtered; I can't bring him back to life, he won't go back into his sty and start eating again as a favor to me just because you've changed your mind, and anyway I've made my arrangements and I won't have them upset. I'm having your room closed up, so you'd better do as I say.

(*Matti has picked up a long broom and begun to sweep the yard*)

TELEPHONE OPERATOR   That gentleman's voice sounds familiar.

MATTI   I should think so. It's your fiancé.

TELEPHONE OPERATOR   It's his voice and then again it isn't. It was different in Kurgela.

MATTI   Oh, in Kurgela? That time when he was looking for legal alcohol?

TELEPHONE OPERATOR   Maybe it seems strange because the circumstances were different and a face went with it. Such a friendly face. He was sitting in a car with the sunrise in his face.

MATTI   I know that face and I know the sunrise. You'd better go home.

(*Bootleg Emma enters the yard. She pretends not to know the telephone operator*)

BOOTLEG EMMA   Is Mr. Puntila here? I wish to speak to him immediately.

MATTI   No, I'm sorry, he's not here. But this is his fiancée. You can speak to her.

TELEPHONE OPERATOR (*playacting*)   Isn't that Emma Takinainen, the bootlegger?

BOOTLEG EMMA   The what? Did you call me a bootlegger? Because I need a bit of alcohol to massage the constable's wife's leg with? The station master's wife uses my alcohol for her fine cherry liqueur, which proves it's legal. And what is this fiancée business? Sandra the telephone girl claiming to be engaged to my fiancé, Mr. Puntila, who resides here, I understand? That's a little too much. You tramp!

TELEPHONE OPERATOR (*beaming*)   And what have I here, you moonshiner? What do you see on my ring finger?

BOOTLEG EMMA   A wart. But what do you see on mine? I'm engaged, not you. With a drink and a ring.

MATTI   Are both you ladies from Kurgela? We seem to have as many fiancées as swallows in May.

(*Lisu the dairymaid and Manda the pharmacist's helper enter the yard*)

DAIRYMAID AND PHARMACIST'S HELPER (*at once*)   Does Mr. Puntila live here?

MATTI   Are you from Kurgela? In that case he doesn't live here. I ought to know, I'm his chauffeur. Mr. Puntila is a gentleman with the same name as the one you seem to be engaged to.

DAIRYMAID   And I'm Lisu Yakkara. Mr. Puntila is really engaged to me, I can prove it. (*Pointing to the telephone operator*) And she can prove it too, she's engaged to him too.

BOOTLEG EMMA AND THE TELEPHONE OPERATOR (*at once*)   We can prove it, we're all his rightful fiancées.

(*All four laugh uproariously*)

MATTI   I'm glad you can prove it. I'll tell you frankly, if there were only one rightful fiancée, I wouldn't be very much interested. But I have an ear for the voice of the masses. I suggest a league of Mr. Puntila's fiancées. And that raises an interesting question: what are you planning to do?

TELEPHONE OPERATOR   Should we tell him? All four of us have a long-standing invitation to the engagement festivities, from Mr. Puntila in person.

MATTI   That kind of invitation is like last year's snow. As far as he's concerned, you'll look like four wild geese from the marshes, turning up after the hunters have gone home.

BOOTLEG EMMA   That's terrible. You mean we won't be welcome?

MATTI   I wouldn't say that. But in a certain sense you're a little early. I'll have to keep an eye open for the right moment to bring you in; then you'll be welcome and recognized, with a clear eye, for the fiancées that you are.

PHARMACIST'S HELPER   We only wanted a bit of a joke, and maybe to kid around a bit on the dance floor.

MATTI   If we pick the right moment, it may turn out all right. Once they begin to get gay, they develop a taste for the grotesque. That's the time for four fiancées to turn up. The parson will be surprised, and the judge will be a new and happier man when he sees the parson surprised. But we've got to maintain order in our ranks or Mr. Puntila may feel a little bewildered when the League of Fiancées marches into the hall singing the Tavastland anthem and waving a petticoat for a flag.

(*They all have a good laugh*)

BOOTLEG EMMA   Do you think there might be a cup of coffee in it for us and maybe a dance or two?

MATTI   That seems like a justifiable demand, because your hopes have been aroused and you've been put to expense. I presume you've come by train.

BOOTLEG EMMA   Passenger train!

(*Fina the chambermaid carries a tub of butter into the house*)

DAIRYMAID   That looks like fine butter.

PHARMACIST'S HELPER   We came straight from the station. I don't know your name, but maybe you could get us a glass of milk?

MATTI   Milk? Not before dinner, you'll spoil your appetite.

DAIRYMAID   Don't worry about that.

MATTI   You'll enjoy your visit more if I get your fiancé a glass of something. And not milk.

TELEPHONE OPERATOR   Yes, his voice did seem rather parched.

MATTI   Sandra of the telephones, you know everything and spread knowledge far and wide, understand why I'm not running to get you milk but racking my brains for a way to get him some aquavit.

DAIRYMAID   But I heard there were ninety cows at Puntila Farms.

TELEPHONE OPERATOR   Yes, Lisu, but you didn't hear his voice.

MATTI   You're all bright girls and I'm sure you'll content yourselves with the smell of food for the moment.

(*The head groom and the cook carry a slaughtered pig into the house*)

THE WOMEN (*applaud*)   That would feed an army.—I only hope they roast it nice and crisp.—Throw in a pinch of marjoram.

BOOTLEG EMMA   Do you think I can unhook my skirt at the table, when nobody's looking? It's too tight even now.

PHARMACIST'S HELPER   Mr. Puntila might take a peek.

TELEPHONE OPERATOR Not when he's eating.

MATTI Do you realize what this dinner is going to be like? You'll be sitting cheek by jowl with the judge of the high court in Viborg. Your Honor, I'll say to him, (*he plants the broom handle in the ground and addresses it*), here before you are four destitute women. They've come here with a just claim, and they're trembling with fear that it might be denied. They've come a long way on a dusty road to see their fiancé. One morning ten days ago a dapper, well-fed gentleman drove into their village in a Studebaker. He exchanged rings with them and pledged his troth, and now he's as likely as not to say he didn't. Do your duty, hand down your verdict, and I'm warning you. If you fail these petitioners, one day, in the not too distant future, there may be no high court in Viborg.

TELEPHONE OPERATOR Bravo.

MATTI The lawyer will drink your health too. What will you say to him, Emma Takinainen?

BOOTLEG EMMA This is what I'll say: I'm glad to meet you, you're a good connection, and would you kindly make out my tax statement, and don't let those bloodsuckers get away with anything. And use your eloquence to make them send my husband home from the army. They're keeping him too long, I can't handle the farm all by myself, and the colonel rubs him the wrong way. And when the storekeeper gives me sugar and kerosene on credit, make him stop padding the bill.

MATTI That's making the most of your opportunity. But you won't have to worry about your taxes if you get Mr. Puntila. Because anyone who gets him can afford to pay. You'll be clinking glasses with the doctor too. What will you say to him?

TELEPHONE OPERATOR Doctor, I'll say to him, I've got those pains in my back again, but don't look so gloomy, calm down, I'll pay my bill as soon as I've married Mr. Puntila. And give my case the time it deserves, we're still on the soup course, they haven't even put on water for the coffee, and you're responsible for public health.

(*Two workmen roll two kegs of beer into the house*)

BOOTLEG EMMA   Say, that's a lot of beer.

MATTI   You'll be sitting with the parson too. What will you say to him?

DAIRYMAID   This is what I'll say: From now on I'll have time to go to church on Sunday if I feel like it.

MATTI   That's too short for a dinner conversation. So I'll put in a few words: Your Reverence, how happy you must be to see Lisu the dairymaid eating off a porcelain plate, because the Good Book says that all are equal before God, so why not before Mr. Puntila? And the new mistress of the farm promises to make sure that a little something comes your way as in the past, for instance a few bottles of white wine on your birthday. That will enable you to go on preaching fine sermons about the heavenly pastures now that she herself is no longer obliged to milk cows in the earthly pastures.

(*While Matti is sounding off, Puntila has come out on the balcony. He has been listening sullenly*)

PUNTILA   When you've finished making speeches, let me know. Who are these people?

TELEPHONE OPERATOR (*laughing*)   Your fiancées, Mr. Puntila. You know us, I hope.

PUNTILA   Never laid eyes on any of you.

BOOTLEG EMMA   Of course you know us. What about these rings?

PHARMACIST'S HELPER   From the pharmacist's curtain rod in Kurgela.

PUNTILA   What have you come here for? To make trouble?

MATTI   Mr. Puntila, this may not be the right time to bring it up, maybe it's too early in the day, but we've just been thinking up a way of contributing to the general merriment at the engagement celebration, and we've founded a league of Mr. Puntila's fiancées.

PUNTILA   Why not a labor union? I wouldn't put it past you. I know you. I know which paper you read.

BOOTLEG EMMA   It was just for a joke and maybe for a cup of coffee.

PUNTILA   I know your jokes! You've come to blackmail me.

BOOTLEG EMMA   Take it easy.

PUNTILA   But I'll show you. You thought you could take advantage of my friendly nature. My advice to you is to get off my property before I drive you off and call the police. I recognize you, you're the telephone operator at Kurgela, I'm going to call up your supervisor and ask him if this is the way he likes his employees to behave. And never fear, I'll find out who the rest of you are.

BOOTLEG EMMA   We understand. But see here, Mr. Puntila. Wouldn't it have been something nice to remember in our old age? I think I'm going to sit right down in your yard, then I'll be able to say: Once I sat down at Puntila Farms, I was invited. (*She sits down on the ground*) There. Now nobody can say different. I don't have to tell them I wasn't sitting in a chair, but on the hard soil of Tavastland, which, as the schoolbooks say, is hard to till but also rewarding, though naturally they don't say who does the tilling and who gets rewarded. Didn't I smell roast pig and see a tub of butter, and wasn't that beer just now? (*She sings*)

And the lake and the hill and the clouds above the hill!
How dear they are to the people of Tavastland,
From the smiling green woods to the Aabo water mill.—

Am I right? And now pick me up, don't leave me sitting here in this historical position.

PUNTILA   Get off my land!
(*The four women throw their straw wreaths on the ground and leave the yard. Matti sweeps up the straw*)

8

Finnish Tales

BOOTLEG EMMA   How can you know what kind of mood you're going to find them in? When they've had plenty to drink, they crack jokes and pinch you God knows where, and it's all you can do to keep them from wrestling you into the raspberry bushes, and five minutes later something has riled them up and they want to call the police. There must be a nail in my shoe.

TELEPHONE OPERATOR   The sole is coming off too.

DAIRYMAID   Those shoes weren't made for a five-hour hike.

BOOTLEG EMMA   Yes, I've worn them out. They'd have done me for another year. I need a stone. (*All sit down, and she hammers in the nail*) As I was saying, you can't figure those people out. First they're one way, then the other. The wife of the former police chief used to send for me in the middle of the night to massage her swollen feet, and every time she was different, depending on how she was getting along with her husband. He was carrying on with the maid. Once she gave me a box of candy, and I knew he had sent the girl away. But soon after that it seems he went back to see her, because nothing could make his wife remember that I'd massaged her ten times that month, and not just six. All of a sudden she'd lost her memory.

PHARMACIST'S HELPER   Sometimes their memory is too good. Like Pekka, who made a fortune in America and came back to see his family twenty years later. They were so poor they begged potato peels from my mother, and when he came to see them they served him roast veal to put him in a good humor. He ate it and told them how he'd once loaned his grandmother twenty marks and said it was a fine how-do-you-do to find them so poor they couldn't even pay their debts.

TELEPHONE OPERATOR   Their heads are screwed on tight. That's how they get rich. One time in the winter of 1908 a land-owner in our district had to cross the lake at night. He got one of his tenants to guide him across the ice. They knew there was a crack in the ice, but they didn't know where, so the tenant had to lead the way. Six miles. The master was so scared he promised him a horse if they made it. When they were in the middle, he spoke up again and said: If you find the way and I don't fall through, I'll give you a calf. Then

they saw the village lights, and he said: Be extra careful now
and you'll earn a watch. Fifty yards from the shore he promised him a sack of potatoes. Then when they were safe on
land, he gave him a mark and said: It's taken you a long
time. We're too dumb for all their tricks. They fool us every
time. The trouble is they look the same as we do, that's what
fools us. If they looked like bears or snakes, we'd be more
careful.

PHARMACIST'S HELPER   The moral is: Don't joke with them and
don't accept anything from them.

BOOTLEG EMMA   Don't accept anything is good. They've got
everything and we haven't got anything. Don't accept anything from the river when you're thirsty.

PHARMACIST'S HELPER   Say, I'm dying of thirst.

DAIRYMAID   So am I. In Kausala there was a girl who was
carrying on with the son of the farmer she was working for.
She had a baby, but when she took him to court in Helsinki
and sued for the child's support, he denied the whole business. Her mother hired a lawyer, and the lawyer produced
the letters he'd written when he was in the army. The letters made everything clear as day, he should have got five
years for perjury. But when the judge read the first letter—
he read it very slowly—she stepped up to him and insisted
on having them back, and she never got a penny. They say
when she came out of the courthouse the tears were running
down her face like a waterfall, her mother was fit to be tied,
and he just laughed. That's love for you.

TELEPHONE OPERATOR   That was stupid.

BOOTLEG EMMA   But the same thing can be smart. It all depends. There was a young fellow from near Viborg who
wouldn't take anything from them. He was with the Reds in
1918, so when it was all over he was sent to a prison camp.
Just a kid. He was so hungry he ate grass, they didn't give
the prisoners anything to eat. His mother came to see him
and brought him food, it was a fifty mile trek. She was a
tenant farmer, the landlord's wife gave her a fish and a pound
of butter. She did the whole fifty miles on foot except when
some peasant picked her up in his cart. She said to the peas-

ant: "I'm going to Tammerfors to see my son Athi, he's in
the camp where they put the Reds, and the landlord's wife
has given me a fish and this pound of butter. Wasn't that
kind of her?" When the peasant heard that, he told her to
get out because her son was a Red, but when she came to
the women who were washing clothes in the river, she told
her story again: "I'm going to Tammerfors to see my son
Athi, he's in the camp where they put the Reds, and the
farmer's wife has given me a fish and this pound of butter."
And when she got to the camp in Tammerfors, she made her
little speech to the commanding officer and he laughed and
let her in, which was normally against the rules. Outside the
camp there was still grass growing, but inside the barbed
wire fence there was no more grass and not a leaf on the
trees, they'd eaten it all up. Yes, you see, that's the truth.
She hadn't seen Athi in two years, first the civil war and then
the camp, and he was very thin. "So there you are, Athi, and
look, here's a fish and this butter, the landlord's wife gave it
to me for you." Athi said hello and asked about her rheuma-
tism and some of the neighbors, but nothing could make
him take the fish or the butter. He got mad and said: "Did
you beg them from the landlord's wife? You can take it back
with you, I don't want it." Hungry as he was, she had to
wrap her presents up again. She said good-bye and went
back home, the whole way on foot again, except when somebody gave her a ride. And now she said to the peasant: "My
Athi in the prison camp wouldn't take my fish and butter
because I'd begged them from the landlord's wife. He won't
accept anything from those people." It was a long trek, and
she was an old woman, and now and then she had to sit
down by the side of the road and eat some of the fish and
butter, but they weren't very good any more, they'd begun
to stink. And when she came to the women by the river she
said: "My Athi in the prison camp didn't want the fish and
butter, because I'd begged them from the landlord's wife.
He won't accept anything from those people." She said the
same thing to everybody she met, and it made a big impression all the way. Fifty miles.

MILKMAID   There are people like her Athi.

BOOTLEG EMMA   Not enough.

(*They stand up and go on in silence*)

9

Puntila Picks a Man to be his Daughter's Fiancé

Dining room with small tables and an enormous buffet table. The parson, the judge and the lawyer are standing, drinking coffee and smoking. Puntila is sitting in the corner, drinking silently. In the next room a phonograph is playing and people are dancing.

PARSON   True faith is rare nowadays. It's given way to doubt and indifference. Sometimes I almost despair of our people. I keep drumming it into them that not a single blueberry would grow if it weren't for God, but they take the fruits of nature for granted and gobble them down as if they were perfectly natural. Partly it's because they don't go to church. I'm always preaching to empty benches, as if there weren't enough bicycles, every milkmaid has one, but partly it's plain innate wickedness. Last week, for instance, I was talking to a man on his deathbed, telling him what to expect in the hereafter. The only answer I got out of him was: Do you think the potatoes will come through this rain all right? Such things make a man wonder if all our effort isn't a waste of time.

JUDGE   I can see what you mean. Trying to bring culture to these yokels is no picnic.

LAWYER   We lawyers haven't an easy time of it either. The source of our livelihood has always been the small peasants, men of iron character, who'd rather end in the poorhouse than let anybody impinge on their rights. They still like to quarrel, but their avarice ruins everything. They'd be glad to insult each other and stick knives into each other and sell each other lame nags, but when they notice that the law costs money, their enthusiasm slips away and they drop the most promising lawsuit. Why? For the sake of vile Mammon.

JUDGE   It's this commercial age. Everything is becoming cheap and tawdry. The good old ways are dying out. It takes a brave man not to give up in despair, but what can we do? We've got to keep on trying to bring these people a little culture.

LAWYER   Puntila's crops come up year after year, nothing can stop them, but a lawsuit is a very sensitive plant; your hair is likely to turn gray before you can coax it to maturity. How many times I've thought: it's all over, it can't go on, another motion for new evidence is out of the question, this little lawsuit is going to die in its cradle, and then suddenly it recovers. When a case is in its infancy, that's when it demands the greatest care, that's when the mortality rate is highest. Once you've coddled it into young manhood, it can look out for itself, it knows its way around. A lawsuit that's more than four, five years old has every prospect of growing to a ripe old age. But in the meantime! Ah, it's a dog's life. (*Enter the attaché with the parson's wife*)

PARSON'S WIFE   Mr. Puntila, you should take better care of your guests. At the moment the foreign minister is busy dancing with Miss Eva, but he's been asking for you. (*Puntila says nothing*)

ATTACHÉ   This charming lady has just said something delightfully witty. The foreign minister asked her if she liked jazz. I can't describe the suspense I was in, wondering how she was going to pass that one off. She thought it over for a moment, then she said: "People can't very well dance to a church organ, so does it really make so much difference what instruments they use?" The minister almost died laughing. What do you think of that, Puntila?

PUNTILA   Nothing, because I don't criticize my guests. (*Motions to the judge*) Fredrik, does that mug appeal to you?

JUDGE   Which one?

PUNTILA   The attaché's. Tell me frankly.

JUDGE Watch your step, Johannes, that punch is pretty powerful.

ATTACHÉ (*hums the tune being played in the next room and moves his feet in time*) It gets you in the legs, doesn't it?

PUNTILA (*motions again to the judge, who tries not to notice*) Fredrik! Tell me the truth. What do you think of it? It's costing me a forest.
(*The other gentlemen join the attaché in humming: "Je cherche après Titine."*)

ATTACHÉ (*unsuspecting*) I can never remember the words, even at school I couldn't, but I've got rhythm in my blood.

LAWYER (*seeing Puntila motioning violently*) It's rather warm in here. Let's go out to the drawing room. (*He tries to draw the attaché away*)

ATTACHÉ The other day I managed to learn a line though: "Yes, we have no bananas." That makes me more optimistic about my memory.

PUNTILA Fredrik! Take a good look at it, and give me your verdict. Fredrik!

JUDGE Do you know the joke about the Jew who left his coat at the café? So the pessimist says: He'll get it back. And the optimist says: He won't get it back.
(*The gentlemen laugh*)

ATTACHÉ And did he get it back?
(*The gentlemen laugh*)

JUDGE I don't think you've quite got the point.

PUNTILA Fredrik!

ATTACHÉ Perhaps you'd explain it to me. You must have got the answers mixed up. The optimist should say, yes, he will get it back.

JUDGE No, the pessimist. Don't you see, the whole point is that it's an old coat, so he's better off if he's lost it.

ATTACHÉ Oh, it's an old coat! You forgot to mention that. Ha ha ha! That's the finest joke I ever heard.

PUNTILA (*stands up glowering*) It's time for me to take a stand. I don't have to put up with a character like that. Fredrik, you refuse to give me an answer to a serious question: What will you think of that face if I have it in the family? But I'm man enough to decide for myself. A man

without humor is no man at all. (*With dignity*) Leave my
house. Yes, you. Don't turn around as if I could possibly be
talking to anybody else.

JUDGE   Puntila, you're going too far.

ATTACHÉ   Gentlemen, please, disregard the incident. You have
no idea how precarious the position of members of the diplomatic corps is. The slightest blot on my reputation, and
down goes my rating. Once in Paris, in Montmartre, the
mother-in-law of the first secretary at the Rumanian legation
beat up her lover with an umbrella. You can hardly imagine
the scandal.

PUNTILA   A grasshopper in a tailcoat. A forest-eating grasshopper.

ATTACHÉ (*eagerly*)   You see, it wasn't because she had a lover,
that was to be expected, or because she thrashed him, that's
perfectly normal, but because she did it with an umbrella.
That's vulgar. It's the nuances that count.

LAWYER   He's right, Puntila. His honor is extremely vulner-
able. He's in the diplomatic service.

JUDGE   The punch is too strong for you, Johannes.

PUNTILA   Fredrik, you don't seem to see the seriousness of the
situation.

PARSON   Mr. Puntila is a little overwrought. Anna, perhaps
you'd better see how things are getting along in the drawing
room.

PUNTILA   My dear lady, there's no cause for alarm. I am in
perfect control. It's the usual punch. The only thing that's
too much for me is this gentleman's face. It gives me the
creeps, tell me you understand.

ATTACHÉ   Princess Bibesco once spoke of my sense of humor
in the most flattering terms. She remarked to Lady Oxford
that when someone tells a joke I always laugh ahead of time,
meaning that I catch on very quickly.

PUNTILA   Fredrik! His sense of humor!

ATTACHÉ   As long as no names are mentioned, nothing is irreparable. Only when names and insults are put together.

PUNTILA (*with heavy sarcasm*)   Fredrik, what can I do? I've
forgotten his name, now I'll never get rid of him, you heard

what he said. Oh, thank the Lord, it's come back to me. Now
I remember, I saw his name on an I.O.U. he wanted me to
buy. Eino Silakka, that's it. Maybe he'll get out of here now,
what do you think?

ATTACHÉ Gentlemen, a name has been pronounced. From now
on you will do well to weigh every word in milligrams.

PUNTILA It's hopeless. (*Suddenly bellowing*) Get out of here
this minute and never show your face again at Puntila Farms.
I'm not marrying my daughter to a grasshopper in a tailcoat!

ATTACHÉ (*turning around to him*) Puntila, that is insulting. If
you throw me out of your house, you will be crossing the
fine dividing line where scandal sets in.

PUNTILA This is too much. My patience is exhausted. I only
meant to inform you, between friends, that your face gets on
my nerves and that you'd better make yourself scarce, but
you force me to make myself plain and say: Get out of here,
you shit!

ATTACHÉ Puntila, I take that amiss. Gentlemen, I bid you good
evening. (*Goes out*)

PUNTILA Get a move on. Let me see you run, I'll teach you to
give me impudent answers. (*He runs after him. All follow
except the judge and the parson's wife*)

PARSON'S WIFE This is developing into a scandal.
(*Enter Eva*)

EVA What's going on? What's all that noise outside?

PARSON'S WIFE (*running up to her*) Oh my poor child. Something dreadful has happened, you must be brave.

EVA What has happened?

JUDGE (*brings a glass of sherry*) Take this, Eva. Your father
drank a whole bottle of punch, and all of a sudden he took a
special dislike to Eino's face and threw him out.

EVA (*drinks*) This sherry tastes of cork. Too bad. What did
he say?

PARSON'S WIFE But Eva, aren't you beside yourself?

EVA Oh yes, of course.
(*The parson comes back*)

PARSON It's too dreadful.

PARSON'S WIFE What? What happened?

PARSON   A dreadful scene in the yard. He threw stones at him.

EVA   Did he hit him?

PARSON   I don't know. The lawyer ran between them. And imagine, the foreign minister right here in the next room.

EVA   Uncle Fredrik, now I'm almost sure he'll leave. It's good we invited the foreign minister. We wouldn't have had half as big a scandal without him.

PARSON'S WIFE   Eva!

(*Enter Puntila with Matti, followed by Laina and Fina*)

PUNTILA   I have just looked deep into the depravity of the world. I went in there with the best of intentions. I announced that I had made a mistake, that I had almost betrothed my only daughter to a grasshopper, but that I now wished to make amends and bestow her hand on a man. The fact is I decided a long time ago to marry my daughter to a good man, Matti Altonen, a fine chauffeur and a good friend of mine. A toast to the happy young couple. Well, what do you think they did? I'd always taken that foreign minister for a cultivated man. He looked at me like a poisonous mushroom, and called for his car. Naturally the rest of them aped him. Sad, sad. I felt like a Christian martyr in the lions' den, and I gave them a good piece of my mind. He left in a hurry, but luckily I caught him before he got to his car and told him that as far as I'm concerned he's a shit too. I trust you would all have said the same in my place.

MATTI   Mr. Puntila, I suggest that we go to the kitchen and discuss the whole thing over a bottle of punch.

PUNTILA   Why in the kitchen? We haven't celebrated your engagement yet, only the wrong one. How stupid. Move the tables together. Set the festive board! Now we'll really celebrate. Fina, you sit next to me.

(*He sits down in the middle of the room and in front of him the others build a long table out of the little ones. Eva and Matti bring chairs*)

EVA   Don't look at me like that, Matti. The way my father looks at a breakfast egg that doesn't smell quite right. I can remember a time when you looked at me very differently.

MATTI   I was only trying to be polite.

EVA   Last night when you were going out to the island with me to catch crayfish, it wasn't for the crayfish.

MATTI   That was at night, and it had nothing to do with getting married.

PUNTILA   Parson, you on the other side of Fina. And you, Mrs. Parson, next to Laina. You too, Fredrik. Sit down at a decent table for once in your life.

(*All sit down reluctantly. Silence*)

PARSON'S WIFE (*to Laina*)   Have you put up your mushrooms yet this year?

LAINA   I don't put them up. I dry them.

PARSON'S WIFE   How do you go about it?

LAINA   I cut them in big chunks and string them with a needle. Then I hang them in the sun.

PUNTILA   I'd like to say a few words about my daughter's fiancé. Matti, I've been studying you in secret and formed a picture of your character. Since you've been here at Puntila Farms, we haven't had the least bit of trouble with our machines, but that's not what I have in mind. It's the man in you that I honor. I haven't forgotten the incident this morning. I watched your expression when I was standing on the balcony like Nero, driving away dear guests in my beclouded blindness. I've told you about my attacks. All through dinner, as you may have noticed, or guessed if you weren't there, I sat there in withdrawn silence, thinking of those four dragging themselves back to Kurgela after I hadn't given them so much as a sip of punch, but only hard words. I wouldn't be surprised to hear that they'd lost faith in Puntila. And now, Matti, I'm asking you a question: Can you forget that?

MATTI   Consider it forgotten, Mr. Puntila. But tell your daughter with all your authority, that she can't marry a chauffeur.

PARSON   Very true.

EVA   Papa, Matti and I had a little argument while you were outside. He doesn't believe you'd give us a sawmill, and he doesn't think I could stand being a plain chauffeur's wife.

PUNTILA   What do you think, Fredrik?

JUDGE   Don't ask me, Johannes, and don't look at me like a wounded stag. Ask Laina.

PUNTILA   Laina, I appeal to you. Do you think I'm capable of stinting on my daughter? Do you think I'd begrudge her a sawmill and a forest to go with it?

LAINA   (*interrupted in a whispered discussion about mushrooms with the parson's wife, as can be gathered from their gestures*)   Of course, Mr. Puntila, I'll be glad to make you a cup of coffee, Mr. Puntila.

PUNTILA   Tell me, Matti, can you fuck properly?

MATTI   So I've been told.

PUNTILA   That's nothing. Can you do it improperly? That's what counts. No, no, I don't expect an answer. I know you're not the man to brag, you hate that kind of thing. But have you fucked Fina? Then I could ask her. No? I can't make you out.

MATTI   Never mind, Mr. Puntila.

EVA   (*who has had a little more to drink, stands up and makes a speech*)   Dear Matti, I beg of you, make me your wife, so I can have a husband like everybody else, and if you like, we can go looking for crayfish right this minute without a net. Whatever you may think, I don't take myself for anything much, and I'll be glad to live with you even if we have to scrimp a little.

PUNTILA   Bravo!

EVA   And if you don't want to go out for crayfish, because maybe it strikes you as frivolous, I'll pack my bag and we'll go and visit your mother. My father won't mind . . .

PUNTILA   Certainly not, I'm all for it.

MATTI   (*also stands up and quickly drains two glasses*)   Miss Eva, I'm game for any kind of nonsense, but I can't take you to see my mother. The poor old thing would have a stroke. Why, you'd be lucky if you got a couch to sleep on. Reverend, tell Miss Eva about a peasant cottage with a spare bed in the kitchen.

PARSON   (*gravely*)   Most uncomfortable.

EVA   Why tell me about it? I'll see for myself.

MATTI   You'll ask my poor old mother where the bathroom is.

EVA   I'll go to the public baths.

MATTI   With Mr. Puntila's money? You're still thinking of me as the owner of a sawmill . . . that's a pipe dream, because Mr. Puntila will be a sensible man when he's himself again tomorrow morning.

PUNTILA Stop right there. Let's not talk about the Puntila who is our common enemy. He has been drowned in a bottle of punch. He was a wicked man. And here I stand. I've turned into a human being. Drink with me, all of you, you will be human too, don't weaken.

MATTI I tell you I can't take you to see my mother. She'll slap down my ears with her slippers if I dare to bring a girl like you into the house, and that's God's truth.

EVA You shouldn't have said that, Matti.

PUNTILA She's right, Matti, you're going too far. Eva has her faults, she may put on a little weight like her mother, but that won't happen before she's thirty or thirty-five, and right now she's fit to be seen anywhere.

MATTI I'm not talking about getting fat, I'm talking about her lack of practical sense. She's not fit to be a chauffeur's wife.

PARSON You've taken the words out of my mouth.

MATTI Don't laugh, Miss Eva. You'll laugh on the other side of your face when my mother starts examining you. You'll crawl.

EVA All right, Matti, let's give it a try. I'm a chauffeur's wife. Tell me what I'm supposed to do.

PUNTILA That's talking. Bring in the sandwiches, Fina. We'll have a bite to eat, and Matti can examine Eva till she's blue in the face.

MATTI Don't move, Fina, there are no servants in our house. When company drops in, there's nothing in the house but what we always eat. Go get the herring, Eva.

EVA (gaily) I'm going on horseback. (Runs out)

PUNTILA (calls after her) Don't forget the butter. (To Matti) I approve your determination to be on your own and not to take anything from me. Most young men wouldn't feel that way about it.

PARSON'S WIFE (to Laina) No, I don't pickle my champignons, I cook them in lemon and butter; they shouldn't be any bigger than buttons. I put up milky caps too.

LAINA Milky caps aren't really fine mushrooms, but they're tasty. The only really fine mushrooms are champignons and boletus.

EVA (*comes back with a platter of herring*) There isn't any butter in our kitchen. Is that right?

MATTI Hm, there he is. I recognize this fellow. (*He takes the platter*) I saw his brother only yesterday and another member of the family the day before yesterday, and so on down through the generations ever since I was old enough to reach for a plate. How many times a week will you want to eat herring?

EVA Three times, Matti, if I have to.

LAINA Then you'll have to eat it more often without wanting to.

MATTI You've got a good deal to learn. My mother, who cooked on a big farm too, served it five times a week, and Laina dishes it up eight times (*he picks up a herring by the tail*). Welcome, O herring, thou sustenance of the poor! Appeaser of hunger at all times of day, salty twister of the bowels! From the sea thou hast come, into the earth wilt thou go. Thou art the power that fells the pine forests and sows the fields, the power that moves the machines known as hired hands, who have not yet achieved perpetual motion. O herring, you dog, if it weren't for you, we'd start asking the boss for pork, and what would become of Finland then? (*He puts it back, cuts it up and gives each of the guests a little piece*)

PUNTILA It tastes like a delicacy to me, because I don't eat it very often. That's inequality and it's not right. If it were up to me, I'd put all the receipts of the farm in a chest, and when any of the help needed something he'd just take what he wanted, because if not for him there wouldn't be anything in the chest. Am I right?

MATTI I wouldn't advise it. You'd go broke before you knew it and the bank would take over.

PUNTILA That's your opinion. I disagree. I'm practically a communist, and if I were a hired hand, I'd make life hell for Puntila. Go on with your examination, I'm enjoying it.

MATTI When I get to thinking about what a woman ought to

know how to do before I can show her to my mother, the first thing that comes to mind is my socks. (*He takes off one shoe and gives Eva the sock*) Could you darn this, for instance?

JUDGE That's asking a good deal. I let the herring pass. But I doubt whether Juliet's love for Romeo would have lasted very long if she had been expected to darn socks. Is that self-sacrificing variety of love really so desirable? It's too intense, too passionate, likely as not to end up in court.

MATTI In the lower classes socks aren't mended for love but for reasons of economy.

FARSON I don't believe the excellent ladies who educated her in Brussels had this kind of situation in mind.

(*Eva has come back with needle and thread and begins to darn*)

MATTI It's time for her to fill in the blanks in her education. (*To Eva*) I won't hold your ignorance against you as long as you make an effort. You've been unlucky in your choice of parents and haven't learned the right things. The herring has already showed the enormous gaps in your education. And I knew what I was doing when I gave you that sock. It'll show me what you're made of.

FINA I'd be glad to give Miss Eva a few pointers.

PUNTILA Buck up, Eva, you've got a good head. You'll figure it out.

(*Hesitantly Eva gives Matti the sock. He lifts it up and examines it with a grim smile. It is hopelessly botched*)

FINA I couldn't have done any better myself without a darning egg.

PUNTILA Why didn't you use one?

MATTI Ignorance. (*To the judge, who is laughing*) Don't laugh. My sock is ruined. (*To Eva*) If you married a chauffeur, this would be a tragedy, because you'll have to make ends meet, and it's not easy, you'll be surprised. But I'll give you another chance. Maybe you'll make out better.

EVA I admit the sock was a failure.

MATTI I'm the chauffeur on an estate, and you help out with the washing and keeping up the fires. I come home at night. How do you welcome me?

EVA   I'll be better at that, Matti. Come home.

(*Matti goes a few steps away, and pretends to come in through the door*)

EVA   Matti! (*She runs up to him and kisses him*)

MATTI   First mistake. Mush and gab when I come home tired. (*He pretends to go to the sink and wash. He holds out his hand for a towel*)

EVA   (*starts chattering*)   Poor Matti, how tired you must be. All day long I've been thinking about you slaving away. I wish I could do your work for you.

(*Fina hands her a tablecloth. Dismayed, she passes it on to Matti*)

EVA   I'm sorry, I didn't understand what you wanted.

(*Matti replies with an unfriendly grunt. He sits down by the table and holds out his legs. She tries to pull his boots off*)

PUNTILA   (*has stood up and is watching eagerly*)   Pull!

PARSON   I regard this as an excellent lesson. You see how unnatural it is.

MATTI   I don't always do this, but today I've been driving the tractor, and I'm half dead. You've got to expect these things. What have you been doing today?

EVA   Washing, Matti.

MATTI   How many big pieces did they give you to do?

EVA   Four big bed sheets.

MATTI   Tell her, Fina.

FINA   You've done at least seventeen, and two tubs of fancy wash.

MATTI   Were you able to use the hose, or did you have to pour the water in with a bucket because the hose is coming apart, like on Puntila Farms?

PUNTILA   Go on, Matti, tell me what you think of me. I'm no good.

EVA   With a bucket.

MATTI   (*picks up her hand*)   You've cracked your nails again— scrubbing the clothes or fixing the fires. You ought to smear a little grease on them. My mother's hands swelled up like ⸱is (*he shows her*) over the years, they're all red too. You ⸱⸱be tired, but you'll have to wash my overalls, I need ⸱⸱n tomorrow.

EVA Yes, Matti.

MATTI They'll be good and dry tomorrow morning and you won't have to get up to iron them until half past five. (*Matti feels about for something on the table*)

EVA (*in alarm*) What's wrong?

FINA The newspaper.

(*Eva jumps up and pretends to hold out a newspaper to Matti. He doesn't take it but continues, sulkily, to grope about on the table*)

FINA On the table.

(*Eva finally puts it on the table, but she hasn't yet pulled the second boot off, and he stamps his booted foot impatiently. She sits down on the floor again to remove it. When she has it off, she stands up relieved, takes a deep breath and smooths her hair*)

EVA I embroidered my apron. A little color is nice, don't you agree? It's easy to have a little color around the house, it doesn't cost much, all you need is the right touch. How do you like it, Matti?

(*Disturbed in his newspaper reading, Matti lowers his paper with a pained look. She is too frightened to speak*)

FINA Don't talk when he's reading the paper.

MATTI (*standing up*) See?

PUNTILA I'm disappointed in you, Eva.

MATTI (*almost pityingly*) Nothing there. Wanting to eat herring only three times a week, mending socks without a darning egg, and when I come home at night, no tact, such as keeping her mouth shut for instance. And then they call me in the middle of the night to go get the old man at the station. Then what?

EVA I'll show you. (*She pretends to go to the window and shouts out, very fast*) What is this! In the middle of the night? When my husband's just got home and needs his sleep? This is the last straw. He can sleep it off in the ditch. I'll hide my husband's pants before I let him out of the house.

PUNTILA You've got to admit that was good.

EVA Waking people up in the dead of night. As if they didn't slave hard enough all day. My husband comes home and drops into bed like a corpse. I'm leaving! Is that better?

MATTI (*laughing*)   Eva, that was good. Naturally I'll get fired, but if you do that for my mother, she'll eat out of your hand. (*Gives her a good-natured smack on the behind*)

EVA (*at first speechless, then furious*)   Stop that!

MATTI   What's wrong?

EVA   How dare you hit me—there?

JUDGE (*stands up and pats Eva on the shoulder*)   Poor Eva, I'm afraid you've flunked after all.

PUNTILA   What's the matter with you?

MATTI   Are you offended? You mean I shouldn't have smacked you?

EVA (*laughs again*)   Papa, I'm afraid it won't work out.

PARSON   She's perfectly right.

PUNTILA   What do you mean you're afraid?

EVA   I can see that I wasn't brought up properly. I think I'll go to bed.

PUNTILA   Time I took a hand. Eva! Sit down immediately!

EVA   Papa, I think I'd better be going. I'm sorry, you can't have your engagement. Good night. (*Goes out*)

PUNTILA   Eva!

(*The parson and the judge also prepare to leave. But the parson's wife is still discussing mushrooms with Laina*)

PARSON'S WIFE (*with enthusiasm*)   You've almost convinced me, but I've always put them up. It seems safer. But I peel them first.

LAINA   There's no need to. Just brush off the dirt.

PARSON   Come, Anna, it's getting late.

PUNTILA   Go, go. Abandon a grief-stricken father. I can't un-man, a fine specimen of a man. She'd be happy, she'd get up every morning singing like a lark, but she's too refined, she's afraid it won't work out. I disown her. (*He runs to the door*) You're disinherited. Pack your rags and get out of my house. Do you think I didn't notice the way you almost took the attaché because I told you to? You haven't any character, you dishrag. You're not my daughter any more.

⸱ON   Mr. Puntila, control yourself.

⸱   Don't bother me. Do your preaching in your church ⸱ere's no one to hear you.

⸱   Puntila, I bid you good evening.

PUNTILA   Go, go. Abandon a grief-stricken father. I can't understand how I ever came by such a daughter. I catch her committing sodomy with a diplomatic grasshopper. Any milkmaid could tell her what God created her rear end for in the sweat of His brow. To lie with a man and water at the mouth with desire when a real man comes her way. (*To the judge*) And you didn't even open your mouth to drive those unnatural sentiments out of her. Make yourself scarce.

JUDGE   That's enough, Puntila. Don't bother me. I wash my hands in innocence. (*He goes out smiling*)

PUNTILA   You've been doing that for thirty years, it's a wonder you have any hands left. Fredrik, you had the hands of a peasant before you got to be a judge and started washing them in innocence.

PARSON   (*tries to take his wife away from the conversation with Laina*)   Anna, it's time to go.

PARSON'S WIFE   No, I don't put them in cold water and, another thing, I don't cook the stems. How long do you cook them?

LAINA   I just bring them to a boil.

PARSON   Anna, I'm waiting.

PARSON'S WIFE   I'm coming. I boil mine for ten minutes.
   (*The parson goes out shrugging his shoulders*)

PUNTILA   (*back at the table*)   People like that aren't human beings. I can't bring myself to regard them as human beings.

MATTI   Oh, they're human all right. I once knew a doctor. When he saw a peasant whipping his horses, he'd say: He's treating them humanly again. Animals don't act like that.

PUNTILA   That's profound wisdom. There's a man I'd have been glad to drink with. Have another drink. I liked that examination you put her through, Matti.

MATTI   I apologize for patting your daughter's rear end, Mr. Puntila. That wasn't part of the examination, it was meant as encouragement, but I guess you noticed, it showed how far apart we are.

PUNTILA   Don't apologize to me. She's not my daughter any more.

MATTI   Don't be unforgiving. (*To the parson's wife and Laina*) Have you at least got together on the mushrooms?

PARSON'S WIFE   And you put in the salt right away?

LAINA   Yes, right away. (*Both go out*)

PUNTILA   Listen, the hired hands are still dancing down by the
pond.

(*Red Surkkala is heard singing*)

SURKKALA

There once was a countess, lived in the northland
As fair as the snow on the leas.
"O woodsman, O woodsman, my garter's come loose
It's come loose, it's come loose.
Won't you kneel down here and fasten it, please."

"O countess, O countess, don't make me do that
I serve you for bread, not for pie.
Your bosom is white, but the ax blade is cold
It is cold, it is cold.
Love's a sweet thing, but it's bitter to die."

The woodsman he fled that very same night.
He rode all the way to the sea.
"O boatman, O boatman, let me ride in your boat
In your boat, in your boat
Carry me off to the ends of the sea."

For such is the love between vixen and cock.
"O sweetheart, do you love me too?"
A beautiful night, but in the gray dawn
The gray dawn, the gray dawn
All on the bushes the cock feathers grew.

PUNTILA   That was a dig at me. Songs like that wound me to
the quick.

(*Meanwhile Matti has taken Fina in his arms and danced off
with her*)

10

Nocturne

In the yard. Puntila and Matti are making water.

PUNTILA   I couldn't live in a city. I like to step out and make water on the open ground, under the stars, or there's no pleasure in it. They say life is primitive in the country, I call it primitive to do it in a porcelain bowl.

MATTI   I can see what you mean. You like to think of it as a sport.

(*Pause*)

PUNTILA   I can't stand people who have no joie de vivre. I'm always studying my help to see if they're capable of enjoying life. When I see a hired hand hanging his head, I've had enough of him.

MATTI   I understand. It's beyond me why the people on this farm look so bad. Pasty-faced, all skin and bones. They look twenty years older than their age. I think they do it to get your goat, or they wouldn't run around loose when we have guests.

PUNTILA   As if anybody went hungry on Puntila Farms.

MATTI   And suppose they did. They ought to be used to hunger by this time in Finland. But they refuse to learn, there's no good will. In 1918, 80,000 of them were wiped out, and after that everything was peaceful and quiet. Why? Because there were that many fewer hungry mouths to feed.

PUNTILA   That kind of thing shouldn't be necessary.

11

Mr. Puntila and Matti, His Hired Man, Climb Mount Hatelma

Library in Puntila's house. Puntila, his head wrapped in a wet towel, is studying bills and groaning. Laina, the cook, is standing beside him with a basin and a second towel.

PUNTILA   If the attaché makes one more of his half-hour phone calls to Helsinki, I'm canceling the engagement. Not another word about the forest he's costing me, but this kind of petty theft sticks in my craw. And why are the figures all blotted in this egg register? Do they expect me to spend my life in the henhouse keeping track?

FINA (*enters*)   The parson and the agent of the milk cooperative wish to speak to you.

PUNTILA   I won't see them. My head is splitting, I think I'm coming down with pneumonia. Bring them in.
(*Enter the parson and the lawyer. Fina goes out quickly*)

PARSON   Good morning, Mr. Puntila, I hope you've slept well. We happened to meet in the village, and we thought we'd drop in to see how you were getting along.

LAWYER   A night of misunderstandings, so to speak.

PUNTILA   I've spoken with Eino on the phone if that's what you're referring to; he's apologized, and there the matter ends.

LAWYER   My dear Puntila, there may be something else. As long as these little misunderstandings here at Puntila Farms concern only your family life and your relations with members of the government, they are your own affair. But unfortunately there's another point.

PUNTILA   Don't beat about the bush, Pekka. If any damage has been done, I'll pay up.

PARSON   Unfortunately there are kinds of damage that can't be made good with money, Mr. Puntila. In a word, we should like to bring up the question of Surkkala—in a spirit of friendship, mind you.

PUNTILA   What about Surkkala?

PARSON   Some time ago, if we are not mistaken, you expressed your intention of dismissing him. You yourself said that he was an out and out Red and a deplorable influence on the community.

PUNTILA   I said I was going to fire him.

PARSON   Yesterday, Mr. Puntila, was the final date for giving notice, but Surkkala has not been dismissed, or I wouldn't have seen his eldest daughter in church yesterday.

PUNTILA   What, he hasn't been dismissed? Is that true, Laina?

LAINA   Yes.

PUNTILA   How's that?

LAINA   You met him at the hiring market and brought him home in the car. Instead of firing him you gave him ten marks.

PUNTILA   What unmitigated gall! Taking ten marks from me after I'd told him time and time again he'd have to clear out by the first of the month. Fina! (*Enter Fina*) Get me Surkkala. (*Fina goes out*) Oh, my head!

LAWYER   Take some coffee.

PUNTILA   That's it, Pekka, I must have been drunk. I always do such things when I've been drinking too much. I could bash my head in. That bastard ought to be in jail, he took advantage of my condition.

PARSON   I'm sure he did, Mr. Puntila. We all know your heart's in the right place. You must have been under the influence of liquor to do such a thing.

PUNTILA   It's horrible. (*Despairingly*) What will I tell my friends in the National Defense Corps? It's a point of honor. I'll be boycotted if it comes out. They'll stop taking my milk. It's the chauffeur's fault, he was sitting next to him, I can see it all. He knew I couldn't abide Surkkala, but he let me give him ten marks.

PARSON   Don't take it to heart, Mr. Puntila. Such things happen.

PUNTILA   Such things happen. Don't give me that. You don't mean it anyway. If things go on like this, I'll have to get the

court to declare me irresponsible and appoint a guardian. I
can't drink up all that milk by myself, I'll be ruined. Pekka,
don't just sit there, you've got to help me, you're the business
agent, I'll give the National Defense Corps a subsidy. Drink,
drink, drink! It doesn't agree with me, Laina.

LAWYER   You'll just have to pay him for the next term. He's
got to go, he's poisoning the atmosphere.

PARSON   I think we'll be leaving, Mr. Puntila. Where there's
good will, no harm is irreparable. It's the good will that
counts, Mr. Puntila.

PUNTILA (*shaking hands with him*)   Thank you.

PARSON   There's nothing to thank us for, we're only doing our
duty. Without loss of time.

LAWYER   And you might be looking into your chauffeur's
record too. He doesn't impress me very favorably either.
(*The parson and the lawyer go out*)

PUNTILA   Laina, I'll never touch a drop of liquor again. Never
I thought it all over when I woke up this morning. It's a
curse. I'm going to the cow barn and make a resolution. I
love my cows. Any promise I make in the cow barn is sacred.
(*Grandly*) Get me the bottles out of the stamp cabinet,
every last one of them. Bring me all the liquor there is in
the house, I'm going to destroy it this minute, I'm going to
smash every single bottle. Don't tell me how much it cost,
think of the farm.

LAINA   Certainly, Mr. Puntila, but are you really sure?

PUNTILA   Imagine my not firing Surkkala. It's scandalous. But
I've learned my lesson. I want to see Altonen too. He's my
evil spirit.

LAINA   My goodness, they were all packed and now they've
unpacked.
(*Laina runs out. Enter Surkkala and his children*)

PUNTILA   I didn't say anything about bringing your kids. I'm
going to settle up with you.

SURKKALA   That's what I thought, Mr. Puntila. That's why I
brought them. I want them to listen. It can't hurt them.
(*Pause. Enter Matti*)

MATTI   Good morning, Mr. Puntila. Is your headache better?

PUNTILA   Here's the son-of-a-bitch now. What's this I hear?

What have you been cooking up behind my back? Didn't
I warn you only yesterday that I'd throw you out without
a reference?

MATTI   Yes, Mr. Puntila.

PUNTILA   Shut up! I've had enough of your backtalk! My
friends have put me wise to you. How much did Surkkala
pay you?

MATTI   I don't know what you mean, Mr. Puntila.

PUNTILA   What?! Are you going to stand there and deny that
you're in cahoots with Surkkala? You're a Red yourself. You
prevented me from firing him before the legal date.

MATTI   I beg your pardon, Mr. Puntila, I only carried out your
orders.

PUNTILA   You must have known there was no rhyme nor reason in those orders.

MATTI   I beg your pardon, it's not as easy as you may think
to tell orders apart. If I only carried out orders that made
sense, you'd fire me for twiddling my thumbs.

PUNTILA   Don't talk back to me, you blackguard. You know
perfectly well that I don't tolerate agitators on my farm.
You Bolshevik, the next thing you know, my help will be
wanting eggs for breakfast before they go to work. It's liquor
that kept *me* from giving him notice on time, so now I have
to pay him three months' wages to get rid of him. With you
it was cold calculation. (*Laina and Fina keep bringing in
bottles*) But this time I'm serious, Laina. You can see that
because I'm not stopping at a mere resolution. I'm physically
exterminating all this liquor. In the past, I have to admit, I
never made a clean sweep, there was always liquor handy
when a fit of weakness came over me. That was the big trouble. I read once that the first step toward abstinence is to
stop buying liquor. That is too little known. But if it's already on hand, there's only one thing to do: wipe it out!
(*To Matti*) I have my reasons for calling you in to watch.
That will frighten you more than anything else.

MATTI   Yes, Mr. Puntila. Would you like me to take the bottles outside and smash them for you?

PUNTILA   No, I'll do it myself, you crook. That would suit
you, wouldn't it? Destroying all this fine liquor (*he holds*

up a bottle and inspects it) by pouring it down your throat.

LAINA   Don't look at that bottle too long, Mr. Puntila. Throw it out the window.

PUNTILA   Right you are. (*Coldly to Matti*) You're not going to start me drinking again, you son-of-a-bitch. You're only happy when you see people wallowing like hogs. Real love for your work is something you never heard of. You wouldn't stir a finger except to keep from starving, you parasite. You fasten on to me, you tell me dirty stories all night, you make me insult my guests. Why? Because you're only happy when you can drag everything into the muck, because that's your element. I've a good mind to call the police. I've heard your confession, I know why you lost every job you ever had, I caught you agitating with those females from Kurgela, you're a subversive. (*Absentmindedly he starts pouring from the bottle into a glass that Matti has dutifully brought him*) You hate me, you think you can take me in with your "Yes, Mr. Puntila." That would suit you.

LAINA   Mr. Puntila!

PUNTILA   Don't worry, I'm only tasting it to make sure the dealer didn't cheat me and to celebrate my unalterable resolution. (*To Matti*) I saw through you the moment I first laid eyes on you. I've been watching you all this time, because I knew you'd give yourself away. You never suspected it, but that's why I spent my time drinking with you. (*He drinks some more*) You thought you could lead me into debauchery and live it up at my expense. You thought I'd spend the rest of my life sopping up liquor with you, but you've made a big mistake, my friends put me wise to you, I owe them a debt of gratitude. Here's to their health! I shudder to think of it, those three days at the Park Hotel and the way I rode around looking for legal alcohol, and the women from Kurgela—is that a reasonable way to live?—and that dairymaid who thought she could take advantage of me because I was tight and she had big tits, her name was Lisu, I think. And this son-of-a-bitch always following me around. Those were good times, you've got to admit, but I won't give you my daughter, you no-good, but you're not a shit, I'll admit that.

LAINA Mr. Puntila, you're drinking again!

PUNTILA Me drinking? You call this drinking? A bottle or two? (*He reaches for the second bottle*) Destroy this one, (*he gives her the empty bottle*) smash it, I never want to see it again, you heard me. And don't look at me like our Saviour looked at Peter, I can't stomach this niggling literal-mindedness. (*With a gesture indicating Matti*) I know he drags me down, but you people want me to sit here like a bump on a log, chewing my toenails with boredom. What kind of a life have I got around here? Driving the help from morning to night, figuring the cost of cow fodder! Get out of here, you midgets!

(*Laina and Fina go out shaking their heads*)

PUNTILA (*looking after them*) Small-minded! No imagination! (*To Surkkala's children*) Steal, rob, grow up to be Reds, but don't be midgets, that's Puntila's advice to you. (*To Surkkala*) Forgive me for meddling in the education of your children. (*To Matti*) Open the bottle.

MATTI I hope the stuff is all right and they haven't put pepper in it like last time. You've got to be on your guard with that dealer, Mr. Puntila.

PUNTILA I know. I'm on my guard all right. I always begin with a tiny sip, I can spit it out if it's no good. An elementary precaution, it's become second nature with me. Without it, God knows what I'd pour into my bowels. For God's sake, Matti, take a bottle, we're going to celebrate my resolutions. They're unalterable and that's always a calamity. Your health, Surkkala.

MATTI You mean they can stay on, Mr. Puntila?

PUNTILA Do we have to talk about that now, among friends? Matti, you disappoint me. What good would it do Surkkala to stay on? This farm is too small for a man like him, he's not happy here and I respect him for it. If I were in his shoes, I'd feel exactly the same way. To me Puntila would be another capitalist, and you know what I'd do to him? I'd put him in a salt mine to find out what it feels like to work, the parasite. Am I right, Surkkala, don't spare my feelings.

SURKKALA'S ELDEST DAUGHTER   But we want to stay here, Mr. Puntila.

PUNTILA   No, no, no, Surkkala is leaving, nothing could stop him. (*He goes to the desk, opens it and takes money from the cash drawer. He hands it to Surkkala*) Minus ten. (*To the children*) You've got a father you can be proud of, a man who stands up for his convictions through thick and thin. You're the oldest, Hella, be a helpmate to him. Well—this is good-bye. (*He holds out his hand to Surkkala, who does not take it*)

SURKKALA   Come along, Hella, we'll go and pack. You've heard all there is to hear on Puntila Farms. (*He goes out with his children*)

PUNTILA (*deeply hurt*)   My hand isn't good enough for him. Did you notice how I was waiting for a sign from him, just some little word? In vain. This farm is so much shit to him. No roots. No feeling for the soil. That's why I let him go when he kept insisting. A sad story. (*He drinks*) You and I, Matti, we're different. You're a friend and guide to me on my thorny path. Just looking at you makes me thirsty. How much do I pay you a month?

MATTI   Three hundred, Mr. Puntila.

PUNTILA   I'm raising you to three fifty. Because I'm really pleased with you. (*Dreamily*) Matti, one of these days you and I ought to climb Mount Hatelma. The view is famous. I want to show you what a beautiful country you live in, you'll kick yourself for not realizing it before. How about it, Matti? Want to climb Mount Hatelma, Matti? Why not? We can do it in spirit. All we need is a few chairs.

MATTI   I'll do anything you can dream up if the day is long enough.

PUNTILA   I'm not sure you've got the imagination for it.
(*Matti says nothing*)

PUNTILA (*erupting*)   Build me a mountain, Matti. Spare no effort, leave no stone unturned, take the biggest boulders, or it won't be Mount Hatelma and we won't have a view.

MATTI   Just as you wish, Mr. Puntila. Even I know that the eight-hour day doesn't count when you want a mountain in this flat country. (*Matti kicks a costly grandfather clock and a massive gun cabinet to pieces. From the wreckage and a few chairs he furiously builds Mount Hatelma on the billiard table*)

PUNTILA   Take that chair. If you want a first-class Mount Hatelma, follow my instructions, because I know what's needed and what isn't, and I'm responsible. If I left you to your own resources, you'd build a mountain that wouldn't pay off—no view, no pleasure for me—because—make a mental note of this—all you care about is having work to do, it's up to me to direct your work toward a useful goal. And now I need a trail up the mountain, and don't make it too steep for my 240 pounds. What good is a mountain without a trail? You see, you don't think hard enough. I know how to handle people, I'd be curious to see you trying to handle yourself.

MATTI   There, the mountain is finished, you can climb up. It's a mountain with a trail, not the unfinished product God made of His mountains because He was in a hurry because He only had six days, so He had to create a lot of hired hands before you could do anything with them, Mr. Puntila.

PUNTILA   (*starting to climb*)   I'm going to break my neck.

MATTI   (*holds him up*)   You can do that on level ground if you haven't got me to hold you up.

PUNTILA   That's why I'm taking you with me, Matti. If I didn't, you'd never see the beautiful country that gave you birth and made you what you are. You wouldn't be worth a plugged nickel without it, be grateful to it.

MATTI   I'll be grateful to my dying day, but maybe that's not enough. I read in the *Helsinki Sanomat* that we should be grateful to the fatherland beyond the grave.

PUNTILA   First the fields and meadows, then the woods. Those pines that grow in rock, with nothing to feed them. It's a miracle how they can thrive in such poverty.

MATTI   They'd be ideal servants, if you see what I mean.

PUNTILA   Up we go, Matti. The works of man are left behind, we're moving into the very heart of nature. The naked purity of it, more naked at every step. Leave all your petty cares behind you, Matti, abandon yourself to this overpowering experience.

MATTI   I'm doing my best, Mr. Puntila.

PUNTILA   O blessed Tavastland . . . One more nip and we'll see
you in all your beauty.

MATTI   Just a second, while I run down the mountain and get
the red wine. (*He climbs down and back up again*)

PUNTILA   Can you really appreciate the beauty of the country?
Are you from Tavastland?

MATTI   Yes.

PUNTILA   Then I ask you. Where is there such a sky as in
Tavastland? I've heard that it's bluer in other places, but the
clouds are lighter here, the Finnish winds are gentler, and I
wouldn't want a different blue even if I could have it. And
when the wild swans fly up whirring from the marsh lakes,
doesn't that mean anything to you? Don't let them tell you
about other places, Matti, you'll be disappointed, stick to
Tavastland, it's good advice I'm giving you.

MATTI   Yes, Mr. Puntila.

PUNTILA   The lakes alone! Forget the woods, that forest over
there is mine, I'm having the section on the point cut down,
just take the lakes, Matti, just a few of them, forget about
the fish they're teeming with, just take the view of those
lakes in the morning, that will keep you from wanting to go
away and eat your heart out among strangers and waste away
with homesickness, and we've got eighty thousand of them
in Finland.

MATTI   All right, I'll just take the view.

PUNTILA   Do you see that little one and the tugboat with a
chest like a bulldog and the tree trunks in the morning light?
The way they float in the clear cool water, all stripped and
bundled, a small fortune? I can smell fresh timber five miles
away, can't you? Ah, the smells we have here in Tavastland,
I could bask in them all day, the berries, for instance. After
the rain. And the birch leaves when you come from the
sauna and you've had yourself whipped with a big bundle
of them, or in the morning as you lie in bed. Where else do
you get such smells? Or a view like this?

MATTI   Nowhere, Mr. Puntila.

PUNTILA   I like it best when it's hazy, it's like sometimes when
you're making love, you half close your eyes, and every-

thing's blurred. As a matter of fact, I think that kind of love only exists in Tavastland.

MATTI   In the place where I was born there were caves with stones in front of them, all polished like bowling balls.

PUNTILA   You crawled in, didn't you? Instead of minding the cows. Look, I can see some now. Swimming across the lake.

MATTI   I see them, there must be fifty of them.

PUNTILA   At least sixty. And there's the train. When I listen hard, I can hear the milk cans clanking.

MATTI   If you listen very hard.

PUNTILA   But I've still got to show you Tavasthus, dear old Tavasthus, we have cities too. Look down there, that's the Park Hotel, they've got good wine, I recommend it. Forget about the castle, they've turned it into a women's prison for political offenders, women shouldn't meddle in politics, but the flour mills make a pretty picture in the distance, they liven up the landscape. And now, what do you see over there on the left?

MATTI   All right, what do I see?

PUNTILA   Fields of course. Fields as far as the eye can see, including mine, especially the peat bog, the soil down there is so rich that if I turn the cows into the clover I can milk them three times a day, and the grain grows up to your chin and yields twice a year. Sing with me!

And the waves of the lovely Roina
Kiss the milk-white sand.

(*Enter Fina and Laina*)

FINA   Jesus Mary!

LAINA   They've wrecked the whole library.

MATTI   We're on the summit of Mount Hatelma, taking in the panorama.

PUNTILA   Sing everybody. Where's your patriotism?

ALL (*except Matti*)

And the waves of the lovely Roina
Kiss the milk-white sand.

PUNTILA O Tavastland, thrice blessed. With its sky, its lakes, its people and its forests! (*To Matti*) Admit that your heart swells when you see all that.

MATTI My heart swells when I see your forests, Mr. Puntila.

12

Matti Turns his Back on Puntila

The yard at Puntila Farms. Early morning. Matti comes out of the house with a suitcase. Laina follows him with a package of food.

LAINA Here, Matti, take this little lunch. I can't make out why you're leaving. Wait at least until Mr. Puntila gets up.

MATTI I'd rather not risk it. Last night he was so drunk that along toward morning he promised before witnesses to sign over half his woods to me. If he hears about it, he'll call the police.

LAINA But if you go off without a reference, what will become of you?

MATTI What good is a reference if it says either that I'm an agitator or a human being. I won't get a job either way.

LAINA He'll be lost without you, he's so used to you.

MATTI He'll just have to do for himself. I'm fed up. Since that business with Surkkala, I can't stomach his friendly ways. Thanks for the lunch, Laina, and good-bye.

LAINA (*sniffling*) Good luck. (*Goes in quickly*)

MATTI (*after taking a few steps*)
This is the end, this morning I
To Puntila must say good-bye.
You're not the worst I ever met
You're almost human when you're tight.
But of course our friendship couldn't last. Sobriety

Sets in and draws the line between you and me.
And even if we shed a tear because
Two kinds of animal can't cross
It doesn't help. It's just a waste of tears.
It's time your hired hands showed you their rears.
They'll quickly find good masters when
The masters are the working men.
(*Goes out quickly*)

Note on the Music

The "Ballad of the Forester and the Countess" was written to the tune of an old Scottish ballad; the "Plum Song" to a folk tune.

The "Puntila Song" was composed by Paul Dessau. During changes of scene the actress playing the part of Laina the cook steps before the curtain with an accordionist and a guitarist and sings the stanza corresponding to the preceding scene. While singing, she performs actions in preparation for the big engagement party, such as sweeping the floor, dusting, stirring batter, beating egg whites, greasing cake tins, washing glasses, grinding coffee, and drying dishes.

PUNTILA SONG

1

Boss Puntila drank for three whole days
His lips were never dry.
But when he left, the poor waiter did
Not even say good-bye.
O waiter, is that nice of you?
Isn't life a delightful treat?
The waiter answered: I couldn't say
My problem is my aching feet.

2

Boss Puntila's daughter read a book
She couldn't help agreeing.
She treasured it because it said
She was a higher being.
But once she looked at the chauffeur
As only a maiden can:
O chauffeur, come and play with me
They tell me that you're a man.

3

And once when Puntila stayed out all night
He met a milkmaid in the early dawn.

O milkmaid with the snow-white breast
Where are you going so soon?
My cows I'm certain you've been milking
While the first dawn glowed red.
But getting up for me is not enough.
Come along and we'll go back to bed.

4

In Puntila there's a Finnish bath
And Finnish baths are fun.
Sometimes a hired hand goes in
To show the daughter how it's done.
Says Puntila, for my daughter I've found
The right husband, an attaché.
He doesn't care who helps my daughter bathe
As long as his debts I pay.

5

The daughter met the hired man
One night when he was free.
My man, I've noticed your manly strength
Come, won't you fish with me?
Young lady, says the hired man
I see you've got the sultry blues.
But goodness, lady, can't you see
I'm trying to read the news?

6

The League of Puntila's Fiancées
Hiked out to the celebration.
But when the landowner sighted them
He bellowed with indignation.
Did ever sheep get a woolen coat
Since first a sheep was shorn?
I'll sleep with you, but at my board
You'll never get your turn.

7

The women of Kurgela sang a song
That did not wish him well.

But by then their shoes were all worn out
And their Sunday shot to hell.
But if you choose to trust the rich
You are lucky if a shoe
Or two is all you have to mourn
And nobody's to blame but you.

8

But Puntila he banged his iron fist
Upon the tablecloth:
I refuse to give this stupid fop
My darling daughter's troth.
He offered her to his hired man:
She's yours if you will agree.
The hired man said no, kind sir
She's not clever enough for me.

The Resistible Rise
of Arturo Ui

A Parable Play

Collaborator: M. Steffin

Translator: Ralph Manheim

CHARACTERS

THE ANNOUNCER
FLAKE
CARUTHER
BUTCHER
MULBERRY
CLARK

} Businessmen, directors of the Cauliflower Trust

SHEET, shipyard owner
OLD DOGSBOROUGH
YOUNG DOGSBOROUGH
ARTURO UI, gang leader
ERNESTO ROMA,
    his lieutenant
EMANUELE GIRI
GIUSEPPE GIVOLA,
    florist

} Gangsters

TED RAGG, reporter on
    the *Star*
DOCKDAISY
BOWL, Sheet's chief
    accountant
GOODWILL and GAFFLES,
    members of the city council

O'CASEY, investigator
AN ACTOR
HOOK, wholesale vegetable
    dealer
DEFENDANT FISH
THE DEFENSE COUNSEL
THE JUDGE
THE DOCTOR
THE PROSECUTOR
A WOMAN
YOUNG INNA, Roma's familiar
A LITTLE MAN
IGNATIUS DULLFEET
BETTY DULLFEET, his wife
DOGSBOROUGH'S BUTLER
BODYGUARDS
GUNMEN
VEGETABLE DEALERS OF CHICAGO
    AND CICERO
REPORTERS

Prologue

The announcer steps before the curtain. Large notices are attached to the curtain: "New developments in dock subsidy scandal"—"The true facts about Dogsborough's will and confession"—"Sensation at warehouse fire trial"—"Friends murder gangster Ernesto Roma"—"Ignatius Dullfeet blackmailed and murdered"—"Cicero taken over by gangsters." Behind the curtain popular dance music.

THE ANNOUNCER
    Friends, tonight we're going to show—
    Pipe down, you boys in the back row!
    And, lady, your hat is in the way!—
    The great historical gangster play
    Containing, for the first time, as you'll see
    The truth about the scandalous dock subsidy.
    Further we give you, for your betterment
    Dogsborough's confession and testament.
    Arturo Ui's rise while the stock market fell
    The notorious warehouse fire trial. What a sell!
    The Dullfeet murder! Justice in a coma!
    Gang warfare: the killing of Ernesto Roma!
    All culminating in our stunning last tableau:
    Gangsters take over the town of Cicero!
    Brilliant performers will portray
    The most eminent gangsters of our day.
    You'll see some dead and some alive
    Some bygone types and others that survive
    Some born, some made—for instance, here we show
    The good old honest Dogsborough!

(*Old Dogsborough steps before the curtain*)
His hair is white, his heart is black.
Corrupt old man, you may step back.
(*Dogsborough bows and steps back*)
The next exhibit on our list
Is Givola—
(*Givola has stepped before the curtain*)
                        the horticulturist.
His tongue's so slippery he'd know how
To sell you a billygoat for a cow!
Short, says the proverb, are the legs of lies.
Look at his legs, just use your eyes.
(*Givola steps back limping*)
Now to Emanuele Giri, the superclown.
Come out, let's look you up and down!
(*Giri steps before the curtain and waves his hand at the audience*)
One of the greatest killers ever known!
Okay, beat it!
(*Giri steps back with an angry look*)
And lastly Public Enemy Number One
Arturo Ui. Now you'll see
The biggest gangster of all times
Whom heaven sent us for our crimes
Our weakness and stupidity!
(*Arturo Ui steps before the curtain and walks out along the footlights*)
Doesn't he make you think of Richard the Third?
Has anybody ever heard
Of blood so ghoulishly and lavishly shed
Since wars were fought for roses white and red?
In view of this the management
Has spared no cost in its intent
To picture his spectacularly vile
Maneuvers in the grandest style.
But everything you'll see tonight is true.
Nothing's invented, nothing's new
Or made to order just for you.
The gangster play that we present

Is known to the whole continent.
(*While the music swells and the sound of a machine-gun
mingles with it, the announcer retires with an air of bustling
self-importance*)

1

(a)

*Financial District. Enter five businessmen, the directors of the
Cauliflower Trust.*

FLAKE
　The times are bad!

CLARK
　　　　　　It looks as if Chicago
　The dear old girl, while on her way to market
　Had found her pocket torn and now she's starting
　To scrabble in the gutter for her pennies.

CARUTHER
　Last Thursday Jones invited me and eighty
　More to a partridge dinner to be held
　This Monday. If we really went, we'd find
　No one to greet us but the auctioneer.
　This awful change from glut to destitution
　Has come more quickly than a maiden's blush.
　Vegetable fleets with produce for this city
　Still ply the lakes, but nowhere will you find
　A buyer.

BUTCHER
　　　　　It's like darkness at high noon.

MULBERRY
　Robber and Clive are being auctioned off.

CLARK
  Wheeler—importing fruit since Noah's ark—
  Is bankrupt.
FLAKE
                    And Dick Havelock's garages
  Are liquidating.
CARUTHER
                        Where is Sheet?
FLAKE
                                    Too busy
  To come. He's dashing round from bank to bank.
CLARK
  What? Sheet?
  (*Pause*)
                        In other words, the cauliflower
  Trade in this town is through.
BUTCHER
                                Come, gentlemen
  Chin up! We're not dead yet.
MULBERRY
                            Call this a life?
BUTCHER
  Why all the gloom? The produce business in
  This town is basically sound. Good times
  And bad, a city of four million needs
  Fresh vegetables. Don't worry. We'll pull through.
CARUTHER
  How are the stores and markets doing?
MULBERRY
                                    Badly.
  The customers buy half a head of cabbage
  And that on credit.
CLARK
                    Our cauliflower's rotting.
FLAKE
  Say, there's a fellow waiting in the lobby—
  I only mention it because it's odd—
  The name is Ui . . .

CLARK

The gangster?

FLAKE

Yes, in person.
He's smelled the stink and thinks he sees an opening.
Ernesto Roma, his lieutenant, says
They can convince shopkeepers it's not healthy
To handle other people's cauliflower.
He promises our turnover will double
Because, he says, the shopkeepers would rather
Buy cauliflower than coffins.
(*They laugh dejectedly*)

CARUTHER

It's an outrage.

MULBERRY (*laughing uproariously*)
Bombs and machine guns! New conceptions of
Salesmanship! That's the ticket. Fresh young
Blood in the Cauliflower Trust. They heard
We had insomnia, so Mr. Ui
Hastens to offer us his services.
Well, fellows, we'll just have to choose. It's him
Or the Salvation Army. Which one's soup
Do you prefer?

CLARK

I tend to think that Ui's
Is hotter.

CARUTHER

Throw him out!

MULBERRY

Politely though.
How do we know what straits we'll come to yet?
(*They laugh*)

FLAKE (*to Butcher*)
What about Dogsborough and a city loan?
(*To the others*)
Butcher and I cooked up a little scheme
To help us through our present money troubles.
I'll give it to you in a nutshell. Why

Shouldn't the city that takes in our taxes
Give us a loan, let's say, for docks that we
Would undertake to build so vegetables
Can be brought in more cheaply? Dogsborough
Is influential. He could put it through.
Have you seen Dogsborough?

BUTCHER

Yes. He refuses
To touch it.

FLAKE

He refuses? Damn it, he's
The ward boss on the waterfront, and he
Won't help us!

CARUTHER

I've contributed for years
To his campaign fund!

MULBERRY

Hell, he used to run
Sheet's lunchroom! Before he took up politics
He got his bread and butter from the Trust.
That's rank ingratitude. It's just like I've been
Telling you, Flake. All loyalty is gone!
Money is short, but loyalty is shorter!
Cursing, they scurry from the sinking ship
Friend turns to foe, employee snubs his boss
And our old lunchroom operator
Who used to be all smiles is one cold shoulder.
Morals go overboard in times of crisis.

CARUTHER

I'd never have expected that of Dogsborough!

FLAKE

What's his excuse?

BUTCHER

He says our proposition
Is fishy.

FLAKE

What's fishy about building docks?
Think of the men we'd put to work.

BUTCHER

                              He says
He has his doubts about our building docks.

FLAKE

Outrageous!

BUTCHER

                    What? Not building?

FLAKE

                              No. His doubts.

CLARK

Then find somebody else to push the loan.

MULBERRY

Sure, there are other people.

BUTCHER

                              True enough.
But none like Dogsborough. No, take it easy.
The man is good.

CLARK

                    For what?

BUTCHER

                              He's honest. And
What's more, reputed to be honest.

FLAKE

                                        Rot!

BUTCHER

He's got to think about his reputation.
That's obvious.

FLAKE

                    Who gives a damn? We need
A loan from city hall. His reputation
Is his affair.

BUTCHER

                    You think so? I should say
It's ours. It takes an honest man to swing
A loan like this, a man they'd be ashamed
To ask for proofs and guarantees. And such
A man is Dogsborough. Old Dogsborough's
Our loan. All right, I'll tell you why. Because they

Believe in him. They may have stopped believing
In God, but not in Dogsborough. A hard-boiled
Broker, who takes a lawyer with him to
His lawyer's, wouldn't hesitate to put his
Last cent in Dogsborough's apron for safekeeping
If he should see it lying on the bar.
Two hundred pounds of honesty. In eighty
Winters he's shown no weakness. Such a man
Is worth his weight in gold—especially
To people with a scheme for building docks
And building kind of slowly.

FLAKE

                          Okay, Butcher
He's worth his weight in gold. The deal he vouches
For is tied up. The only trouble is:
He doesn't vouch for ours.

CLARK

                          Oh no, not he!
"The city treasury is not a grab bag!"

MULBERRY

And "All for the city, the city for itself!"

CARUTHER

Disgusting! Not an ounce of humor.

MULBERRY

                              Once
His mind's made up, an earthquake wouldn't change it.
To him the city's not a place of wood
And stone, where people live with people
Struggling to feed themselves and pay the rent
But words on paper, something from the Bible.
The man has always gotten on my nerves.

CLARK

His heart was never with us. What does he care
For cauliflower and the trucking business!
Let every vegetable in the city rot
You think he'd lift a finger? No, for nineteen years
Or is it twenty, we've contributed
To his campaign fund. Well, in all that time
The only cauliflower he's ever seen

Was on his plate. What's more, he's never once
Set foot in a garage.

BUTCHER

                    That's right.

CLARK

                                The devil

Take him!

BUTCHER

              Oh no! We'll take him.

FLAKE

                                But Clark says

It can't be done. The man has turned us down.

BUTCHER

That's so. But Clark has also told us why!

CLARK

The bastard doesn't know which way is up.

BUTCHER

Exactly. What's his trouble? Ignorance.
He hasn't got the faintest notion what
It's like to be in such a fix. The question
Is therefore how to put him in our skin.
In short, we've got to educate the man.
I've thought it over. Listen, here's my plan.

(*A sign appears, recalling certain incidents in the recent past*)*

(b)

Outside the produce exchange. Flake and Sheet in conversation.

SHEET

I've run from pillar to post. Pillar was out
Of town, and Post was sitting in the bathtub.
Old friends show nothing but their backs. A brother
Buys wilted shoes before he meets his brother
For fear his brother will touch him for a loan.

* See historical table at the end of the play, p. 302–03.

Old partners dread each other so they use
False names when meeting in a public place.
Our citizens are sewing up their pockets.

FLAKE
So what about my proposition?

SHEET
                              No. I
Won't sell. You want a full-course dinner for the
Price of the tip. And to be thanked for the tip
At that. You wouldn't like it if
I told you what I think of you.

FLAKE
                              Nobody
Will pay you any more.

SHEET
                        And friends won't be
More generous than anybody else.

FLAKE
Money is tight these days.

SHEET
                        Especially
For those in need. And who can diagnose
A friend's need better than a friend?

FLAKE
                                   You'll lose
Your shipyard either way.

SHEET
                     And that's not all
I'll lose. I've got a wife who's likely to
Walk out on me.

FLAKE
                  But if you sell . . .

SHEET
. . . she'll last another year. But what I'm curious
About is why you want my shipyard.

FLAKE
                              Hasn't
It crossed your mind that we—I mean the Trust—
Might want to help you?

SHEET

                    No, it never crossed
My mind. How stupid of me to suspect you
Of trying to grab my property, when you
Were only trying to help.

FLAKE

                    Such bitterness
Dear Sheet, won't save you from the hammer.

SHEET

At least, dear Flake, it doesn't help the hammer.
(*Three men saunter past: Arturo Ui, the gangster, his lieu-*
tenant Ernesto Roma, and a bodyguard. In passing, Ui stares
at Flake as though expecting to be spoken to, and in leaving
Roma turns his head and gives Flake an angry look)

SHEET

Who's that?

FLAKE

                    Arturo Ui, the gangster.—How
About it? Are you selling?

SHEET

                         He seemed eager
To speak to you.

FLAKE (*laughing angrily*)

                    And so he is. He's been
Pursuing us with offers, wants to sell
Our cauliflower with his tommy-guns.
The town is full of types like that right now
Corroding it like leprosy, devouring
A finger, then an arm and shoulder. No one
Knows where it comes from, but we all suspect
From deepest hell. Kidnapping, murder, threats
Extortion, blackmail, massacre:
"Hands up!" "Your money or your life!" Outrageous!
It's got to be wiped out.

SHEET (*looking at him sharply*)

                    And quickly. It's contagious.

FLAKE

Well, how about it? Are you selling?

SHEET (*stepping back and looking at him*)

No doubt about it: A resemblance to
Those three who just passed by. Not too pronounced
But somehow there, one senses more than sees it.
Under the water of a pond sometimes
You see a branch, all green and slimy. It
Could be a snake. But no, it's definitely
A branch. Or is it? That's how you resemble
Roma. Don't take offense. But when I looked
At him just now and then at you, it seemed
To me I'd noticed it before, in you
And others, without understanding. Say it
Again, Flake: "How about it? Are you selling?"
Even your voice, I think . . . No, better say
"Hands up!" because that's what you really mean.
(*He puts up his hands*)
All right, Flake. Take the shipyard!
Give me a kick or two in payment. Hold it!
I'll take the higher offer. Make it two.

FLAKE
  You're crazy!

SHEET
                I only wish that that were true!

2

*Back room in Dogsborough's restaurant. Dogsborough and his
son are washing glasses. Enter Butcher and Flake.*

DOGSBOROUGH
  You didn't need to come. The answer is no.
  Your proposition stinks of rotten fish.

YOUNG DOGSBOROUGH
  My father turns it down.

BUTCHER
                        Forget it, then.
  We ask you. You say no. So no it is.

DOGSBOROUGH
  It's fishy. I know your kind of docks.
  I wouldn't touch it.

YOUNG DOGSBOROUGH
                    My father wouldn't touch it.

BUTCHER
                                        Good.
  Forget it.

DOGSBOROUGH
            You're on the wrong road, fellows.
  The city treasury is not a grab bag
  For everyone to dip his fingers into.
  Anyway, damn it all, your business is
  Perfectly sound.

BUTCHER
                  What did I tell you, Flake?
  You fellows are too pessimistic.

DOGSBOROUGH
                            Pessimism
  Is treason. You're only making trouble for
  Yourselves. I see it this way: What do you
  Fellows sell? Cauliflower. That's as good
  As meat and bread. Man doesn't live by bread
  And meat alone, he needs his green goods.
  Suppose I served up sirloin without onions
  Or mutton without beans. I'd never see
  My customers again. Some people are
  A little short right now. They hesitate
  To buy a suit. But people have to eat.
  They'll always have a dime for vegetables.
  Chin up! If I were you, I wouldn't worry.

FLAKE
  It does me good to hear you, Dogsborough.
  It gives a fellow courage to go on.

BUTCHER
  Dogsborough, it almost makes me laugh to find you

So staunchly confident about the future
Of cauliflower, because quite frankly we
Have come here for a purpose. No, don't worry.
Not what you think, that's dead and buried. Something
Pleasant, or so at least we hope. Old man
It's come to our attention that it's been
Exactly twenty years this June, since you—
Well known to us for having operated
The lunchroom in one of our establishments for
More than three decades—left us to devote
Your talents to the welfare of this city.
If not for you our town would not be what
It is today. Nor, like the city, would
The Trust have prospered as it has. I'm glad
To hear you call it sound, for yesterday
Moved by this festive occasion, we resolved
In token of our high esteem, as proof
That in our hearts we somehow still regard you
As one of us, to offer you the major share
Of stock in Sheet's shipyard for twenty thousand
Dollars, or less than half its value.
(*He lays the packet of stocks on the bar*)

DOGSBOROUGH

I

Don't understand.

BUTCHER

Quite frankly, Dogsborough
The Cauliflower Trust is not reputed
For tenderness of heart, but yesterday
After we'd made our . . . well, our
Stupid request about the loan, and heard
Your answer, honest, incorruptible
Old Dogsborough to a hair, a few of us—
It's not an easy thing to say—were close
To tears. Yes, one man said—don't interrupt
Me, Flake, I won't say who.—"Good God"
He said, "the man has saved us from ourselves."
For some time none of us could speak. Then this
Suggestion popped up of its own accord.

DOGSBOROUGH

I've heard you, friends. But what is there behind it?

BUTCHER

What should there be behind it? It's an offer.

FLAKE

And one that we are really pleased to make.
For here you stand behind your bar, a tower
Of strength, a sterling name, the model of
An upright citizen. We find you washing
Glasses, but you have cleansed our souls as well.
And yet you're poorer than your poorest guest.
It wrings our hearts.

DOGSBOROUGH

I don't know what to say.

BUTCHER

Don't say a word. Just take this little package.
An honest man can use it, don't you think?
By golly, it's not often that the gravy train
Travels the straight and narrow. Take your boy here:
I know a good name's better than a bank
Account, and yet I'm sure he won't despise it.
Just take the stuff and let us hope you won't
Read us the riot act for *this!*

DOGSBOROUGH

Sheet's shipyard!

FLAKE

Look, you can see it from right here.

DOGSBOROUGH (*at the window*)

I've seen it

For twenty years.

FLAKE

We thought of that.

DOGSBOROUGH

And what is

Sheet going to do?

FLAKE

He's moving into beer.

BUTCHER

Okay?

DOGSBOROUGH
     I certainly appreciate
Your oldtime sentiments, but no one gives
Away a shipyard for a song.
FLAKE
                     There's something
In that. But now the loan has fallen through
Maybe the twenty thousand will come in handy.
BUTCHER
And possibly right now we're not too eager
To throw our stock upon the open market . . .
DOGSBOROUGH
That sounds more like it. Not a bad deal if
It's got no strings attached.
FLAKE
              None whatsoever.
DOGSBOROUGH
The price you say is twenty thousand?
FLAKE
                      Is it too much?
DOGSBOROUGH
No. And imagine, it's the selfsame shipyard
Where years ago I opened my first lunchroom.
As long as there's no nigger in the woodpile . . .
You've really given up the loan?
FLAKE
               Completely.
DOGSBOROUGH
I might consider it. Hey, look here, son
It's just the thing for you. I thought you fellows
Were down on me and here you make this offer.
You see, my boy, that honesty sometimes
Pays off. It's like you say: When I pass on
The youngster won't inherit much more than
My name, and these old eyes have seen what evil
Can spring from penury.
BUTCHER
             We'll feel much better
If you accept. The ugly aftertaste

Left by our foolish proposition would be
Dispelled. In future we could benefit
By your advice. You'd show us how to tide
The slump by honest means, because our business
Would be your business, Dogsborough, because
You too would be a cauliflower man
And want the Cauliflower Trust to win.
(*Dogsborough takes his hand*)

DOGSBOROUGH
Butcher and Flake, I'm in.

YOUNG DOGSBOROUGH

My father's in.

(*A sign appears*)

3

Bookmaker's office on 122nd Street. Arturo Ui and his lieuten-
ant Ernesto Roma, accompanied by bodyguards, are listening
to the racing news on the radio. Next to Roma is Dockdaisy.

ROMA
I wish, Arturo, you could cure yourself
Of this black melancholy, this inactive
Dreaming. The whole town's talking.

UI (*bitterly*)

Talking? Who's talking?
Nobody talks about me any more.
This city's got no memory. Short-lived
Is fame in such a place. Two months without
A murder and a man's forgotten.
(*He whisks through the newspapers*)

When
The rod falls silent, silence strikes the press.
Even when I deliver murders by the
Dozen, I'm never sure they'll print them.

It's not accomplishment that counts; it's
Influence, which in turn depends on my
Bank balance. Things have come to such a pass
I sometimes think of chucking the whole business.

ROMA

The boys are chafing too from lack of cash.
Morale is low. This inactivity's
No good for them. A man with nothing but
The ace of spades to shoot at goes to seed.
I feel so sorry for those boys, Arturo
I hate to show my face at headquarters. When
They look at me, my "tomorrow we'll see action"
Sticks in my throat. Your vegetable idea was
So promising. Why don't we start right in?

UI

Not now. Not from the bottom. It's too soon.

ROMA

"Too soon" is good. For four months now—
Remember?—since the Cauliflower Trust
Gave you the brush-off, you've been idly brooding.
Plans! Plans! Half-hearted feelers! That rebuff
Frizzled your spine. And then that little mishap—
Those cops at Harper's Bank—you've never gotten
Over it.

UI

      But they fired!

ROMA

                      Only in
The air. That was illegal.

UI

                 Still too close
For me. I'd be in stir if they had plugged
My only witness. And that judge! Not two
Cents worth of sympathy.

ROMA

                   The cops won't shoot
For grocery stores. They shoot for banks. Look here
Arturo, we'll start on Eleventh Street
Smash a few windows, wreck the furniture

Pour kerosene on the veg. And then we work
Our way to Seventh. Two or three days later
Giri, a posy in his buttonhole
Drops in and offers our protection for
A suitable percentage on their sales.

UI

No. First I need protection for myself
From cops and judges. Then I'll start to think
About protecting other people. We've
Got to start from the top. (*Gloomily*) Until I've put the
Judge in my pocket by slipping something
Of mine in his, the law's against me. I
Can't even rob a bank without some two-bit cop
Shooting me dead.

ROMA

You're right. Our only hope is
Givola's plan. He's got a nose for smells
And if he says the Cauliflower Trust
Smells promisingly rotten, I believe
There's something in it. And there *was* some talk
When, as they say, on Dogsborough's recommendation
The city made that loan. Since then I've heard
Rumors about some docks that aren't being built
But ought to be. Yet on the other hand
Dogsborough recommended it. Why should
That do-good peg for fishy business? Here comes
Ragg of the *Star*. If anybody knows
About such things, it's him. Hi Ted.

RAGG (*slightly drunk*)

Hi, boys!
Hi, Roma! Hi, Arturo! How are things in
Capua?

UI

What's he saying?

RAGG

Oh, nothing much.
That was a one-horse town where long ago
An army went to pot from idleness
And easy living.

UI
> Go to hell!

ROMA (*to Ragg*)
> No fighting.

Tell us about that loan the Cauliflower
Trust wangled.

RAGG
> What do you care? Say! Could you

Be going into vegetables? I've got it!
You're angling for a loan yourselves. See Dogsborough.
He'll put it through. (*Imitating the old man*) "Can we allow
    a business
Basically sound but momentarily
Threatened with blight, to perish?" Not an eye
At city hall but fills with tears. Deep feeling
For cauliflower shakes the council members
As though it were a portion of themselves.
Too bad, Arturo, guns call forth no tears.
(*The other customers laugh*)

ROMA
Don't bug him, Ted. He's out of sorts.

RAGG
> I shouldn't

Wonder. I hear that Givola has been
To see Capone for a job.

DOCKDAISY
> You liar!

You leave Giuseppe out of this!

RAGG
> Hi, Dockdaisy!

Still got your place in Shorty Givola's harem?
(*Introducing her*)
Fourth super in the harem of the third
Lieutenant of a (*points to Ui*) fast-declining star
Of second magnitude! Oh, bitter fate!

DOCKDAISY
Somebody shut the rotten bastard up!

RAGG
Posterity plaits no laurels for the gangster!

New heroes captivate the fickle crowd.
Yesterday's hero has been long forgotten
His mug-shot gathers dust in ancient files.
"Don't you remember, folks, the wounds I gave you?"—
"When?"—"Once upon a time."—"Those wounds have turned
To scars long since." Alas, the finest scars
Get lost with those who bear them.—"Can it be
That in a world where good deeds go unnoticed
No monument remains to evil ones?"—
"Yes, so it is."—"Oh, lousy world!"

UI (*bellows*)

                          Shut
Him up!
(*The bodyguards approach Ragg*)

RAGG (*turning pale*)
          Be careful, Ui. Don't insult
The press.
(*The other customers have risen to their feet in alarm*)

ROMA
            You'd better beat it, Ted. You've said
Too much already.

RAGG (*backing out, now very much afraid*)
                See you later, boys.
(*The room empties quickly*)

ROMA
Your nerves are shot, Arturo.

UI
                  Those bastards
Treat me like dirt.

ROMA
              Because of your long silence.
No other reason.

UI (*gloomily*)
           Say, what's keeping Giri
And that accountant from the Cauliflower
Trust?

ROMA
     They were due at three.

UI

       And Givola?
What's this I hear about him seeing Capone?

ROMA

 Nothing at all. He's in his flower shop
 Minding his business, and Capone comes in
 To buy some wreaths.

UI

      Some wreaths? For who?

ROMA

           Not us.

UI

 I'm not so sure.

ROMA

    You're seeing things too black.
 Nobody's interested in us.

UI

     Exactly.
 They've more respect for dirt. Take Givola.
 One setback and he blows. By God
 I'll settle his account when things look up.

ROMA

 Giri!
 (*Enter Emanuele Giri with a rundown individual, Bowl*)

GIRI

 I've got him, boss.

ROMA (*to Bowl*)

     They tell me you
 Are Sheet's accountant at the Cauliflower
 Trust.

BOWL

   Was. Until last week that bastard . . .

GIRI

 He hates the very smell of cauliflower.

BOWL

 Dogsborough . . .

UI (*quickly*)

    Dogsborough! What about him?

ROMA
What have you got to do with Dogsborough?
GIRI
That's why I brought him.
BOWL

Dogsborough
Fired me.
ROMA
Fired you? From Sheet's shipyard?
BOWL
No, from his own. He took it over on
September first.
GIRI

Sheet's shipyard
Belongs to Dogsborough. Bowl here was present
When Butcher of the Cauliflower Trust
Handed him fifty-one percent of the stock.
UI
So what?
BOWL
So what? It's scandalous . . .
GIRI

Don't you
Get it, boss?
BOWL
. . . Dogsborough sponsoring that
Loan to the Cauliflower Trust . . .
GIRI
. . . when he
Himself was secretly a member of
The Cauliflower Trust.
UI (*who is beginning to see the light*)
Say, that's corrupt.
By God, the old man hasn't kept his nose
Too clean.
BOWL
The loan was to the Cauliflower

Trust, but they did it through the shipyard. Through
Me. And I signed for Dogsborough. Not for Sheet
As people thought.

GIRI

By golly, it's a killer.
Old Dogsborough. The trusty and reliable
Signboard. So honest. So responsible!
Whose handshake was an honor and a pledge!
The staunch and incorruptible old man!

BOWL

I'll make the bastard pay. Can you imagine?
Firing me for embezzlement when he himself . . .

ROMA

Cool it! You're not the only one whose blood
Boils at such abject villainy. What do
You say, Arturo?

UI (*referring to Bowl*)

Will he testify?

GIRI

He'll testify.

UI (*grandly getting ready to leave*)

Keep an eye on him, boys. Let's go
Roma. I smell an opening.
(*He goes out quickly, followed by Ernesto Roma and the
bodyguards*)

GIRI (*slaps Bowl on the back*)

Bowl, I
Believe you've set a wheel in motion, which . . .

BOWL

I hope you'll pay me back for any loss . . .

GIRI

Don't worry about that. I know the boss.

(*A sign appears*)

4

Dogsborough's country house. Dogsborough and his son.

DOGSBOROUGH

I should never have accepted this estate.
Taking that package as a kind of gift was
Beyond reproach.

YOUNG DOGSBOROUGH

Of course it was.

DOGSBOROUGH

And sponsoring
That loan, when I discovered to my own
Detriment that a thriving line of business
Was languishing for lack of funds, was hardly
Dishonest. But when, confident the shipyard
Would yield a handsome profit, I accepted
This house before I moved the loan, so secretly
Acting in my own interest—that was wrong.

YOUNG DOGSBOROUGH

Yes, father.

DOGSBOROUGH

That was faulty judgment
Or might be so regarded. Yes, my boy
I should never have accepted this estate.

YOUNG DOGSBOROUGH

No.

DOGSBOROUGH

We've stepped into a trap.

YOUNG DOGSBOROUGH

Yes, father.

DOGSBOROUGH

That
Package of stocks was like the salty tidbit
They serve free gratis at the bar to make
The customer, appeasing his cheap hunger

Work up a raging thirst.
(*Pause*)
                              That inquiry
At city hall about the docks, has got
Me down. The loan's used up. Clark helped
Himself; so did Caruther, Flake, and Butcher
And so, I'm sad to say, did I. And no
Cement's been bought yet, not a pound! The one
Good thing is this: at Sheet's request I kept
The deal a secret; no one knows of my
Connection with the shipyard.

A BUTLER (*enters*)
                              Telephone
Sir, Mr. Butcher of the Cauliflower
Trust.

DOGSBOROUGH
        Take it, son.
(*Young Dogsborough goes out with the butler. Church bells
are heard in the distance*)

DOGSBOROUGH
                    Now what can Butcher want?
(*Looking out the window*)
Those poplars are what tempted me to take
The place. The poplars and the lake down there, like
Silver before it's minted into dollars.
And air that's free of beer fumes. The fir trees
Are good to look at too, especially
The tops. Gray-green and dusty. And the trunks—
Their color calls to mind the leathers that we used to wrap
    around
The taps when drawing beer. It was the poplars, though
That turned the trick. Ah yes, the poplars.
It's Sunday. Hm. The bells would sound so peaceful
If the world were not so full of wickedness.
But what can Butcher want on Sunday?
I should never have . . .

YOUNG DOGSBOROUGH (*returning*)
                              Father, Butcher says
Last night the city council voted to

Investigate the Cauliflower Trust's
Projected docks. Father, what's wrong?

DOGSBOROUGH

My smelling salts!

YOUNG DOGSBOROUGH (*gives them to him*)
Here.

DOGSBOROUGH

What does Butcher want?

YOUNG DOGSBOROUGH

He wants to come here.

DOGSBOROUGH

Here? I refuse to see him. I'm not well.
My heart. (*He stands up. Grandly*) I haven't anything to do
With this affair. For sixty years I've trodden
The narrow path, as everybody knows.
They can't involve me in their schemes.

YOUNG DOGSBOROUGH

No, father.

Do you feel better now?

THE BUTLER (*enters*)

A Mr. Ui.

Desires to see you, sir.

DOGSBOROUGH

The gangster!

THE BUTLER

Yes

I've seen his picture in the papers. Says he
Was sent by Mr. Clark of the Cauliflower
Trust.

DOGSBOROUGH

Throw him out! Who sent him? Clark? Good God!
Is he threatening me with gangsters now? I'll . . .
(*Enter Arturo Ui and Ernesto Roma*)

UI

Mr.

Dogsborough.

DOGSBOROUGH

Get out!

ROMA

> I wouldn't be in such
A hurry, friend. It's Sunday. Take it easy.

DOGSBOROUGH

> Get out, I said!

YOUNG DOGSBOROUGH

> My father says: Get out!

ROMA

> Saying it twice won't make it any smarter.

UI (*unruffled*)

> Mr. Dogsborough.

DOGSBOROUGH

> Where are the servants? Call the
Police.

ROMA

> I wouldn't leave the room if I
Were you, son. In the hallway you might run
Into some boys who wouldn't understand.

DOGSBOROUGH

> Ho! Violence!

ROMA

> I wouldn't call it that.
Only a little emphasis perhaps.

UI

> Mr. Dogsborough. I am well aware that you
Don't know me, or even worse, you know me but
Only from hearsay. Mr. Dogsborough
I have been very much maligned, my image
Blackened by envy, my intentions disfigured
By baseness. When about fourteen years ago
Yours truly, then a modest, unemployed
Son of the Bronx, appeared within the gates
Of this your city to launch a new career
Which, I may say, has not been utterly
Inglorious, my only followers
Were seven youngsters, penniless like myself
But brave and like myself determined
To cut their chunk of meat from every cow
The Lord created. I've got thirty now

And will have more. But now you're wondering: What does
Arturo Ui want of me? Not much. Just this.
What irks me is to be misunderstood
To be regarded as a fly-by-night
Adventurer and heaven knows what else.
(*Clears his throat*)
Especially by the police, for I
Esteem them and I'd welcome their esteem.
And so I've come to ask you—and believe me
Asking's not easy for my kind of man—
To put a word in for me with the precinct
When necessary.

DOGSBOROUGH (*incredulously*)
                    Vouch for you, you mean?

UI

If necessary. That depends on whether
We strike a friendly understanding with
The vegetable dealers.

DOGSBOROUGH
                    What is your
Connection with the vegetable trade?

UI

That's what I'm coming to. The vegetable
Trade needs protection. By force if necessary.
And I'm determined to supply it.

DOGSBOROUGH
                    No
One's threatening it as far as I can see.

UI

Maybe not. Not yet. But I see further. And
I ask you: How long with our corrupt police
Force will the vegetable dealer be allowed
To sell his vegetables in peace? A ruthless
Hand may destroy his little shop tomorrow
And make off with his cash-box. Would he not
Prefer at little cost to arm himself
Before the trouble starts, with powerful protection?

DOGSBOROUGH
I doubt it.

UI
>   That would mean he doesn't know
> What's good for him. Quite possible. The small
> Vegetable dealer, honest but shortsighted
> Hard-working but too often unaware
> Of his best interest, needs strong leadership.
> Moreover, toward the Cauliflower Trust
> That gave him everything he has, he feels
> No sense of responsibility. That's where I
> Come in again. The Cauliflower Trust
> Must likewise be protected. Down with the welshers!
> Pay up, say I, or close your shop! The weak
> Will perish. Let them, that's the law of nature.
> In short the Trust requires my services.

DOGSBOROUGH
> But what's the Cauliflower Trust to me?
> Why come to me with this amazing plan?

UI
> We'll get to that. I'll tell you what you need.
> The Cauliflower Trust needs muscle, thirty
> Determined men under my leadership.

DOGSBOROUGH
> Whether the Trust would want to change its typewriters
> For tommy-guns I have no way of knowing.
> You see, I'm not connected with the Trust.

UI
> We'll get to that. You say: With thirty men
> Armed to the teeth, at home on our premises
> How do we know that we ourselves are safe?
> The answer's very simple. He who holds
> The purse strings holds the power. And it's you
> Who hand out the pay envelopes. How could
> I turn against you even if I wanted
> Even without the high esteem I bear you?
> For what do I amount to? What
> Following have I got? A handful. And some
> Are dropping out. Right now it's twenty. Or less.
> Without your help I'm finished. It's your duty
> Your human duty to protect me from

My enemies, and (I may as well be frank)
My followers too! The work of fourteen years
Hangs in the balance! I appeal to you
As man to man.

DOGSBOROUGH

As man to man I'll tell
You what I'll do. I'm calling the police.

UI

What? The police?

DOGSBOROUGH

Exactly, the police!

UI

Am I to understand that you refuse
To help me as a man? (*Bellows*) Then I demand
It of you as a criminal. Because
That's what you are! I'm going to expose you!
I've got the proofs! There's going to be a scandal
About some docks. And you're mixed up in it! Sheet's
Shipyard—that's you. I'm warning you! Don't
Push me too far! They've voted to investigate!

DOGSBOROUGH (*very pale*)

They never will. They can't. My friends . . .

UI

You haven't got any. You had some yesterday.
Today you haven't got a single friend
Tomorrow you'll have nothing but enemies.
If anybody can rescue you, it's me
Arturo Ui! Me! Me!

DOGSBOROUGH

Nobody's going to
Investigate. My hair is white.

UI

But nothing else
Is white about you, Dogsborough.
(*Tries to seize his hand*)
Think, man! It's now or never! Let me save you!
One word from you and any bastard who
Touches a hair of yon white head, I'll drill him!
Dogsborough, help me now. I beg you. Once!

Just once! Oh, say the word, or I shall never
Be able to face my boys again.
(*He weeps*)

DOGSBOROUGH

                     Never!
I'd sooner die than get mixed up with you!

UI

I'm washed up and I know it. Forty
And still a nobody. You've got to help me.

DOGSBOROUGH

Never.

UI

        I'm warning you. I'll crush you.

DOGSBOROUGH

                    Never.
Never while I draw breath will you get away with
Your greengoods racket!

UI (*with dignity*)

               Mr. Dogsborough
I'm only forty. You are eighty. With God's
Help I'll outlast you. And one thing I know:
I'll break into the greengoods business yet!

DOGSBOROUGH

Never!

UI

       Come, Roma. Let's get out of here.
(*He makes a formal bow and leaves the room with Ernesto Roma*)

DOGSBOROUGH

Air! Give me air. Oh, what a mug!
Oh, what a mug! I should never have accepted
This country house. But they won't dare. I'm sunk
If they investigate, but they won't dare.

THE BUTLER (*enters*)

Goodwill and Gaffles of the city council.
(*Enter Goodwill and Gaffles*)

GOODWILL

Hello, Dogsborough!

DOGSBOROUGH

Hello, Goodwill and Gaffles!
Anything new?

GOODWILL

Plenty, and not so good, I fear.
But wasn't that Arturo Ui who
Just passed us in the hall?

DOGSBOROUGH (*with a forced laugh*)

Himself in person.
Hardly an ornament to a country home.

GOODWILL

No.
Hardly an ornament. It's no good wind
That brings us. It's that loan we made to the Trust
To build their docks with.

DOGSBOROUGH (*stiffly*)

What about the loan?

GAFFLES

Well, certain council members said—don't get
Upset—the thing looked kind of fishy.

DOGSBOROUGH

Fishy.

GOODWILL

Don't worry! The majority flew off
The handle. Fishy! We almost came to blows.

GAFFLES

Dogsborough's contracts fishy! they shouted. What
About the Bible? Is that fishy too?
It almost turned to an ovation for you
Dogsborough. When your friends demanded an
Investigation, some, infected with
Our confidence, withdrew their motion and
Wanted to shelve the whole affair. But the
Majority, resolved to clear your name
Of every vestige of suspicion, shouted:
Dogsborough's more than a name. It stands for more than
A man. It's an institution! In an uproar
They voted the investigation.

DOGSBOROUGH
                              The
  Investigation.
GOODWILL
                    O'Casey is in charge.
  The cauliflower people merely say
  The loan was made directly to Sheet's shipyard.
  The contracts with the builders were to be
  Negotiated by Sheet's shipyard.
DOGSBOROUGH
                              By Sheet's shipyard.

GOODWILL
  The best would be for you to send a man
  Of flawless reputation and impartiality
  Someone you trust, to throw some light on this
  Unholy rat's nest.
DOGSBOROUGH
                    So I will.
GAFFLES
                         All right
  That settles it. And now suppose you show us
  This famous country house of yours. We'll want
  To tell our friends about it.
DOGSBOROUGH
                         Very well.

GOODWILL
  What blessed peace! And church bells! All one can
  Wish for.
GAFFLES (*laughing*)
                No docks in sight.
DOGSBOROUGH
                         I'll send a man.
  (*They go out slowly*)

  (*A sign appears*)

5

City Hall. Butcher, Flake, Clark, Mulberry, Caruther. Across from them Dogsborough, who is as white as a sheet, O'Casey, Gaffles, and Goodwill. Reporters.

BUTCHER (*in an undertone*)
    He's late.

MULBERRY
               He's bringing Sheet. Quite possibly
    They haven't come to an agreement. I
    Believe they've been discussing it all night.
    Sheet *has* to say the shipyard still belongs
    To him.

CARUTHER
             It's asking quite a lot of Sheet
    To come here just to tell us *he's* the scoundrel.

FLAKE
    He'll never come.

CLARK
              He's got to.

FLAKE
                     Why should he
    Ask to be sent to prison for five years?

CLARK
    It's quite a pile of dough. And Mabel Sheet
    Needs luxury. He's still head over heels
    In love with Mabel. He'll play ball all right.
    And anyway he'll never serve his term.
    Old Dogsborough will see to that.
    (*The shouts of newsboys are heard. A reporter brings in a paper*)

GAFFLES
    Sheet's been found dead. In his hotel. A ticket
    To San Francisco in his pocket.

BUTCHER

Sheet

Dead?

O'CASEY (*reading*)

Murdered.

MULBERRY

My God!

FLAKE (*in an undertone*)

He didn't come.

GAFFLES

What is it, Dogsborough?

DOGSBOROUGH (*speaking with difficulty*)

Nothing. It'll pass.

O'CASEY

Sheet's death . . .

CLARK

Poor Sheet. His unexpected death

Would seem to puncture your investigation . . .

O'CASEY

Of course the unexpected often looks
As if it were expected. Some indeed
Expect the unexpected. Such is life.
This leaves me in a pretty pickle and
I hope you won't refer me and my questions
To Sheet, for Sheet, according to this paper
Has been most silent since last night.

MULBERRY

Your questions?

You know the loan was given to the shipyard
Don't you?

O'CASEY

Correct. But there remains a question:

Who is the shipyard?

FLAKE (*under his breath*)

Funny question! He's

Got something up his sleeve.

CLARK (*likewise*)

I wonder what.

O'CASEY

Something wrong, Dogsborough? Could it be the air?
(*To the others*)
I only mean: some people may be thinking
That several shovelsful of earth are not
Enough to load on Sheet and certain muck
Might just as well be added. I suspect . . .

CLARK

Maybe you'd better not suspect too much
O'Casey. Ever hear of slander? We've
Got laws against it.

MULBERRY

What's the point of these
Insinuations? Dogsborough, they tell me
Has picked a man to clear this business up.
Let's wait until he comes.

O'CASEY

He's late. And when
He comes, I hope Sheet's not the only thing
He'll talk about.

FLAKE

We hope he'll tell the truth
No more no less.

O'CASEY

You mean the man is honest?
That suits me fine. Since Sheet was still alive
Last night, the whole thing should be clear. I only
(*To Dogsborough*)
Hope that you've chosen a good man.

CLARK (*cuttingly*)

You'll have
To take him as he is. Ah, here he comes.
(*Enter Arturo Ui and Ernesto Roma with bodyguards*)

UI

Hi, Clark! Hi, Dogsborough! Hi, everybody!

CLARK

Hi, Ui.

UI

Well, it seems you've got some questions.

O'CASEY (*to Dogsborough*)
  Is this your man?
CLARK
                    That's right. Not good enough?
GOODWILL
  Dogsborough, can you be . . . ?
  (*Commotion among the reporters*)
O'CASEY
                              Quiet over there!
A REPORTER
  It's Ui!
  (*Laughter. O'Casey bangs his gavel for order. Then he musters the bodyguards*)
O'CASEY
        Who are these men?
UI
                          Friends.
O'CASEY (*to Roma*)
                              And who
  Are you?
UI
          Ernesto Roma, my accountant.
GAFFLES
  Hold it! Can you be serious, Dogsborough?
  (*Dogsborough is silent*)
O'CASEY
                                  Mr.
  Ui, we gather from Mr. Dogsborough's
  Eloquent silence that you have his confidence
  And desire ours. Well then. Where are the contracts?
UI
  What contracts?
CLARK (*seeing that O'Casey is looking at Goodwill*)
                    The contracts that the shipyard no doubt
  Signed with the builders with a view to enlarging
  Its dock facilities.
UI
            I never heard
  Of any contracts.

O'CASEY
                    Really?

CLARK
                            Do you mean
    There are no contracts?

O'CASEY (*quickly*)
                        Did you talk with Sheet?

UI (*shaking his head*)
    No.

CLARK
        Oh. You didn't talk with Sheet?

UI (*angrily*)
                                    If any-
    One says I talked with Sheet, that man's a liar.

O'CASEY
    Ui, I thought that Mr. Dogsborough
    Had asked you to look into this affair?

UI
    I have looked into it.

O'CASEY
                        And have your studies
    Borne fruit?

UI
                    They have. It wasn't easy to
    Lay bare the truth. And it's not a pleasant truth.
    When Mr. Dogsborough, in the interest of
    This city, asked me to investigate
    Where certain city funds, the hard-earned savings
    Of taxpayers like you and me, entrusted
    To a certain shipyard in this city, had gone to
    I soon discovered to my consternation
    That they had been embezzled. That's Point One.
    Point Two is who embezzled them. All right
    I'll answer that one too. The guilty party
    Much as it pains me, is . . .

O'CASEY
                        Well, who is it?

UI
                                    Sheet.

O'CASEY
Oh, Sheet! The silent Sheet you didn't talk to!

UI
Why look at me like that? The guilty party
Is Sheet.

CLARK
              Sheet's dead. Didn't you know?

UI
                                                    What, dead?
I was in Cicero last night. That's why
I haven't heard. And Roma here was with me.
(*Pause*)

ROMA
That's mighty funny. Do you think it's mere
Coincidence that . . .

UI
                        Gentlemen, it's not
An accident. Sheet's suicide was plainly
The consequence of Sheet's embezzlement.
It's monstrous!

O'CASEY
              Except it wasn't suicide.

UI
What then? Of course Ernesto here and I
Were in Cicero last night. We wouldn't know.
But this we know beyond a doubt: that Sheet
Apparently an honest business man
Was just a gangster.

O'CASEY
                        Ui, I get your drift.
You can't find words too damaging for Sheet
After the damage he incurred last night.
Well, Dogsborough, let's get to you.

DOGSBOROUGH
                                    To me?

BUTCHER (*cuttingly*)
What about Dogsborough?

O'CASEY

As I understand Mr.
Ui—and I believe I understand
Him very well—there was a shipyard which
Borrowed some money which has disappeared.
But now the question rises: Who is this
Shipyard? It's Sheet, you say. But what's a name?
What interests us right now is not its name
But whom it actually belonged to. Did it
Belong to Sheet? Unquestionably Sheet
Could tell us. But Sheet has buttoned up
About his property since Ui spent
The night in Cicero. But could it be
That when this swindle was put over someone
Else was the owner. What is your opinion
Dogsborough?

DOGSBOROUGH

Me?

O'CASEY

Yes, could it be that you
Were sitting in Sheet's office when a contract
Was . . . well, suppose we say, not being drawn up?

GOODWILL

O'Casey!

GAFFLES (*to O'Casey*)

Dogsborough? You're crazy!

DOGSBOROUGH

I . . .

O'CASEY

And earlier, at city hall, when you
Told us how hard a time the cauliflower
People were having and how badly they
Needed a loan—could that have been the voice
Of personal involvement?

BUTCHER

Have you no shame?
The man's unwell.

CARUTHER
                    Consider his great age!
FLAKE
  His snow-white hair confounds your low suspicions.
ROMA
  Where are your proofs?
O'CASEY
                    The proofs are . . .
UI
                                        Quiet, please!
  Let's have a little quiet, friends!
GAFFLES (*in a loud voice*)
                            For God's sake
  Say something, Dogsborough!
A BODYGUARD (*suddenly roars*)
                            The chief wants quiet!
  Quiet!
  (*Sudden silence*)
UI
        If I may say what moves me in
  This hour and at this shameful sight—a white-
  Haired man insulted while his friends look on
  In silence—it is this: I trust you, Mr.
  Dogsborough. And I ask: Is this the face
  Of guilt? Is this the eye of one who follows
  Devious ways? Can you no longer
  Distinguish white from black? A pretty pass
  If things have come to such a pass!
CLARK
                            A man of
  Untarnished reputation is accused
  Of bribery!
O'CASEY
                    And more: of fraud. For I
  Contend that this unholy shipyard, so
  Maligned when Sheet was thought to be the owner
  Belonged to Dogsborough at the time the loan
  Went through.

MULBERRY
>A filthy lie!

CARUTHER
>I'll stake my head
For Dogsborough. Summon the population!
I challenge you to find one man to doubt him.

A REPORTER (*to another who has come in*)
Dogsborough's under suspicion!

THE OTHER REPORTER
>Dogsborough?
Why not Abe Lincoln?

MULBERRY AND FLAKE
>Witnesses!

O'CASEY
>Oh
It's witnesses you want? Hey, Smith, where *is*
Our witness? Is he here? I see he is.
(*One of his men has stepped into the doorway and made a
sign. All look toward the door. Short pause. Then a burst of
shots and noise are heard. Tumult. The reporters run out*)

THE REPORTERS It's outside. A machine-gun.—What's your
witness's name, O'Casey?—Bad business.—Hi, Ui.

O'CASEY (*going to the door*) Bowl! (*Shouts out the door*)
Come on in!

THE MEN OF THE CAULIFLOWER TRUST What's going on?—
Somebody's been shot.—On the stairs.—God damn it!

BUTCHER (*to Ui*)
More monkey business? Ui, it's all over
Between us if . . .

UI
>Yes?

O'CASEY
>Bring him in!
(*Policemen carry in a corpse*)

O'CASEY
It's Bowl. My witness, gentlemen, I fear
Is not in a fit state for questioning.
(*He goes out quickly. The policemen have set down Bowl's
body in a corner*)

DOGSBOROUGH
For God's sake, Gaffles, get me out of here!
(*Without answering Gaffles goes out past him*)
UI (*Going toward Dogsborough with outstretched hand*)
Congratulations, Dogsborough. Don't doubt
One way or another, I'll get things straightened out.

(*A sign appears*)

6

Mammoth Hotel. Ui's suite. Two bodyguards lead a ragged actor to Ui. In the background Givola.

FIRST BODYGUARD   It's an actor, boss. Unarmed.

SECOND BODYGUARD   He can't afford a rod. He was able to get tight because they pay him to declaim in the saloons when they're tight. But I'm told that he's good. He's one of them classical guys.

UI   Okay. Here's the problem. I've been given to understand that my pronunciation leaves something to be desired. It looks like I'm going to have to say a word or two on certain occasions, especially when I get into politics, so I've decided to take lessons. The gestures too.

THE ACTOR   Very well.

UI   Get the mirror.

(*A bodyguard comes front stage with a large standing mirror*)

UI   First the walk. How do you guys walk in the theater or the opera?

THE ACTOR   I see what you mean. The grand style. Julius Caesar, Hamlet, Romeo—that's Shakespeare. Mr. Ui, you've come to the right man. Old Mahonney can teach you the classical manner in ten minutes. Gentlemen, you see before you a tragic figure. Ruined by Shakespeare. An English poet.

If it weren't for Shakespeare, I could be on Broadway right
now. The tragedy of a character. "Don't play Shakespeare
when you're playing Ibsen, Mahonney! Look at the calendar! This is 1912, sir!"—"Art knows no calendar, sir!" say
I. "And art is my life." Alas.

GIVOLA   I think you've got the wrong guy, boss. He's out of
date.

UI   We'll see about that. Walk around like they do in this
Shakespeare.
(*The actor walks around*)

UI   Good!

GIVOLA   You can't walk like that in front of cauliflower men.
It ain't natural.

UI   What do you mean it ain't natural? Nobody's natural in
this day and age. When I walk I want people to know I'm
walking. (*He copies the actor's gait*)

THE ACTOR   Head back. (*Ui throws his head back*) The foot
touches the ground toe first. (*Ui's foot touches the ground
toe first*) Good. Excellent. You have a natural gift. Only the
arms. They're not quite right. Stiff. Perhaps if you joined
your arms in front of your private parts. (*Ui joins his arms
in front of his private parts*) Not bad. Relaxed but firm. But
head back. Good. Just the right gait for your purposes, I believe, Mr. Ui. What else do you wish to learn?

UI   How to stand. In front of people.

GIVOLA   Have two big bruisers right behind you and you'll be
standing pretty.

UI   That's the bunk. When I stand I don't want people looking at the two bozoes behind me. I want them looking at me.
Correct me! (*He takes a stance, his arms crossed over his
chest*)

THE ACTOR   A possible solution. But common. You don't want
to look like a barber, Mr. Ui. Fold your arms like this. (*He
folds his arms in such a way that the backs of his hands remain visible. His palms are resting on his arms not far from
the shoulder*) A trifling change, but the difference is incalculable. Draw the comparison in the mirror, Mr. Ui.
(*Ui tries out the new position before the mirror*)

UI   Not bad.

GIVOLA

           What's all this for, boss? Just for those
Fancy-pants in the Trust?

UI

                  Hell, no! It's for
The little people. Why, for instance, do
You think this Clark makes such a show of grandeur?
Not for his peers. His bank account
Takes care of them, the same as my big bruisers
Lend me prestige in certain situations.
Clark makes a show of grandeur to impress
The little man. I mean to do the same.

GIVOLA

But some will say it doesn't look inborn.
Some people stick at that.

UI

                I know they do.
But I'm not trying to convince professors
And smart alecks. My object is the little
Man's image of his master.

GIVOLA

               Don't overdo
The master, boss. Better the democrat
The friendly, reassuring type in shirtsleeves.

UI

I've got old Dogsborough for that.

GIVOLA

                 His image
Is kind of tarnished, I should say. He's still
An asset on the books, a venerable
Antique. But people aren't as eager as they
Were to exhibit him. They're not so sure
He's genuine. It's like the family Bible
Nobody opens any more since, piously
Turning the yellowed pages with a group
Of friends, they found a dried-out bedbug. But
Maybe he's good enough for Cauliflower.

UI

I decide who's respectable.

GIVOLA

Sure thing, boss.
There's nothing wrong with Dogsborough. We can
Still use him. They haven't even dropped him
At city hall. The crash would be too loud.

UI   Sitting.

THE ACTOR   Sitting. Sitting is almost the hardest, Mr. Ui. There
are men who can walk; there are men who can stand; but
find me a man who can sit. Take a chair with a backrest,
Mr. Ui. But don't lean against it. Hands on thighs, at right
angles, elbows away from body. How long can you sit like
that, Mr. Ui?

UI   As long as I please.

THE ACTOR   Then everything's perfect, Mr. Ui.

GIVOLA

You know, boss, when old Dogsborough passes on
Giri could take his place. He's got the
Popular touch. He plays the funny man
And laughs so loud in season that the plaster
Comes tumbling from the ceiling. Sometimes, though
He does it out of season, as for instance
When you step forward as the modest son of
The Bronx you really were and talk about
Those seven determined youngsters.

UI

Then he laughs?

GIVOLA

The plaster tumbles from the ceiling. Don't
Tell him I said so or he'll think I've got
It in for him. But maybe you could make
Him stop collecting hats.

UI

What kind of hats?

GIVOLA

The hats of people he's rubbed out. And running
Around with them in public. It's disgusting.

UI

Forget it. I would never think of muzzling
The ox that treads my corn. I overlook

The petty foibles of my underlings.
(*To the actor*)
And now to speaking! Speak a speech for me!
THE ACTOR   Shakespeare. Nothing else. Julius Caesar. The Ro-
man hero. (*He draws a little book from his pocket*) What
do you say to Mark Antony's speech? Over Caesar's body.
Against Brutus. The ringleader of Caesar's assassins. A model
of demagogy. Very famous. I played Antony in Zenith in
1908. Just what you need, Mr. Ui. (*He takes a stance and
recites Mark Antony's speech line for line*)
Friends, Romans, countrymen, lend me your ears!
(*Reading in the little book, Ui speaks the lines after him.
Now and then the actor corrects him, but in the main Ui
keeps his rough staccato delivery*)
THE ACTOR
I come to bury Caesar, not to praise him.
The evil that men do lives after them;
The good is oft interred with their bones;
So let it be with Caesar. The noble Brutus
Hath told you Caesar was ambitious.
If it were so, it was a grievous fault,
And grievously hath Caesar answer'd it.
UI (*continues by himself*)
Here, under leave of Brutus and the rest—
For Brutus is an honorable man;
So are they all, all honorable men—
Come I to speak in Caesar's funeral.
He was my friend, faithful and just to me;
But Brutus says he was ambitious;
And Brutus is an honorable man.
He hath brought many captives home to Rome,
Whose ransoms did the general coffers fill;
Did this in Caesar seem ambitious?
When that the poor have cried, Caesar hath wept;
Ambition should be made of sterner stuff.
Yet Brutus says he was ambitious;
And Brutus is an honorable man.
You all did see that on the Lupercal

I thrice presented him a kingly crown,
Which he did thrice refuse. Was this ambition?
Yet Brutus says he was ambitious;
And sure he is an honorable man.
I speak not to disprove what Brutus spoke,
But here I am to speak what I do know.
You all did love him once, not without cause;
What cause withholds you then, to mourn for him?

(*During the last lines the curtain slowly falls*)

(*A sign appears*)

7

*Offices of the Cauliflower Trust. Arturo Ui, Ernesto Roma,
Giuseppe Givola, Emanuele Giri, and bodyguards. A group of
small vegetable dealers is listening to Ui. Old Dogsborough,
who is ill, is sitting on the platform beside Ui. In the background Clark.*

UI (*bellowing*)
   Murder! Extortion! Highway robbery!
   Machine-guns sputtering on our city streets!
   People going about their business, law-abiding
   Citizens on their way to city hall
   To make a statement, murdered in broad daylight!
   And what, I ask you, do our town fathers do?
   Nothing! These honorable men are much
   Too busy planning their shady little deals
   And slandering respectable citizens
   To think of law enforcement.
GIVOLA
                    Hear!

UI

                                        In short
Chaos is rampant. Because if everybody
Can do exactly what he pleases, if
Dog can eat dog without a second thought
I call it chaos. Look. Suppose I'm sitting
Peacefully in my vegetable store
For instance, or driving my cauliflower truck
And someone comes barging not so peacefully
Into my store: "Hands up!" Or with his gun
Punctures my tires. Under such conditions
Peace is unthinkable. But once I know
The score, once I recognize that men are not
Innocent lambs, then I've got to find a way
To stop these men from smashing up my shop and
Making me, when it suits them, put 'em up
And keep 'em up, when I could use my hands
For better things, for instance, counting pickles.
For such is man. He'll never put aside
His hardware of his own free will, say
For love of virtue, or to earn the praises
Of certain silver tongues at city hall.
If I don't shoot, the other fellow will.
That's logic. Okay. And maybe now you'll ask:
What's to be done? I'll tell you. But first get
This straight: What you've been doing so far is
Disastrous: Sitting idly at your counters
Hoping that everything will be all right
And meanwhile disunited, bickering
Among yourselves, instead of mustering
A strong defense force that would shield you from
The gangsters' depredations. No, I say
This can't go on. The first thing that's needed
Is unity. The second is sacrifices.
What sacrifices? you may ask. Are we
To part with thirty cents on every dollar
For mere protection? No, nothing doing.
Our money is too precious. If protection
Were free of charge, then yes, we'd be all for it.

Well, my dear vegetable dealers, things
Are not so simple. Only death is free:
Everything else costs money. And that includes
Protection, peace and quiet. Life is like
That, and because it never will be any different
These gentlemen and I (there are more outside)
Have resolved to offer you protection.
(*Givola and Roma applaud*)

                                                      But
To show you that we mean to operate
On solid business principles, we've asked
Our partner, Mr. Clark here, the wholesaler
Whom you all know, to come here and address you.
(*Roma pulls Clark forward. A few of the vegetable dealers
applaud*)

GIVOLA

Mr. Clark, I bid you welcome in the name
Of this assembly. Mr. Ui is honored
To see the Cauliflower Trust supporting his
Initiative. I thank you, Mr. Clark.

CLARK

We of the Cauliflower Trust observe
Ladies and gentlemen, with consternation
How hard it's getting for you vegetable
Dealers to sell your wares. "Because" I hear
You say, "they're too expensive." Yes, but why
Are they expensive? It's because our packers
And teamsters, pushed by outside agitators
Want more and more. And that's what Mr. Ui
And Mr. Ui's friends will put an end to.

FIRST DEALER

But if the little man gets less and less
How is he going to buy our vegetables?

UI

Your question is a good one. Here's my answer:
Like it or not, this modern world of ours
Is inconceivable without the working man
If only as a customer. I've always
Insisted that honest work is no disgrace.

Far from it. It's constructive and conducive
To profits. As an individual
The working man has all my sympathy.
It's only when he bands together, when he
Presumes to meddle in affairs beyond
His understanding, such as profits, wages
Etcetera, that I say: Watch your step
Brother, a worker is somebody who works.
But when you strike, when you stop working, then
You're not a worker any more. Then you're
A menace to society. And that's
Where I step in.
(*Clark applauds*)
                          However, to convince you
That everything is open and above
Board, let me call your attention to the presence
Here of a man well known, I trust, to
Everybody here for his sterling honesty
And incorruptible morality.
His name is Dogsborough.
(*The vegetable dealers applaud a little louder*)
                          Mr. Dogsborough
I owe you an incomparable debt
Of gratitude. Our meeting was the work
Of providence. I never will forget—
Not if I live to be a hundred—how
You took me to your arms, an unassuming
Son of the Bronx and chose me for your friend
Nay more, your son.
(*He seizes Dogsborough's limply dangling hand and shakes it*)
GIVOLA (*in an undertone*)
                          How touching! Father and son!
GIRI (*steps forward*)
Well, folks, the boss has spoken for us all.
I see some questions written on your faces.
Ask them! Don't worry. We won't eat you. You
Play square with us and we'll play square with you.
But get this straight: we haven't got much patience
With idle talk, especially the kind

That carps and cavils and finds fault
With everything. You'll find us open, though
To any healthy, positive suggestion
On ways and means of doing what must be done.
So fire away!
(*The vegetable dealers don't breathe a word*)
GIVOLA (*unctuously*)
                    And no holds barred. I think
You know me and my little flower shop.
A BODYGUARD
    Hurrah for Givola!
GIVOLA
                    Okay, then. Do
You want protection? Or would you rather have
Murder, extortion and highway robbery?
FIRST DEALER
    Things have been pretty quiet lately. I
    Haven't had any trouble in my store.
SECOND DEALER
    Nothing's wrong in my place.
THIRD DEALER
                    Nor in mine.
GIVOLA
    That's odd!
SECOND DEALER
                    We've heard that recently in bars
    Things have been happening just like Mr. Ui
    Was telling us, that glasses have been smashed
    And gin poured down the drain in places that
    Refused to cough up for protection. But
    Things have been peaceful in the greengoods business.
    So far at least, thank God.
ROMA
                    And what about
    Sheet's murder? And Bowl's death? Is that
    What you call peaceful?
SECOND DEALER
                    But is that connected
    With cauliflower, Mr. Roma?

ROMA

No. Just a minute.

(*Roma goes over to Ui, who after his big speech has been sitting there exhausted and listless. After a few words he motions to Giri to join them. Givola also takes part in a hurried whispered conversation. Then Giri motions to one of the bodyguards and goes out quickly with him*)

GIVOLA

Friends, I've been asked to tell you that a poor
Unhappy woman wishes to express
Her thanks to Mr. Ui in your presence.

(*He goes to the rear and leads in a heavily madeup and flashily dressed woman—Dockdaisy—who is holding a little girl by the hand. The three stop in front of Ui, who has stood up*)

GIVOLA

Speak, Mrs. Bowl.

(*To the vegetable dealers*)

It's Mrs. Bowl, the young
Widow of Mr. Bowl, the late accountant
Of the Cauliflower Trust, who yesterday
While on his way to city hall to do
His duty, was struck down by hand unknown.
Mrs. Bowl!

DOCKDAISY   Mr. Ui, in my profound bereavement over my husband who was foully murdered while on his way to city hall in the exercise of his civic duty, I wish to express my heartfelt thanks for the flowers you sent me and my little girl, aged six, who has been robbed of her father. (*To the vegetable dealers*) Gentlemen, I'm only a poor widow and all I have to say is that without Mr. Ui I'd be out in the street as I shall gladly testify at any time. My little girl, aged five, and I will never forget it, Mr. Ui.

(*Ui gives Dockdaisy his hand and chucks the child under the chin*)

GIVOLA

Bravo!

(*Giri wearing Bowl's hat cuts through the crowd, followed*

*by several gangsters carrying large gasoline cans. They make
their way to the exit*)

UI

Mrs. Bowl, my sympathies. This lawlessness
This crime wave's got to stop because . . .

GIVOLA (*as the dealers start leaving*)

Hold it!

The meeting isn't over. The next item
Will be a song in memory of poor Bowl
Sung by our friend James Greenwool, followed by
A collection for the widow. He's a baritone.
(*One of the bodyguards steps forward and sings a sentimental song in which the word "home" occurs frequently.
During the performance the gangsters sit rapt, their heads in
their hands, or leaning back with eyes closed, etc. The meager
applause at the end is interrupted by the howling of police
and fire sirens. A red glow is seen in a large window in the
background*)

ROMA

Fire on the waterfront!

A VOICE

Where?

A BODYGUARD (*entering*)

Is there a vegetable

Dealer named Hook in the house?

SECOND DEALER

That's me. What's wrong?

THE BODYGUARD

Your warehouse is on fire.
(*Hook, the dealer, rushes out. A few follow him. Others go
to the window*)

ROMA

Hold it!

Nobody leave the room! (*To the bodyguard*) Is it arson?

THE BODYGUARD

It must be. They've found some gasoline cans.

THIRD DEALER

Some gasoline cans were taken out of here!

ROMA (*in a rage*)
  What's that? Is somebody insinuating
  We did it?
A BODYGUARD (*pokes his automatic into the man's ribs*)
             What was being taken out
  Of here? Did you see any gasoline cans?
OTHER BODYGUARDS (*to other dealers*)
  Did you see any cans?—Did you?
THE DEALERS

                         Not I.—

  Me neither.
ROMA

                 That's better.
GIVOLA (*quickly*)

                         Ha. The very man
  Who just a while ago was telling us
  That all was quiet on the greengoods front
  Now sees his warehouse burning, turned to ashes
  By malefactors. Dòn't you see? Can you
  Be blind? You've got to get together. And quick!
UI (*bellowing*)
  Things in this town are looking very sick!
  First murder and now arson! This should show
  You men that no one's safe from the next blow!

  (*A sign appears*)

8

*The warehouse fire trial. Press. Judge. Prosecutor. Defense
counsel. Young Dogsborough. Giri. Givola. Dockdaisy. Bodyguards. Vegetable dealers and Fish, the accused.*

(a)

Emanuele Giri stands in front of the witness's chair, pointing at Fish, the accused, who is sitting in utter apathy.

GIRI (*shouting*)
   There sits the criminal who lit the fire!
   When I challenged him he was slinking down the street
   Clutching a gasoline can to his chest.
   Stand up, you bastard, when I'm talking to you.
   (*Fish is pulled to his feet. He stands swaying*)
THE JUDGE   Defendant, pull yourself together. This is a court of law. You are on trial for arson. That is a very serious matter. Bear that in mind.
FISH (*in a thick voice*)   Arlarlarl.
THE JUDGE   Where did you get that gasoline can?
FISH   Arlarl.
   (*At a sign from the judge an excessively well-dressed, sinister-looking doctor bends down over Fish and exchanges glances with Giri*)
THE DOCTOR   Simulating.
DEFENSE COUNSEL   The defense moves that other doctors be consulted.
THE JUDGE (*smiling*)   Denied.
DEFENSE COUNSEL   Mr. Giri, how did you happen to be on the spot when this fire, which reduced twenty-two buildings to ashes, broke out in Mr. Hook's warehouse?
GIRI   I was taking a walk for my digestion.
   (*Some of the bodyguards laugh. Giri joins in the laughter*)
DEFENSE COUNSEL   Are you aware, Mr. Giri, that Mr. Fish, the defendant, is an unemployed worker, that he had never been in Chicago before and arrived here on foot the day before the fire?
GIRI   What? When?
DEFENSE COUNSEL   Is the registration number of your car XXXXXX?
GIRI   Yes.
DEFENSE COUNSEL   Was this car parked outside Dogsborough's restaurant on 87th Street during the four hours preceding

the fire, and was defendant Fish dragged out of that restaurant in a state of unconsciousness?

GIRI   How should I know? I spent the whole day on a little excursion to Cicero, where I met fifty-two persons who are all ready to testify that they saw me.

(*The bodyguards laugh*)

DEFENSE COUNSEL   Your previous statement left me with the impression that you were taking a walk for your digestion in the Chicago waterfront area.

GIRI   Any objection to my eating in Cicero and digesting in Chicago?

(*Loud and prolonged laughter in which the judge joins*)

(*Darkness. An organ plays Chopin's "Funeral March" in dance rhythm*)

(b)

When the lights go on, Hook, the vegetable dealer, is sitting in the witness's chair.

DEFENSE COUNSEL   Did you ever quarrel with the defendant, Mr. Hook? Did you ever see him before?

HOOK   Never.

DEFENSE COUNSEL   Have you ever seen Mr. Giri?

HOOK   Yes. In the office of the Cauliflower Trust on the day of the fire.

DEFENSE COUNSEL   Before the fire?

HOOK   Just before the fire. He passed through the room with four men carrying gasoline cans.

(*Commotion on the press bench and among the bodyguards*)

THE JUDGE   Would the gentlemen of the press please be quiet.

DEFENSE COUNSEL   What premises does your warehouse adjoin, Mr. Hook?

HOOK   The premises of the former Sheet shipyard. There's a passage connecting my warehouse with the shipyard.

DEFENSE COUNSEL   Are you aware, Mr. Hook, that Mr. Giri

lives in the former Sheet shipyard and consequently has access to the premises?

HOOK   Yes. He's the stockroom superintendent.

(*Increased commotion on the press bench. The bodyguards boo and take a menacing attitude toward Hook, the defense, and the press. Young Dogsborough rushes up to the judge and whispers something in his ear*)

JUDGE   Order in the court! The defendant is unwell. The court is adjourned.

(*Darkness. The organ starts again to play Chopin's "Funeral March" in dance rhythm*)

(c)

When the lights go on, Hook is sitting in the witness's chair. He is in a state of collapse, with a cane beside him and bandages over his head and eyes.

THE PROSECUTOR   Is your eyesight poor, Hook?

HOOK   (*with difficulty*)   Yes.

THE PROSECUTOR   Would you say you were capable of recognizing anyone clearly and definitely?

HOOK   No.

THE PROSECUTOR   Do you, for instance, recognize this man? (*He points at Giri*)

HOOK   No.

THE PROSECUTOR   You're not prepared to say that you ever saw him before?

HOOK   No.

THE PROSECUTOR   And now, Hook, a very important question. Think well before you answer. Does your warehouse adjoin the premises of the former Sheet shipyard?

HOOK   (*after a pause*)   No.

THE PROSECUTOR   That is all.

(*Darkness. The organ starts playing again*)

(d)

When the lights go on, Dockdaisy is sitting in the witness's chair.

DOCKDAISY (*mechanically*)   I recognize the defendant perfectly because of his guilty look and because he is five feet eight inches tall. My sister-in-law has informed me that he was seen outside city hall on the afternoon my husband was shot while entering city hall. He was carrying a Webster sub-machine-gun and made a suspicious impression.
(*Darkness. The organ starts playing again*)

(e)

When the lights go on, Giuseppe Givola is sitting in the witness's chair. Greenwool, the bodyguard, is standing near him.

THE PROSECUTOR   It has been alleged that certain men were seen carrying gasoline cans out of the offices of the Cauliflower Trust before the fire. What do you know about this?

GIVOLA   It couldn't be anybody but Mr. Greenwool.

THE PROSECUTOR   Is Mr. Greenwool in your employ?

GIVOLA   Yes.

THE PROSECUTOR   What is your profession, Mr. Givola?

GIVOLA   Florist.

THE PROSECUTOR   Do florists use large quantities of gasoline?

GIVOLA (*seriously*)   No, only for plant lice.

THE PROSECUTOR   What was Mr. Greenwool doing in the offices of the Cauliflower Trust?

GIVOLA   Singing a song.

THE PROSECUTOR   Then he can't very well have carried any gasoline cans to Hook's warehouse at the same time.

GIVOLA   It's out of the question. It's not in his character to start fires. He's a baritone.

THE PROSECUTOR   If it please the court, I should like witness Greenwool to sing the fine song he was singing in the offices of the Cauliflower Trust while the warehouse was being set on fire.

THE JUDGE   The court does not consider it necessary.

GIVOLA   I protest.
(*He rises*)
The bias in this courtroom is outrageous.
Cleancut young fellows who in broadest daylight
Fire a well-meant shot or two are treated
Like shady characters. It's scandalous.
(*Laughter. Darkness. The organ starts playing again*)

(f)

When the lights go on, the courtroom shows every indication of utter exhaustion.

THE JUDGE   The press has dropped hints that this court might be subject to pressure from certain quarters. The court wishes to state that it has been subjected to no pressure of any kind and is conducting this trial in perfect freedom. I believe this will suffice.

THE PROSECUTOR   Your honor! In view of the fact that defendant Fish persists in simulating dementia, the prosecution holds that he cannot be questioned any further. We therefore move . . .

DEFENSE COUNSEL   Your honor. The defendant is coming to!
(*Commotion*)

FISH (*seems to be waking up*)   Arlarlwaratarlawatrla.

DEFENSE COUNSEL   Water! Your honor! I ask leave to question defendant Fish!
(*Uproar*)

THE PROSECUTOR   I object! I see no indication that Fish is in his right mind. It's all a machination on the part of the defense, cheap sensationalism, demagogy!

FISH   Watr.
(*Supported by the defense counsel, he stands up*)

DEFENSE COUNSEL   Fish. Can you answer me?

FISH   Yarl.

DEFENSE COUNSEL   Fish, tell the court: Did you, on the 28th of last month, set fire to a vegetable warehouse on the waterfront? Yes or no?

FISH   N-n-no.

DEFENSE COUNSEL   When did you arrive in Chicago, Fish?

FISH   Water.

DEFENSE COUNSEL   Water!

(*Commotion. Young Dogsborough has stepped up to the judge and is talking to him emphatically*)

GIRI (*stands up square-shouldered and bellows*)   Frame-up! Lies! Lies!

DEFENSE COUNSEL   Did you ever see this man (*he indicates Giri*) before?

FISH   Yes. Water.

DEFENSE COUNSEL   Where? Was it in Dogsborough's restaurant on the waterfront?

FISH (*faintly*)   Yes.

(*Uproar. The bodyguards draw their guns and boo. The doctor comes running in with a glass. He pours the contents into Fish's mouth before the defense counsel can take the glass out of his hand*)

DEFENSE COUNSEL   I object. I move that this glass be examined.

THE JUDGE (*exchanging glances with the prosecutor*)   Motion denied.

DOCKDAISY (*screams at Fish*)   Murderer!

DEFENSE COUNSEL
Your Honor!
Because the mouth of truth cannot be stopped with earth
They're trying to stop it with a piece of paper
A sentence to be handed down as though
Your Honor—that's their hope—should properly
Be titled Your Disgrace. They cry to justice:
Hands up! Is this our city, which has aged
A hundred years in seven days beneath
The onslaught of a small but bloody brood
Of monsters, now to see its justice murdered
Nay, worse than murdered, desecrated by
Submission to brute force? Your Honor!
Suspend this trial!

THE PROSECUTOR
I object!

GIRI
You dog!

You lying, peculating dog! Yourself
A poisoner! Come on! Let's step outside!
I'll rip your guts out! Gangster!

DEFENSE COUNSEL
The whole

Town knows this man.

GIRI (*fuming*)
Shut up!

(*When the judge tries to interrupt him*)
You too!

Just keep your trap shut if you want to live!
(*He runs short of breath and the judge manages to speak*)

THE JUDGE   Order in the court. Defense counsel will incur
charges of contempt of court. Mr. Giri's indignation is quite
understandable. (*To the defense counsel*) Continue.

DEFENSE COUNSEL   Fish! Did they give you anything to drink
at Dogsborough's restaurant? Fish! Fish!

FISH (*his head hanging limp*)   Arlarlarl.

DEFENSE COUNSEL   Fish! Fish! Fish!

GIRI (*bellowing*)

Go on and shout! Looks like his tire's gone down!
We'll see who's running things in this here town!
(*Uproar. Darkness. The organ starts again to play Chopin's
"Funeral March" in dance rhythm*)

(g)

*As the lights go on for the last time, the judge stands up and
in a toneless voice delivers the sentence. The defendant is deathly
pale.*

THE JUDGE   Charles Fish, I find you guilty of arson and sentence
you to fifteen years at hard labor.

(*A sign appears*)

9

(a)

Cicero. A woman climbs out of a shot-up truck and staggers forward.

THE WOMAN
Help! Help! Don't run away. Who'll testify?
My husband's in that truck! They got him! Help!
My arm is smashed . . . and so's the truck. I need
A bandage for my arm. They gun us down
Like rabbits! God! Won't anybody help?
You murderers! My husband! I know who's
Behind it! Ui! (*raging*) Fiend! Monster! Shit!
You'd make an honest piece of shit cry out:
Where can I wash myself? You lousy louse!
And people stand for it! And we go under!
Hey you! It's Ui!
(*A burst of machine-gun fire nearby. She collapses*)
          Ui did this job!
Where's everybody? Help! Who'll stop that mob?

(b)

Dogsborough's country house. Night toward morning. Dogsborough is writing his will and confession.

DOGSBOROUGH
And so I, honest Dogsborough, acquiesced
In all the machinations of that bloody gang
After full eighty years of uprightness.
I'm told that those who've known me all along

Are saying I don't know what's going on
That if I knew I wouldn't stand for it.
Alas, I know it all. I know who set
Fire to Hook's warehouse. And I know who dragged
Poor Fish into the restaurant and doped him.
I know that when Sheet died a bloody death
His steamship ticket in his pocket, Roma
Was there. I know that Giri murdered Bowl
That afternoon outside of City Hall
Because he knew too much about myself
Honest old Dogsborough. I know that he
Shot Hook, and saw him with Hook's hat.
I know that Givola committed five
Murders, here itemized. I also know
All about Ui, and I know he knew
All this—the deaths of Sheet and Bowl, Givola's
Murders and all about the fire. All this
Your honest Dogsborough knew. All this
He tolerated out of sordid lust
For gain and fear of forfeiting your trust.

10

*Mammoth Hotel. Ui's suite. Ui is sitting slumped in a deep
chair, staring into space. Givola is writing and two bodyguards
are looking over his shoulder, grinning.*

GIVOLA

And so I, Dogsborough, bequeath my bar
To good hard-working Givola. My country
House to the brave, though somewhat hot-headed Giri.
And I bequeath my son to honest Roma.
I furthermore request that you appoint
Roma police chief, Giri judge, and Givola

Commissioner of welfare. For my own
Position I would warmly recommend
Arturo Ui, who, believe your honest
Old Dogsborough, is worthy of it.—That's
Enough, I think, let's hope he kicks in soon.
This testament will do wonders. Now that the old
Man's known to be dying and the hope arises
Of laying him to rest with relative
Dignity, in clean earth, it's well to tidy up
His corpse. A pretty epitaph is needed.
Ravens from olden time have battened on
The reputation of the fabulous
White raven that somebody saw sometime
And somewhere. This old codger's their white raven.
I guess they couldn't find a whiter one.
And by the way, boss, Giri for my taste
Is too much with him. I don't like it.

UI (*starting up*)

                                   Giri?
What about Giri?

GIVOLA

                         Only that he's spending
A little too much time with Dogsborough.

UI

                                              I
Don't trust him.
(*Giri comes in wearing a new hat, Hook's*)

GIVOLA

                    I don't either. Hi, Giri
How's Dogsborough's apoplexy?

GIRI

                                   He refuses
To let the doctor in.

GIVOLA

                    Our brilliant doctor
Who took such loving care of Fish?

GIRI

                                   No other
Will do. The old man talks too much.

UI
   Maybe somebody's been talking too much to him . . .

GIRI
   What's that? (*To Givola*) You skunk, have you been stink-
      ing up
   The air around here again?

GIVOLA (*alarmed*)
                       Just read the will
   Dear Giri.

GIRI (*snatches it from him*)
            What! Police chief? Him? Roma?
   You must be crazy.

GIVOLA
              He demands it. I'm
   Against it too. The bastard can't be trusted
   Across the street.
   (*Roma comes in followed by bodyguards*)
              Hi, Roma. Take a look at
   This will.

ROMA (*grabbing it out of his hands*)
          Okay, let's see it. What do you know!
   Giri a judge! But where's the old man's scribble?

GIRI
   Under his pillow. He's been trying to
   Smuggle it out. Five times I've caught his son.

ROMA (*holds out his hand*)
   Let's have it, Giri.

GIRI
             What? I haven't got it.

ROMA
   Oh yes, you have!
   (*They glare at each other furiously*)
             I know what's on your mind.
   There's something about Sheet. That concerns me.

GIRI
   Bowl figures in it too. That concerns *me*.

ROMA
   Okay, but you're both jerks, and I'm a man.
   I know you, Giri, and you too, Givola.

I'd even say your crippled leg was phony.
Why do I always find you bastards here?
What are you cooking up? What lies have they
Been telling you about me, Arturo? Watch
Your step, you pipsqueaks. If I catch you trying
To cross me up, I'll rub you out like blood spots!

GIRI
Roma, you'd better watch your tongue! I'm not
One of your two-bit gunmen.

ROMA (*to his bodyguards*)
                                        That means you!
That's what they're calling you at headquarters!
They hobnob with the Cauliflower Trust—
(*Pointing to Giri*)
That shirt was made to order by Clark's tailor—
You two-bit gunmen do the dirty work—
And you (*to Ui*) put up with it.

UI (*as though waking up*)
                                        Put up with what?

GIVOLA
His shooting up Caruther's trucks! Caruther's
A member of the Trust!

UI
                            Did you shoot up
Caruther's trucks?

ROMA
                        I gave no orders. Just
Some of the boys. Spontaneous combustion.
They don't see why it's always the small grocers
That have to sweat and bleed. Why not the big wheels?
Damn it, Arturo, I myself don't get it.

GIVOLA
The Trust is good and mad.

GIRI
                                Clark says they're only
Waiting for it to happen one more time.
He's put in a complaint with Dogsborough.

UI (*morosely*)
Ernesto, these things mustn't happen.

GIRI

Crack down, boss!
These guys are getting too big for their britches!

GIVOLA

The Trust is good and mad, boss!

ROMA (*pulls his gun. To Giri and Givola*)

Okay. Hands up! (*To their bodyguards*) You too!
Hands up the lot of you. No monkey business!
Now back up to the wall.
(*Givola, his men, and Giri raise their hands and with an air
of resignation back up to the wall*)

UI (*indifferently*)

What is all this?
Ernesto, don't make them nervous. What are you guys
Squabbling about? So some palooka's wasted
Some bullets on a cauliflower truck.
Such misunderstandings can be straightened out.
Everything is running smooth as silk.
The fire was a big success. The stores
Are paying for protection. Thirty cents
On every dollar. Almost half the city
Has knuckled under in five days. Nobody
Raises a hand against us. And I've got
Bigger and better projects.

GIVOLA (*quickly*)

Projects? What
For instance?

GIRI

Fuck your projects. Get this fool
To let me put my hands down.

ROMA

Safety first, Arturo.
We'd better leave them up!

GIVOLA

Won't it look sweet
If Clark comes in and sees us here like this!

UI

Ernesto, put that rod away!

ROMA

No dice!
Wake up, Arturo. Don't you see their game?
They're selling you out to the Clarks and Dogsboroughs.
"If Clark comes in and sees us!" What, I ask you
Has happened to the shipyard's funds? We haven't
Seen a red cent. The boys shoot up the stores
Tote gasoline to warehouses and sigh:
We made Arturo what he is today
And he doesn't know us any more. He's playing
The shipyard owner and tycoon. Wake up
Arturo!

GIRI

Right. And speak up. Tell us where
You stand.

UI (*jumps up*)

Are you boys trying to pressure me
At gunpoint? Better not, I'm warning you
You won't get anywhere with me like that.
You'll only have yourselves to blame for
The consequences. I'm a quiet man. But
I won't be threatened. Either trust me blindly
Or go your way. I owe you no accounting.
Just do your duty, and do it to the full.
The recompense is up to me, because
Duty comes first and then the recompense.
What I demand of you is trust. You lack
Faith, and where faith is lacking, all is lost.
How do you think I got this far? By faith!
Because of my fanatical, my unflinching
Faith in the cause! With faith and nothing else
I flung a challenge at this city and forced
It to its knees. With faith I made my way
To Dogsborough. With faith I climbed the steps
Of City Hall. With nothing in my naked
Hands but indomitable faith!

ROMA

And
A tommy-gun!

UI

No, other men have them
But lack firm faith in their predestination
To leadership! And that is why you too
Need to have faith in me! Have faith! Believe that
I know what's best for you and that I'm
Resolved to put it through. That I will find
The road to victory. If Dogsborough
Passes away, then I decide who gets to
Be what. I say no more, but rest assured:
You'll all be satisfied.

GIVOLA (*puts his hand on his heart*)

Arturo!

ROMA (*sullenly*)

Scram

You guys!
(*Giri, Givola, and Givola's bodyguard go out slowly with
their hands up*)

GIRI (*leaving, to Roma*)

I like your hat.

GIVOLA (*leaving*)

Dear Roma . . .

ROMA

Scram!

Giri, you clown, don't leave your laugh behind.
And Givola, you crook, be sure to take
Your clubfoot, though I'm pretty sure you stole it.
(*When they are gone, Ui relapses into his brooding*)

UI

I want to be alone.

ROMA (*standing still*)

Arturo, if I
Hadn't the kind of faith you've just described
I'd sometimes find it hard to look my
Men in the face. We've got to act. And quickly.
Giri is cooking up some dirty work.

UI

Don't worry about Giri. I am planning
Bigger and better things. And now, Ernesto

To you, my oldest friend and trusted lieutenant
I will divulge them.
ROMA (*beaming*)

        Speak, Arturo. Giri
And what I had to say of him can wait.
(*He sits down with Ui. Roma's men stand in the corner,
waiting*)
UI
We're finished with Chicago. I need more.
ROMA
More?
UI

      Vegetables are sold in other cities.
ROMA
But how are you expecting to get in?
UI

                    Through
The front door, through the back door, through the windows.
Resisted, sent away, called back again.
Booed and acclaimed. With threats and supplications
Appeals and insults, gentle force and steel
Embrace. In short, the same as here.
ROMA

                Except
Conditions aren't the same in other places.
UI
I have in mind a kind of dress rehearsal
In a small town. That way we'll see
Whether conditions are so different. I
Doubt it.
ROMA

      And where have you resolved to stage
This dress rehearsal?
UI

         In Cicero.
ROMA

           But there
They've got this Dullfeet with his Journal

For Vegetables and Positive Thinking
Which every Saturday accuses me
Of murdering Sheet.

UI

That's got to stop.

ROMA

It will. These journalists have enemies.
Their black and white makes certain people
See red. Myself, for instance. Yes, Arturo
I think these accusations can be silenced.

UI

I'm sure they can. The Trust is negotiating
With Cicero right now. For the time being
We'll just sell cauliflower peacefully.

ROMA

Who's doing this negotiating?

UI

Clark.

But he's been having trouble. On our account.

ROMA

I see. So Clark is in it. I wouldn't trust
That Clark around the corner.

UI

In Cicero
They say we're following the Cauliflower
Trust like its shadow. They want cauliflower, but
They don't want us. The shopkeepers don't like us.
A feeling shared by others: Dullfeet's wife
For instance, who for years now has been running
A greengoods wholesale house. She'd like to join
The Trust, and would have joined except for us.

ROMA

You mean this plan of moving in on Cicero
Didn't start with you at all, but with the Trust?
Arturo, now I see it all. I see
Their rotten game.

UI

Whose game?

ROMA

       The Trust's.
The goings-on at Dogsborough's! His will!
It's all a machination of the Trust.
They want the Cicero connection. You're in
The way. But how can they get rid of you?
You've got them by the balls, because they needed
You for their dirty business and connived at
Your methods. But now they've found a way:
Old Dogsborough confesses and repairs
In ash and sackcloth to his coffin.
The cauliflower boys with deep emotion
Retrieve this paper from his hands and sobbing
Read it to the assembled press: How he repents
And solemnly adjures them to wipe out
The plague which he—as he confesses—brought
In, and restore the cauliflower trade
To its time-honored practices.
That's what they plan, Arturo. They're all in it:
Giri, who gets Dogsborough to scribble wills
And who is hand in glove with Clark, who's having
Trouble in Cicero because of us
And wants pure sunshine when he shovels shekels.
Givola, who smells carrion.—This Dogsborough
Honest old Dogsborough with his two-timing will
That splatters you with muck has got to be
Rubbed out, Arturo, or your best-laid plans
For Cicero are down the drain!

UI

       You think
It's all a plot? It's true. They've kept me out
Of Cicero. I've noticed that.

ROMA

      Arturo
I beg you: let me handle this affair!
I tell you what: my boys and I will beat
It out to Dogsborough's tonight
And take him with us. To the hospital
We'll tell him—and deliver him to the morgue.

UI

But Giri's with him at the villa.

ROMA

He

Can stay there.
(*They exchange glances*)

Two birds one stone.

UI

And Givola?

ROMA

On the way back I'll drop in at the florist's
And order handsome wreaths for Dogsborough.
For Giri too, the clown. And I'll pay cash.
(*He pats his gun*)

UI

Ernesto, this contemptible project of
The Dogsboroughs and Clarks and Dullfeets
To squeeze me out of Cicero's affairs
By coldly branding me a criminal
Must be frustrated with an iron hand.
I put my trust in you.

ROMA

And well you may.

But you must meet with us before we start
And give the boys a talk to make them see
The matter in its proper light. I'm not
So good at talking.

UI (*shaking his hand*)

It's a deal.

ROMA

I knew it

Arturo! This was how it had to be
Decided. Say, the two of us! Say, you
And me! Like in the good old days.
(*To his men*)

What did

I tell you, boys? He gives us the green light.

UI

I'll be there.

ROMA
> At eleven.

UI
> ### Where?

ROMA
> At the garage.
> I'm a new man. At last we'll see some fight!
> (*He goes out quickly with his men*)
> (*Pacing the floor, Ui prepares the speech he is going to make
> to Roma's men*)

UI
> Friends, much as I regret to say it, word
> Has reached me that behind my back perfidious
> Treason is being planned. Men close to me
> Men whom I trusted most implicitly
> Have turned against me. Goaded by ambition
> And crazed by lust for gain, these despicable
> Fiends have conspired with the cauliflower
> Moguls—no, that won't do—with who? I've got it!
> With the police, to coldly liquidate you
> And even, so I hear, myself! My patience
> Is at an end. I therefore order you
> Under Ernesto Roma who enjoys
> My fullest confidence, tonight . . .
> (*Enter Clark, Giri, and Betty Dullfeet*)

GIRI (*noticing that Ui looks frightened*)
> It's only
> Us, boss.

CLARK
> Ui, let me introduce
> Mrs. Dullfeet of Cicero. The Trust
> Asks you to give her your attention, and hopes
> The two of you will come to terms.

UI (*scowling*)
> I'm listening.

CLARK
> A merger, as you know, is being considered
> Between Chicago's Cauliflower Trust

And Cicero's purveyors. In the course
Of the negotiations, Cicero
Objected to your presence on the board.
The Trust was able, after some discussion
To overcome this opposition. Mrs. Dullfeet
Is here . . .

MRS. DULLFEET
                    To clear up the misunderstanding.
Moreover, I should like to point out that
My husband Mr. Dullfeet's newspaper
Campaign was not directed against you
Mr. Ui.

UI
                    Against who was it directed?

CLARK
I may as well speak plainly, Ui. Sheet's
"Suicide" made a very bad impression
In Cicero. Whatever else Sheet may
Have been, he was a shipyard owner
A leading citizen, and not some Tom
Dick or Harry whose death arouses no
Comment. And something else. Caruther's
Garage complains of an attack on one of
Its trucks. And one of your men, Ui, is
Involved in both these cases.

MRS. DULLFEET
                              Every child in
Cicero knows Chicago's cauliflower
Is stained with blood.

UI
                    Have you come here to insult me?

MRS. DULLFEET
No, no. Not you, since Mr. Clark has vouched
For you. It's this man Roma.

CLARK (*quickly*)
                    Cool it, Ui!

GIRI
Cicero . . .

UI

You can't talk to me like this!
What do you take me for? I've heard enough!
Ernesto Roma is my man. I don't
Let anybody tell me who to pal with.
This is an outrage.

GIRI

Boss!

MRS. DULLFEET

Ignatius Dullfeet
Will fight the Romas of this world to his
Last breath.

CLARK (*coldly*)

And rightly so. In that the Trust
Is solidly behind him. Think it over.
Friendship and business are two separate things.
What do you say?

UI (*likewise coldly*)

You heard me, Mr. Clark.

CLARK

Mrs. Dullfeet, I regret profoundly
The outcome of this interview.
(*On his way out, to Ui*)

Most unwise, Ui.
(*Left alone, Ui and Giri do not look at each other*)

GIRI

This and the business with Caruther's truck
Means war. That's plain.

UI

I'm not afraid of war.

GIRI

Okay, you're not afraid. You'll only have
The Trust, the papers, the whole city, plus
Dogsborough and his crowd against you!
Just between you and me, boss, I'd think twice . . .

UI

I know my duty and need no advice.

(*A sign appears*)

11

Garage. Night. The sound of rain. Ernesto Roma and young Inna. In the background gunmen.

INNA

It's one o'clock.

ROMA

He must have been delayed.

INNA

Could he be hesitating?

ROMA

He could be.
Arturo's so devoted to his henchmen
He'd rather sacrifice himself than them.
Even with rats like Givola and Giri
He can't make up his mind. And so he dawdles
And wrestles with himself. It might be two
Or even three before he gets a move on.
But never fear, he'll come. Of course he will.
I know him, Inna. (*Pause*) When I see that Giri
Flat on the carpet, pouring out his guts
I'll feel as if I'd taken a good leak.
Oh well, it won't be long.

INNA

These rainy nights are
Hard on the nerves.

ROMA

That's what I like about them.
Of nights the blackest
Of cars the fastest
And of friends
The most resolute.

INNA

How many years have
You known him?

ROMA
> Going on eighteen.

INNA
> > That's a long time.

A GUNMAN (*comes forward*)
The boys want whisky.

ROMA
> No. Tonight I need
Them sober.
(*A little man is brought in by the bodyguards*)

THE LITTLE MAN (*out of breath*)
> Dirty work at the crossroads!
Two armored cars outside police h.q.
Jam-packed with cops.

ROMA
> Okay, boys, get the
Bulletproof shutter down. Those cops have got
Nothing to do with us, but foresight's better
Than hindsight.
(*Slowly an iron shutter falls, blocking the garage door*)
> Is the passage clear?

INNA (*nods*)
It's a funny thing about tobacco. When a man
Is smoking, he looks calm. And if you imitate
A calm-looking man and light a cigarette, you
Get to be calm yourself.

ROMA (*smiling*)
> Hold out your hand.

INNA (*does so*)
It's trembling. That's no good.

ROMA
> Don't worry. It's all
Right. I don't go for bruisers. They're unfeeling.
Nothing can hurt them and they won't hurt you.
Not seriously. Tremble all you like.
A compass needle is made of steel but trembles
Before it settles on its course. Your hand
Is looking for its pole. That's all.

A SHOUT (*from the side*)

                                Police car
  Coming down Church Street!

ROMA (*intently*)

                                Is it stopping?

THE VOICE

                                     No.

A GUNMAN (*comes in*)

  Two cars with blacked-out lights have turned the corner.

ROMA

  They're waiting for Arturo. Givola and
  Giri are laying for him. He'll run straight
  Into their trap! We've got to head him off!
  Let's go!

A GUNMAN

           It's suicide.

ROMA

                   If suicide it is
  Let it be suicide! Hell! Eighteen years
  Of friendship!

INNA (*loud and clear*)

                Raise the shutter!
  Machine-gun ready?

A GUNMAN

               Ready.

INNA

                 Up she goes!
  (*The bulletproof shutter rises slowly. Ui and Givola enter
  briskly, followed by bodyguards*)

ROMA

  Arturo!

INNA (*under his breath*)

           Yeah, and Givola!

ROMA

                 What's up?
  Arturo, man, you had us worried. (*Laughs loudly*) Hell!
  But everything's okay.

UI (*hoarsely*)

                Why wouldn't it be okay?

INNA

We thought
Something was wrong. If I were you I'd give him
The glad-hand, boss. He was going to lead
Us all through fire to save you. Weren't you, Roma?
(*Ui goes up to Roma, holding out his hand. Roma grasps it, laughing. At this moment, when Roma cannot reach for his gun, Givola shoots him from the hip*)

UI

Into the corner with them!
(*Roma's men stand bewildered. Inna in the lead, they are driven into the corner. Givola bends down over Roma, who is lying on the floor*)

GIVOLA

He's still breathing.

UI

Finish him off.
(*To the men lined up against the wall*)
Your vicious plot against me is exposed.
So are your plans to rub out Dogsborough.
I caught you in the nick of time. Resistance
Is useless. I'll teach you to rebel against me!
You bastards!

GIVOLA

Not a single one unarmed!
(*Speaking of Roma*)
He's coming to. He's going to wish he hadn't.

UI

I'll be at Dogsborough's country house tonight.
(*He goes out quickly*)

INNA

You stinking rats! You traitors!

GIVOLA (*excitedly*)

Let 'em have it!
(*The men standing against the wall are mowed down by machine-gun fire*)

ROMA (*comes to*)

Givola! Christ,
(*Turns over, his face chalky-white*)

What happened over there?

GIVOLA

Nothing. Some traitors have been executed.

ROMA

You dog! My men! What have you done to them?
(*Givola does not answer*)
And where's Arturo? You've murdered him. I knew it!
(*Looking for him on the floor*)
Where is he?

GIVOLA

He's just left.

ROMA (*as he is being dragged to the wall*)
You stinking dogs!

GIVOLA (*coolly*)
You say my leg is short, I say your brain is small.
Now let your pretty legs convey you to the wall!

(*A sign appears*)

12

Givola's flower shop. Ignatius Dullfeet, a very small man, and Betty Dullfeet come in.

DULLFEET

I don't like this at all.

BETTY

Why not? They've gotten rid
Of Roma.

DULLFEET

Yes, they've murdered him.

BETTY

That's how
They do it. Anyway, he's gone. Clark says
That Ui's years of storm and stress, which even

The best of men go through, are over. Ui
Has shown he wants to mend his uncouth ways.
But if you persevere in your attacks
You'll only stir his evil instincts up
Again, and you, Ignatius, will be first
To bear the brunt. But if you keep your mouth shut
They'll leave you be.

DULLFEET
                    I'm not so sure my silence
Will help.

BETTY
          It's sure to. They're not beasts.
(*Giri comes in from one side, wearing Roma's hat*)

GIRI
Hi. Here already? Mr. Ui's inside.
He'll be delighted. Sorry I can't stay.
I've got to beat it quick before I'm seen.
I've swiped a hat from Givola.
(*He laughs so hard that plaster falls from the ceiling, and
goes out, waving*)

DULLFEET
Bad when they growl. No better when they laugh.

BETTY
Don't say such things, Ignatius. Not here.

DULLFEET (*bitterly*)
                                    Nor
Anywhere else.

BETTY
              What can you do? Already
The rumor's going around in Cicero
That Ui's stepping into Dogsborough's shoes.
And worse, the greengoods men of Cicero
Are flirting with the Cauliflower Trust.

DULLFEET
And now they've smashed two printing presses on me.
Betty, I've got a dark foreboding.
(*Givola and Ui come in with outstretched hands*)

BETTY
Hi, Ui!

UI

     Welcome, Dullfeet!

DULLFEET

                        Mr. Ui

I tell you frankly that I hesitated

To come, because . . .

UI

               Why hesitate? A man

Like you is welcome everywhere.

GIVOLA

                     So is a

Beautiful woman!

DULLFEET

           Mr. Ui, I've felt

It now and then to be my duty to

Come out against . . .

UI

             A mere misunderstanding!

If you and I had known each other from

The start, it never would have happened. It

Has always been my fervent wish that what

Had to be done should be done peacefully.

DULLFEET

Violence . . .

UI

        No one hates it more than I do.

If men were wise, there'd be no need of it.

DULLFEET

My aim . . .

UI

       Is just the same as mine. We both

Want trade to thrive. The small shopkeeper whose

Life is no bed of roses nowadays

Must be permitted to sell his greens in peace.

And find protection when attacked.

DULLFEET (*firmly*)

                   And be

Free to determine whether he desires

Protection. I regard that as essential.

UI

And so do I. He's *got* to be free to choose.
Why? Because when he chooses his protector
Freely, and puts his trust in somebody he himself
Has chosen, then confidence, which is
As necessary in the greengoods trade
As anywhere else, will prevail. That's always been
My stand.

DULLFEET

      I'm glad to hear it from your lips.
For, no offense intended, Cicero
Will never tolerate coercion.

UI

                Of course not.
No one unless he has to tolerates
Coercion.

DULLFEET

       Frankly, if this merger with the Trust
Should mean importing the ungodly bloodbath
That plagues Chicago to our peaceful town
I never could approve it.
(*Pause*)

UI

       Frankness calls
For frankness, Mr. Dullfeet. Certain things
That might not meet the highest moral standards
May have occurred in the past. Such things
Occur in battle. Among friends, however
They cannot happen. Dullfeet, what I want
Of you is only that in the future you should
Trust me and look upon me as a friend
Who never till the seas run dry will forsake
A friend—and, to be more specific, that
Your paper should stop printing these horror stories
That only make bad blood. I don't believe
I'm asking very much.

DULLFEET

        It's easy not
To write about what doesn't happen, sir.

UI

    Exactly. And if now and then some trifling
    Incident should occur, because the earth
    Is inhabited by men and not by angels
    You will abstain, I hope, from printing lurid
    Stories about trigger-happy criminals.
    I wouldn't go so far as to maintain that
    One of our drivers might not on occasion
    Utter an uncouth word. That too is human.
    And if some vegetable dealer stands
    One of our men to a beer for punctual
    Delivery of his carrots, let's not rush
    Into print with stories of corruption.

BETTY

                      Mr.
    Ui, my husband's human.

GIVOLA

                  We don't doubt it.
    And now that everything has been so amiably
    Discussed and settled among friends, perhaps
    You'd like to see my flowers . . .

UI (*to Dullfeet*)

                After you.
    (*They inspect Givola's flower shop. Ui leads Betty, Givola leads Dullfeet. In the following they keep disappearing behind the flower displays. Givola and Dullfeet emerge*)

GIVOLA

    These, my dear Dullfeet, are Malayan fronds.

DULLFEET

    Growing, I see, by little oval ponds.

GIVOLA

    Stocked with blue carp that stay stock-still for hours.

DULLFEET

    The wicked are insensitive to flowers.
    (*They disappear. Ui and Betty emerge*)

BETTY

    A strong man needs no force to win his suit.

UI

    Arguments carry better when they shoot.

BETTY
  Sound reasoning is bound to take effect.
UI
  Except when one is trying to collect.
BETTY
  Intimidation, underhanded tricks . . .
UI
  I prefer to speak of pragmatic politics.
  (*They disappear. Givola and Dullfeet emerge*)
DULLFEET
  Flowers are free from lust and wickedness.
GIVOLA
  Exactly why I love them, I confess.
DULLFEET
  They live so quietly. They never hurry.
GIVOLA (*mischievously*)
  No problems. No newspapers. No worry.
  (*They disappear. Ui and Betty emerge*)
BETTY
  They tell me you're as abstinent as a vicar.
UI
  I never smoke and have no use for liquor.
BETTY
  A saint perhaps when all is said and done.
UI
  Of carnal inclinations I have none.
  (*They disappear. Givola and Dullfeet emerge*)
DULLFEET
  Your life with flowers must deeply satisfy.
GIVOLA
  It would, had I not other fish to fry.
  (*They disappear. Ui and Betty emerge*)
BETTY
  What, Mr. Ui, does religion mean to you?
UI
  I am a Christian. That will have to do.
BETTY
  Yes. But the Ten Commandments, where do they
  Come in?

UI
>   In daily life they don't, I'd say.

BETTY
> Forgive me if your patience I abuse
> But what exactly are your social views?

UI
> My social views are balanced, clear and healthy.
> What proves it is: I don't neglect the wealthy.
> (*They disappear. Givola and Dullfeet emerge*)

DULLFEET
> The flowers have their life, their social calls.

GIVOLA
> I'll say they do. Especially funerals!

DULLFEET
> Oh, I forgot that flowers were your bread.

GIVOLA
> Exactly. My best clients are the dead.

DULLFEET
> I hope that's not your only source of trade.

GIVOLA
> Some people have the sense to be afraid.

DULLFEET
> Violence, Givola, brings no lasting glory.

GIVOLA
> It gets results, though.

DULLFEET
>   That's another story.

GIVOLA
> You look so pale.

DULLFEET
>   The air is damp and close.

GIVOLA
> The heavy scent affects you, I suppose.
> (*They disappear. Ui and Betty emerge*)

BETTY
> I am so glad you two have worked things out.

UI
> Once frankness showed what it was all about . . .

BETTY
 Foul-weather friends will never disappoint . . .
UI (*putting his arm around her shoulder*)
 I like a woman who can get the point.
 (*Givola and Dullfeet, who is deathly pale, emerge. Dullfeet
 sees the hand on his wife's shoulder*)
DULLFEET
 Betty, we're leaving.
UI (*comes up to him, holding out his hand*)
                    Mr. Dullfeet, your
 Decision honors you. It will redound to
 Cicero's welfare. A meeting between such men
 As you and I can only be auspicious.
GIVOLA (*giving Betty flowers*)
 Beauty to beauty!
BETTY
                    Look, how nice, Ignatius!
 Oh, I'm so happy. 'Bye, 'bye!
GIVOLA
                    Now we can
 Start going places.
UI (*darkly*)
                    I don't like that man.
 (*A sign appears*)

13

*Bells. A coffin is being carried into the Cicero funeral chapel,
followed by Betty Dullfeet in widow's weeds, and by Clark,
Ui, Giri, and Givola bearing enormous wreaths. After handing
in their wreaths, Ui, Giri and Givola remain outside the chapel.
The pastor's voice is heard from inside.*

VOICE
 And so Ignatius Dullfeet's mortal frame
 Is laid to rest. A life of charily

Rewarded toil is ended, of toil expended
For others than the toiler who has left us.
The angel at the gates of heaven will set
His hand upon Ignatius Dullfeet's shoulder
Feel that his cloak has been worn thin and say:
This man has borne the burdens of his neighbors.
And in the city council for some time
To come, when everyone has finished speaking
Silence will fall. For so accustomed are
His fellow citizens to listen to
Ignatius Dullfeet's voice that they will wait
To hear him. 'Tis as though the city's conscience
Had died. This man who met with so untimely
An end could walk the narrow path unseeing.
Justice was in his heart. This man of lowly
Stature but lofty mind created in
His newspaper a rostrum whence his voice
Rang out beyond the confines of our city.
Ignatius Dullfeet, rest in peace! Amen.

GIVOLA

A tactful man: no word of how he died.

GIRI (*wearing Dullfeet's hat*)

A tactful man? A man with seven children.

(*Clark and Mulberry come out of the chapel*)

CLARK

God damn it! Are you mounting guard for fear
The truth might be divulged beside his coffin?

GIVOLA

Why so uncivil, my dear Clark? I'd think
This holy place would curb your temper. And
Besides, the boss is out of sorts. He doesn't
Like the surroundings here.

MULBERRY

You murderers!
Ignatius Dullfeet kept his word—and silence.

GIVOLA

Silence is not enough. The kind of men
We need must be prepared not only to
Keep silent for us but to speak—and loudly.

MULBERRY
    What could he say except to call you butchers?
GIVOLA
    He had to go. That little Dullfeet was
    The pore through which the greengoods dealers oozed
    Cold sweat. He stank of it unbearably.
GIRI
    And what about your cauliflower? Do
    You want it sold in Cicero or don't
    You?
MULBERRY
            Not by slaughter.
GIRI
                        Hypocrite, how else?
    Who helps us eat the calf we slaughter, eh?
    You're funny bastards, clamoring for meat
    Then bawling out the cook because he uses
    A cleaver. We expect you guys to smack
    Your lips and all you do is gripe. And now
    Go home!
MULBERRY
            A sorry day, Clark, when you brought
    These people in!
CLARK
            You're telling me?
    (*The two go out, deep in gloom*)
GIRI
                        Boss
    Don't let those stinkers keep you from enjoying
    The funeral!
GIVOLA
            Pst! Betty's coming!
    (*Leaning on another woman, Betty comes out of the chapel.*
    Ui steps up to her. Organ music from the chapel)
UI
                        Mrs.
    Dullfeet, my sympathies!
    (*She passes him by without a word*)

GIRI (*bellowing*)

Hey, you!
(*She stops still and turns around. Her face is white*)

UI

I said, my
Sympathies, Mrs. Dullfeet. Dullfeet—God
Have mercy on his soul—is dead. But cauliflower—
Your cauliflower—is still with us. Maybe you
Can't see it, because your eyes are still
Blinded with tears. This tragic incident
Should not, however, blind you to the fact
That shots are being fired from craven ambush
On law-abiding vegetable trucks.
And kerosene dispensed by ruthless hands
Is spoiling sorely needed vegetables.
My men and I stand ready to provide
Protection. What's your answer?

BETTY (*looking heavenward*)

This
With Dullfeet hardly settled in his grave!

UI

Believe me, I deplore the incident:
The man by ruthless hand extinguished was
My friend.

BETTY

The hand that felled him was the hand
That shook his hand in friendship. Yours!

UI

Am I
Never to hear the last of these foul rumors
This calumny which poisons at the root
My noblest aspirations and endeavors
To live in harmony with my fellow men!
Oh, why must they refuse to understand me?
Why will they not requite my trust? What malice
To speak of threats when I appeal to reason!
To spurn the hand that I hold out in friendship!

BETTY

You hold it out to murder!

UI
                                    No!
  I plead with them and they revile me!
BETTY
                                                You
  Plead like a serpent pleading with a bird!
UI
  You've heard her. That's how people talk to me.
  It was the same with Dullfeet. He mistook
  My warm, my openhearted offer of friendship
  For calculation and my generosity
  For weakness. How, alas, did he requite
  My friendly words? With stony silence. Silence
  Was his reply when what I hoped for
  Was joyful appreciation. Oh, how I longed to
  Hear him respond to my persistent, my
  Well-nigh humiliating pleas for friendship, or
  At least for a little understanding, with
  Some sign of human warmth. I longed in vain.
  My only reward was grim contempt. And even
  The promise to keep silent that he gave me
  So sullenly and God knows grudgingly
  Was broken on the first occasion. Where
  I ask you is this silence that he promised
  So fervently? New horror stories are being
  Broadcast in all directions. But I warn you:
  Don't go too far, for even my proverbial
  Patience has got its breaking point!
BETTY
                                        Words fail me.
UI
  Unprompted by the heart, they always fail.
BETTY
  You call it heart that makes you speak so glibly?
UI
  I speak the way I feel.
BETTY
                          Can anybody feel
  The way you speak? Perhaps he can. Your murders

Come from the heart. Your blackest crimes are
As deeply felt as other men's good deeds!
As we believe in faith, so you believe in
Betrayal! No good impulse can corrupt you!
Unwavering in your inconstancy!
True to disloyalty, staunch in deception!
Kindled to sacred fire by bestial deeds!
The sight of blood delights you! Violence
Exalts your spirit! Sordid actions move you
To tears, and good ones leave you with deep-seated
Hatred and thirst for vengeance!

UI

                              Mrs. Dullfeet
I always—it's a principle of mine—
Hear out my opponent, even when
His words are gall. I know that in your circle
I'm not exactly loved. My origins—
Never have I denied that I'm a humble
Son of the Bronx—are held against me.
"He doesn't even know," they say, "which fork
To eat his fish with. How then can he hope
To be accepted in big business? When
Tariffs are being discussed, or similar
Financial matters, he's perfectly capable
Of reaching for his knife instead of his pen!
Impossible! We can't use such a man!"
My uncouth tone, my manly way of calling
A spade a spade are used as marks against me.
These barriers of prejudice compel me
To bank exclusively on my own achievement.
You're in the cauliflower business, Mrs.
Dullfeet, and so am I. There lies the bridge
Between us.

BETTY

                    And the chasm to be bridged
Is only foul murder!

UI

                    Bitter experience
Teaches me not to stress the human angle

But speak to you as a man of influence
Speaks to the owner of a greengoods business.
And so I ask you: How's the cauliflower
Business? For life goes on despite our sorrows.

BETTY

Yes, it goes on—and I shall use my life
To warn the people of this pestilence!
I swear to my dead husband that in future
I'll hate my voice if it should say "Good morning"
Or "Pass the bread" instead of one thing only:
"Extinguish Ui!"

GIRI (*in a threatening tone*)
                    Don't overdo it, kid!

UI

Because amid the tombs I dare not hope
For milder feelings, I'd better stick to business
Which knows no dead.

BETTY

                    O Dullfeet, Dullfeet! Now
I truly know that you are dead.

UI

                    Exactly.
Bear well in mind that Dullfeet's dead. With him
Has died the only voice in Cicero
That would have spoken out in opposition
To crime and terror. You cannot deplore
His loss too deeply! Now you stand defenseless
In a cold world where, sad to say, the weak
Are always trampled. You've got only one
Protector left. That's me, Arturo Ui.

BETTY

And this to me, the widow of the man
You murdered! Monster! Oh, I knew you'd be here
Because you've always gone back to the scene of
Your crimes to throw the blame on others. "No
It wasn't me, it was somebody else."
"I know of nothing." "I've been injured"
Cries injury. And murder cries: "A murder!
Murder must be avenged!"

UI

My plan stands fast.
Protection must be given to Cicero.

BETTY (*feebly*)

You won't succeed.

UI

I will! That much I know.

BETTY

From this protector God protect us!

UI

Give
Me your answer.
(*He holds out his hand*)
Is it friendship?

BETTY

Never while I live!
(*Cringing with horror, she runs out*)

(*A sign appears*)

14

*Ui's bedroom at the Mammoth Hotel. Ui tossing in his bed,
plagued by a nightmare. His bodyguards are sitting in chairs,
their revolvers on their laps.*

UI (*in his sleep*)

Out, bloody shades! Have pity! Get you gone!
(*The wall behind him becomes transparent. The ghost of
Ernesto Roma appears, a bullet hole in his forehead*)

ROMA

It will avail you nothing. All this murder
This butchery, these threats and slaverings
Are all in vain, Arturo, for the root of

Your crimes is rotten. They will never flower.
Treason is bad manure. Murder, lie
Deceive the Clarks and slay the Dullfeets, but
Stop at your own. Conspire against the world
But spare your fellow conspirators.
Trample the city with a hundred feet
But trample not the feet, you treacherous dog!
Cozen them all, but do not hope to cozen
The man whose face you look at in the mirror!
In striking me, you struck yourself, Arturo!
I cast my lot with you when you were hardly
More than a shadow on a barroom floor.
And now I languish in this drafty
Eternity, while you sit down to table
With sleek and proud directors. Treachery
Made you, and treachery will unmake you.
Just as you betrayed Ernesto Roma, your
Friend and lieutenant, so you will betray
Everyone else, and all, Arturo, will
Betray you in the end. The green earth covers
Ernesto Roma, but not your faithless spirit
Which hovers over tombstones in the wind
Where all can see it, even the gravediggers.
The day will come when all whom you struck down
And all you will strike down will rise, Arturo
And bleeding but made strong by hate, take arms
Against you. You will look around for help
As I once looked. Then promise, threaten, plead.
No one will help. Who helped me in my need?

UI (*jumping up with a start*)

Shoot! Kill him! Traitor! Get back to the dead!

(*The bodyguards shoot at the spot on the wall indicated
by Ui*)

ROMA (*fading away*)

What's left of me is not afraid of lead.

15

Financial district. Meeting of the Chicago vegetable dealers. They are deathly pale.

FIRST VEGETABLE DEALER
Murder! Extortion! Highway robbery!
SECOND VEGETABLE DEALER
And worse: submissiveness and cowardice!
THIRD VEGETABLE DEALER
What do you mean, submissiveness? In January
When the first two came barging into
My store and threatened me at gunpoint, I
Gave them a steely look from top to toe
And answered firmly: I incline to force.
I made it plain that I could not approve
Their conduct or have anything to do
With them. My countenance was ice.
It said: So be it, take your cut. But only
Because you've got those guns.
FOURTH VEGETABLE DEALER
                              Exactly!
I wash my hands in innocence! That's what
I told my missus.
FIRST VEGETABLE DEALER *(vehemently)*
                         What do you mean, cowardice?
We used our heads. If we kept quiet, gritted
Our teeth and paid, we thought those bloody fiends
Would put their guns away. But did they? No! It's
Murder! Extortion! Highway robbery!
SECOND VEGETABLE DEALER
Nobody else would swallow it. No backbone!
FIFTH VEGETABLE DEALER
No tommy-gun, you mean. I'm not a gangster.
My trade is selling greens.

THIRD VEGETABLE DEALER
                          My only hope
Is that the bastard some day runs across
Some guys who show their teeth. Just let him try his
Little game somewhere else!
FOURTH VEGETABLE DEALER
                          In Cicero
For instance!
(*The Cicero vegetable dealers come in. They are deathly pale*)
THE CICERONIANS
Hi, Chicago!
THE CHICAGOANS
              Hi, Cicero!
What brings *you* here?
THE CICERONIANS
                    We were told to come.
THE CHICAGOANS
By who?
THE CICERONIANS
          By him.
FIRST CHICAGOAN
              Who says so? How can he command
You? Throw his weight around in Cicero?
FIRST CICERONIAN
                                With
His gun.
SECOND CICERONIAN
          Brute force. We're helpless.
FIRST CHICAGOAN
                              Stinking cowards!
Can't you be men? Is there no law in Cicero?
FIRST CICERONIAN
No.
SECOND CICERONIAN
        No longer.
THIRD CHICAGOAN
              Listen, friends. You've got
To fight. This plague will sweep the country
If you don't stop it.

FIRST CHICAGOAN
                    First one city, then another.
   Fight to the death! You owe it to your country!
SECOND CICERONIAN
   Why us? We wash our hands in innocence.
FOURTH CHICAGOAN
   We only hope with God's help that the bastard
   Some day comes across some guys that show
   Their teeth.
   (*Fanfares. Enter Arturo Ui and Betty Dullfeet—in mourning
   —followed by Clark, Giri, Givola, and bodyguards. Flanked
   by the others, Ui passes through. The bodyguards line up in
   the background*)
GIRI
                    Hi, friends! Is everybody here
   From Cicero?
FIRST CICERONIAN
                    All present.
GIRI
                                And Chicago?
FIRST CHICAGOAN
   All present.
GIRI (*to Ui*)
                    Everybody's here.
GIVOLA
   Greetings, my friends. The Cauliflower Trust
   Wishes you all a hearty welcome. Our
   First speaker will be Mr. Clark. (*To Clark*) Mr. Clark.
CLARK
   Gentlemen, I bring news. Negotiations
   Begun some weeks ago and patiently
   Though sometimes stormily pursued—I'm telling
   Tales out of school—have yielded fruit. The wholesale
   House of B. Dullfeet, Cicero, has joined
   The Cauliflower Trust. In consequence
   The Cauliflower Trust will now supply
   Your greens. The gain for you is obvious:
   Secure delivery. The new prices, slightly
   Increased, have already been set. It is

With pleasure, Mrs. Dullfeet, that the Trust
Welcomes you as its newest member.
(*Clark and Betty Dullfeet shake hands*)

GIVOLA

And now: Arturo Ui.
(*Ui steps up to the microphone*)

UI

                                Friends, countrymen!
Chicagoans and Ciceronians! When
A year ago old Dogsborough, God rest
His honest soul, with tearful eyes
Appealed to me to protect Chicago's green-
Goods trade, though moved, I doubted whether
My powers would be able to justify
His smiling confidence. Now Dogsborough
Is dead. He left a will which you're all free
To read. In simple words therein he calls me
His son. And thanks me fervently for all
I've done since I responded to his appeal.
Today the trade in vegetables—
Be they kohlrabi, onions, carrots, or what
Have you—is amply protected in Chicago.
Thanks, I make bold to say, to resolute
Action on my part. When another civic
Leader, Ignatius Dullfeet, to my surprise
Approached me with the same request, this time
Concerning Cicero, I consented
To take that city under my protection.
But one condition I stipulated, namely:
The dealers had to want me. I would come
Only pursuant to their free decision
Freely arrived at. Cicero, I told
My men, in no uncertain terms, must not be
Subjected to coercion or constraint!
The city has to elect me in full freedom!
I want no grudging "Why not?" no teeth-gnashing
"We might as well." Half-hearted acquiescence
Is poison in my books. What I demand
Is one unanimous and joyful "Yes"

Succinct and, men of Cicero, expressive.
And since I want this and everything else I want
To be complete, I turn again to you
Men of Chicago, who, because you know
Me better, hold me, I have reason to believe
In true esteem, and ask you: Who is for me?
And just in passing let me add: If anyone's
Not for me he's against me and has only
Himself to blame for anything that happens.
Now you may vote!

GIVOLA

               But first a word from Mrs.
Dullfeet, the widow, known to all of you, of
A man beloved by all.

BETTY

             Dear friends
Your faithful friend and my beloved husband
Ignatius Dullfeet is no longer with us to . . .

GIVOLA

God rest his soul!

BETTY

                . . . sustain and help you. I
Advise you all to put your trust in Mr.
Ui, as I do now that in these grievous days
I've come to know him better.

GIVOLA

             Time to vote!

GIRI

All those in favor of Arturo Ui
Raise your right hands!
(*Some raise their hands*)

A CICERONIAN

Is it permissible to leave?

GIVOLA

          Each man
Is free to do exactly as he pleases.
(*Hesitantly the Ciceronian goes out. Two bodyguards follow
him. A shot is heard*)

GIRI

All right, friends. Let's have your free decision!
(*All raise both hands*)

GIVOLA

They've finished voting, boss. With deep emotion
Teeth chattering for joy, the greengoods dealers
Of Cicero and Chicago thank you
For your benevolent protection.

UI

                    With
Pride I accept your thanks. Some fifteen years
Ago, when I was only a humble, unemployed
Son of the Bronx; when following the call
Of destiny I sallied forth with only
Seven staunch men to brave the Windy City
I was inspired by an iron will
To create peace in the vegetable trade.
We were a handful then, who humbly but
Fanatically strove for this ideal
Of peace! Today we are a multitude.
Peace in Chicago's vegetable trade
Has ceased to be a dream. Today it is
Unvarnished reality. And to secure
This peace I have put in an order
For more machine-guns, rubber truncheons
Etcetera. For Chicago and Cicero
Are not alone in clamoring for protection!
There are other cities: Washington and Milwaukee!
Detroit! Toledo! Pittsburgh! Cincinnati!
And other towns where vegetables are traded!
Philadelphia! Baltimore! St. Louis! Little Rock!
Minneapolis! Columbus! Charleston! And New York!
They all demand protection! And no "Phooey!"
No "That's not nice!" will stop Arturo Ui!
(*Amid drums and fanfares the curtain falls*)

(*A sign appears*)

Epilogue

Therefore learn how to see and not to gape.
To act instead of talking all day long.
The world was almost won by such an ape!
The nations put him where his kind belong.
But don't rejoice too soon at your escape—
The womb he crawled from still is going strong.

Chronological Table

1. 1929–32. Germany is hard hit by the world crisis. At the height of the crisis a number of Prussian Junkers try to obtain government loans, for a long time without success. The big industrialists in the Ruhr dream of expansion.

2. By way of winning President Hindenburg's sympathy for their cause, the Junkers make him a present of a landed estate.

3. In the fall of 1932, Adolf Hitler's party and private army are threatened with bankruptcy and disintegration. To save the situation Hitler tries desperately to have himself appointed chancellor, but for a long time Hindenburg refuses to see him.

4. In January 1933 Hindenburg appoints Hitler chancellor in return for a promise to prevent the exposure of the East Aid scandal, in which Hindenburg himself is implicated.

5. After coming to power legally, Hitler surprises his high patrons by extremely violent measures, but keeps his promises.

6. The gang leader quickly transforms himself into a statesman. He is believed to have taken lessons in declamation and bearing from one Basil, a provincial actor.

7. February 1933, the Reichstag fire. Hitler accuses his enemies of setting the fire and gives the signal for the "Night of the Long Knives."

8. The Supreme Court in Leipzig condemns an unemployed worker to death for setting the fire. The real incendiaries get off scot free. From then on the German judiciary work for Hitler.

9. and 10. The impending death of the aged Hindenburg provokes bitter struggles in the Nazi camp. The Junkers and industrialists demand Röhm's removal. The occupation of Austria is planned.

11. On the night of June 30, 1934, Hitler overpowers his friend Röhm at an inn where Röhm has been waiting for him. Up to the last moment Röhm thinks that Hitler is coming

to arrange for a joint strike against Hindenburg and Göring.

12. Under compulsion the Austrian Chancellor Engelbert Dollfuss agrees to stop the attacks on Hitler that have been
appearing in the Austrian press.

13. Dollfuss is murdered at Hitler's instigation, but Hitler goes
on negotiating with Austrian rightist circles.

15. The occupation of Austria is the first of many European
conquests. It is followed by the seizure of Czechoslovakia,
Poland, Denmark, Norway, Holland, Belgium, France, Ro-
mania, etc.

Dansen

Translators: Rose and Martin Kastner

CHARACTERS

DANSEN
THE STRANGER

On the stage are three house fronts. One is a tobacco store with the sign: "Austrian—Tobacconist." In the second is a shoe store with the sign: "Czech—Boots and Shoes." In the third there is no store, but a sign in the window reads: "Fresh ham." Next to this house front there is a large iron door with a sign saying: "Svendson. Iron."

1

Beside the door sits Dansen. He is a small man. In front of him is a tub. He is holding a pig under his arm.

DANSEN (*to the audience*)   I'm a little man, respected, well-off and independent. I get along perfectly with my neighbors. We settle all disagreements between us peacefully through an organization to which almost all of us belong. We have pacts that cover everything. So far we've been doing fine. I have my freedom and my business connections, I have my friends and my customers, I have my principles and I raise pigs. (*He starts scrubbing the pig in the tub*) There. And now, my boy, hold still and let me wash your rosy ears. We've got to look nice when the customers turn up: healthy, happy, and succulent. If we're good and eat properly, we'll go far in life. The customer will say: That's a good little pig. After all, what do you want in this world? What does your little heart desire? You desire to be sold. Oh, you're clever. Whenever you suspect that I'm neglecting you, that I've forgotten your heart's desire for one moment, you let out

a loud squeal and remind me. If anyone passes by who looks the least bit as if he hadn't eaten yet, you squeal. That way I myself have nothing to worry ab . . .
(*The pig squeals*)

DANSEN (*looks up, pleased*)   What is it? What is it? Is somebody coming? A customer?
(*Stealthily, looking anxiously around, an armed man approaches the tobacco store; his hat is drawn down over his eyes. He stops outside the closed door and takes a bunch of passkeys out of his trouser pocket. He tries them one after another, meanwhile smiling at Dansen, whose hair is beginning to stand on end. Finally the burglar loses patience and climbs in through the window, holding a large pistol. Immediately a terrible din is heard from inside: a falling chair, loud cries for help. Dansen jumps up in horror. With the pig under his arm, he runs around wildly. Then he rushes to the telephone*)

DANSEN   Svendson, Svendson! What should I do? They're shouting for help in the tobacco store across the street. A stranger has broken in before my very eyes.—What, you can hear the screams from where you are?—No, of course I can't go in, I have no right to barge into someone else's house. But what should I do when he comes out? I'm trembling with indignation.—Don't worry, I'll give him a good piece of my mind. You know my policy, no, not insurance policy, policy . . . (*after warily looking around, he sings into the telephone in a muffled voice*)

A Dansen does his duty
In every town and land
For his sincere opinions
He bravely takes his stand.

In short, I'll fling my loathing in his face. As I said, I'm trembling with indignation.
(*The calls for help have stopped. A scream, a pistol shot, and a loud thud are heard*)

DANSEN   I've got to hang up. I have to sit down. I think my hair has turned gray.

(*Deep in gloom, he sits down again outside the house, his pig under his arm. The stranger comes out of the tobacco store, quickly crosses out the word "Austrian" with chalk and writes "Ostmarker & Co." over it. Then he steps up to Dansen*)

THE STRANGER   Why are you looking so pale?

DANSEN   My dear fellow, I'll tell you. I'm pale with pent-up agitation.

THE STRANGER   You could learn from your charming little pig. He's pink and he stays pink.

DANSEN   But a pig isn't human. I'm pale with human emotion, and you know why.

THE STRANGER   What a *good* little pig!

DANSEN (*points accusingly at the tobacco store*)   What . . . what . . . happened in there?

THE STRANGER   Do you really want to know?

DANSEN   Of course I want to know! Anything that happens to my fellow man . . .

(*The pig squeals a second time*)

DANSEN   What is it? What is it?

THE STRANGER   You mean you don't want to know!

DANSEN (*to the pig*)   But that man . . . (*He points at the to-bacco store*)

THE STRANGER   Did you know him?

DANSEN   Did I know him? No, yes, I'm sorry, I'm all mixed up. (*Reproachfully*) We belonged to the same club.

THE STRANGER   What did you do in your club? Sell pigs?

DANSEN (*morosely*)   We played cards. We played noninter-vention.

THE STRANGER   I can't afford that game. Too expensive.

DANSEN   We only play once a week. On Saturdays. (*Points at the tobacco store*) He comes too.

THE STRANGER   I don't think he'll be coming any more.

DANSEN   Are you going to tell him not to? That would be an outrage. I mean it. Austrian is a free man.

THE STRANGER (*hesitantly*)   Nobody'll be telling him anything now. (*He laughs mirthlessly*)

DANSEN (*indignantly*)   What do you mean by that?

THE STRANGER   Do you really want to know?

DANSEN   Do I want to know? Yes, no. I don't know, my head
is swimming. You stand here talking as if . . . and just a
minute ago, with my own eyes, I saw . . . Of course I want
to know! Abso . . .
(*The pig under his arm squeals a third time in terror, as
though cruelly maltreated*)

DANSEN (*tonelessly completes the word*)   . . . lutely. (*His confidence is gone; he is afraid to meet the eyes of the stranger,
who is now stroking the pig*)

DANSEN   I don't understand the world any more. I'm a peace-
loving man. I loathe violence and respect agreements. I have
business connections and I have my freedom, a few customers
and a few friends, I have my pig farm and my . . . (*Almost
without thinking*) Would you care to buy a pig?

THE STRANGER (*flabbergasted*)   I beg your pardon?

DANSEN   A pig? Three or four pigs? I could let you have them
cheap. I've got so many. Too many. I've got pigs to burn.

THE STRANGER   Let's have one.

DANSEN (*intently*)   Sure you don't want two?

THE STRANGER   One.

DANSEN   But what will I do with the rest? They breed like
rabbits. Every night I drown half a dozen in the manure pit,
and every morning another dozen are born. (*Gestures to
the stranger to look into the pigsty*) You see, there are fourteen of them again.

THE STRANGER   *One*.

DANSEN   Take a good look at them. Aren't they healthy,
amiable, and succulent? Don't they make your mouth water?

THE STRANGER (*whose mouth is watering, with an effort*)
They're a luxury.

DANSEN   How can you say such a thing when they're a hundred percent edible? Even the ears. Even the toes. Fried
pig's toes.

THE STRANGER   A luxury.

DANSEN (*grieved, to the pig*)   You a luxury! (*Disappointed,
to the stranger*) In that case, we'll make it just two.

THE STRANGER (*loudly*)   One. I don't waste money on luxuries.

DANSEN   You buy iron, though. You buy all the iron my
friend Svendson can deliver.

THE STRANGER   Iron isn't a luxury. Iron is a necessity.

DANSEN   (*gives him the pig; his hands are trembling*)   My nerves are shot. That terrible experience just now . . . (*He wipes the sweat off his neck with a red handkerchief*)

THE STRANGER   What's that red rag you've got there?

DANSEN   This?

THE STRANGER   (*roughly*)   Yes, that. (*He puts the pig back in the tub*)

DANSEN   (*eager to please*)   It's not red. Look, it's got a white cross on it. (*He points at it*)

THE STRANGER   Okay. (*He throws money down*)

DANSEN   I'll wrap it up for you.

THE STRANGER   Take this paper. Otherwise you'll charge me for the wrapping. (*He hands him a large sheet of paper he has taken out of his pocket*)

DANSEN   (*smoothing out the paper*)   But this is a pact!

THE STRANGER   What kind of a pact?

DANSEN   With Mr. Austrian, I think. Friendship pact, it says. Don't you need it any more?

THE STRANGER   No. What's the use of a friendship pact with a stiff? (*He takes the paper away from him and tears it up*)

DANSEN   (*almost fainting*)   Quick, take the pig. I'm feeling sick.

(*The stranger takes the pig from his hands. Dansen puts his handkerchief on his head*)

THE STRANGER   (*looking at the cross with irritation*)   Put that cross away!

(*Dansen puts the handkerchief back in his pocket*)

THE STRANGER   I'll take the pig as it is. Maybe I'll cut off a chunk on the way. (*He takes it under his arm. But before he goes, he looks at the shoe store*)   Nice place, that shoe store.

DANSEN   Yes, very nice.

THE STRANGER   Plenty of room. Your house isn't bad either.

DANSEN   (*without thinking*)   I like it.

THE STRANGER   (*looking at it dreamily*)   Well, I'll be seeing you. (*Goes out*)

DANSEN   (*wiping his forehead, unnerved*)   I'll be seeing you!— I was so indignant I went and sold him a pig. Look what he's

done to that nice peace-loving Mr. Austrian. Just simply . . .
The damn brute! (*Looking anxiously around, he goes into
the corner between his house and the warehouse door and
grumbles*) Barbarian! Inhuman monster! What a way to
treat a pact!

2

Dansen is sitting in front of his house with a pig on his lap.

DANSEN   I'm a respected man, but a little one. I have a feeling
things aren't right any more. The dreadful incidents lately
have really got me down. Pacts are wonderful things, but if
they're not held sacred . . . My two friends next door and I
have been toying with the idea of arming ourselves. We're
not entirely helpless. There aren't many suppliers of iron
beside my friend Svendson. Right here in the warehouse (*he
points to Svendson's warehouse*) we've got quite a supply of
iron. If we used it to forge weapons . . . It would be sheer
madness to bury our heads in the sand. On the other hand,
we can't afford a repetition of those dreadful events. What's-
his-name can't do such a thing twice.
(*Stealthily, looking anxiously around, the stranger approaches the shoe store; his cap is drawn down over his eyes.
He stops outside the closed door and takes a bunch of passkeys out of his trouser pocket. He tries them one after another, shaking his head now and then and smiling at Dansen,
whose hair is beginning to stand on end. Finally the stranger
loses patience and climbs in through the window, holding a
large pistol. Immediately a terrible din is heard from inside:
a falling chair, loud cries for help*)
DANSEN   He's done it again. This is terrible. And to think that
the poor old woman had an agreement with him. There's
something sick about that man's greed. Whatever he sees he
wants. What about my own house? Not bad, he said. I'll

have to take very firm steps immediately. And whatever I do, I mustn't attract his attention. I'll have to disappear. But how can I prevent him from seeing me? Ah, the tub! (*With the pig under his arm, he pulls the tub, which he ordinarily uses to wash his pigs in, over his head*)

(*The stranger steps out of the shoe store. He hurriedly crosses out the name "Czech" with chalk and writes "Protectorate, Inc."*)

(*At this moment Dansen's pig is heard squealing inside the tub*)

DANSEN'S VOICE   What is it? What is it? Is somebody coming? A customer? (*He looks out cautiously, sees the stranger writing, and ducks back in again*)

(*The stranger steps forward, takes a sheet of paper from his pocket and tears it up. The scraps fall to the ground*)

THE STRANGER   Hey, what's become of that pig farmer? Probably stepped out for a drink. Good chance to take a look at Svendson's iron warehouse. (*Looking around, he saunters over to the warehouse door and, turning his back to it, tries the handle. But the door is locked*)

(*Suddenly Dansen's phone rings. At first Dansen sits motionless. When it goes on ringing, he is obliged to answer it. With extreme caution he gets up and with the tub still over him goes to the phone. The stranger looks with amazement at the walking tub*)

THE STRANGER (*instantly*)   Mighty suspicious!

(*Since Dansen, under the tub, cannot see the stranger, he almost bumps into him, but the stranger, grinning, steps out of his way. Reaching the telephone, which rests on a low lard crate in front of the house, Dansen settles down, bent over the crate*)

DANSEN (*under his breath into the telephone, but the receiver reverberates slightly under the tub*)   That you, Svendson? —Oh, you've heard the latest terrible news?—No, good God, not my place. Why do you keep thinking it happened at my place? It gives me the creeps.—Of course we've got to do something together. We'll have to consider taking very firm action. No, not take, consider—Arm ourselves? Out of the question!—Stand united, yes, but arm, no.—United in what? In not arming! That would only attract his attention, and I've done everything in my power to avoid that.—Yes, I said we've got to be united. Our unity must be iron-clad and directed against no one. (*Very emphatically*) Against no one. Then it can't attract attention.—Yes, Svendson, you can rely on me.—I understand perfectly that your mind wouldn't be at ease about your warehouse, no, not for a minute, if I were to give up one grain of my independence. I'll keep my nose strictly out of the whole business. And stick to selling my pigs, period.—Where I keep the key to your warehouse? Where I always keep it, of course, on a string around my neck, under my shirt.—Naturally I'm keeping my eyes open.—That burglary the other day, when your letter to me was stolen? Yes, but that was a burglary, there's nothing we can do about that.—Of course I won't give anybody the key, never!—Let somebody take it? What do you think I am?—Under pressure? Nobody has ever put pressure on me, I've never given anyone reason to.—I'm being watched? Ridiculous! Nobody's watching me, I'd notice it, wouldn't I?—You insist on strong action? I'm all for it. I suggest we sign a pact. Before the day's over we must absolutely sign a pact.—That's it, against everybody who doesn't keep their pacts. Listen. I have a brilliant idea, we'll agree not to sell any more iron to a certain notorious troublemaker and disturber of the peace, we'll offer it to decent people instead.—Not so brilliant? Why?—You say the big shots are already discussing effective measures?

(*The stranger, who has sat down and has been quietly listening, knocks on the tub*)

DANSEN (*in his tub, alarmed*) Hold on! I'll have to break off for a second.—No, I've got to wait on a customer. We'll go on with our discussion right away.

(*The stranger pulls him out of the tub by the seat of his pants*)

THE STRANGER Looks like I got here in the nick of time. How did you get stuck in that tub? If I hadn't come along, you'd have suffocated.

(*Dansen sits on the ground in sullen silence*)

THE STRANGER Why are you so quiet? Is something worrying

you? You know, Dansen, I've been thinking the two of us ought to get better acquainted. It's really nice sitting here with you. The house is small but not at all bad. What would you say to a mutual friendship pact?

DANSEN (*his hair standing on end*)   Friendship pact . . .

THE STRANGER   Friendship pact. (*He strokes Dansen's pig*) You're a good little pig! Are you a good little pig? I suggest we sign a pact. Saying we're friends. (*He takes a pencil stub from his vest pocket, stands up and picks up one of the paper scraps from the ground. On the back of the scrap he scribbles a few words*) You simply agree not to attack me under any circumstances, if for instance I take one of your pigs or something. And I agree in return that you can call on me for protection at any time. Well, what do you say?

DANSEN   No offense, but I wouldn't want to make that kind of decision on the spur of the moment.

THE STRANGER   You wouldn't?

(*Dansen's pig squeals for the second time*)

DANSEN (*aside to his pig*)   You keep quiet! (*To the stranger*) I'd have to phone my friend Svendson first.

THE STRANGER   Oh, so you won't sign? (*Dansen is silent*) That's funny. Didn't I hear you say you wanted a pact before the day's over? (*To Dansen's pig, stroking it*) You're a smart little pig. We understand each other. There'd never be any disagreement between us. But I guess it's no go. I don't force myself on anyone. If my offers of friendship are trampled underfoot, there's nothing for me to do but leave. (*Looking offended, he stands up*)

(*The pig squeals a third time*)

DANSEN (*wipes the sweat from his neck with his red handkerchief*)   Wait! (*The stranger turns around*) Maybe I was a little hasty. I've been so confused by the recent events. You wanted to buy a pig?

THE STRANGER   Why not?

DANSEN (*hoarsely*)   Then give me the pact. (*He signs*) But don't you need a duplicate?

STRANGER   Not necessary. (*He takes the pig under his arm*) Send me the bill after New Year's. (*On his way out*) And kindly don't forget that you're friends with *me* now and you're to choose your company accordingly. I'll be seeing you.

DANSEN (*in amazement*) Now I've made a friendship pact with *him*. (*Holding the pact, he returns hesitantly to the phone*) Hello, Svendson. It's Dansen. I've got something to tell you. No sooner said than done, I've made a pact.—With whom? With What's-his-name.—He doesn't keep agreements? But I've got his personal signature. Hold on, let's see what it says . . . I haven't read it through yet . . . oh yes, *he* agrees not to attack me, and *I* agree not to help anyone he attacks.—If he attacks you? Out of the question. He can't keep on doing these things. Your warehouse is as safe as the Bank of England.—Who you can rely on? On me! You can rely on me. And I can rely on him.

3

Dansen is standing in front of his house, still on the phone.

DANSEN I don't see how you can say our unity is in danger when I've been telling you now for three days and three nights that it's not in danger.—All right, let me tell you this: if he doesn't keep *this* pact, I won't hesitate for one moment to invest every penny I've saved out of my pig business in the last five years on arming ourselves to the teeth with your iron. What do you think of that?—Right now it would be madness. There's no reason for it.—What *about* the sky? (*He looks around*) Yes, my goodness, it really is red.
(*During the conversation the sky has turned slightly red. Muffled thunder in the distance*)

DANSEN Say, that's funny thunder. I think we'll have to break off. Got to take a look at my pigs.—Yes, of course, your warehouse too. I'm really glad about that pact now, especially for your sake.—Now you'll see what a shrewd move I made. Want to bet that What's-his-name is beginning to feel sorry he made me that promise? In any case we'll keep in tou . . . Hello! Are you there, Svendson? (*He shakes the telephone, but the line has gone dead*) Damn it, this is a fine time for the phone to go dead! (*He goes to the tub and fishes out his pact. Then he unties the rope attaching the pig to the tub*) Yes, sir, where would I be now without this paper? I'm dog-tired. The pigs were so restless I had to tie them up, and all this phoning has been a strain. And to make matters worse I'll have to stand guard outside the warehouse tonight, I owe that to my friend Svendson. (*Shouldering the rolled-up pact like a rifle, he marches up and down in front of the warehouse, occasionally shading his eyes with one hand and peering into the distance. He soon begins to drag his feet*) If I let my vigilance flag for so much as one second, the consequences for myself and my friends up the street will be incalculable. (*He sits down with his back to the warehouse wall; the pig is now on his lap. He yawns*) It's unbelievable. Now he's even picking a fight with Pollack, the horse trader. (*Dozes off, wakes with a start, reaches for the big warehouse key that he is wearing around his neck, under his shirt, and pulls it out*) Anyway I've got the key. (*He puts it back*) I don't see why Pollack doesn't just sign . . . a pact . . . with him . . . (*He falls asleep*)

(*It gets dark. Only the reddish horizon remains visible. Slowly a sign with the words "Dansen's Dream" on it comes down from the flies*)

(*A rosy light fills the stage. Dansen and the stranger stand facing each other. Dansen is leading his pig on a rope and shouldering his pact. The stranger, still in civilian clothes, is armed to the teeth. He is wearing a steel helmet; he has hand grenades in his belt, and a tommy-gun under his arm*)

THE STRANGER   I've been attacked. I was paying an innocent little visit to a certain Pollack, I'd arranged to meet a friend of mine at his place. While I was in the house, the neighbors surrounded me and attacked me. You've got to help me.

DANSEN   But . . .

THE STRANGER   Don't talk so much. I haven't a moment to lose. There's not enough iron in my house. I need the key to my friend Svendson's warehouse right away.

DANSEN   But I can't let it out of my hands.

THE STRANGER   You can give it to me. The warehouse definitely needs protection, it's full of iron and you're in no position to defend it. Give me the key! Quick!

DANSEN   But the key was given to me for safekeeping. I'll at least have to phone my friend Svendson first . . .

THE STRANGER   Your safekeeping is my safekeeping. This is no time to quibble. Hands up! (*He threatens him with his tommy-gun*)

(*Dansen suddenly aims his pact at the stranger and stands motionless in this menacing position*)

THE STRANGER   (*not believing his eyes*)   Are you out of your mind? What's that you've got there?

DANSEN   My pact!

THE STRANGER   (*contemptuously*)   Pacts! Who says I have to respect pacts?

DANSEN   Maybe you don't have to respect the others. But you've got to respect this one with me!

THE STRANGER   (*letting his gun drop*)   This is terrible! I *need* that iron. Everybody's against me.

DANSEN   I'm sorry.

THE STRANGER   But I'm lost without it. I'll be trampled to a pulp, do you hear me, a pulp!

DANSEN   You should have thought of that before, my friend.

THE STRANGER   My whole livelihood is at stake! I've got to get in there! I've got to, I've got to!

DANSEN   (*holds up the paper*)   I'm sorry, it can't be done.

THE STRANGER   I'll buy all your pigs, Dansen, if you'll cooperate!

DANSEN   I can't do it, friend.

(*Dansen's pig squeals. A gong sounds in the distance*)

DANSEN   Shut up! When freedom is at stake. (*To the stranger*) We're sorry.

THE STRANGER   (*going down on his knees, sobbing*)   Please, I beg you, the key! Don't be heartless! My family, my wife, my children, my mother, my grandmother! My aunts!

DANSEN   It can't be done. I deeply sympathize, but it can't be done. A pact's a pact.

THE STRANGER (*broken, stands up with difficulty*) There's only one thing left for me to do: hang myself. This pact is costing me, one of your best customers, my life. (*Crushed, he turns to go*)
(*The pig squeals a second time. Again the distant gong*)

DANSEN Shut up. You make me sick. You haven't got a penny's worth of morality. (*To the stranger*) And you, don't come to me any more with your immoral demands, understand! They won't go down with me, the next time I might lose my patience! (*As the stranger staggers away, Dansen, clutching the pact in his fist, sings the third stanza of* "King Christian Stood by the Tall Mast")

Niels Juel he shouted to the gale
"The time has come!"
Hoisted the red flag like a sail
And bade the enemy turn tail.
Aloud he shouted in the gale
"The time has come!"
"Vile knaves," he shouted, "leave the stage!
For who will not to Dansen's rage
Succumb!"

(*But when he comes to the last line, he is horrified to hear the pig squeal a third time*)
(*The stranger suddenly turns around looking triumphant. Darkness. Another sign is lowered. On it is written* "And Dansen's Awakening")
(*The light goes on. The pig has gone on squealing. Beside Dansen, who is still leaning against the warehouse door asleep, stands the stranger, armed to the teeth. He gives Dansen a kick. Dansen wakes up with a start*)

THE STRANGER Give me that key!

DANSEN I can't let anyone have it!

THE STRANGER Then you're breaking the pact, you swine. You think you can make a friendship pact with me and then refuse me your friendship? (*Kicks him*) You think you can defraud me of the key I need to get at the iron? Now you've proved you're my enemy, one of the worst. (*He grabs the pact out of his hands and tears it up*) And now for the last time: give me that key!

(*Dansen reaches for the key and, staring at the stranger, takes it out. The stranger grabs it and opens the door*)

DANSEN (*amazed*)   Goodness, I've honored the pact by giving him Svendson's key!

THE STRANGER (*in the doorway, turns around to Dansen, takes the pig's rope out of his hands and says menacingly*)   I expect you to hand over the rest of the pigs without being asked, and don't let me see any bills! (*He goes into Svendson's warehouse with Dansen's pig*)

How Much
Is Your Iron?

Translators: Rose and Martin Kastner

CHARACTERS

SVENDSON
THE CUSTOMER
MR. AUSTRIAN, a tobacconist
MRS. CZECH, owner of a shoe store
THE GENTLEMAN
THE LADY

Prologue

An Englishman, dear friends, not long ago
Spun out a fable, which we soon will show.
With two young Swedes he'd met near the Old Vic
He downed a few, and talked of politics;
But though they quaffed much brandy, ale, and rye
He and the Swedes could not see eye to eye.
Next day, the Englishman took pen in hand
And wrote a parable that all could understand.
This fable made his point both sharp and clear—
For your diversion, now, we'll show it here.
The scene: a shop with iron bars for sale.
You'll recognize the merchant without fail.
The shoe store lady and the tobacconist
Are figures that can't easily be missed.
And by our playlet's end—if not before—
You'll know which fellow's grabbing all the ore.
Even a simpleton, we dare to say
Will get the point: so now let's start the play!

An iron dealer's store. A wooden door and a wooden table.

1

*On the table lie iron bars. The storekeeper is polishing them
with a cloth. On an easel an enormous calendar showing the
date: 1938.*
A tobacconist comes in with cigar boxes under his arm.

MR. AUSTRIAN   Good morning, Mr. Svendson. How are you
for smokes? I've got some fine cigars here, thirty cents
apiece, genuine Austrillos.

SVENDSON   Good morning, Mr. Austrian. Let's have a look!
What an aroma. You know how crazy I am about your
cigars. Unfortunately my business hasn't been doing very
well. I'll have to cut down on my smoking. No, I can't take
any today. I can't see my way clear. No hard feelings, Mr.
Austrian. Maybe next time.

MR. AUSTRIAN   This is a bit of a disappointment. But of course
I understand. (*He packs up his wares*)

SVENDSON   Been having a pleasant round, Mr. Austrian?

MR. AUSTRIAN   Not very pleasant, Mr. Svendson. I'm afraid
your store is rather out of the way.

SVENDSON   Out of the way? Nobody ever told me that before.

MR. AUSTRIAN   I'd never thought of it before myself. The fact
is, we all live pretty far from each other. But today I met a
man on the way here and I've had a funny feeling ever since.

SVENDSON   How come? Was he rude to you?

MR. AUSTRIAN   Far from it. He spoke to me like an old friend.
He called me by my first name and said we were related.
News to me, I told him. What, he says, you didn't know?
And he glares at me like I was a bad oyster. And then he
starts explaining exactly how we're related and the longer he
talks the more related we are.

SVENDSON   Is that so bad?

MR. AUSTRIAN   No, but he said he'd be coming to see me soon.

SVENDSON   You make it sound like a threat.

MR. AUSTRIAN   There was nothing unusual about his words.
He said that maybe he had one weakness, an over-developed
family sense. When he discovers he's even remotely related
to somebody he just can't live without him.

SVENDSON   That's not such a bad thing to say.

MR. AUSTRIAN   No, but he shouted so when he said it.

SVENDSON   And that frightened you?

MR. AUSTRIAN   To tell you the truth, it did.

SVENDSON   Good Lord, you're shaking. Like a leaf.

MR. AUSTRIAN   Because I can't get him out of my head.

SVENDSON   Nerves. You ought to live up here, in this pure air.

MR. AUSTRIAN   Maybe. The one good thing is that he didn't seem to be armed. If he were, I might be really worried. Oh, well, we all have our headaches, and no one can have them for us.

SVENDSON   No.

MR. AUSTRIAN   Another thing that struck me as odd was that before he let me go he suggested we sign an agreement never to say anything detrimental about each other.

SVENDSON   That sounds fair enough. Honest give-and-take.

MR. AUSTRIAN   Think so?

(*Pause*)

MR. AUSTRIAN   Maybe I ought to have some kind of weapon.

SVENDSON   Yes. It might come in handy.

MR. AUSTRIAN   Unfortunately weapons are expensive.

SVENDSON   That's a fact.

MR. AUSTRIAN   Well, good-bye, Mr. Svendson.

SVENDSON   Good-bye, Mr. Austrian.

(*Mr. Austrian goes out*)

(*Svendson stands up and does Swedish exercises with his iron bars, in time to monotonous music*)

(*A customer in an ill-fitting suit enters*)

THE CUSTOMER (*in a hoarse voice*)   How much is your iron?

SVENDSON   A crown a bar.

THE CUSTOMER   Expensive.

SVENDSON   I've got to earn my living.

THE CUSTOMER   I see.

SVENDSON   Your face looks familiar.

THE CUSTOMER   You knew my brother. He often came here.

SVENDSON   How's he getting along?

THE CUSTOMER   Dead. He left me the business.

SVENDSON   I'm sorry to hear it.

THE CUSTOMER (*menacingly*)   Really?

SVENDSON   I didn't mean about your having the business, I meant about his being dead.

THE CUSTOMER   You seem to have been very close friends with him.

SVENDSON   Not really. But he was a good customer.

THE CUSTOMER   And now I'm your customer.

SVENDSON   At your service. I suppose you want two bars, same as your brother?

THE CUSTOMER   Four.

SVENDSON   That will be four crowns.

THE CUSTOMER   (*pulls some bills out of his pocket. Hesitantly*) They've got a few spots on them. Coffee stains. Do you mind?

SVENDSON   (*examining the bills*)   This isn't coffee.

THE CUSTOMER   What is it then?

SVENDSON   It's reddish.

THE CUSTOMER   Then it must be blood. (*Pause*) I cut my finger. (*Pause*) Do you want the money or not?

SVENDSON   I don't think I'll have any trouble getting rid of it.

THE CUSTOMER   No. I'm sure you won't.

SVENDSON   Very well. (*He puts the bills in the cash drawer while the customer takes his bars under his arm. Casually*) Oh, by the way. My old friend the tobacconist dropped in a little while ago. He complained of being stopped and molested by a stranger on the way here. Has anybody molested you?

THE CUSTOMER   No. No one has molested me. No one even spoke to me, which rather surprised me, I must say. Your friend seems to be a liar of the worst kind.

SVENDSON   (*taking offense*)   You have no right to say that.

THE CUSTOMER   The world is full of liars, thieves, and murderers.

SVENDSON   I don't subscribe to that. My friend seemed really worried. I was even thinking of giving him one of my iron bars to defend himself with if necessary.

THE CUSTOMER   I wouldn't advise you to do that. It would make for bad blood in the neighborhood if you started arming everybody free of charge. Take it from me, they're all a lot of thieves and murderers. And liars. Your best bet is to keep your nose clean and peacefully attend to your iron business. I'm speaking as a peace-loving individual. Just don't put any weapons into those people's hands! They don't know where the next meal is coming from. You put weapons into the hands of a hungry man and . . .

SVENDSON   I see what you mean.

THE CUSTOMER   Say, aren't we related?

SVENDSON (*surprised*)   What makes you think that?

THE CUSTOMER   I'm pretty sure. Through our great-grand-
fathers or something.

SVENDSON   I believe you're mistaken.

THE CUSTOMER   Really? Well, I'll be going now. Good iron
you've got here. It's expensive, but I need it. What can I do
if I need it? You think the price will come down?

SVENDSON   I doubt it.

(*The customer turns toward the door. A rumbling sound is
heard*)

SVENDSON   Did you say something?

THE CUSTOMER   Me? No, that's my stomach. I'd been eating
too much for a while. Now I'm fasting.

SVENDSON (*laughs*)   Oh! Well, good day.

(*The customer goes out*)

SVENDSON (*picks up the phone*)   Is that you, Dansen? Listen,
that new man has just been here.—Oh, he's been at your
place too? He bought some of my merchandise.—Oh, he's
bought from you too? Well, as long as he pays he's good
enough for me.—Of course he's good enough for you too
as long as he pays.

(*The stage grows dark*)

2

The calendar in the iron shop reads 1939.
Mrs. Czech comes in with some shoe boxes under her arm.

MRS. CZECH   Good morning, Mr. Svendson. Can I interest you
in some shoes? (*She takes out a pair of large yellow shoes*)
Good sturdy oxfords, eleven crowns a pair, genuine Czech
workmanship.

SVENDSON　Good morning, Mrs. Czech. I'm always glad to see you. My business hasn't been doing very well lately, so I'm afraid I can't afford new shoes at the moment, but rest assured, I won't buy from anyone else. But you look rather upset, Mrs. Czech.

MRS. CZECH　(*looking around fearfully from time to time*) Does that surprise you? Haven't you heard the terrible news about the tobacconist?

SVENDSON　What about him?

MRS. CZECH　This tobacconist, a Mr. Austrian, was attacked on the street. Robbed and murdered.

SVENDSON　You don't say so! Why, that's terrible.

MRS. CZECH　The whole neighborhood's talking about it. They want to organize a police force. We must all join up. You too, Mr. Svendson.

SVENDSON　(*dismayed*)　Me? No, that's impossible. I'm not cut out for police work, Mrs. Czech, not in the least. I'm a peace-loving man. Besides, my iron business takes up all my time. I want to sell my iron in peace, that's enough for me.

MRS. CZECH　The man who attacked the tobacconist must have been well armed. I want a weapon too, I'm frightened. Send me one of your iron bars, Mr. Svendson.

SVENDSON　Glad to. With the greatest pleasure, Mrs. Czech. One iron bar, that will be one crown.

MRS. CZECH　(*fumbling in her purse*)　Goodness, there must be a crown in here.

SVENDSON　Why, your hands are trembling, Mrs. Czech.

MRS. CZECH　Here it is. (*She has brought out the crown*) On my way here a man spoke to me. He offered me his protection. It scared me out of my wits.

SVENDSON　Why?

MRS. CZECH　Well, you see, I haven't any enemies among the people I know. But this was somebody I didn't know. He wanted to come home with me to protect me, so he said. Isn't that creepy? Tell me: don't you feel threatened?

SVENDSON　Me? No. They all have to keep on good terms with me, because they all need my iron in these uncertain times. Even when they're at each other's throats, they've got to use kid gloves with me. Because they need my iron.

MRS. CZECH   Yes, you're a lucky man. Good day, Mr. Svendson. (*She goes out*)

SVENDSON (*calls after her*)   Good day, Mrs. Czech. I'll have your bar delivered. (*He stands up and does Swedish exercises in time to the monotonous music*)
(*The customer comes in. He has something hidden under his coat*)

THE CUSTOMER   How much is your iron?

SVENDSON   A crown a bar.

THE CUSTOMER   Price hasn't come down yet? Let's have it.

SVENDSON   Four bars again?

THE CUSTOMER   No, eight.

SVENDSON   That will be eight crowns.

THE CUSTOMER (*slowly*)   I'd like to make you a proposition, in view of the fact that after all we're slightly related.

SVENDSON   Not that I know of, Mr. . . .

THE CUSTOMER   You may not know it yet, but never mind. I'd like to suggest a new way of doing business: barter. I bet you smoke cigars. Well, I've got cigars. (*He takes a box full of big cigars from under his coat*) I can let you have them cheap, because I got them for nothing. I've inherited them from a relative. And I don't smoke.

SVENDSON   You don't smoke. You don't eat. You don't smoke. And these are Austrillos.

THE CUSTOMER   Ten cents apiece. That makes ten crowns for a box of a hundred. But between cousins I'll let you have it for eight, the price of your iron. Is it a deal?

SVENDSON   The tobacconist was a good friend of mine. How did he die?

THE CUSTOMER   Peacefully, my friend, very peacefully. Quietly and peacefully. A peace-loving man. He suddenly sent for me. And then a Higher Power sent for him. It all happened very quickly. He barely had time to say: Brother, don't let the tobacco dry out, and then he was gone. He'd hung a wreath on the door to welcome me. I laid it on his coffin. (*He wipes a tear from his eye. As he does so, a revolver falls out of his sleeve. He puts it back hastily*) He has departed this cruel world. A world where everyone distrusts everyone else. A world of violence, where the streets aren't safe any

more. I always carry a weapon nowadays. Unloaded, just as
a deterrent. How about the cigars?

SVENDSON   I can't afford cigars. If I could buy anything, I'd
buy myself a pair of shoes.

THE CUSTOMER   I haven't got any shoes. I have cigars. And I
need the iron.

SVENDSON   What do you need so much iron for?

THE CUSTOMER   Oh, iron always comes in handy. (*Again his
stomach rumbles loudly*)

SVENDSON   Maybe you'd better buy some food instead?

THE CUSTOMER   All in good time. All in good time. I've got to
go now, it looks like rain, and my suit is made out of syn-
thetic wool, my own invention, it won't stand up under rain.
Would you be interested in a bolt of this excellent material?

SVENDSON   All right, I'll take the Austrillos. My business isn't
doing very well. (*He takes the box*)

THE CUSTOMER   (*laughs scornfully and picks up his eight iron
bars*)   Good day, Mr. Svendson.

SVENDSON   (*picks up the phone, voluptuously puffing on an
Austrillo*)   Is that you, Dansen? What do you say about the
recent events?—Yes, that's what I say. I don't say anything.
—Oh, you're not sticking your neck out? Right, I'm not
sticking my neck out either.—Oh, you're still doing business
with him? Right, I'm still doing business with him too.—So
you're not worried? Fine, I'm not worried either.
(*The stage grows dark*)

3

The calendar in the iron store reads February 1939.
*Svendson sits smoking an Austrillo. A lady and a gentleman
come in.*

THE GENTLEMAN   My dear Mr. Svendson, Mrs. Gall and I
would like a word with you if you can spare the time.

SVENDSON   Rest assured, Mr. Britt, that I always have time for my best customer.

(*The lady and the gentleman sit down*)

THE GENTLEMAN   We wished to speak to you about the dreadful assault on Mrs. Czech.

SVENDSON   An assault on Mrs. Czech?

THE GENTLEMAN   Last night our neighbor Mrs. Czech was assaulted, robbed, and murdered by What's-his-name. He was armed to the teeth.

SVENDSON   What, Mrs. Czech murdered? How can that be?

THE GENTLEMAN   How indeed? We're quite beside ourselves, we just don't understand. Mrs. Gall was a special friend of hers. Last night Mrs. Gall heard loud cries for help coming from her house. She rushed straight over to my place and we sat there for hours discussing what we could do. Then we went to the poor woman's house and found her engaged in a violent argument with that What's-his-name. He was asking for something that supposedly belonged to a relative of his, and we advised her to let him have it if he promised to leave her in peace. She consented and he promised. But later in the night he seems to have come back and murdered the poor woman.

THE LADY   Of course we'd never have left if we hadn't trusted him to keep his promise.

THE GENTLEMAN   Now we've decided to form an organization of all our neighbors to make sure such a thing never happens again. We've come to ask if you wish to join our law-enforcement organization and add your name to our membership list. (*He hands him the list*)

SVENDSON (*takes it hesitantly. Uneasily*)   But you see, I've only got a small iron business. I can't get mixed up in the quarrels of the big corporations. Some of my customers might take it amiss if I were to join this kind of organization.

THE LADY   I see. You wish to sell your iron no matter what happens, to no matter whom?

SVENDSON   Not at all. How can you say such a thing? My conscience, it seems to me, is as sensitive as yours. But I'm just not the warlike type, don't you see. My business has nothing to do with it. Let's be a little more relaxed about all this. (*To the gentleman*) Do you smoke?

THE GENTLEMAN   Austrillos.

THE LADY   I'd appreciate it if the gentlemen didn't smoke.

SVENDSON (*annoyed, puts away the box and his own cigar*)   I beg your pardon.

THE GENTLEMAN   You were speaking of your conscience, Mr. Svendson.

SVENDSON   Was I? Yes, of course. I can assure you that I abhor all violence. I haven't had a good night's sleep since these dreadful things started happening. To tell you the truth, madame, it's only on account of my nerves that I've been smoking so much.

THE LADY   Then you have no basic objection to the idea of an organization to combat violence?

SVENDSON   Basic or not, my motives are of the purest.

THE GENTLEMAN   We wouldn't think of questioning the purity of your motives. It's obvious that if you sell your iron to What's-his-name it's not because you approve of his conduct.

SVENDSON   Of course not. I abominate it.

THE GENTLEMAN   And you don't consider yourself related to him, as he allegedly claims?

SVENDSON   Certainly not.

THE GENTLEMAN   You only sell because he pays and you'll only sell as long as he pays.

SVENDSON   That's right.

THE GENTLEMAN   And you think What's-his-name wouldn't need your iron any more if you were to join our peace league that would guarantee your security and everyone else's?

SVENDSON   Of course he needs my iron. I honestly don't know what he does with it . . .

THE LADY (*amiably*)   He makes machine-guns!

SVENDSON (*ignoring her information*)   As I've said, I don't know, but he'd probably have to buy it even then. Only, as I said before, it might make him angry, and, you see, I just happen to be the peaceful kind. To be perfectly frank, I'm expecting him now, and I'd rather he didn't find you in my

store. He's uncommonly sensitive and quick to take offense.
So you'd be doing me a big favor if . . .
(*The customer comes in with a package under his arm*)

THE CUSTOMER   How much is your iron?

SVENDSON   A crown a bar.

THE CUSTOMER   Ah, I see we have company. Friends of yours,
Svendson?

SVENDSON   Hm. Yes. No. In a way. A business call.

THE GENTLEMAN   We've been talking about Mrs. Czech, the
lady you murdered, sir.

THE CUSTOMER   Me?

THE LADY   Yes.

THE CUSTOMER   Lies! Calumny! Slander!

THE GENTLEMAN   What, you deny that you murdered Mrs.
Czech?

THE CUSTOMER   Of course I deny it. Mrs. Czech was recommended to me by some close relatives of mine who roomed
in her house. She asked me for protection. When my relatives got down on their knees and begged me, I gave in, and
yesterday I started protecting her. It was her last great joy
on earth. A few minutes later she died peacefully of old age
in my arms. That's the truth, and that's what you and certain
other people choose to represent as murder! What's more,
it was because of you that Mrs. Czech came to me! You let
her down and you'll let all your friends down. That ought
to give you pause, Mr. Svendson.

THE LADY   So you just took care of Mrs. Czech?

THE CUSTOMER   Why would I have wanted to hurt her? (*His
stomach rumbles*)

THE GENTLEMAN   And you really mean to deny that you
threaten everyone who lives anywhere near you?

THE CUSTOMER   Of course I deny it! I've come here to buy
sixteen bars of iron, Mr. Svendson. But I find an atmosphere
of hostility. Obviously you can't be expected to sell iron to
anyone who threatens you. So let me ask you a question;
think carefully before you answer: Do you feel threatened
by me?

SVENDSON   Me? How can you ask? How many bars did you

say? Oh yes, sixteen. Do I feel threatened by you? Whatever
put that into your head? Do you really want an answer?

THE GENTLEMAN, THE LADY, AND THE CUSTOMER   Yes.

SVENDSON (*counting out the bars*)   In that case I'll tell you:
No. I don't feel threatened.

(*The lady and the gentleman leave in indignation*)

THE CUSTOMER (*while Svendson wipes off the bars with the
membership list*)   Splendid. There's a man who still has the
courage of his convictions. We must be related in some way,
Svendson. Even if you deny it. People deny a lot of things.
By the way, since we're both so passionately devoted to
peace, couldn't we make a little pact entitling you to attack
anyone you please with iron bars except me, and me to attack anyone but you?

SVENDSON (*in a dying voice*)   I wouldn't like to do that. My
biggest customer . . .

THE CUSTOMER   But I need more iron, Svendson. People are
plotting against me. They're planning to attack me. They all
want to attack me. Because they can't bear to see how well
I'm getting along. (*His stomach rumbles again*) They accuse
me of killing that woman! Lies! Lies! Lies! And do you
know what I found in her house afterwards? An iron bar!
She was going to attack me! You're right to keep out of
these disgusting quarrels. You're an iron dealer, not a politician, Svendson. You sell your iron to anyone who can pay.
And I buy from you because I like you and because I see
that you have to make a living. Because you're not against
me and don't let my enemies incite you against me—that's
why I buy your iron. Why else would I buy it? You've no
reason to make an enemy of me! Weren't you saying something about shoes? Here, I've brought you some shoes. (*He
takes out a pair of large yellow oxfords*) Just what you need,
Svendson. I can let you have them cheap. Do you know how
much they cost me?

SVENDSON (*feebly*)   How much?

THE CUSTOMER   Nothing. See. And you get the benefit, Svendson. Oh yes, you and I are going to be great friends, especially when we've come to a perfect agreement about the
price of iron. And we will, Svendson, we will. Give me a

hand with these bars, Svendson. (*Svendson helps him to pick up the bars. He takes six under each arm, loads the rest on his back, and thus heavily laden hobbles out*)

SVENDSON   Good day.

THE CUSTOMER (*turning with difficulty in the doorway. Smiling*)   See you soon.

4

The calendar in the iron store now reads 19??.
Svendson is strolling around, smoking an Austrillo and wearing Mrs. Czech's shoes. Suddenly the sound of guns is heard. Very much upset, Svendson tries in vain to telephone. The telephone is dead. He turns on the radio. The radio is dead. He looks out the window and sees the glow of flames.

SVENDSON   War!
(*He hurries to the blackboard showing the price of iron, rubs out the figure 3 with a sponge and in feverish haste writes in a 4. The customer comes in with all sorts of things under his coat. His face is chalky-white*)

SVENDSON (*listening*)   Do you know where that gunfire is coming from?

THE CUSTOMER   It's coming from my rumbling stomach. I'm on my way to get some food. But for that I need more iron. (*He throws open his coat, uncovering machine-guns at the ready*)

SVENDSON   Help! Help!

THE CUSTOMER   How much is your iron?

SVENDSON (*broken*)   Nothing.

Practice Pieces
for Actors

Translator: Ralph Manheim

PARALLEL SCENES

The following transpositions of the murder scene from *Macbeth* and the quarrel between the queens in *Maria Stuart* into a prosaic setting are intended to help with the alienation of classical scenes. In our theaters such scenes have long been played with a view, not to the happenings represented, but to the outbreaks of temperament these happenings make possible. The transpositions restore interest in the happenings themselves and also refresh the actor's interest in the stylization and poetic speech of the originals, which he now comes to see as something special, something added.

THE MURDER IN THE PORTER'S LODGE
(Parallel to Shakespeare's *Macbeth*, Act 2, Scene 2)

A porter's lodge. The porter, his wife, and a sleeping beggar. A chauffeur has brought in a large package.

THE CHAUFFEUR Careful. This thing is fragile.

THE PORTER'S WIFE (*taking it*) What is it?

THE CHAUFFEUR They say it's a Chinese good-luck god.

THE WIFE A present from *her*?

THE CHAUFFEUR Yes, for his birthday. The maids will come and get it. Make sure you tell them to handle it with care, Mrs. Fersen; it's worth more than this whole porter's lodge. (*He goes out*)

THE WIFE What do they need a good-luck god for when they've got money to burn, that's what I'd like to know! It's us that could do with one.

THE PORTER Complain, complain. You ought to be glad we've

got a job; that's all the good luck we need. Put it in the bedroom.

THE WIFE (*going out with the package under her arm, turns her head and speaks over her shoulder*)   It's disgraceful. The likes of them can buy good-luck gods that are worth more than a whole house. When we're the ones that need good luck or we wouldn't even have a roof over our heads, though we work from morning to night. It makes my blood boil. (*She stumbles in trying to open the door and the package slips out of her hands*)

THE PORTER   Careful!

THE WIFE   It's broken!

THE PORTER   Hell! Why can't you be careful!

THE WIFE   This is terrible. They'll throw us out when they see it. The head's fallen off. I'll kill myself.

THE PORTER   This sure won't get us a reference. We might as well hit the road (*points to the beggar who has woken up*) with him. You'll never explain this away.

THE WIFE   I'll kill myself.

THE PORTER   That won't mend it.

THE WIFE   What could we say?

THE BEGGAR (*groggy with sleep*)   Something wrong?

THE PORTER   Shut up. (*To his wife*) There's nothing you *can* say. It was entrusted to us, and now it's broken. What do you want to say? Just pack.

THE WIFE   But maybe there's something we could say. No matter what. We could say it was broken already.

THE PORTER   He's been with them for ten years. They'll believe him sooner than us.

THE WIFE   There are two of us. Two witnesses against one.

THE PORTER   Nonsense. My testimony is worthless, because I'm your husband. I know the mistress. She'll have our three sticks of furniture auctioned off from under us, just for spite.

THE WIFE   We've got to think of something.

(*The bell rings outside*)

THE PORTER   They're coming.

THE WIFE   I'll hide it. (*She rushes into the bedroom with the package and comes back. Referring to the beggar, who has fallen asleep again*) Was he awake?

THE PORTER   Yes, just for a second.

THE WIFE   Did he see "it"?

THE PORTER   I don't know. Why?

(*The bell rings again*)

THE WIFE   Take him into the bedroom.

THE PORTER   I've got to open up. They'll get ideas if I don't.

THE WIFE   Keep them outside for a minute. (*Referring to the beggar*) He did it. In there. When they come in, we don't know a thing. (*Shakes the beggar*) Hey, you! (*The porter starts to go out*) Take the paper, like you'd been reading. (*He goes out with the newspaper. The wife pushes the groggy beggar into the bedroom. Comes back and goes out through another door, opposite*)

THE PORTER   (*comes back with two maids from the manor house*) It's cold out there, and you haven't even got your coats on.

THE HOUSEKEEPER   We've just run over for the package.

THE PORTER   We put it in the bedroom.

THE HOUSEKEEPER   The mistress can't wait to see it. Where is it?

THE PORTER   I'd better take it to her myself.

THE HOUSEKEEPER   Don't bother, Mr. Fersen.

THE PORTER   I'll be glad to.

THE HOUSEKEEPER   I know you would, Mr. Fersen. But there's no need. Is it in there?

THE PORTER   Yes, the big package. (*She goes in*) They say it's a good-luck god. Is that right?

THE MAID   Yes, the mistress is furious with the chauffeur for not bringing it an hour ago. They do it to spite her, she can't count on anyone, all they think of is their own convenience, and if anything goes wrong not one of them takes the blame, and so on. Oh well, some people just don't want to knock themselves out for such masters. Am I right?

THE PORTER   Yes, that's the way it is. They're not all alike.

THE MAID   My aunt always says: He who sups with the devil needs a long spoon.

THE HOUSEKEEPER   (*from the bedroom*)   This is dreadful.

THE PORTER AND THE MAID   What's the matter?

THE HOUSEKEEPER   Someone must have done it on purpose!
The head's been pulled off!

THE PORTER   Pulled off?

THE MAID   The good-luck god?

THE HOUSEKEEPER   Just look at it. The minute I picked it up,
I knew it was in two pieces. I was wondering whether to
open it. I just undid one corner of the paper and the head
fell out!

(*The porter and the maid go in*)

THE HOUSEKEEPER   Her birthday present. And her so super-
stitious.

THE WIFE (*comes in*)   What's the matter? You're all upset.

THE HOUSEKEEPER   Mrs. Fersen, I wish I didn't have to tell
you. I know what a fine woman you are. But the good-luck
god has been broken.

THE WIFE   What? Broken? In my house?

THE PORTER (*comes back with the maid*)   I just don't understand. We're finished. They entrust a valuable article to our
safekeeping, and then this happens! I won't be able to look
the mistress in the face!

THE HOUSEKEEPER   Who could have done it?

THE MAID   It must have been that beggar, that peddler. He pretended he'd been asleep and suddenly woken up, but he still
had the string on his lap. He probably thought he'd look
inside the package to see if there was anything worth stealing.

THE PORTER   Damn it, I shouldn't have thrown him out!

THE HOUSEKEEPER   Why didn't you grab him?

THE PORTER   I could kick myself, but who can think of everything? Nobody can! My temper ran away with me. There
was the good-luck god, and there was the head three feet
away, and there, lying on the bench, that beggar, playing
innocent. I could only think of the mistress.

THE HOUSEKEEPER   The police will pick him up in no time.

THE WIFE   I feel sick.

THE BATTLE OF THE FISHWIVES

(Parallel to Schiller's *Maria Stuart*, Act 3)

1

A street. Mrs. Zwillich and her neighbor, walking.

MRS. ZWILLICH   No, Mr. Koch, I can't do it. I can't humiliate myself like that. I've lost everything, but I still have my pride. They'd point their fingers at me in the fish market. That's the one that licked the boots of Mrs. Scheit—the hypocritical monster!

MR. KOCH   Don't work yourself up so, Mrs. Zwillich. You'll have to go and see Mrs. Scheit. If her nephew testifies against you in court, they'll give you four months.

MRS. ZWILLICH   But I didn't give false weight. It's a pack of lies.

MR. KOCH   Of course it is, Mrs. Zwillich. We know that, but do the police know it? Mrs. Scheit is a lot slyer than you are. She's too much for you.

MRS. ZWILLICH   Cheap tricks.

MR. KOCH   Nobody claims it was decent of Mrs. Scheit to send that no-good nephew of hers to buy a flounder from you and take it to the police and tell them to weigh it. Of course the police know Mrs. Scheit was only trying to get rid of a competitor. But unfortunately your two-pound flounder was three ounces short. Those fatal three ounces!

MRS. ZWILLICH   Because I was talking with her nephew while weighing the flounder, so I didn't check the weight carefully. I got myself into this trouble by being friendly to a customer!

MR. KOCH   We all admire your friendliness. Nobody says any different.

MRS. ZWILLICH   It's true the customers came to me and not to her. Because I'm attentive, because I inject a personal note.

That's what drove her crazy. It wasn't enough for the market police to take my stand away and stop me from selling; oh no, she had to get her nephew to drag me into court—that was too much.

MR. KOCH   And another thing: You'll have to be very careful, take it from me. Very careful. Choose your words!

MRS. ZWILLICH   "Choose your words!" With her! Things have come to a pretty pass. With a miserable creature that ought to be put in jail for defamation of character, you want me to choose my words!

MR. KOCH   With care! It's a good deal that she's letting me take you to see her. Don't spoil it now with your temper and righteous indignation.

MRS. ZWILLICH   I can't do it, Mr. Koch. I just feel that I can't do it. All day I've been waiting for you to come and tell me if she'll condescend to listen to me. Pull yourself together, I said to myself, she can send you to the clink. I went over the whole scene, how I'd appeal to her and wring her heart. But now I can't do it. All I know is that I hate her, she's a shameless hussy, and I'd like to scratch her eyes out.

MR. KOCH   Control yourself, Mrs. Zwillich, I beg you. Grit your teeth. She has you at her mercy. Beg her to be magnanimous. For God's sake, forget your pride, this is no time for pride.

MRS. ZWILLICH   I know you're trying to help me. All right, I'll go. But believe me, no good will come of it. We're like cats and dogs. She's done me wrong and I'd like to scratch her . . . (*They walk away*)

2

Fish market in the late afternoon. Only a single fishwife, Mrs. Scheit, is sitting there. Beside her, her nephew.

MRS. SCHEIT   No, I won't talk to her. Why should I? Now that I'm finally rid of her. What heavenly peace there's been in the fish market yesterday and today, now that she's gone with her mincing ways: A gorgeous eel, ma'am? Your husband's well, I hope. Goodness me, how lovely you're looking today, as usual! It makes my blood boil to hear her.

A CUSTOMER   Here I've spent a whole hour chewing the fat. What will I cook for supper? Isn't that pike rather small?

MRS. SCHEIT   Then catch yourself a bigger one, madam. It's not my fault if he didn't live longer. If you don't want it, leave it be, I won't tear my hair out.

THE CUSTOMER   Don't get offended right away. I only said it looked rather small.

MRS. SCHEIT   And what's more it hasn't got a moustache. It doesn't suit you, and that's that. Hugo, pack up the baskets; we're closing.

THE CUSTOMER   All right, I'll take it. Don't fly off the handle.

MRS. SCHEIT   One-thirty. (*Gives her the pike. To her nephew*) Some people come around after closing time. Then to make matters worse they get picky and choosy. I like that. Come on, let's shove off.

THE NEPHEW   But, auntie, you said you'd speak to Mrs. Zwillich.

MRS. SCHEIT   At closing time, I said, and is she here?

(*Mrs. Zwillich and Mr. Koch come in and stop a little way off*)

THE NEPHEW   There she is now.

MRS. SCHEIT (*pretending not to notice Mrs. Zwillich*)   Pack up the baskets. We haven't done at all badly today, sold twice as much as last Thursday. They grabbed them out of my hands. "My husband always says: this carp comes from Mrs. Scheit's, I can tell by the taste." People are really idiotic. As if one carp didn't taste just like another.

MRS. ZWILLICH (*shuddering, to Mr. Koch*)   No one with a spark of human feeling would talk like that!

MRS. SCHEIT   Would the lady and gentleman wish to buy a flounder?

THE NEPHEW   But auntie, it's Mrs. Zwillich.

MRS. SCHEIT   What? Who told her to come here and bother me?

THE NEPHEW   But now she's here, auntie. The Bible says to love thy neighbor.

MR. KOCH   You must show forebearance, Mrs. Scheit. There
stands an unhappy woman. She doesn't dare open her mouth.

MRS. ZWILLICH   I can't do it, Mr. Koch.

MRS. SCHEIT   What did she say? Did you hear that, Mr. Koch?
An unhappy woman, who's been crying her eyes out day
and night and wants to beg for mercy. Isn't that what you
said? Don't make me laugh! Haughty, that's what she is! As
impudent as ever!

MRS. ZWILLICH   All right. I'll even put up with that. (*To Mrs.
Scheit*) You've got what you wanted. You can thank your
lucky stars. But don't overdo it. Give me your hand, Mrs.
Scheit. (*She holds out her hand*)

MRS. SCHEIT   You've wheedled yourself into this situation, Mrs.
Zwillich.

MRS. ZWILLICH   Don't forget, Mrs. Scheit, that luck can change.
Even yours. Mine has changed already. Besides, people are
listening. Look. We were in the same business. Nothing like
this ever happened in the fish market! Good God, don't
stand there like a rock! What more can I do than beg you
on bended knee? It's bad enough that I'll go to jail if I don't
move you. But just looking at you the words stick in my
throat.

MRS. SCHEIT   Make it short, if you please. I have no desire to
be seen with you. I only consented out of Christian charity.
For two years you filched my customers away from me.

MRS. ZWILLICH   I don't know what to say. If I tell the truth,
you'll take offense. You haven't done right by me. When
you sent your nephew to buy a flounder, you only wanted
to get me in trouble. I'd never have expected such a thing
of you or anyone else. Never. I sold fish here just the same
as you. And now you're dragging me into court.—Look, I'm
willing to put the whole thing down to bad luck. You're not
to blame. I'm not to blame. We wanted to sell fish, and the
customers came between us. They told you this and they
told me that. Supposedly you said my fish stank, and I said
you kind of gave false weight, or the other way around.—
Now there's no one between us. We could just as well be
sisters. You the older, me the younger. It would never have

come to this if we'd had a heart to heart talk before it was
too late.

MRS. SCHEIT   A fine snake I'd have nurtured in my bosom!—A
creature like you doesn't belong in the fish market! You use
unfair methods! You want to hog all the business! You
wheedled one customer after another away from me with
your mincing ways and your simpering "just another little
perch, madam?" And when I told you so, you threatened to
have me up for slander. But now you're getting yours!

MRS. ZWILLICH   I'm in the hands of God, Mrs. Scheit. Surely
you wouldn't want to commit such a sin—

MRS. SCHEIT   Who's going to stop me? You were the first one
to talk about the police, with your complaint about slander!
If I let you go and tell my nephew to withdraw the complaint, you'll be sitting here again tomorrow. I know you.
You won't show repentance; oh no, you'll buy a lipstick to
make the waiter at the "Red Lion" buy your haddock!
That's what will happen if I put mercy before justice.

MRS. ZWILLICH   Keep the fish market! Sell fish all by yourself,
for all I care. All right, I'll give up my stand. You've had
your way with me. You've broken me. I'm a mere shadow
of the Mrs. Zwillich I used to be. But now stop persecuting
me and say: go in peace, I've shown you what's what, and
now I'll show you how a Christian behaves. If you say that,
I'll say thank you and mean it. But don't keep me waiting too
long for those little words. If you don't say them and go to
the police—I wouldn't want to face the people in your shoes
for all the world!

MRS. SCHEIT   So you finally see that I've got you down? Have
you run out of tricks? Has the policeman from the market
place cooled off a bit? Haven't you any more admirers? You
who go to the movies with anybody that gets you an order,
even if he's married ten times over!

MRS. ZWILLICH   Now I really have to control myself. You're
going too far.

MRS. SCHEIT   (*after giving her a long contemptuous look*)
Hugo, can this be the Mrs. Zwillich that's always so friendly?
That everybody comes running to as if the likes of me were

nothing but an old bag, a pile of shit in the market place that everybody steers clear of! A common whore, that's what she is.

MRS. ZWILLICH   This is too much!

MRS. SCHEIT (*laughing scornfully*)   Ah, so that's her true face. The dainty mask has fallen off.

MRS. ZWILLICH (*seething with rage, but dignified*)   Mr. Koch, I admit that I'm young and I have my faults. I may have given a man a friendly look now and then when he bought my fish, but I've never done anything in secret. If that's my reputation, I can only say that I'm better than my reputation. You'll be getting it too, Mrs. Scheit! You cover up your pleasures. The whole market knows you're a bad lot. Your mother wasn't in jail for nothing!

MR. KOCH   For God's sake! That does it! You haven't controlled yourself as you promised, Mrs. Zwillich.

MRS. ZWILLICH   Controlled myself is good, Mr. Koch. I've stood for as much as a mortal woman can bear. Now I'm going to talk. Now I'm going to get it all off my chest. The whole . . .

MR. KOCH   She's gone out of her mind. She doesn't know what she's saying, Mrs. Scheit!

THE NEPHEW   Don't listen to her, auntie! Come on, let's go home. I'll take the baskets.

MRS. ZWILLICH   Stinking fish she sent to the "Red Lion"! She's a disgrace to the whole fish market! She only got her stand because her no-good brother gets drunk with one of the market cops!

INTERCALARY SCENES

The intercalary scenes for Shakespeare's *Hamlet* and *Romeo and Juliet* are not, of course, to be added to performances of these plays, but only to be played by the actors in rehearsal. The Ferry Scene for Hamlet, to be intercalated between scenes 3 and 4, Act 4, and the recitation of the Concluding Report are intended to prevent actors from heroizing Hamlet in their performance. Bourgeois *Hamlet* critics usually look on Hamlet's hesitation as the interesting new element in this play, but regard the massacre in Act 5, in which he exchanges reflection for "action," as a positive solution. But the massacre is a regression, for this action is criminal. The little practice scene provides an explanation for Hamlet's hesitation: it corresponds to the new political and social attitude that had made its appearance among the bourgeoisie. The intercalary scenes for *Romeo and Juliet* are not, of course, intended to demonstrate the simple maxim, "One man's joy is another man's sorrow," but to enable the actors playing Romeo and Juliet to build up these characters in a contradictory manner.

FERRY SCENE
(To be played between Scenes 3 and 4, Act 4 of Shakespeare's *Hamlet*.)

A ferry. Hamlet and the ferryman. Hamlet's confidant.

HAMLET   What's that building on the shore over there?
FERRYMAN   It's a fort, Your Highness; they built it for the coast guard.
HAMLET   But what's that wooden chute running down to the sound?

FERRYMAN   That's for loading fish into the boats that go to Norway.

HAMLET   Funny fort. Do the fish live in it?

FERRYMAN   They're salted in it. Your noble father, the new king, has signed a trade pact with Norway.

HAMLET   Our soldiers used to go there. So now they've been salted. Funny war.

FERRYMAN   The war is over. We backed down; we ceded the coast and now they've agreed to take our fish. Since then we've had a bigger say over there than we did before; indeed we have, sire.

HAMLET   Then the fishermen must be all for the new king?

FERRYMAN   They say: The alarums of war don't fill the belly, sire. They're for the king.

HAMLET   But the ambassador of my noble first father, whom you must distinguish from the second, was slapped in the face at the court of Norway, so I hear. Has that been straightened out?

FERRYMAN   Your noble second father, so to speak, sire, is said to have said that the ambassador's face was too big for the ambassador of a country with so much fish.

HAMLET   Wise restraint.

FERRYMAN   For half a year we were worried sick here on the coast. The king hesitated to sign.

HAMLET   Really? He hesitated?

FERRYMAN   He hesitated. Once they even reinforced the guard in the fort. Everybody said: Now there'll be war and no fish business. Oh, how the pendulum swung between hope and despair! But God guided the good king, and he signed the treaty.

HAMLET'S CONFIDANT   But what of honor?

HAMLET   Quite frankly, I see no offense to honor. The new methods, friend. They're coming in everywhere. People don't like the smell of blood any more. A change of taste.

THE CONFIDANT   Unwarlike times, a sickly generation.

HAMLET   Why unwarlike? Maybe the fish do the fighting now. An amusing idea, salting soldiers. A slight disgrace and plenty of honor. And those who slap the ambassador's face have to buy fish. Disgrace digs his grave, and honor eats plenty of fish. Likewise, the murderer gains popularity by smilingly rubbing his face, and the unworthy son points to the money received for fish well sold. His scruples toward the murderer, not toward the murdered, are beginning to honor him; his cowardice is his best quality; he'd be a scoundrel if he were not a scoundrel, and so on and so on, so let's go to sleep and not interfere with the fishing.

As commerce thrives, the sumptuous tomb crumbles.
Oh, how much more accusing when it crumbles!
One piece of business still unfinished, yet
Writing it off, you can cancel yet another
Quite prematurely. Is there a postmaturely?
And yet a scoundrel breathes easy, and turns almost
Into a good man. Not only seems, but is!
And you, tear down what has been built, because
It stands on ruins (and grows and bears rich fruit!).
Fill up the fort again with butchers. Go back
To bloody deeds, because *he* got his start with blood!
Oh, had he only hesitated!

Concluding Report

And so, cautiously using the sound of accidental
Drums and the battle cry of unknown butchers
By accident set free at last from his
So sensible and human inhibition
Running amuck in one horrendous race
He kills the king, his mother and himself
So justifying his successor's contention
That, had he mounted the throne, he surely would have
Comported himself most royally.

THE SERVANTS

(To be played between Scenes 1 and 2, Act 2 of Shakespeare's *Romeo and Juliet*.)

1

Romeo and one of his tenants.

ROMEO   I've already told you, old fellow, that I need the money and for no unworthy purpose.

TENANT   But where are we to go if your lordship sells the land from one minute to the next? There are five of us.

ROMEO   Can't you hire out somewhere? You're a good worker, I'll give you an excellent reference. I must have the money, I have obligations, you don't understand these things, or do I have to explain that when a lady has given me her all I can't put her out in the street without so much as a present? Just bye-bye, my love, and that's all? Would you want me to do anything so contemptible? Then you're a worthless blackguard, a selfish dog. Farewell presents cost money. And you'll have to admit they're unselfish, one gets nothing in return. Am I right, old friend? Don't be a spoilsport. Who rocked me on his knees and carved my first bow, remember? Shall I say to myself: even Gobbo doesn't understand me any more, lets me down, wants me to play the cad? My friend, I'm in love! There's nothing I wouldn't sacrifice. I'd even commit a crime for the girl I love, a murder. And I'd be proud of it, but you don't understand. You're too old, old Gobbo, dried out. Don't you see, I have to get rid of the other one. Now I've taken you into my confidence, and I ask you: are you still the old Gobbo you used to be, or not? Answer me.

TENANT   I'm no good at making speeches, sire. But where will I take my family if you drive me off your land?

ROMEO   Poor old Gobbo. He's too old to understand. I tell him

I'm dying of love and he mumbles something about land. Do I own a piece of land? I've forgotten. No, I own no land, or rather, my land must go. What's land to me? I'm burning.

TENANT   And we're starving, sire.

ROMEO   Dolt. Is it impossible to talk sense to you? Have you animals no feelings? In that case, away with you, the sooner the better.

TENANT   Yes, away with us. Here, do you want my coat too? (*He takes it off*) My hat? My boots? Animals you say? Even animals have to eat.

ROMEO   Ah, so that's the tune you sing? So that's your true face? That you've hidden for twenty-five years like a leprous spot? So that's my reward for speaking to you like a human being? Get out of my sight, or I'll thrash you, you animal. (*He chases him away, but during the love scene the tenant lurks in the background*)

ROMEO   He jests at scars that never felt a wound.

2

Juliet and her lady's maid.

JULIET   And you love your Thurio? How do you love him?

MAID   At night when I've said my "Our Father" and the nurse has begun to snore, begging your pardon, I get up again and go to the window in my bare feet, mistress.

JULIET   Just because he might be standing outside?

MAID   No, because he was standing there before.

JULIET   Oh, how well I understand that. I like to look at the moon because we've looked at it together. But tell me some more about how you love him. If he were in danger, for instance . . .

MAID   You mean if he were dismissed for instance? I'd run straight to the master.

JULIET   No, if his life were in danger . . .

MAID   Oh, if there were a war? Then I'd keep at him until he pretended to be sick and took to his bed and stayed there.

JULIET   But that would be cowardly.

MAID　I'd make a coward of him all right. If I lay down with him, he'd stay in bed all right.

JULIET　No, I mean if he were in danger and you could save him by sacrificing your life.

MAID　You mean if he got the plague? I'd put a rag soaked in vinegar in my mouth and I'd care for him, of course.

JULIET　But would you remember the rag?

MAID　What do you mean by that?

JULIET　Since it won't help, anyway.

MAID　Not much, but it does help some.

JULIET　Anyway, you'd risk your life for him, and so would I for my Romeo. But one more thing: If for instance he went to war and came back and something was missing . . .

MAID　What?

JULIET　I can't say it.

MAID　Oh, that! I'd scratch his eyes out.

JULIET　Why?

MAID　For going to war.

JULIET　And then it would be all over between you?

MAID　Well, wouldn't it be all over?

JULIET　You don't love him.

MAID　What, you don't call it love that I like to be with him so much?

JULIET　That's earthly love.

MAID　But isn't earthly love nice?

JULIET　Oh yes, but I love my Romeo more, I assure you.

MAID　You think because I like so much to be with my Thurio I don't really love him? But maybe I'd even forgive him for what you said. I mean, after the first excitement was over. Oh yes. My love is too strong.

JULIET　But you hesitated.

MAID　That was because of love.

JULIET　(embraces her)　That's true too. You must go to him tonight.

MAID　Oh yes, on account of that other girl. I'm so glad you're letting me off. If he meets her, it will be all over.

JULIET　You're sure you can catch him at the back door in the wall?

MAID   Oh yes, he can't get out any other way. And he wasn't to meet her until eleven.

JULIET   If you leave now, you can't miss him. Here, take this kerchief, it's pretty. And which stockings have you got on?

MAID   My best. And I'll put on my sweetest smile, and I'll be nicer to him than ever. I love him so.

JULIET   Wasn't that a branch crackling?

MAID   It sounded like someone jumping down from the wall. I'll look.

JULIET   But don't miss your Thurio.

MAID   (*at the window*)   Who do you think has jumped down off the wall and there he is in the garden?

JULIET   It's Romeo! Oh, Nerida, I must go out on the balcony and talk to him.

MAID   But the gatekeeper sleeps downstairs, mistress. He'll hear everything. Suddenly there won't be steps in your room, but there will be on the balcony. And voices, too.

JULIET   Then you must walk up and down in here and rattle the basin as if I were washing.

MAID   But then I won't meet my Thurio and it will be all over for me.

JULIET   Maybe they'll keep him in tonight. After all, he's a servant too. Just walk up and down and rattle the basin. Dear, dear Nerida! Don't let me down, I must speak to him.

MAID   Can't you make it quick? Please make it quick!

JULIET   Very quick, Nerida, very quick. Walk up and down here in the room.

(*Juliet appears on the balcony. During the love scene the maid walks back and forth rattling the basin now and then. When the clock strikes eleven, she falls in a faint*)

Notes and Variants

THE GOOD PERSON
OF SZECHWAN

Texts by Brecht

The Song from the Opium Den

1

THE GIRL
In those distant days of loving-kindness
Which they say are now forever gone
I adored the world, and sought for blindness
Or a heaven, the very purest one.
Soon enough, at dawn, I got my warning:
Blindness strikes the inquisitive offender
Who would see the heaven's pure bright dawning.
And I saw it. And I saw its splendor.
How can scrounging crumbs make people happy?
What's the good if hardships last for ever?
Must we never pluck the crimson poppy
Just because its blooms are sure to wither?
    And so I said: drop it.
    Breathe in the smoke twisting black
    Towards colder heavens. Look up: like it
    You'll not come back.

2

THE MAN
My enemy who 'mid the poppies molders—
I think of him when lighting up the drug.

And my bull? I've harnessed his great shoulders
And I've marched before a crimson flag.
By midday I'd tired of strife and rancor
Thought they offered nothing much to go on
You meantime were being so much franker
Saying they could be of use to no one.
Why smite enemies? I have no doubt mine
Nowadays could smite me without trying.
Nobody grows fatter than his outline.
Why, too, put on weight when you are dying?
    And so I said: drop it.
    Breathe in the smoke twisting black
    Towards colder heavens. Look up: like it
    You'll not come back.

3

THE OLD MAN

Ever since those distant days I've hurried
Sown my millet, reaped it where it grew
Lain with women, cried to gods when worried
Fathered sons who now sow millet too.
Late enough, at night, I got the lesson:
Not a cock will crow, for they're ignoring
My end, nor will the most complete confession
Rouse a single god where he lies snoring.
Why keep sowing millet on this gravel
Soil whose barrenness can't be corrected
If my tamarisk is doomed to shrivel
Once I'm dead and it is left neglected?
    And so I said: drop it.
    Breathe in the smoke twisting black
    Towards colder heavens. Look up: like it
    You'll not come back.

["Der Gesang aus der Opiumhöhle," GW *Gedichte*, pp. 90–91, tr. by John Willett. Brecht's typescript is dated by

BBA "About 1920." This song, unpublished till after Brecht's death, is the origin of the "Song of the Smoke" (p. 18–19) and would appear to have been the first of his known writings on Chinese and Japanese themes. The opium motif will be found to recur in the Santa Monica version of the play (see pp. 385, 391, 394, 396 ff.).]

Fragment of a Story

However as the dearth increased and the cries of all living creatures asserted themselves the gods grew uneasy. For there were many complaints that there can be no fear of the gods where the shortage is excessive. And they said "Were we to alter the world, which cost so much effort to create, a great disorder would ensue. Therefore if we can find people who are steadfast in time of dearth and keep our commandments in spite of poverty then the world shall remain as it is and there will be no disorder in it."

Three of the highest thereupon set forth to discover god-fearing people such as might keep their commandments and display resistance in time of dearth.

And they came to the city of Szechwan, where they found a water seller who feared the gods, and he went around seeking a shelter for them. And he hunted round the city on their behalf for an entire day and could find no shelter.

And he said "I thought that it would be simple, for these are among the highest of the gods, and it is only for one night. But there is not a house in Szechwan that will give them shelter."

And he came back to them and comforted them, and went again and turned to a girl whom he knew by the name of Mi Lung to ask her for shelter.

And they saw that the measuring cup from which he sold water had a false bottom.

[From Werner Hecht (ed.): *Materialien zu Brechts "Der gute Mensch von Sezuan,"* Frankfurt, Suhrkamp, 1968, p. 95. There described as "probably written very early on." The name Mi Lung never recurs.]

Press Report

A strange story has been reported from Szechwan province. Mr. Lao Go, a manufacturer of tobacco products in the provincial capital, has been standing trial for the murder of his cousin, a certain Miss Li Gung. According to witnesses this Miss Li Gung was known among the common populace of the slum quarters as a "good person." She even acquired the romantic sobriquet of "angel of the slums." Starting out as a simple woman of the streets, she was put in possession of a little capital by an alleged donation from the gods. She bought a tobacco shop, which however she ran on such altruistic lines that a few days later it was on the brink of ruin. Not only did she feed and maintain a number of persons from her extremely poor and overcrowded neighborhood, but she also proved incapable of refusing lodging in her little shop to a family of nine with whom she was barely acquainted. Shortly before the disaster a young man turned up describing himself to her numerous hangers-on as Miss Li Gung's cousin, and intervened so drastically as to put her confused affairs into comparative order. The following incident will provide an example of his methods. The family sent an adolescent boy out to steal bottles of milk from the neighbors' doorsteps. The cousin voiced no objection but called a policeman into the shop and chatted to him until the boy came back with the stolen milk. The visitors were forthwith taken off to the police station and Miss Li Gung was rid of them. The young lady for her part stayed away while her cousin was saving her business for her.

After her own return and her cousin Mr. Lao Go's departure, she resumed her charitable activities but on a very reduced scale. Instead she entered into an intimate relationship with an unemployed airmail pilot named Yü Schan whom she was locally rumored to have saved from an attempted suicide. Unfortunately her hopes of making him a loan which would help him to secure a post as a mail pilot in Peking were cut short when her shop turned out not to be the little gold mine that people usually imagine such small concerns to be. There was a further threat to her shop in the shape of the methods employed by Mr. Feh Pung, the so-called "Tobacco King of Szechwan," a man who is not unduly inhibited by humanitarian scruples. When one of Mr. Feh Pung's shops opened in her immediate vicinity, selling tobacco fifty percent cheaper, she once again bowed to outside advice and summoned her cousin to help. He did indeed . . . [A break in the typescript follows, during which there was presumably some mention of the other small tobacconists and their decision to unite.]

. . . On his first visit he had deliberately omitted to tell them of the threats already made to the shop by Feh Pung on the day of its opening; otherwise he would not have been admitted to their mutual aid association. While accepting their tobacco, which was intended to help him to hold out, he now nonetheless negotiated with Feh Pung and induced the tobacco king to make a special bid for the shop to the disadvantage of the other members. However, he was not anxious to effect his cousin's intended purchase of the desired post for her lover Yü Schan, even though the sale of the shop had put him in a position to do so. Apparently this Yü Schan had made it all too plain to him that he was counting on Li Gung's money. Rather than gratify Yü Schan's wishes her conscientious cousin arranged a sensible marriage between Miss Li Gung and the prosperous Mr. Kau, a barber. However, it seems that he had underestimated the extent of Yü Schan's power over his cousin. At any rate the pilot succeeded in gaining her complete confidence and persuading her to make a love marriage with himself. This marriage was much discussed in the neighborhood, because it never came about. When the small tobacconists heard of Mr. Lao Go's plan to hand over to the tobacco king Li Gung's shop, which had been kept afloat only by their joint efforts, they had little difficulty in persuading Li Gung to cancel it. Here her lover's power over her proved quite ineffective. Mr. Lao Go, sent for by the lover to make his cousin "see reason," failed to appear; then Li Gung realized how Schan's behavior had hurt her, and made no secret of the fact that her cousin thought him a bad person and a fortune hunter; at which point the whole marriage blew up. Perhaps if the whole neighborhood had not been so enchanted by its "angel of the slums" it would by now have realized the amazing fact underlying the situation: that Mr. Lao Go was none other than Miss Li Gung herself. She was the conscientious "cousin" whose sometimes equivocal manipulations made possible the good deeds for which people so admired her. However, it was to be a long time before Szechwan understood this. Unhappily the other tobacconists were not able to benefit from Li Gung's self-sacrifice. The short time spent on her efforts at marriage had been enough to make them doubt her loyalty. Undercutting one another's prices, they had handed their shops on a plate to the tobacco king, to the good old refrain of "devil take the hindmost." Li Gung meanwhile was forced to admit to her old friend Sun the water seller that she thought she was pregnant. The situation was desperate. Her shop was on the brink of total ruin. For the third (and, as it turned out, last) time her cousin appeared. His task was to rescue the shop on behalf of the expected child, object now of all the girl's love. The means selected by him were wholly unscrupulous. Taking every financial advantage both of the barber's admiration for his "cousin" and of the faith placed by many small people in the "angel of the slums," he organized a sweat shop of the worst sort in which her former friends and dependents were to process tobacco at starvation wages. Yü Schan, the child's father, was likewise roped into the rapidly booming business. Before her third disappearance Li Gung had promised his mother to find him a post where he might "improve himself by honest work." Under the strict hand of Mr. Lao Go he was made foreman in the new factory. The effect of such employment was to bring him into continual close contact with Mr. Lao Go. Finally this was to be Mr. Lao Go's downfall. Yü Schan had been led by an occasional small personal gift to believe that Mr. Lao Go was keeping his cousin locked up in a room at the back of the shop. He made an attempt at blackmail, which the tobacconist naturally rejected. Thwarted, he ended up by sending for the police, whereupon the back room proved to contain all Li Gung's clothing and personal possessions. The only way for Mr. Lao Go to answer the charge of murder was by making a clean breast of the true facts: that he and Miss Li Gung were one and the same. Before the astonished eyes of the court, Lao Go changed back into Li Gung: the scourge of the slums and the angel of the slums were identical. Badness was only the reverse face of goodness, good deeds were made possible only by bad—a shattering testimonial to the unhappy condition of this world.

A poetic light is cast on the episode, which Szechwan regards as highly humorous, by the utterances of a water seller who claims that Li Gung's initial capital had indeed been a present from three gods, who told him that they had come to Szechwan to search for a good person, and also appeared more than once in his dreams to ask how the good person was faring. He claims that the three judges before whom the secret was finally unmasked were those same gods.

Whatever the real nature of the gods in question, they will no doubt have been somewhat surprised to find out in what way, in Szechwan, one sets about the problem of being a good person.

[GW *Schriften zum Theater*, pp. 1157–61. Typescript is dated September 15, 1939, and in effect resumes the state of the story when Brecht abandoned it in order to write *Mother Courage*.]

Working Plan

1. swamped

the little boat presented by the gods quickly fills with unfortunates to the point of capsizing / a family is given lodging / the former owner looked after / former suppliers arrive with demands / the landlady wants a guarantee /

2. crisis and advertisement

the cousin arrives to disentangle things / the family are handed over to the police / the suppliers paid off / the landlady placated / but as nastiness is neither a substitute for capital nor a shield against the powerful an advertisement must be drafted to get li gung a well-to-do husband.

3. *love*

quarrel about li gung's profession / she is off to an assignation with a well-to-do suitor / meets the unemployed pilot schan who is about to hang himself / comforts him / falls in love with him and buys him a glass of water from sun the water carrier /

4. *the flier has to fly*

sun's hand is broken / li gung tells of her love and buys a shawl / the barber falls desperately in love with her / but she discovers sun's wound and tries to find witnesses / without success / she offers to perjure herself / the carpet dealer and his wife overhear her talking to schan's mother about a job for schan which will cost 400 yen / they offer to guarantee the shop / the flier has to fly /

5. *love triumphs*

the cousin finds schan the money / sells the already mortgaged business to the landlady / gets to know schan and sees through him / talks things over with the barber / sun is disappointed / li gung should have a chance to do good / schan and the barber address the audience / li gung decides for schan/

6. *the wedding*

schan wants to get married and sell out / everybody is waiting for the cousin / the carpet dealers hurry in and are calmed down by li gung / whenever li gung is present her cousin is not/

7. *maternal joys*

maternal joys / schan's mother / the guarantee / the garbage pail / the carpenter / li gung's little son will be looked after by her cousin /

8. *the tobacco factory*

the carpenter's children are hauling bales of tobacco / schan gets a job and distinguishes himself as foreman / song of the tobacco workers /

9. *the rumor*

rain / the landlady / schan makes a discovery / the monarchs smoke and the mob assembles / the police act /

10. *the trial*

the gods appear in the role of judges / the tobacco king is scared / the trial / the denouement / the gods depart on a cloud/

> [From Werner Hecht (ed.): *Materialien zu Brechts "Der gute Mensch von Sezuan*," Frankfurt, Suhrkamp, 1968, pp. 22–23. This is a typical big structural plan, probably dating from the summer of 1940 and used for the main work on the play, with the ten scenes set out in ten vertical columns across a wide sheet of paper. Under each Brecht has penciled further notes and suggestions, of which Hecht provides a photographic reproduction and a transcription.]

From Brecht's Journal

making minor corrections to *The Good Person* is costing me as many weeks as writing the scenes did days. not easy, given the definite objective, to imbue the tiny sub-scenes with that element of irresponsibility, accident, transitoriness which we call "life." moreover in the end there is a basic question to be settled: how to handle the *li gung – lao go* problem. one can either (a) extend the parable aspect so as to have a straightforward conflict, *gods – li gung – lao go*, which would keep it all on a moral plane and allow two conflicting principles ("two souls") to figure separately, or else (b) have a plain story about how *li gung* masquerades as her cousin and to that end makes use of the experiences and qualities which her gutter existence has brought out in her. in fact only (b) is possible unless one is to abandon mrs. shin's discovery (scene 7), her conversation with the pregnant lao go and the whole theme of how this pregnancy makes the double game impossible to maintain. the transformation scene before the curtain (4a) is not in any way mystical but merely a technical solution in terms of mime and a song. where the difficulty becomes acute is wherever *lao go* directly addresses the audience. the question is whether he ought not to do this using li gung's voice and consequently her attitude too. at bottom it all depends on how scene 5 is handled. this is where lao go must make some remark to explain his change of attitude. however, he has no confidant, nor can he make a confidant of the audience—not as lao go. what is more, li gung's debacle at the end of that scene is harder to understand if the solution adopted is (b) rather than (a). the only possible explanation is that here too she is being addressed as li gung. when you come down to it the elements *good* and *evil* are too segregated for a realistic drama of masquerade. an occasional slip would be unavoidable. the most realistic scene in this respect is the ninth. a further consideration could be that li gung has to make strenuous efforts to play the part of lao go and is no longer capable of appearing unpleasant when dressed in her own clothes and before the eyes of those who know and address her as li gung. herein lies an important lesson: how easy it is for her to be good and how hard to be evil.

[*Bertolt Brecht Arbeitsjournal*, vol. 1, 1938–42, Frankfurt, Suhrkamp, 1973, pp. 144–5. From the entry for August 9, 1940, roughly seven weeks after the completion of the first script and (obviously) before the changing of the characters' names.]

The Good Person of Szechwan

Prologue

Three gods enter the city of Szechwan. They are looking for a good person, having heard a rumor to the effect that to be good on this earth has become more and more difficult. Aided by an obliging water seller they make the acquaintance of a good person, to wit the poor prostitute Chen Teh. Even she, however, complains that she finds it almost impossible to respect all the commandments of the gods, since she is so badly off. In order to give her a chance, the gods make her a present of money, convey their best wishes and leave her.

1

The good Chen Teh uses the gods' present of money to fit out a small tobacco shop. Concerned from the outset to obey the gods' commandments, to help her neighbors, to put her own interests second and to satisfy every request from her none too good-natured fellow humans, no matter how far-fetched, she finds her shop close to ruin the very evening after it has opened. A family of eight has chosen to take refuge there. In order to keep out further cadgers her "visitors" cynically advise her to invent a cousin who will supposedly be a hard man and the real owner of the shop. By bedtime there is no room in her own shop for Chen Teh, and she has to go away.

2

Next morning, greatly to the "visitors'" astonishment, the door opens and an extremely hard-looking young business man comes into the shop. He introduces himself as Chen Teh's cousin. Politely but firmly he invites the family to leave the premises, as this is where his cousin must conduct her business. When they prove reluctant to go he promptly summons the police, who jail one or two of the family's members on some trivial charge. To justify himself to the audience he demonstrates that they were bad people: certain of the sacks which the family has left behind contain opium.—The friendly relations that have grown up between the cousin and the police bear fruit at once. A grateful policeman draws his attention to the flattering interest being taken in his pretty cousin by the prosperous barber Chu Fu from across the way. He is prepared to help set up an assignation in the public park. The cousin expresses interest: Chen Teh is clearly incompetent to run the shop without some protection, and he himself has to go off again and will probably not be able to come back.

3

We see Chen Teh in the park on her way to her assignation with the wealthy barber. Under a tree she sees, to her horror, a down-at-heel young man about to hang himself. He tells her that he is an unemployed pilot and is unable to raise the $500 needed to get him a pilot's job in Peking. A shower of rain forces Chen Teh to take shelter under his tree. A tender conversation ensues. For the first time Chen Teh samples the joy of a man-woman relationship unclouded by material interests. And before she goes home she has promised the pilot to help him get the Peking job. She thinks her cousin may be able to provide the $500. Radiant with joy, she tells her confidant the water seller that in setting out to meet a man who might be able to help her she met a man she is able to help.

Interlude

Before the eyes of the audience Chen Teh transforms herself into her cousin Chui Ta. As she sings a song to explain how impossible it is to perform good deeds without toughness and force she is meantime donning costume and mask of the evil Chui Ta.

4

Chen Teh has asked her friend, the pilot Sun, to come to her shop. In place of the girl he finds her cousin Chui Ta. The latter says he is prepared to provide the $500 for the Peking job, which he reckons a sound financial basis for Sun and Chen Teh. He has asked Mi Tzu to come, a lady tobacco wholesaler who at once offers $300 for the shop. Since Sun evidently has no hesitations the deal is soon agreed. He is radiant as he pockets the $300. Admittedly there is the problem of finding the remaining $200. The cousin's somewhat unscrupulous solution is to make money from the opium which the family of eight have left behind in Chen Teh's shop. Picture his horror, however, not to mention astonishment, when it emerges as a result of a more or less accidental question that the pilot is not thinking of taking the girl to Peking with him. He of course breaks off all further negotiations. The pilot is not all that easily dealt with. Not only does he fail to return the $300 he has been given, but he also expresses himself easily confident of getting the balance from the girl, since she is blindly obsessed with him. Triumphantly he leaves the shop in order to wait for her outside. Chui Ta, whom anger and despair have driven to distraction, sends for Chu Fu the barber and tells him that his cousin's unbridled goodness has been the ruin of her, so that she needs a powerful patron right away. The infatuated barber is prepared to discuss the young lady's problems "over a small supper for two." As Chui Ta goes off "to notify his cousin" the pilot Sun smells trouble and reappears in the shop. When Chen Teh emerges from the back room for her outing with the barber she is confronted by Sun. He reminds her of their love; he recalls that wet evening in the park where they first met. Poor Chen Teh! All that Chui Ta has found out about the pilot's bare-faced egotism is washed away by Chen Teh's feelings of love. She leaves, not with the barber her clever cousin has designated, but with the man she loves.

5

At first light, following a night of love, a happy Chen Teh is discovered outside a local teahouse. She is carrying a small sack of opium which she proposes to sell so as to raise the extra $200 needed to get her flier flying. In a kind of mime to musical accompaniment she and we see the opium smokers leaving the teahouse after a night of indulgence, lonely, stumbling, ravaged, and shivering. The sight of these wrecks brings her to her senses. She is quite incapable of buying happiness for herself by trafficking in such deadly poison. Sun will surely understand. He won't reject her if she comes back to him empty-handed. Charged with this hope she hastens away.

6

Chen Teh's hope has not been fulfilled. Sun has left her. In low dives he is drinking all the money raised by the sale of the shop. We next see Chen Teh in the yard, loading her few possessions on a cart. She has lost her little shop, gift of the gods. As she takes down her washing she becomes giddy, and a woman neighbor remarks mockingly that her fine upstanding lover has no doubt put her in the family way. The discovery fills Chen Teh with indescribable joy. She hails the pilot's son as a pilot of the future. Turning round, she can scarcely believe her eyes when she sees a neighbor's child fishing for scraps of food in the garbage pail; it is hungry. The sight brings about a complete transformation in her. She makes a big speech to the audience proclaiming her determination to turn herself into a tigress for the sake of the child in her womb. That, it seems to her, is the only way to shield it from poverty and degeneracy. The only one who can help is her cousin.

Interlude

The water seller asks the audience whether they have seen Chen Teh. It is now five months since she vanished. Her cousin has grown rich and is now known as the Tobacco King. Rumor however has it that his prosperity is due to shady dealings. The water seller is sure it is the opium traffic.

7

The Tobacco King, Chui Ta, is sitting in solitude in Chen Teh's old but newly smartened-up shop. He has grown fat. Only his housekeeper knows why. The autumn rain seems to make him incline to melancholy. The housekeeper pokes fun at him. Is the master perhaps thinking about that rainy evening in the park? Is he still waiting for the pilot to reappear? The shop door opens and a decrepit individual comes in; it is Sun. Chui Ta is greatly agitated and asks what he can do for him. The ex-pilot brusquely refuses food and clothing. He wants just one thing: opium. Chui Ta, seeing in this unforgotten lover a victim of his own shady traffic, has just begged him to give up this suicidal vice when Wang the water seller appears with his regular monthly enquiry as to the whereabouts of Chen Teh. Reproachfully he informs Chui Ta that she herself told him she was pregnant, and swears that Chen Teh's friends are never going to give up enquiring about her, for good people are both rare and desperately needed. This is too much for Chui Ta. Without a word he goes into the back room. Sun has overheard that Chen Teh is expecting a child. He at once sees an opening for blackmail. Then he hears sobs from the back room; undoubtedly it is Chen Teh's voice. When Chui Ta reenters the shop Sun once again demands opium, and because Chui Ta refuses he goes off uttering threats. Chui Ta's secret is on the verge of being discovered. He must get away. He is just leaving the shop and Szechwan when Sun comes back with the police. A quick search reveals Chen Teh's clothing. The Tobacco King is taken away on suspicion of murder.

8

The water seller has a dream. The three gods appear to him and ask about Chen Teh. He is forced to tell them that she has been murdered by her cousin. The gods are appalled. During their entire trip across the province they failed to find a single other good person. They will return at once.

9

At the trial of Chui Ta the Tobacco King, which has aroused the entire neighborhood, the three gods appear as judges. As it proceeds Chen Teh's good works are universally lauded and Chui Ta's misdeeds condemned. Chui Ta is forced to justify his harshness by his desire to help his unworldly cousin. He regards himself as her one genuinely disinterested friend. Asked where she is staying at that moment, he has no answer. When cornered he promises to make a statement if the court can be cleared. Once alone with his judges he takes off his disguise: he is Chen Teh. The gods are horrified. The one good person they found is the most detested man in the entire city. It can't be true. Incapable of facing the reality they send for a pink cloud and hastily mount it in order to journey back up to their heaven. Chen Teh falls on her knees, imploring them for help and advice. "How can I be good and yet survive without my cousin, Enlightened Ones?"—"Well, do your best" is the gods' embarrassed answer.—"But I've got to have my cousin, Enlightened Ones!"—"Not too often, not too often."—"At least once a week!"—"Once a month, that will do." And despairingly she watches her gods disappear into the sky, waving and smiling.

When the court doors are once again opened the crowd delightedly hails the return of the good person of Szechwan.

[From Werner Hecht (ed.): *Materialien zu Brechts "Der gute Mensch von Sezuan,"* Frankfurt, Suhrkamp, 1968, pp. 100–106. This outline corresponds to the "Santa Monica 1943" version of the play, as discussed below, pp. 383 ff.]

Editorial Note

1. Preliminary Ideas

This appears to be the first play conceived by Brecht as a "parable," and it originates in the notion of a prostitute, "Fanny Kress, or the Whores' Only Friend," who disguises herself as a man, a cigar merchant, in order to help her sisters. Some three or four years later, in 1931, he noted that "economic pressure or a falling demand for labor will make people sacrifice even their sex," a point developed further in the short story "Der Arbeitsplatz" which he wrote around 1934 about a woman who dresses as a man in order to take over her dead husband's job. The play idea next surfaced as one of a pair of short plays, the first being planned as *Der Gelegenheitskauf*, about the sale of a secondhand car, while the second, in five scenes, would be called *Die Ware Liebe*, a pun roughly equivalent to *Love is the Goods:*

> A young prostitute realizes that she cannot be both goods and saleswoman. A stroke of luck puts a small sum of money in her way. She uses it to open a cigar store, and dresses as a man in order to pose as its proprietor, meanwhile continuing to practice as a prostitute.

One of various possible plots which Brecht noted for it involved the proprietor's assistant, who was to make the prostitute pregnant, thus forcing her to disappear (much like Shen Teh), and then to blackmail his employer on this account. It is not clear what induced Brecht to shift the setting of this story from Berlin during the world economic crisis to a semi-mythical Chinese city. Possibly the images conjured up in the "Song of the Smoke" (pp. 18 f.), whose derivation from the "Song from the Opium Den" (pp. 359 f.) makes it the oldest element in the final play, may have haunted his thinking even though it was added only in the 1941 revision. But it seems likelier that, as with *The Caucasian Chalk Circle* three years later, the impulse derived from Klabund's *The Chalk Circle* with its prostitute heroine, modified to some extent by the "counterplay" *Tai-Yang erwacht* which Friedrich Wolf wrote as a "Lehrstück" (or didactic play) and whose staging by Piscator in 1931 made a considerable impression on Brecht. Wolf's Shanghai factory scenes, his heroine's character and role as her employer's mistress, certainly seem echoed in Brecht's Szechwan, as also does the un-Brechtian sweetness of Klabund's very successful exercise in chinoiserie. At the same time Brecht's interest in Chinese settings had already shown itself in unfinished prose projects such as his "Book of Changes," while in August 1938 he published the "Six Chinese Poems" based on Arthur Waley's translations, of which one, Po Chü-yi's "The Big Rug," was to be incorporated in the play (p. 23).

At any rate by the following March, when his journal shows him returning to the play idea in earnest, he had given it the new title of *The Good Person of Szechwan*, so the transposition away from Europe had evidently already been settled in his mind. Four of the five planned scenes seemed usable for what he now envisaged as a "thin structure of steel," an ambitious, precisely calculated piece of engineering which would have nothing pretty-pretty about it. Not much could be done before he left Denmark, but once safely lodged in Sweden he devoted much of the summer of 1939 to working on it while the world round him headed for war. He was clear about the need to avoid chinoiserie:

> the girl must be a big powerful person. the city must be a big, dusty, uninhabitable place . . . the vision is of a chinese city's outskirts where there are cement works and so on. they still have gods, but airplanes have come in. perhaps the lover should be an out-of-work pilot?

The scenes too now expanded to eight in number, an early but undated scheme giving them as:

Prologue
1. The whore gets a tobacco shop.
2. Her cousin must rescue it.

3. The whore falls in love.
4. The cousin must foot the bill.
5. The whore's one friend.
6. The whore's marriage.
7. Suspicion.
8. Trial.

This plot however became too elaborate, the personality of the cousin too simply bad, the whole play much too long. From Brecht's journal it sounds as if such writing as got done was patchy, and certainly no complete script of this version seems to have survived. It looks as though there was to have been a large-scale tobacco merchant called Feh Pung trying to squeeze the heroine and other small traders out of business, while neither the landlady nor the family of eight appeared in the story, the former being replaced by a male landlord and the latter by giving a more important role to the two prostitutes of scene 3. The barber too would have been more sympathetic, as he was to help the heroine combat Feh Pung. The names all through differed from those in our version (and were indeed changed mainly at a relatively late stage); thus Shen Teh/Shui Ta was (or were) Li Gung/Lao Go; the pilot Yu Schan or Schan Yu; the water seller Sun; Mrs. Shin at first Mrs. Si; and the barber Kau or Kiau. Finally, in September, at the time of the German invasion of Poland and the allied declaration of war, the work ground to a halt. Within a fortnight of summing it all up in the "Press Report" printed on pp. 362 ff., Brecht was hard at work on *Mother Courage* instead.

2. The Finnish Version

He picked up the threads again the next spring, after moving to Finland in April 1940. "No play has ever given me so much trouble," he noted in June after he and Margarete Steffin had been working on it concentratedly for some six weeks:

the material presented many difficulties, and in the (roughly) ten years since i first tackled it i made several false starts.

the main danger was of being over-schematic. li gung had to be a person if she was to become a good person. as a result her goodness is not of a conventional kind; she is not wholly and invariably good, not even when she is being li gung. nor is lao go conventionally bad, etc. the continual fusion and dissolution of the two characters, and so on, comes off reasonably well, i think. the gods' great experiment of extending love of one's neighbor to embrace love of one's self, adding "be good to thyself" to "be good to others," needed to stand apart from the story and at the same time to dominate it . . .

The first complete script in the Brecht Archive dates from this period, but as it is one of Brecht's characteristic pasted-up typescripts, with many later additions and corrections stuck in and yet others written in by hand, much detective work will be needed before we know just what stages it went through. Originally the characters bore the earlier names (apart from Mrs. Si, who had already become Mrs. Shin), which Brecht at some point amended by hand. His journal suggests that this change was decided between August 9 and September 6, 1940, in other words at the last moment before he moved on to intensive work on *Puntila*. However, the addition of the three songs "Song of the Smoke," "Song of the Eighth Elephant," and "Trio of the Vanishing Gods on their Cloud," which were written in January 1941, suggest that the final amendments were probably made during that month. Thereafter it was retyped and mimeographed, copies being sent to Switzerland, Sweden, and the U.S., with the text virtually as we now have it. Until the 1950s the play bore a dedication to Helene Weigel, Brecht's wife.

The most elaborate of the "working schemes" used for the play is reproduced on pp. 365 ff. Its penciled additions include Li Gung's "Praise of the Rain" in scene 3 (possibly the origin of the water seller's song on p. 35) and a sketch for the "Song of the Defenselessness of the Gods and the Good People" (p. 45 f.). The January revision too seems to have been concerned (to judge from a journal entry of the 25th) with "introducing a poetic element, a few verses and songs. this should make it lighter and less tedious, even if it cannot be shortened." Besides this variation of the texture and the changing of the names it seems that Brecht's reworking of the draft completed the previous June concentrated on four main points: the treatment of the stocks of raw tobacco brought in by the family of eight, the exact details of Shen Teh's borrowings and payments, the direct addressing of the audience, and minor questions of local color: e.g., should the characters feed on bread and milk or on rice and tea? "i have taken care to avoid any element of folklore," he noted at one point. "on the other hand i don't want people to make a joke of yellow men eating white french bread . . . that would be using china as a mere disguise, and a ragged disguise at that." What he was striving for rather, he said, was something equivalent to the imaginary London of *The Threepenny Opera* or the Kiplingesque Kilkoa of *A Man's a Man*, both of which he considered successful "poetic conceptions."

3. Account of the First Script

To resume this 1940–41 script scene by scene, the chief points of interest are:

Prologue

Dated by Brecht June 11, 1940 and followed by a photograph of a Chinese water carrier.

1

Here as elsewhere the rice distributed by Shen Teh was originally milk. Sacks of tobacco are brought in by the "elderly couple" on p. 12, also by the grandfather and the niece. The "Song of the Smoke" (p. 18) was inserted with the title "Song of the impoverished family." The verse "They are wicked" was likewise a later addition (p. 14).

2

The details of Mrs. Mi Tzu's demand for the rent in advance
(p. 27) were added to the script, as was the passage with the
old woman (p. 29). All sums were originally in yen, not silver
dollars.

3

At the start Brecht cut eleven lines in which the young prostitute told Shen Teh that her family had seven sacks of tobacco
to restart in business, and asked her to look after them. Thereafter the rain, Shen Teh's references to her tame crane, her
speech beginning "There are still friendly people" (p. 34)
and the verses "In our country" and "I'm rich" (both on p. 33)
were all later additions to the script. The verse "No sooner
was there" in the ensuing interlude (p. 37) was originally at
the end of scene 1, where it was spoken by Shen Teh.

4

The episode where the two old people lend Shen Teh the rent
money (pp. 41 f.) was certainly reworked, if not actually added
to the script. The passage where Shen Teh hands the money to
Mrs. Yang, proposes to sell her tobacco stocks and wonders
how to raise a further $300 (from "You can take them" to
"a flier must fly" on pp. 44 f.) appears to be an addition too.

5

In various schemes for the complex finances of this scene it
appears that Mrs. Mi Tzu was to buy not only the shop but also
the sacks of tobacco left by the family of eight, who would
then be reluctant to claim them. This was cut on the script.
Brecht also deleted an appearance of the old woman early in the
scene to inquire about her loan, substituting instead the ex-

change between Sun and Shui Ta (p. 49); both versions stress
that there was no agreement in writing. Notes made after the
change of names show Brecht concerned to reconcile Sun's
more "hooligan-like" features with his genuine keenness for
flying. At that stage his boasting about his hold over Shen
Teh was primarily intended to impress Mrs. Mi Tzu, not (as
now) Shui Ta. The barber, too, was at this point to suggest
turning his empty houses into a tobacco factory for the general
benefit of the neighborhood.

6

Brecht added Sun's references to the "three gremlins" (p. 60 f.)
and the mention of the old couple (on p. 62). Shen Teh's
demand that Sun repay the $200 is not in this script, and only
appears in that of the Zurich production.

7

The first six lines, with their further mention of repayment, are
not in this script. Shu Fu's gift of the blank check (p. 69) is
not in the working plan, and it appears that the whole ending
of the scene, with its installation of the factory in Shu Fu's
shacks, was extensively worked over. Previously this develop-
ment was to have been left to scene 8, while the sacks (subsequently bales) of tobacco would already have been sold in
scene 5. The script specifies that Shen Teh's big verse speech on
p. 74 should be accompanied by the music of the "Song of
the Defenselessness of the Gods and the Good People," which
would continue softly after its end. Her little rhyme about
"Once there was a juicy plum" (p. 71) was added in revision.

8

Though the scene is dated May 21, 1940, the "Song of the
Eighth Elephant" (p. 83) was added in January. Most of the

indications that Mrs. Yang's remarks were to be addressed to the audience were likewise additions.

9

Bears the dates May 23 and June 17 and seems to have been scarcely revised since.

10

Dated Helsingfors, May 29 and June 17, 1940, but bears signs of considerable subsequent reworking. Shen Teh's big speech (pp. 100 ff.) looks like a separate insertion, and the reference to her as "strong and strapping" (p. 101) is added in Brecht's hand. Originally on this script the scene ended with "Once a month, that will do" (p. 102), followed by the final quatrain. The gods' trio, initially with a slightly different first verse, was added in the January revision.

The epilogue is not included in this script, whose finally amended version is otherwise to all intents and purposes the same as the final text used in our edition.

4. The Zurich Script of 1943

For the play's first production at the Zurich Schauspielhaus a duplicated script was made by the Reiss-Verlag of Basel. Subtitled "A Parable by Bertold Brecht" this again is very close to the final text, but includes a number of small dramaturgical changes due presumably to the theater. Thus it runs most of the interludes into the immediately preceding scenes, puts an intermission after scene 5 and makes the following cuts:

1

The sacks of tobacco previously brought by the elderly couple were omitted.

6

Cut from Sun's "Why not?" (p. 60) to the start of Mrs. Yang's next speech (p. 61).

8

Cut stage direction and Mrs. Yang's speech, following the song.

9

Cut from "SHUI TA (*pitifully*)" to "*in Mrs. Shin's arms*" (p. 85), also the stage direction and Wang's first speech in the interlude following.

10

Cut from "Mr. Shui Ta, on the other hand" to "from committing sheer perjury" (p. 96). Again, there was no epilogue.

5. The Santa Monica Version

Even before the Zurich production Brecht had tried to arouse interest in the play in the U.S., but without yet attempting to modify it for the very different audience there. It was only later, when Kurt Weill thought he might be able to arrange a Broadway production, that Brecht in New York hurriedly made what he termed "a szechwan version for here." Though this has not been firmly identified, it could well be the "story" printed on p. 361, which was found inside one of the duplicated copies of the Finnish version, from which however it differs extensively. The full script embodying this story, typed by Brecht himself and marked "only copy," was headed "1943

version" and datelined Santa Monica 1943, so that it must have
been written after his return there from New York at the end
of May, probably once the main work on *Schweyk* had been
completed. By September 20 Brecht's journal shows that Christopher Isherwood had read the play but was not interested
enough to want to translate it as its author had hoped. Thereafter, as Weill began to think rather of making a "semi-opera"
of it, the new script was set aside and apparently forgotten,
subsequent U.S. translations and productions being based, so
far as we know, on the previous version. This seems surprising
in view of Brecht's success here, not only in shortening and
simplifying the play but also in shedding a more critical light
on the heroine's goodness, and thus interweaving the ideas of
good and evil as he wanted in the earlier journal entry printed
on pp. 367 ff. The principal differences from our text are as
follows:

Prologue

As before.

1

The stage direction for the entry of the elderly couple on p.
12 adds "*The wife and the shabbily dressed man are carrying sacks on their shoulders.*" Then there is a long cut from
Mrs. Mi Tzu's entry (p. 16) to the nephew's "About the shelves"
(p. 17), after which the former's exit speech, starting "I shall
be very glad," and the wife's ensuing comment, ending "all about
you by tomorrow morning," (p. 17) are likewise cut.

2

Unchanged up to where Shui Ta bows (p. 26). Thereafter the
rest of the scene is different, thus:

SHUI TA There's just one thing: aren't you going to take your sacks?

THE HUSBAND (*giving him a conspiratorial look*) What sacks? You know we didn't bring any sacks with us.

SHUI TA (*slowly*) Oh. Then either my cousin got it wrong or I must have misunderstood her. (*To the policeman*) It's quite all right.

THE POLICEMAN Get going, you! (*He drives them out*)

THE GRANDFATHER (*solemnly, from the doorway*) Good morning.

(*All go out except Shui Ta*)

(*Shui Ta hastens backstage and brings out a sack*)

SHUI TA (*showing the sack to the audience*) Opium! (*He hears somebody approaching and quickly hides the sack*)

THE POLICEMAN (*reentering*) I've handed those crooks over to my colleague. Forgive my coming back. I would like to thank you in the name of the police.

SHUI TA It is for me to thank you, officer.

THE POLICEMAN (*negligently*) You were saying something about sacks. Did those crooks leave anything here, Mr. Shui Ta?

SHUI TA Not a button. Do you smoke?

THE POLICEMAN (*putting two cigars in his pocket*) Mr. Shui Ta, I must admit we at the station began by viewing this shop with mixed feelings, but your decisive action on the side of the law just now showed us the sort of man you are. We don't take long to find out who is to be relied on as a friend of law and order. I only hope you will be staying here.

SHUI TA Unfortunately I shall not be staying here and I cannot come again. I was able to give my cousin a hand just because I was passing through; I merely saved her from the worst. Any minute now she will be thrown back on her own resources. I am worried as to what will happen.

THE POLICEMAN All you have to do is find a husband for her.

SHUI TA A husband?

THE POLICEMAN (*eagerly*) Why not? She's a good match. Between you and me I had a hint only yesterday from Mr. Shu Fu, the barber next door, that he is taking a flattering interest in the young lady, and he's a gentleman who owns twelve houses and has only one wife and an old one at that. He went so far as to ask about her financial standing. That shows real affection . . .

SHUI TA (*cautiously*) It's not a bad idea. Could you arrange a meeting?

THE POLICEMAN I think so. It would have to be done delicately, of course. Mr. Shu Fu is very sensitive. I'd say, a meeting by accident outside the teahouse by the city lake. There's a bath-hut there; I know because I had the good fortune to make an arrest there last week. Miss Shen Teh could be looking at the goldfish and in her delight could let drop some remark such as . . . well, what?

SHUI TA Look at the pretty goldfish.

THE POLICEMAN Brilliant. And Mr. Shu Fu could reply, let's say, for example . . .

SHUI TA All I can see is a pretty face mirrored in the water, madam.

THE POLICEMAN Perfect. I'll speak to Mr. Shu Fu at once. Don't think, Mr. Shui Ta, that the authorities have no sympathy for the honest businessman.

SHUI TA Indeed I foresaw a black outlook for this little shop which my cousin regards as a gift of the gods. But now I see a way out. It is almost frightening how much luck one needs in order to live, what brilliant ideas, what good friends.

3

Up to p. 34 f. the first two-thirds of the scene are unchanged, except that on p. 31 and again on p. 33 Shen Teh "has got" to marry the man she is meeting at the teahouse, not merely "is going" to. Then from "Have you got a friend?" at the end of Sun's speech (p. 34) to Shen Teh's "Yes" (p. 34) there is a cut and the following is substituted:

SHEN TEH They say that to speak without hope is to speak without kindness.

SUN I have no hope. I need 500 silver dollars to be human. This morning when a letter came saying there was a job for me the first thing I did was to get myself a rope; you see, it costs 500 dollars.

SHEN TEH   Is it a flier's job? (*He nods, and she slowly goes on*) I have a friend, a cousin of mine, who might be able to raise that amount. This friend is too cunning and hard. It really would have to be the last time. But a flier must fly, that's obvious.

SUN   What do you think you are talking about?

SHEN TEH   Please come tomorrow to Sandalmakers' Street. You'll find a small tobacco shop. If I'm not there my cousin will be.

SUN (*laughs*)   And if your cousin isn't there nobody will be, is that it? (*He looks at her*) Your shawl's really the prettiest thing about you.

SHEN TEH   Yes? (*Pause*) And now I've felt a raindrop.

And so on as in our text, up to the end of the poem on p. 35. The scene then finishes thus:

WANG   Weren't you meeting somebody in the park who was going to be able to help you?

SHEN TEH   Yes, but now I've found somebody I am going to be able to help, Wang.

After that come the stage direction (*She pays . . .*) and her last laughing remark to Wang as we have them.

4

Is omitted, only the first six lines from Shen Teh's monologue about the city (p. 40) being kept and transposed to a new interlude before scene 7.

The interlude before the curtain which follows remains unchanged.

5

Instead of as on our pp. 46–47 Mrs. Shin's first speech reads:

MRS. SHIN   I may be an old gossip, Mr. Shui Ta, but I think you should know what's going on. Once people start talking about how Miss Shen Teh never comes home before morning—and you know we have all the scum of the district hanging round the shop at crack of dawn to get a plate of rice—then a shop like this gets a bad name, and where do you go from there?

On page 47 for Sun's "Man, I'm going to fly again" substitute "Neat, very neat." For 300 silver dollars (three times) read 500. For the two lines "it was decent of her" to "get me anywhere" read "Nothing for it, we'll have to sell." Then omit Shui Ta's next two sentences (from "Perhaps" to "her shop") and for Sun's "Which is all to her credit" below substitute "Really." About a page further on delete Shui Ta's sentence about the 200 dollars and the rent, and for both mentions of 250 dollars (amount of Sun's pay in Peking) substitute 150 dollars. In Shui Ta's next speech, for "the owner of the house" (p. 49) substitute "the lady tobacco merchant" (Tabakhändlerin). The dialogue from that point reads:

THE LADY TOBACCO MERCHANT (*enters*) Good morning, Mr. Shui Ta. Are you really wanting to sell the shop?

SHUI TA Mrs. Mi Tzu, my cousin is contemplating marriage, and her future husband—(*he introduces Yang Sun*) —Mr. Yang Sun, is taking her to Peking where they wish to start a new life. If I can get a good price for my tobacco I shall sell it.

THE LADY TOBACCO MERCHANT How much do you need?

SHUI TA 500 in cash.

THE LADY TOBACCO MERCHANT How much did your stock cost?

SHUI TA My cousin originally paid 1000 silver dollars, and very little of it has been sold.

THE LADY TOBACCO MERCHANT 1000 silver dollars! She was swindled of course. I'll make you an offer: you can have 300 silver dollars for the whole business, if you move out the day after tomorrow.

SUN All right. That's it, old boy!

SHUI TA It's too little.

SUN We'd consider that, certainly, but 300 isn't enough. (*Like an auctioneer*) First-class tobacco, recently acquired, in admirable condition, price 1000 dollars F.O.B.

Together with complete shop fittings and a growing clien-
tèle, attracted by the good looks of the proprietress. The
whole to be knocked down for only 500 dollars due to
special circumstances. It's an opportunity that mustn't be
missed. Now you're an intelligent woman, you know what
life's about, it's written all over you. (*He strokes her*)
You know what love is, it's plain to see. The shop's got
to go, selling below cost price due to hasty marriage—the
sort of chance that occurs once in a business lifetime.

THE LADY TOBACCO MERCHANT (*not unaffected, but still firmly*)
300 dollars.

SUN (*with a sidelong glance at Shui Ta*) Not enough, but
better than nothing, what? 300 in hand would give us
room to turn round in.

SHUI TA (*alarmed*) But 300 won't get us the job.

SUN OK, but what good is a shop to me?

SHUI TA But everything would have gone, there'd be nothing to live on.

SUN But I'd have the 300 dollars. (*To the lady tobacco
merchant*) It's a deal. Lock, stock, and barrel for 300 dollars, and our troubles are over. How soon can we have
the 300?

THE LADY TOBACCO MERCHANT Right away. (*She pulls notes
from her bag*) Here, 300 dollars, and that's because I'm
glad to help where it seems to be a case of young love.

SUN (*to Shui Ta*) Write down 300 on the contract. Shen
Teh's signature's already on it, I see.
(*Shui Ta fills in the figure and hands the contract to the
lady tobacco merchant. Sun takes the notes away from
him*)

THE LADY TOBACCO MERCHANT Good-bye, Mr. Yang Sun;
good-bye, Mr. Shui Ta. Please remember me to Miss Shen
Teh. (*Goes out*)

SUN (*sits down exhausted on the counter*) We've made it,
old boy.

SHUI TA But it's not enough.

SUN Your cousin certainly thought you were the right man
them.

SHUI TA How am I to do that without stealing?

SUN Your cousin certainly thought you were the right man
to find them.

SHUI TA Perhaps I am. (*Slowly*) I took it that the point at issue was Shen Teh's happiness. A person's goodness, they said, doesn't have to be denied to that person and the same applies to his or her compassion.

SUN   Right, partner. O boy, I'm going to be flying again!

SHUI TA *(smiling and with a bow)*   A flier has to fly. *(Negligently)* Have you got the money for both your tickets, and enough to tide you over?

Thereafter the dialogue continues as we have it from Sun's "Of course" (p. 50) to the *(Pause)* on p. 50. Then Shui Ta continues:

I should like you to hand me back the 300 dollars, Mr. Yang Sun, and leave them in my custody until you are able to show me two tickets to Peking.

SUN   Why? You mean you don't trust me?

SHUI TA   I don't trust anybody.

SUN   Why specially me?
(They look at each other)

SUN   My dear brother-in-law, I would prefer it if you didn't meddle in the intimate affairs of people in love. We don't understand one another, I see. As for the other 200 I'll have to rely on the girl.

SHUI TA *(incredulously)*   Do you really expect her to give up everything for you if you aren't even thinking of taking her along?

SUN   She will. Even so.

SHUI TA   And you are not afraid of what I might have to say against it?

Then back to our text from Sun's "Come off it" (p. 51), but with the following modifications. First of all Sun's exit speech (p. 51) ends, after *(puts the box under his arm)*

And now I'm going to go and wait outside the shop, and don't let it worry you if we're a bit late tonight. We're having supper together and we'll be talking about that missing 200.

Then Mrs. Shin's second sentence ("And all Yellow Street") is cut, as is her speech following the poem (p. 52). Instead

Shen Teh concludes the poem by saying "Fetch Mr. Shu Fu the barber at once," and Shin (*dashes off*). About a page later there is a long cut from Wang's entry with the policeman (p. 53) to immediately before Shui Ta's "I shall hasten to notify my cousin" (p. 54). Roughly two pages after that Sun's "But I'm not going to" (p. 56) is followed by a new insertion "Look me in the eyes. Do you really believe I can't be in love with you without a dowry?" before continuing "They're ruining" and so on as in our text. Finally, after Shen Teh's "I'm going away with Sun" (p. 56) Sun says "Bring your shawl, the blue one," and (*Shen Teh fetches the shawl she wore in the park*) before Sun goes on "We love each other" and so on to the end.

The ensuing interlude (pp. 57–58) is partly absorbed in the new interlude outside a teahouse (see below).

6

Is omitted, as is the interlude (pp. 66–68) which follows it.

Interlude Outside a Teahouse

This is mainly new. Carrying a small sack, Shen Teh addresses the audience as at the beginning of our scene 4 (p. 40), from "I'd never seen the city in the early morning," but omitting the sentence "I've come a long way" etc. After "filling his lungs with fresh air and reaching for his tools" (p. 40) she continues:

And here is the Teahouse of Bliss where I am supposed to sell this little sack so that Sun may fly again. (*She tries to enter, but guests are leaving. They are opium smokers, human wrecks, stumbling and freezing. A young man takes out his purse, finds it empty and throws it away. A hideous old woman escorts a very young drugged girl*) That's terrible. It's opium that has ruined them like that. (*She looks at her sack in horror*) It's poison. How could I think of selling this? It doesn't even belong to me. How could I forget that too?

Then she goes into the monologue on p. 57, starting at "In a surge of feeling," omitting the sentence "How could I simply forget those two good old people?" and ending after "he'll understand" (p. 58) with:

He would rather get a job at the cement works than owe his flying to a filthy deal. I must go to him at once.

7 [renumbered 6]

After the opening stage direction, which is as in our text, Mrs. Shin's speech is changed to read: "There you are, your shop's gone and the whole district knows that for weeks that pilot of yours has been boozing away the money in the lowest sort of bar." Shen Teh (*says nothing*). Then Shin continues "Then everything's gone" etc., as in our text (p. 68), down to Shen Teh's "earn a little sorting tobacco." Then:

(*A child appears in the gateway to the yard*)
MRS. SHIN (*shooing it away*) Clear out, you! (*To Shen Teh*) Those gutter vultures only need to get one sniff of bankruptcy and before you know it they come around stuffing their pockets.
SHEN TEH Oh, let him look through my junk. He might find something worth taking.
MRS. SHIN If there's anything worth taking I'm taking it. You haven't paid me for the washing yet. Beat it or I'll call the police! (*Child disappears*)

Shen Teh then asks "Why are you so mean?" introducing the poem as on p. 72. After it Mrs. Shin comments "A pity your cousin didn't hear that," and goes on "How did Mr. Shui Ta's pants get here" etc., as on p. 68. After Shen Teh's "No" seven lines further on there is another new passage:

(*Lin To the carpenter appears in the gateway*)
THE CARPENTER Good morning, Miss Shen Teh. There's a story going round the district that you have got permis-

sion for the homeless to move into Shu Fu the barber's houses. Is that right?

MRS. SHIN   It was right. But now we've given Shu Fu the brushoff there ain't going to be no accommodation.

THE CARPENTER   That's a pity. I don't know what I can do with my family.

MRS. SHIN   It looks as if Miss Shen Teh will be in the happy position of being able to ask *you* for accommodation. (*The carpenter goes out, disappointed*) There'll be a lot more of them coming along.

SHEN TEH   This is dreadful.

MRS. SHIN   You think you're too good for the barber, so the plague huts down by the river are going to have to be good enough for Lin To and his family. If you ask me you're not giving up that pilot of yours in spite of the bad way he has behaved to you. Don't you mind him being such a bad person?

SHEN TEH   It all comes from poverty.

Then she addresses the poem to the audience as on p. 69, after which the text continues, with one exception, as we have it until after the plum rhyme that ends her big speech (p. 71). The exception is that the mention of the barber's check is cut; thus after Mrs. Shin's "If only it's not a little stranger" (p. 70) the speaker (*laughs*) and continues: "Your pilot has fixed you good and proper. Landed you with a kid, that's what he's done!" Then (*She goes to the rear*) and so on. But once past the plum rhyme this version is different:

(*The child reappears in the gateway. It seems surprised by Shen Teh's play-acting. Suddenly she observes it and beckons it into the yard*)

THE CHILD   Where are you going?

SHEN TEH   I don't know, Ni Tzu.

(*The child rubs its stomach and looks expectantly at her*)

SHEN TEH   I haven't any more rice, Ni Tzu, not a grain.

THE CHILD   Don't go.

SHEN TEH   I'd like to stay.

(*The water seller is heard calling "Buy water!"*)

SHEN TEH   That's something I can still do for you. Come on, little man. (*To the audience*)

Hey, you people. Someone is asking for shelter.
A citizen of tomorrow is asking you for a today.

(*To the child*) Wait a moment. (*She hurries to the gateway, where the water seller has appeared*)

WANG   Good morning, Shen Teh. Is it true that you're having to clear out of your shop?

SHEN TEH   That's not important: happiness has come to me, I am to have a child, Wang. I'm so glad you came; I had to tell somebody about it. But don't repeat that or Yang Sun may hear of it, and he won't want us. Give me a cupful.

(*He gives her a cup of water. When she turns round with it she sees the child and stiffens. It has gone over to the garbage pail and is fishing around in it. It picks out something which it eats*)

SHEN TEH (*to Wang*)   Please go at once; I'm not well. (*She pushes him out*) He's hungry. Fishing in the garbage.

Then (*She lifts up the child*) (p. 73) and makes her big verse speech as in our text, and the scene ends with "for the last time, I hope" on p. 74.

A new, much shorter interlude follows in lieu of the present one (pp. 78–79). It goes thus:

(*The water seller walks slowly along before the curtain as if it were a street. He stops and addresses the audience*)

WANG   Can any of you good people tell me where to find Miss Shen Teh, formerly of Sandalmakers' Street? It's five months since she completely vanished. That was when her cousin suddenly popped up—must have been for the third time—what's more [?] there have been some queer business dealings in her tobacco shop, very profitable but dirty. (*Softly*) Opium. The worst of it is I'm no longer in touch with the Enlightened Ones. It may be because I'm so worried I can't sleep a wink, so that I no longer have dreams. Anyway, if you do see Shen Teh, could you tell her to get in touch with me? We miss her badly in our district; she is such a good person, you see. (*He walks worriedly on*)

8

Is omitted.

9 [renumbered 7]

This is the scene in Shen Teh's shop (pp. 84 ff.), but with changes. It starts thus:

(*The shop has been transformed into an office, with easy chairs and fine carpets. Shui Ta, fat and expensively dressed, is ushering out the elderly couple and the nephew who called on Shen Teh the day the shop was opened. Mrs. Shin, in noticeably new clothes, is watching with amusement. Outside it is raining*)

SHUI TA   I tell you for the tenth time I never found any sacks in the back room.

THE WIFE   Then we'd better write to Miss Shen Teh. What's her address?

SHUI TA   I'm afraid I don't know.

THE NEPHEW   So that's it. The sacks have gone, but you've done all right for yourself.

SHUI TA   That indeed is it.

MRS. SHIN   Better watch your step. Mr. Shui Ta found jobs in his factory for some of your family, didn't he? His patience might suddenly give out.

THE WIFE   But the work's ruining my boy's health. It's more than he can take.

(*Shui Ta and Mrs. Shin say nothing*)

THE HUSBAND   Come along, we've got nothing to prove those were our sacks. But Shen Teh may be back some day.

(*Shui Ta shrugs his shoulders. The elderly couple and the nephew go off angrily*)

SHUI TA (*feebly*)   Working in a factory unhealthy? Work's work.

MRS. SHIN   Those people wouldn't have got anywhere with their couple of sacks. That sort of thing is just a foundation, and it takes very special talents to build any real prosperity on it. *You* have them.

SHUI TA (*has to sit down because he feels sick*)   I feel dizzy again.

MRS. SHIN (*bustling around him*)   You're six months gone! You mustn't let yourself get worked up. Lucky for you you've got me. We can all do with a helping hand. Yes, when your time comes I shall be at your side. (*She laughs*)

SHEN TEH (*feebly*)   Can I count on that, Mrs. Shin?

MRS. SHIN   You bet. It'll cost money, of course.

(*A smartly dressed man enters. He is the unemployed man who was given cigarettes the day the shop was opened*)

THE AGENT   Our accounts, Mr. Shui Ta. From street-corner clients 50 dollars. From the Teahouse of Bliss . . .

SHUI TA (*laboriously*)   Go away. Tomorrow.

MRS. SHIN   Can't you see Mr. Shui Ta isn't up to it?

THE AGENT   But we've got a little problem with the police in District Four. One consignment got into the wrong hands, Mr. Shui Ta.

MRS. SHIN   Can't you ever handle anything by yourself? (*The agent starts to go, nervously*)

SHUI TA   Wait! Hand over the money! (*The agent hands over money and goes*)

Then as in our text from "SHUI TA (*pitifully*)" down to "Everyone's watching the shop" (p. 85), after which Mrs. Shin says:

Have a drop of water, dear. (*She gets some water*) Why don't you move out of this place and take a villa in a better district? Oh, but I know why. You're still waiting for that broken-down pilot. That's a weakness.

SHUI TA   Nonsense.

(*Enter a decrepit figure, the former pilot Yang Sun. He is amazed to see Shui Ta in Mrs. Shin's arms, being made to drink by her*)

SUN (*hoarsely*)   Am I disturbing you? (*Shui Ta gets up with difficulty and stares at him*)

MRS. SHIN   Mr. Yang Sun in person.

SUN (*respectfully*)   Excuse me coming to see you dressed like this, Mr. Shui Ta. My luggage got held up, and I didn't want the rain to stop my calling on one or two of my old acquaintances, you see.

SHUI TA (*draws Mrs. Shin aside before she can open her mouth*)   Go and find him some clothes.

MRS. SHIN   Chuck him out right away. I'm telling you.

SHUI TA (*sharply*)   You do what you're told. (*Mrs. Shin goes out, protesting*)

SUN   Woolen rugs. What riches. I'm told people are calling you the Tobacco King, Mr. Shui Ta.

SHUI TA   I've been lucky.

SUN   Oh, Mr. Shui Ta, it isn't just luck; you've earned it. Ah yes, some get fat and others get thin, that's it, isn't it?

SHUI TA   I take it that fate has not been kind to you, Mr. Yang Sun; but are you ill?

SUN   Me? No, my health is fine.

SHUI TA   Good. Damage to one's health is the only thing that cannot sooner or later be repaired, I would say.

(*Enter Mrs. Shin from the back room with clothing*)

SHUI TA   I hope these things will fit you. Isn't that hat rather big?

(*Mrs. Shin tries a hat on Sun*)

SHUI TA   Yes, it's too big. Get another, Mrs. Shin.

SUN   I don't want a hat. (*Suddenly angry*) What are you up to? Trying to buy me off with an old hat? (*Controlling himself*) Why should I want your hat? It's something else I need. (*Ingratiatingly*) Mr. Shui Ta, would you grant just one favor to a man down on his luck?

SHUI TA   What can I do for you?

MRS. SHIN   It's written all over him. I can tell you what kind of a favor he means.

SHUI TA (*beginning to understand*)   No!

MRS. SHIN   Opium, eh?

SHUI TA   Sun!

SUN   Only a little packet, enough for two or three pipes. That's all I need. I don't care about clothes or food. But I've got to have my pipe.

SHUI TA (*in the depths of horror*)   Not opium? Don't tell me you're a victim of that vice. Listen to me, those wretches who think it may help them escape their miseries for an hour or two are plunged in misery by it forever, so that in no time they need the drug not to make them happy but simply to reduce their worst sufferings.

SUN   I see you know all about it. That's how it is with me.

SHUI TA   Turn back at once! You must be ruthless and control your craving; never touch the drug again, you can do it.

SUN   All very well for you to say that, Mr. Shui Ta; you
deal in it and know all about it. Your livelihood depends
on us smokers not finding the way back.

SHUI TA   Water! I feel sick.

MRS. SHIN   You haven't been in form lately, not in your old
form. (*Mockingly*) Perhaps it's Mr. Yang Sun's fault for
bringing the rain with him. Rain always makes you so
touchy and melancholic. I expect you know why.

SHUI TA   Go away.

Then Wang's voice is heard singing, as on p. 86–87, but this time
it is Mrs. Shin who comments: "There comes that damned
water seller. He's going to start agitating again." She then (*goes
out at a sign from Shui Ta*) as his voice continues with his
speech (*from outside*), after which Sun says (*pressingly*):

We'll make a bargain. Give me what I asked for, and I'll
shut him up. What business is it of his, where she is?

Then Wang enters, and with two minor changes the text is the
same as ours up to Shui Ta's "Have you dropped that idea?"
on p. 88. The first change is the addition of the words "(*as if
transformed*)" after "SUN (*to the audience*)" on p. 88. The
second is the substitution seven lines on of "left here rotting" for
"left here slaving" and the addition of "So that lousy water
seller can't even recognize me" before "(*He flies into a rage*)."
Then after "dropped that idea?" the next four pages of our
text are considerably changed and shortened, going on thus:

SUN (*cautiously*)   Why do you ask that? Want to buy me
a pilot's job? Now? What makes you think anyone can fly
with hands like this? (*He shows his; they are trembling*)
Where's my fiancée? Do you hear me? I said, where is my
fiancée Shen Teh?

SHUI TA   Do you really want to know?

SUN   I should think so.

SHUI TA   My cousin might be pleased to hear that.

SUN   Anyway, I'm concerned enough not to be able to shut
my eyes if, for instance, I find that she is being deprived
of her freedom.

SHUI TA   By whom?

SUN By you.
(*Pause*)

SHUI TA What would you do in such an eventuality?

SUN (*crudely*) I'd say you had better meet my request and no arguing about it.

SHUI TA Your request for . . .

SUN (*hoarsely*) The stuff, of course.

SHUI TA Aha. (*Pause*) Mr. Yang Sun, you will not get a single pinch of that drug out of me.

SUN In that case perhaps your cousin wouldn't deny the father of her child a few pipes of opium every day and a bench to sleep on? Dear cousin-in-law, my longing for the lady of my heart cannot be suppressed. I feel I shall be forced to take steps if I am to enfold her in my arms once more. (*He calls*) Shen Teh! Shen Teh!

SHUI TA Didn't they tell you Shen Teh has gone away? Do you want to search the back room?

SUN (*giving him a peculiar look*) No, I don't, anyway not by myself. I'm not physically in any condition to fight with you. The police are better fed. (*He leaves quickly, taking care not to present his back to Shui Ta*)
(*Shui Ta looks at him without moving. Then he goes quickly into the back room once more and brings out all kinds of things belonging to Shen Teh: underwear, toilet articles, a dress. He looks lengthily at the shawl which Sun once commented favorably on in the park, then packs it all up in a bundle. Then he gets a suitcase and some men's clothes which he stuffs into it*)

SHUI TA (*with the bundle and the suitcase*) So this is the finish. After all my efforts and triumphs I am having to leave this flourishing business which I developed from the dirty little shop thought good enough by the gods. Just one weak moment, one unforeseeable attack of softness, and I'm pitched into the abyss. I just had to let that broken-down creature open his mouth, instead of instantly handing him over to the police for having embezzled $300, and I was ruined. No amount of toughness and inhumanity will do unless it is total. That's the kind of world it is. (*On hearing sounds from outside, he hurriedly stuffs the bundle under the table. Somebody throws a stone through the window. Voices of an excited crowd outside. Enter Sun, Wang and the policeman*)

The scene then ends virtually as it does after their entry in our text (p. 91). The policeman in his first speech says "we" instead of "I" and omits the words "communicated by a member of your own firm." Then in place of Mrs. Mi Tzu's speech Sun (*points at the bundle*) saying, "He's packed his things. He wanted to clear out." Finally Shui Ta's last speech is cut and he simply "(*bows and goes out ahead of the policeman*)."

The interlude which follows (pp. 93–94) is as we have it.

10 [*renumbered 8*]

This is very largely the last scene as we have it, less the epilogue. Minor changes in the first part are:

P. 94, for Wang's first speech substitute "I've collected as many witnesses as I could."

Three lines below, for "property owner," substitute "lady tobacco merchant."

P. 95, for "THE OLD WOMAN" substitute "THE YOUNG PROSTITUTE."

P. 96, in the policeman's evidence cut the two sentences beginning "His cousin had trustingly" down to "perjury."

P. 96, Mrs. Mi Tzu's evidence goes:

"As president of the United District Charities, I wish to bring to the attention of the court that Mr. Shui Ta is giving bread and work to a considerable number of people in his tobacco factories. This Shen Teh person, by contrast, was not in particularly good repute."

Five lines below, Wang steps forward with (*the carpenter and the family of eight*).

On p. 97, l. 13, for "bales" read "sacks."

There are also still slighter changes in the German which would not affect the translation. After the sister-in-law's "But we had no place to go," however (p. 96), the scene goes on thus:

SHUI TA   There were too many of you. The lifeboat was on the point of capsizing. I got it afloat again. There wasn't a single morning when the poor of the district failed to get their rice. My cousin regarded her shop as a gift of the gods.

WANG That didn't prevent you from wanting to sell it off.

SHUI TA Because my cousin was helping an airman to get back into the air again. I was supposed to find the money.

WANG She may have wanted that, but you had your eye on that good job in Peking. The shop wasn't good enough for you.

SHUI TA My cousin had no idea of business.

MRS. SHIN Besides, she was in love with the airman.

SHUI TA Hadn't she the right to love?

WANG Of course she had. So why did you try to make her marry a man she didn't love, the barber here?

SHUI TA The man she loved was a crook.

THE FIRST GOD (*showing interest*) Who was it she was in love with?

MRS. SHIN (*pointing at Sun, who is sitting like some kind of animal*) That's him. They say birds of a feather flock together. So much for the private life of your Angel of the Slums.

WANG It wasn't the fact that he was like her that made her love him, but the fact that he was miserable. She didn't just help him because she loved him; she also loved him because she helped him.

THE SECOND GOD You are right. Loving like that was not unworthy of her.

SHUI TA But it was mortally dangerous.

THE FIRST GOD Isn't he the one who accused you of her murder?

SUN Of restricting her freedom. He couldn't have murdered her. A few minutes before his arrest I heard Shen Teh's voice from the room behind the shop.

Then from the first god's remark (on p. 97) for ten lines, down to Shui Ta's "Because you didn't love her," the text is the same as ours, after which:

SUN I was out of work.

WANG (*to Shui Ta*) You were just out for the barber's money.

SHUI TA But what was the money needed for, your worships? (*To Sun*) You wanted her to sacrifice everything, but the barber offered his buildings and his money so that she could help the poor. Even to let her do good I had to promise her to the barber. But she didn't want to.

WANG   Are you blaming Shen Teh because not enough good was done?

SHUI TA   Much of the time.

MRS. SHIN   A lot of good she did! There's somebody she wanted to help for you; look at him. (*Points at Sun*) Then look at Mr. Li Gung (*pointing at the agent*) who was helped by Mr. Shui Ta. Nine months back he came into the shop in rags, out of work and begging for a cigarette. Now he is a fully accredited agent.

WANG   Quite right, that's how you help people, Shui Ta. And it was to help you start up your opium business that Shen Teh had to be got out of the way. Come clean; you've gone into the drug traffic.

SHUI TA   It was for the child's sake.

THE WOMAN (*furious*)   And *my* child?

THE CARPENTER   What about our children? Whom Shen Teh looked after? You shoved them into your insanitary sweat-shops, your tobacco factory, you tobacco king!
(*Shui Ta remains silent*)

THE GRANDFATHER (*at a sign from Wang, steps forward with dignity*)   It's unhealthy work. The boy's coughing.

Then from Wang's "Now you have nothing to say" (p. 99) to the end of the scene is the same as our text, apart from a cut ten lines on from "How many good people" to "her deadly enemy" (p. 99).

There is no epilogue.

PUNTILA AND MATTI, HIS HIRED MAN

Texts by Brecht

A Note of 1940

The reader and, more important, the actor may be inclined to skim over passages such as the short dialogue between judge and lawyer (about the Finnish summer) in the sixth scene, because they use a homely way of speaking. However, the actor will not be performing the passage effectively unless he treats it as a prose poem, since it is one. Whether it is a good or a bad poem is not at this point relevant; the reader or actor can make up his own mind about that. The relevant thing is that it has to be treated as a poem, i.e., in a special manner, "presented on a silver platter." Matti's hymn of praise to the herring in scene 9 is an even better instance, perhaps. There is more than one situation in *Puntila* which would undoubtedly seem crude in a naturalistic play; for instance, any actor who plays the episode where Matti and Eva stage a compromising incident (scene 4) as if it were an episode from a farce will entirely fail to bring it off. This is exactly the kind of scene that calls for real virtuosity, as again do the tests to which Matti subjects his betrothed in scene 8. To cite the casket scene in *The Merchant of Venice* is not to propose any kind of qualitative comparison; though the scene may fall a long way short of Shakespeare's it can still only be made fully effective if one finds a way of acting something like that demanded by a play in verse. Admittedly it is hard to speak of artistic simplicity rather than primitiveness when a play is written in prose and deals with "ordinary" people. All the same the expulsion of the four vil-

lage women (in scene 7) is not a primitive episode but a simple
one, and as with the third scene (quest for legal alcohol and
fiancées) it has to be played poetically; in other words the
beauty of the episode (once again, be it big or be it small) must
come across in the set, the movements, the verbal expression.
The characters too have to be portrayed with a certain grandeur, and this again is something that will be none too easy for
the actor who has only learnt to act naturalistically or fails to
see that naturalistic acting is not enough in this case. It will
help him if he realizes that it is his job to create a national
character, and that this is going to call for all his sensitivity,
daring, and knowledge of humanity. One last point: *Puntila*
is far from being a play with a message. The Puntila part therefore must not for an instant be in any way deprived of its
natural attractiveness, while particular artistry will be needed
to make the drunk scenes delicate and poetic, with the maxi-
mum of variety, and the sober scenes as ungrotesque and un-
brutal as possible. To put it in practical terms: Puntila has if
possible to be staged in a style combining elements of the old
commedia dell' arte and of the realistic play of mores.

> [GW *Schriften zum Theater*, pp. 1167–68. This is the
> section bearing specifically on *Puntila* from the general
> essay "Notes on the Folk Play," written in 1940, which
> will be included in Brecht's theatrical writings (and can
> meanwhile be found in *Brecht on Theatre*, pp. 153–7). It
> was originally prefaced by the words "To take some in-
> stances from *Puntila*. . . ."]

Notes on the Zurich Première

1

Instead of the conventional curtain falling like a guillotine to
chop the play into separate scenes, back to the lightly fluttering
half-height linen curtain with the scene titles projected on it.
During scene changes this curtain was somewhat lit so as to
make it come to life and allow the audience to become more
or less aware of the busy preparations being made for them on

the stage. In particular they saw the upper parts of the big wall sections as they were shifted in, and they saw the sun's disk and the moon's sickle being lowered on wires, not yet illuminated and therefore visibly made of metal; they also saw the various little clouds being changed around.

2

These emblems for sun, moon, and clouds hung, like inn or shop signs, before the high broad wall of birch bark that constituted the background of the *Puntila* stage. According as to whether it was day, half-light, or night the wall was lit strongly, feebly, or not at all; the acting area being fully illuminated the while. In this way the atmospheric element was established in the background, independently of the rest of the performance.

3

No use was made of colored light of any sort. Provided the lighting equipment is up to it the light should be as uniform as for a variety performance which includes the display of acrobatics. Sharply defined spotlighting would blot out the faces. Areas of darkness, even if only relative, detract from the words issuing from them. It is a good idea to have photographs taken to find out what kind of lighting is liable to strain the audience.

4

Color and contrast can be supplied by the stage designer without having recourse to colored light. The color scheme for *Puntila* comprised blue, gray, and white for the stage, and black, gray, and white for the costumes. On top of this the latter were strictly realistic, with particular respect for details (the village women's handbags; the farm workers working barefoot on Sunday in their best trousers, shirts, and waist-coats, etc.).

5

All working processes must be shown in proper detail. (An actress who happened to have the figure of a child turned Fina the maid into a memorable character by showing her working late at the washing (6), carrying butter (7) and falling asleep exhausted during Mr. Puntila's engagement party (9).

6

The permanent framework consisted of the great birch bark wall at the back already mentioned with thin structures of gold rods on either side downstage. The sets were composed of separate elements, those in the first scene for instance being (a) a wooden paneled wall with table, chairs, tablecloth covered with bottles of red wine, and a dozen empties grouped on the floor; and (b) a potted palm (the luxury element). Elements like those of the sixth scene, with its courtyard gateway and its main entrance to the house, could be definitively placed during the rehearsals. A further luxury element was a trashy plaster statuette in the second scene, whereas the slaughtered pig of scene 5, suspended from a scaffolding made of carmine-colored joists and a brass rod, was no luxury element since it told of the preparations for the engagement banquet and was to be carried across the courtyard in the next scene. Importance was attached to the beauty and ease of the elements and the charm of their combination. At the same time they had to be realistic. Though the car in scene 3 consisted only of a truncated fore-part it had been made from authentic components.

7

That the various stage elements, the costumes, and the props should all look worn not only contributes to realism but also relieves the stage of that new, untested look.

8

Meaning, spatial dispositions, and color must be such that every glimpse of the stage captures an image worth seeing.

9

The German language has no term for that aspect of mime which is known to the English stage as "business," and we tend to insinuate it half-heartedly, in an embarrassed way. Our word Kiste [literally, "box"] which we use instead, shows the contempt in which it is held. All the same, Kisten [pieces of business] are essential components of narrative theater. (*Puntila walks dryshod across the aquavit* (1); *Puntila hires a forestry worker because he likes his eyes* (4); *the women of Kurgela see butter, meat, and beer entering their fiancé's house* (7), and so on.) Such things were of course played for all they were worth. This was greatly helped by the "one thing after another" principle, which any dramaturgy founded on exposition, climax, and thickening of the plot is always having to disregard.

10

The decisive point is the establishment of the class antagonism between Puntila and Matti. Matti must be so cast as to bring about a true balance, i.e., so as to give him intellectually the upper hand. The actor playing Puntila must be careful not to let his vitality or charm in the drunk scenes so win over the audience that they are no longer free to look at him critically.

11

Among the play's nobler characters are the four women from Kurgela. It would be completely wrong to portray them as comic; rather they are full of humor. They would anyway have to be attractive, if only because their expulsion must be attributable to no other cause than their inferior status.

12

Possible cuts: Scene 4 (The Hiring Market) is deleted. But parts of it are used in the following scene (Scandal at Puntila Farms).

Then scene 5 begins as follows:

The yard at Puntila Farms. A bath-hut, the interior of which is visible. Forenoon. Over the door leading into the house Laina the cook and Fina the chambermaid are nailing a sign saying "Welcome to the Engagement Celebration!"

Puntila and Matti come in through the gate, followed by a few workers.

LAINA   Welcome home! Miss Eva and His Excellency and His Honor are here already. They're having breakfast.

PUNTILA   The first thing I want to know is what's the matter with Surkkala. Why is he packing?

LAINA   But you promised the parson you'd fire him because he's a Red.

PUNTILA   What? Surkkala? The only intelligent tenant I've got. Besides, he has four children. What must he think of me? My house is closed to the parson from now on, he's inhuman. Send Surkkala here right away, I want to apologize to him and his family. Send the children too, all four of them. I want them to hear from me in person how sorry I am for all the worry and anxiety they must have gone through.

LAINA   That's not necessary, Mr. Puntila.

PUNTILA (*gravely*)   Oh yes, it is. (*Pointing to the workers*) These gentlemen will be staying. Bring them some aquavit, Laina, I'm taking them on to work in the forest.

LAINA   I thought you were selling the forest.

PUNTILA   Me? Me sell a forest? My daughter's got her dowry between her legs. Am I right? And I've brought these men home because the hiring market makes me sick. When I want to buy horses or cows, I go to the market and think nothing of it. But you're men, and that shouldn't be. Human beings weren't made to be marketed. Am I right?

A SICKLY-LOOKING WORKER   Dead right.

MATTI   I beg your pardon, Mr. Puntila, you're not right. They need work and you have work to be done, that's a business proposition: whether you attend to it in a church or in a market or right here, it's still a market.

PUNTILA   Brother, do you look at *me* to see if my legs are straight like you were looking into a horse's mouth?

MATTI   No, I take you on faith.

PUNTILA (*indicating the sickly-looking worker*)   This man's not bad. I like his eyes.

MATTI   Mr. Puntila, I don't want to interfere, but he won't do. He couldn't take it.

THE SICKLY-LOOKING WORKER   What do you mean? How do you know I couldn't take it?

MATTI   Eleven and a half hours a day in the summer. I just wouldn't want you to be disappointed, Mr. Puntila. You'll only have to fire him when you find out that he can't take it.

PUNTILA   I'm going to the sauna. Tell Fina to get me some coffee. While I'm undressing, go get two or three more, so I can take my pick.

(*He goes into the bath-hut and undresses. Fina brings the workers aquavit*)

MATTI (*to Fina*)   Get him some coffee.

A REDHAIRED WORKER   What's it like at Puntila Farms?

MATTI   Not bad. Four quarts of good milk. I'm told they give you potatoes too. The room isn't very big.

THE REDHEAD How far is the schoolhouse? I've got a little girl.

MATTI About an hour's walk.

THE REDHEAD That's nothing in good weather. What's *he* like?

MATTI Too familiar. It won't make much difference to you, you'll be out in the woods, but he's got me with him in the car, I'm at his mercy, and before I know it he's acting human. I won't be able to take it much longer.

(*Surkkala comes in with his four children*)

MATTI Surkkala! For God's sake get out of here quick. By the time he's had his bath and his coffee, he'll be stone sober, and God help you if he lays eyes on you. My advice is to keep out of his sight for the next few days.

(*Surkkala nods and starts off with his children*)

PUNTILA (*who has listened while undressing and not heard the last, looks out of the bath-hut and sees Surkkala and the children*) Surkkala! I'll be with you in a minute. (*To Matti*) Give him ten marks earnest money.

MATTI Yes, but couldn't you make up your mind about these men here? They'll miss the hiring market.

PUNTILA Don't rush me. I don't buy human beings in cold blood, I'm offering them a home at Puntila Farms.

THE REDHEAD In that case I'd better be going. I need a job.

(*He goes out*)

PUNTILA Stop! Now he's gone. I could have used that man. (*To the sickly-looking worker*) Don't let him scare you away. You'll do the work all right. I give you my word of honor. Do you know what that means, the word of a Tavastland farmer? Mount Hatelma can crumble, it's not likely, but it's possible, but the word of a Tavastland farmer stands firm, everybody knows that. (*To Matti*) Come in here, I need you to pour on water. (*To the sickly-looking worker*) You can come in too.

(Unchanged from p. 134, line 19, to p. 137, line 21. Then:)

PUNTILA (*to Fina*) I've made a decision. Listen carefully, or they'll twist my words around the way they always do. (*Pointing to one of the workers*) I'd have taken that one, but his pants are too good, he won't work. Always take a good look at the clothing; too fancy and they think they're too good to work, too ragged and the character's bad. It's all right for a gardener, for instance, to run around in patched pants, provided the knees are patched and not the backside, yes, with a gardener it's got to be the knees. I can see through a man at a glance, I don't care about his age, your oldtimers will carry just as much or more, because they're afraid of being fired. The main thing, in my opinion, is the man himself. I'm not interested in intelligence, the smart ones spend the whole day figuring out how many hours they've worked. I don't like that, I like to be on friendly terms with my help. (*To a husky worker*) You can come along, I'll give you your earnest money inside. Which reminds me. (*To Matti, who has come out of the bath-hut*) Give me your jacket. Yes, your jacket, do you hear? (*Matti gives him his jacket*) I've got you now, you crook. (*Shows him the wallet*) What do I find in your pocket? The first time I laid eyes on you I knew you for a jailbird. Is this my wallet, or isn't it?

MATTI Yes, Mr. Puntila.

PUNTILA That does it: ten years in jail: all I need to do is call the police.

MATTI Yes, Mr. Puntila.

PUNTILA But I won't do you the favor. So you can lounge around in a cell, taking it easy and eating the taxpayers' bread. That would suit you, wouldn't it? Especially now at harvest time. It would keep you away from the tractor. But I'll put it in your reference, see?

MATTI Yes, Mr. Puntila.

(*Puntila in a rage starts for the house. Eva is standing in the doorway with a straw hat over her arm. She has been listening*)

THE SICKLY-LOOKING WORKER Want me to come along, Mr. Puntila?

PUNTILA No, I can't use you. The work would be too much for you.

THE SICKLY-LOOKING WORKER But the hiring market's over now.

PUNTILA You should have thought of that before, instead of trying to take advantage of my friendly humor. I never forget the people who try to do that. (*To the worker who has followed him*) I've changed my mind. I'm not taking anybody. I'll probably sell the forest, and you can lay the blame on that no-good (*points at Matti*), who deliberately kept me in the dark about something I should have known. I'll show him. (*He goes off gloomily into the house*)

(Unchanged from p. 138, line 19.)

> [GW *Schriften zum Theater*, pp. 1169–73, and GW *Stücke*, pp. 1713–17, which originally were consecutive. Written in 1948 and first published in *Versuche 10*, 1950. For the Zurich première of June 5, 1948, the scene designer was Teo Otto. Puntila was played by Leonard Steckel, Matti by Gustav Knuth.]

Notes on the Berliner Ensemble Production

1. PROLOGUES, INTER-SCENE SONGS, AND SCENE TITLES

Our new audience, being engaged in building a new life for itself, insists on having its say and not just accepting what happens on the stage ("That's how things are, and what's to change them?"); it doesn't like having to guess the playwright's viewpoint. Prologues, songs during scene changes, and the occasional projection of scene titles on the half-curtain all make for direct contact with the audience. The actress playing the dairymaid, Regine Lutz, delivered a short verse prologue with a bunch of everlastings in her hand. For the Zurich production there were scene titles [examples as in our text are cited]. Prologues are to be found in the classic drama, scene titles however only in the classic adventure story. They put the audience in a state of mild suspense and lead them to look for something definite in the scene that follows. In the Berliner Ensemble production the scene titles were dropped in favor of the singing of the Puntila song. Annemarie Hase, playing the cook, stepped before the curtain carrying whatever household utensils she happened to be working with, thus making it possible to follow the various stages of the great Puntila engagement party. Her song was accompanied on the other side of the stage by two musicians who had appeared before the curtain carrying a guitar and a piano accordion. The song gave a running commentary on events at Puntila Farms as viewed from the kitchen, and by making them celebrated as it were, turned Mr. Puntila's escapades into aspects of local history.

2. SOME PRINCIPLES OF THE PRODUCTION ILLUSTRATED

This play's satire is of a poetic kind. The director's task therefore is to translate its poetic features into memorable images.

At the beginning of the play, for instance, we encounter a Puntila of almost mythological grandeur. He is the triumphant last survivor of a true flood of spirituous liquors, in which all his drinking companions have drowned. [. . .]

The director accordingly must conjure up Puntila's moan of isolation and his berating of the inadequate judge; Puntila's encounter with a real man (Puntila is on the dining table demonstrating how one walks across a sea of aquavit when he catches sight of Matti. He has to clamber down and steer a wide course round the gratuitously large table in order to greet Matti and bring him back to the table); the revealing of his dreadful malady (Puntila formally creeps into the protesting Matti); Matti's ghost story (while he eats he recalls those who are being starved on the big landed estates); Puntila promoting Matti to be a friend and then consulting him about his own personal affairs (to solve his shabby problems Puntila keeps Matti up when he would much rather go home and go to bed); Matti leading a subdued Puntila out of the hotel (again a wide tour of the table, Puntila having confidingly and ceremoniously handed him the wallet containing his despised money).

3. THE WAY PEOPLE WORK

Showing how work is actually done is something the bourgeois theater finds uninteresting; the usual solution is to botch up any old thing. It is essential that Matti, the chauffeur, should work deftly, whether he is changing a tire as he talks to the landowner's daughter, or sweeping out the yard, or massaging Puntila, or dragging out the drunken judge. Likewise the kitchenmaid's serving of coffee, soaking of linen, and carrying of butter all have to be got right.

4. PUNTILA'S DRUNKENNESS

The actor playing Puntila will find that his chief problem is how to portray the drunkenness which makes up 90 percent of the part. It would seem unacceptably repellent were he to contribute the conventional drunk act, in other words to demonstrate a state of intoxication blurring over and devaluing every physical and mental process. The drunkenness played by Steckel was the drunkenness specific to Puntila, i.e., that through which the landowner achieves his semblance of humanity. Far from exhibiting the usual impairments of speech and physical movement, he displayed a rhythmical, almost musical way of speaking and relaxed, almost ballet-like movements. Admittedly a certain handicap was imposed on his inspiration by the weight of his limbs, which was too great for those superterrestrial motions which he had in mind. He ascended Mount Hatelma on wings, albeit slightly defective ones. Each of the monster's drunken gests—of meekness, anger at injustice, generosity in giving and taking, comradeship, and what not—was developed with gusto. Puntila abandoned his possessions like a Buddha, disowned his daughter as in the Bible, invited the Kurgela women to be his guests like some Homeric monarch.

5. STECKEL'S TWO PUNTILAS

Before playing Puntila in Berlin Steckel had played him in Zurich. There he played almost without makeup, and the impression gained by most of the audience was of a likeable man subject to the occasional nasty turn when in a state of sobriety, which state being tantamount to a hangover the turns seemed excusable. In Berlin, in view of these effects, he opted for a foully shaped bald head and made himself up with debauched and debased features. Only now did his drunken charm seem menacing and his sociable approaches like those of a crocodile. Nearly all German performances of this play, whether before or after the Berlin production, suffered from the same mistake as was made in Zurich.

6. SOCIALLY BASED HUMOR

There is little that a play like *Puntila* can take from the old-clothes cupboard of "timeless humor." True, even in "timeless humor" there is a social element—the clown sets out brimming with self-confidence and falls flat on his face—but it has become overlaid to the point where the clown's fall appears like something purely biological, something that is humorous to all people under all conditions. The actors who perform *Puntila and Matti, His Hired Man* must derive their humor from the prevailing class situation, even if that means there are one or two classes whose members will not laugh. When the happily reintoxicated landowner gets Matti to build him a Mount Hatelma from the billiard-room furniture, Matti does so with anger, because even in the depths of drunkenness Puntila did not omit to sack Red Surkkala. Relentlessly he demolishes gun cabinet and grandfather clock; this is going to be an expensive mountain. At each crash Puntila winces and his smile becomes forced.—In the village Puntila listens to the life stories of the Kurgela girls, but he does not listen properly because he knows what is coming and takes a long pull of "legal alcohol" after every story. The humor is of a gloomy sort.—If the landowner takes the women's "Plum" song as a personal tribute that is traditional humor and unexceptionable. But there is added depth if he appears somehow interested in folklore and adopts a knowledgeable expression. It shows up the cleft which is the theme of the play.—In scene 4 Puntila brings a group of agricultural workers back from the hiring market. It is the one day in the year when they are able to find jobs, and Puntila has no use for them; he just wants company. He at once raises one man's hopes ("I like his eyes"). Then he breaks through the ring of workers surrounding him and hastens into the sauna in order to sober up enough to get the strength to throw the workers out. The cravenness of this flight into sobriety is a stroke of humor that can scarcely be achieved except by an actor with social understanding and socialist principles.

7. THE WOMAN OF KURGELA

From the outset the portrayal of those women of Kurgela whom Puntila invites to his estate when drunk and throws off it when sober presented great problems. These are the noblest characters in the play, and in planning their costumes and makeup we hesitated a long time between the beautiful and the characteristic before realizing that these are not really opposites. To give a fairy-tale quality to the story of the four early risers we started by making stylized costumes with very delicate colors, then thought them boring and plumped for naturalism without regard for beauty. This led to outsize boots and long noses. Then Caspar Neher intervened. Full of skepticism, he came to the rehearsals and produced a batch of scene designs that are among the most beautiful things which our generation has created for the theater. He solved the problem of how to reconcile the women's naive behavior with their practical worldly wisdom by having them play a light-hearted game with the landowner. With jokes and a bit of playacting they confronted the landowner as a body, as the legendary "Women of Kurgela," biblical brides hoping for a dance and a coffee from their bridegroom on high. Neher made them don straw garlands, and he endowed the chauffeur Matti too with imagination, devising the broom which he sticks in the ground and addresses as the High Court at Viborg, and also uses to sweep up the garlands when they have thrown them down in the yard following their unpleasant reception. Now that their behavior had been got right there was virtually no problem in making the costumes and makeup beautiful. The cut of the costumes remained realistic, but their contours were somewhat emphasized and identical material was used for all of them. The faces were given a certain uncouth, peasant quality—we began by testing the effect of crumbled cement which we tried out on plaster casts—while a golden complexion was created by covering them with warm-toned pounded ochre. The big shoes, retained for one of the women, in no way detracted from the beauty which came above all from the dignity of these working women. Starting as poor guests, they became rich in kindliness, ready and willing to bestow their humor even on a landowner; from poetic figures they turned into real people with a feeling for poetry. Composed by a great painter, the groupings lent grace and power to their natural, realistic demeanor.

8. CASPAR NEHER'S PUNTILA STAGE

The symbolist stage of Expressionists and Existentialists, which expresses general ideas, is of no use to a realistic theater, nor can we go back to the naturalistic stage with its crude mixture of the relevant and the irrelevant. A mere echo of the real world is not enough; it must be not only recognizable but also understandable. This means that the images have to be artistically valid and to display an individual handwriting. Wit and imagination are specially desirable in the designer of a comedy.

9. THE MASKS

Puntila, the attaché, the parson, parson's wife, lawyer, and judge all wore more or less grotesque masks and moved in a foolish, regal manner. Matti, the women of Kurgela, the hired hands, and the agricultural workers wore no masks and moved normally. An exception was made for Eva, the landowner's daughter; she had no mask. Any suggestion that this amounts to symbolism would be unfounded. No hidden significance is intended. The theater is simply adopting an attitude and heightening significant aspects of reality, to wit, certain physiognomical malformations to be found in parasites.

10. IS A PLAY LIKE *Puntila and Matti, His Hired Man* STILL RELEVANT TO US NOW THAT THE BIG ESTATES HAVE BEEN GOT RID OF?

There is an attractive kind of impatience which would have the theater only present things in their current real-life state. Why waste time on an estate owner? Haven't we got rid of such people? Why show a proletarian like Matti? Don't we have more active fighters? Likeable as such impatience is, it should not be given way to. The fact that alongside those works of art which we have to organize there are certain works of art that have come down to us is only a valid argument if the usefulness of the latter can be proved, never mind how much time is needed to organize the former. Why can *Puntila and Matti, His Hired Man* still be regarded as a play with relevance? Because not only the struggle but the history of that struggle is instructive. Because past eras leave a deposit in people's souls for a long time. Because the class struggle demands that victory in one area of conflict be exploited so as to promote victory in another, and in both cases the situation prior to victory may be similar. Because, like all pioneers, people who have been liberated from their oppressors may at first have a hard life, since they have to replace the oppressors' system with a new one. These are the sorts of arguments that can be adduced to show the relevance of plays like *Puntila and Matti, His Hired Man.*

[1, 4 and 10 from GW SzT 1173–75, the rest from pp. 18–45 of *Theaterarbeit* (1950), for which these notes were written. They refer to the Berliner Ensemble production of 1949, in which Puntila was played initially by Steckel once more and later by the comedian Curt Bois. Paul Dessau's setting of the songs was written for this. The last note is an answer to some of Brecht's East German critics.]

Notes on the Puntila Film

1. ABOUT THE SCRIPT FOR *Puntila*

As it stands the script doesn't seem right to me. It is true that it follows the general line which Pozner and I agreed on, but in the course of its realization the story has lapsed into a genre which makes it not so much comic as ridiculous. It has become a drawing-room comedy in which the crude jokes of the play jar and seem merely crude. Nor is it clear *who* is telling the entire story or from what point of view. The film company, it would seem, and from the point of view of making a film. The Puntila tales have of course to be told from below, from the position of the people. Then characters like Matti and Eva Puntila can be seen in the right light. The present script turns Matti into a feeble, indefinite figure; it fails to bring out how despite and because of their master/man relationship he is in continual opposition to his employer in every line he says. What makes Eva Puntila "love" him is not his muscles—it would be all the same if he had none—but the fact that he is a proper man, humorous, dominating, and so forth. Nor of course must he for one instant imagine that Eva is the right wife for him or that Mr. Puntila would really let him have her. His *test* is simply a way of deflating Eva's and Puntila's romantic notion. It has to remain a game if Matti is not to be made into an idiot.

We have made a new outline, since I realize that the studio cannot wait. As the poetic material is already at hand the preparation of a new shooting script would be a remarkably quick business. Given the script as it is I would find it quite impossible to turn the new dialogue (which makes up at least half the total dialogue and is entirely naturalistic) into Puntila-German, because the situations are naturalistic and in my view false. Nor if this script were used could I under any circumstances allow the use of my name or the name *Puntila*. I am not by any means out to make difficulties, but neither do I wish to damage my reputation as a writer. I am sure you will understand this.

2. NEW STORY LINE FOR *Puntila*

1. *Hotel Tavasthus*

Surrounded by passed-out drunks and dead-tired waiters, a man is traversing a vast table covered with plates of meat and bottles: it is Mr. Puntila. He claims to be able to walk dry-shod across the sea of aquavit represented to him by the table top. Another man addresses him, and turns out to be his chauffeur whom he has left waiting outside for two days and a night. Feeling lonely and abandoned by his too easily intoxicated friends—the judge, the teacher, and so on—Puntila instantly becomes bosom pals with his chauffeur Matti and discusses with him his most intimate concerns, i.e., his daughter Eva's forthcoming engagement to an attaché. For this a dowry is required, so he must sell a forest. To postpone the decision Puntila has got drunk. They decide to have another look at the forest.

2. *Forest*

Puntila realizes that the forest is too beautiful to sell. Sooner than that he will marry Widow Klinckmann, who is rich and the owner of the Kurgela estate, but whom he last saw fifty years ago. Off to Kurgela.

3. *Kurgela*

Rousing the sleepy domestics Puntila pushes his way through them into Widow Klinckmann's bedroom. One look is enough: the widow is too hideous to sell himself to.

4. *The Village of Kurgela Next Day*

Fleeing from Widow Klinckmann and avid for beauty, Puntila meets three young women, is upset by the sadness of their lives and instantly becomes engaged to them. He tells them to come to the Puntila estate on the following Sunday. The young women take this as a jest on the part of a well-to-do drunk gentleman, and laughingly promise they will come. The telephone operator, last of the three, advises him to drive to the hiring market at Lammi, where he will meet another estate owner called Bibelius who wants to buy his forest. He will recognize him by his butterfly tie-pin. Since the forest has to be sold after all, Puntila decides to drive to Lammi.

5. Hiring Market

The alcoholic effects are wearing off. Puntila gives vent to some intelligent and ill-natured remarks about servants. Drinks coffee laced with rum, and apologizes to Matti. Discloses his malady and asks Matti for moral support. Engages four cripples because he likes them as people. Sees a fat man beating a horse and tells him where to get off. On Matti and the workers expressing their enthusiastic approval he learns that he has just beaten up the man who wants to buy his forest. This sobers him up, and he gets gloomily into his car without offering a lift to the laborers.

"Home," he says curtly. "I'm selling the forest to Widow Klinckmann."

6. Puntila Farms

Preparations for the engagement party are in full swing. Pigs are being slaughtered, windows cleaned, and Matti is helping the cook to nail up a garlanded sign which says "Welcome to the Engagement Celebration." Miss Puntila would like to know what Matti thinks of her engagement to the attaché. She herself has no use for him. With considerable ingenuity she induces Matti to help her stage a scandal in order to frighten off the attaché, who is now staying at Puntila Farms. The scandal is staged (sauna) but clearly the attaché must have enormous debts: he overlooks it. Puntila is very angry, takes his wallet from Matti, and threatens to tell the police. Eva blames Matti for not sticking up for himself like a gentleman.

7. Summer Nights in Tavastland

The combination of the feigned love scene with Matti and the erotic ambience of the summer night has put fresh thoughts into Eva's head. On the pretext of catching crayfish she takes Matti rowing to a somewhat notorious island. Once there however the thought that she is behaving like a dairymaid disconcerts her; she insists on catching crayfish and is eventually rowed back by a frustrated Matti.

8. Puntila Farms

Puntila turns his three "fiancées" off the estate, then tells Matti to collect the entire stock of liquor so that it can be destroyed. Thousands of bottles are collected in an operation involving the entire staff. Puntila drinks extravagantly and sends Matti off to bring back his "fiancées." Beaming, he announces that in his view they are much better suited than certain other people to the sort of engagement party he has in mind.

9. Country Road

Matti drives off after the young women, but fails to persuade them to return.

10. Inside Puntila's House

All the guests have arrived, including the foreign minister Eva has locked herself in her room, so that the attaché has to receive them on his own. Enter like a whirlwind a totally drunk Puntila, who throws the attaché out. Thereafter he throws out the minister, parson, judge, and so on, and sends for the domestics. Matti on his return is offered Eva as his wife. Matti insists on testing Eva's matrimonial capacities. She shows herself incompetent to do her own housework. Eventually when Matti slaps her on the backside she takes it badly and runs off in tears. Left alone, Puntila hears his hired hands singing the ballad of the Woodsman and the lovely Countess. He resolves to show Matti what a beautiful country they live in, and with this object they climb Mount Hatelma.

11. In the Courtyard

Matti puts the Puntila estate behind him.

[Brecht: *Texte für Filme II*, Frankfurt, Suhrkamp, 1969, pp. 636–40. The Puntila film, under the same title as the play, was made in Austria by Wien-Film with Alberto Cavalcanti as director and Curt Bois in the title part (which he had also played in the second Berliner Ensemble production), and was first shown in Brussels on March 29, 1955. Vladimir Pozner was one of the scriptwriters. A new musical score was written by Hanns Eisler, and the text of the Puntila Song somewhat varied for the purpose.]

Editorial Note

1. Preliminary Ideas

Though the Puntila theme was not Brecht's own it none the less struck several long-standing chords in his mind, among them being Faustian Man (with his twin souls), Chaplin's film *City Lights*, and the ironic discursive style of Hašek's *Schweik*. They may well moreover (as Jost Hermand has suggested) have included Carl Zuckmayer's bucolic "Volksstück" of 1925, *Der fröhliche Weinberg*, and the falsely jovial personality of Reichsmarschall Hermann Göring. There is, however, no sign of such elements coming together before Brecht met Hella Wuolijoki in 1940. Stimulated, so it appears, by the Finnish Dramatists' League's play competition, she then showed him her play *The Sawdust Princess* together with the film treatment from which it derived, with the result that by August 27 they had agreed to collaborate on a new version. For her the theme went back to the early 1930s when (according to evidence gathered by Hans-Peter Neureuter in the *Mitteilungen aus der deutschen Bibliothek*, Helsinki, numbers 7, 1973 and 8, 1974), she wrote a story in English, based possibly on the personality of one of her own relatives, and called it "A Finnish Bacchus." This was worked up into a treatment for Suomi-Film, which however was never made. Its central character, says Margaret Mare in her edition of the play (Methuen, 1962), was to be

> Puntila, a Tavastland estate owner, who, mellowed by drink, went one night to the village and engaged himself to several young women with the help of liquor and curtain rings. Puntila has a daughter, Eva . . . who is wooed both by a young diplomat and by a chauffeur. She chooses the latter, and all ends well when he turns out to be an engineer, masquerading in his own chauffeur's uniform.

Puntila himself was to marry "Aunt Hanna," the owner of the house where he arrives drunk early in the story (and where he also confronts his village "fiancées").

How far the play *The Sawdust Princess* was complete when Brecht first saw it is not entirely clear. Some commentators think that it was, but Brecht himself referred to it as a draft and in his journal (entry for September 2) describes it thus:

> hw's half-finished play is a comedy, a conversation piece. (puntila sober is puntila drunk plus a hangover, hence in a bad temper, the stereotype of a drinker. his chauffeur is a *gentleman* who had applied for the chauffeur's job after having seen a photograph of his daughter, etc.) but there is also a film of hers which yields some useful epic elements (the mountain climb and the trip for legal alcohol). it is my job to bring out the underlying farce, dismantle the psychologically-orientated conversations, make room for opinions and for stories from finnish popular life, find scenic terms for the master/man antithesis, and restore the poetry and comedy proper to this theme.

This was not, of course, the job as Hella Wuolijoki herself saw it, but in Brecht's view she was handicapped by a hopelessly conventional dramatic technique. A fortnight before, he had already tried to give her an idea of "non-Aristotelian" dramaturgy while discussing a plan of hers to write a play about the early Finnish nationalist J. V. Snellman, a work which she never completed. Now he took over *The Sawdust Princess* and within three weeks had turned it into something very different from what he had found.

He started with a German translation which Wuolijoki, an excellent linguist, dictated to Margarete Steffin. From this orthodox four-act play he took the characters of Puntila, Eva (the Sawdust Princess of the title), the attaché, the doctor, Fina the maid, and all the village women apart from the pharmacist's helper. Initially he also took Kalle the pseudo-chauffeur, whom he turned into a genuine chauffeur and later renamed Matti, while from the treatment he took Aunt Hanna, first turning her into Puntila's housekeeper, then banishing her from the play altogether except in the shadowy form of the unseen Mrs. Klinckmann. The setting and the Swedish-style place names—Tavastland or Häme in southwest Finland, Kurgela, Lammi, Tammerfors (Tampere), Mount Hatelma (Hattelmala near Tavasthus) and so on—are likewise taken from Wuolijoki, Kurgela indeed being the nearest sizeable town to her own Marlebäck estate.

A succession of plans shows Brecht isolating the crucial incidents in her story, switching them and building on them until he had the framework of a ten-scene play. One of the earliest goes thus:

1. Mr. von P. gets engaged to the churchgoers.
2. The league of Mr. von P's fiancées.
3. Playing with fire (those who pretend to be in love fall in love).
4. Driving out the materialists.
5. Mr. von P. sits in judgment.
6.
7. Climbing the mountain.
8. Mr. von P's funeral speech.

Thereafter (it would seem) two new scenes were added at the start (the first being described as "gethsemaneh/a chauffeur with dignity/the engagement"), while the center of the play was left undetermined. According as to whether Puntila was to be mainly drunk or sober, Brecht now started marking the scenes "d" or "s"—that is, in German "b" or "n." Kalle's new role became clearer and something like the final play began to take shape:

1. puntila finds a human being and hires him as his chauffeur (d).
2.
3. puntila finds legal alcohol and gets engaged to the early risers. (d).
4. p engages his daughter to a human being/in the sauna/the league of mr von p's fiancées/kalle and eva conduct a test. (d and s).
5. p engages his daughter to an attaché/the attaché is uncongenial to him/k refuses to marry eva/puntila rejects her. (s and d).
6. judgment on kalle/kalle says goodbye to e/the mountain climb.
7. k leaves p and makes a speech about him.

Next the two main events of this scene 4, the engagement and the league of fiancées, are separated, the former being shifted to a separate scene immediately before or after scene 5. One scheme introduces "p gets engaged to his housekeeper" as the theme of the last scene but one. Finally there is a characteristic big working plan in columns, such as Brecht used to pin up before starting to write in earnest:

1. p finds a human being.
2. p and his daughter.
3. p gets engaged to the early risers.
4. p engages his daughter to an attaché.
5. p at the hiring market.
6. kalle goes on strike.
7. the league of p's fiancées.
8. p engages his daughter to a human being.
9. p sits in judgment and climbs mount hatelma.
10. kalle turns his back on p.

Though two further scenes were to be added, initially as 7a and 8a, while 9 and 10 became run together, the above is in effect the play as Brecht first wrote it. He also kept before him three examples of what he called "Puntila's way of speaking"

(the passage starting "I'd be ashamed," p. 142), "Kalle's way
of speaking" (a passage in scene 6 starting "Your father only
wants what's best for you," p. 150), and "the gentry's way of
speaking" (the judge's passage in the same scene starting "Paternity suits," p. 147). Once these tones of voice had been fixed
"the work went very smoothly," he noted, even though the
tone was not original:

> it is hašek's way of speaking in schweik, as already used by
> me in courage. the plan for the scenes was quickly settled.
> their length was predetermined and fairly closely kept to.
> the visit to the hiring market was an afterthought; it took
> place a few days ago near here.

So he wrote in his journal on September 19, the day when he
had finished the play and handed it to Hella Wuolijoki to read.
At first her reactions were far from favorable. "She seems
extremely alarmed," says a journal entry five days later:

> it is undramatic, unfunny, etc. all the characters speak alike,
> not differently as they do in real life and in hw's plays. pas-
> sages like the conversation between judge and lawyer in the
> kitchen are boring (something the finns are not unused to)
> and do nothing to further the plot. kalle is not a finnish
> chauffeur. the landowner's daughter cannot attempt to bor-
> row money from the chauffeur (but can presumably at-
> tempt to marry him, as in hw's play): it's all so epic as to
> be undramatic.

Brecht tried to encourage her, not least because she still had
to produce a Finnish text for submission to the jury. Though
she accepted something of what he said, he felt,

> the point i could not get across was that my scenes' gait and
> garb corresponded to the gait and garb of puntila himself,
> with all his aimlessness, looseness, his detours and delays, his
> repetitions and improprieties. she wants to bring on the
> women of kurgela earlier, immediately they have been in-
> vited, so as to make sure the audience has not forgotten
> them. she fails to see the beauty of having them virtually
> forgotten, not only by the audience but by puntila too, then

making them pop up long after the morning of the invitation.

None the less she did embark on the translation, and only ten days later seemed very happy about the whole undertaking. She told Brecht (who again noted it in his journal) that the play was full of riches and Puntila himself on the way to becoming "a national figure."

In the Finnish version published in 1946 (by Tammi of Helsinki) the name Puntila is changed to Iso-Heikkilä and the title of the play to *The Landowner Iso-Heikkilä and His Servant Kalle*, subtitled "A comic tale of Tavastland drunkenness in nine scenes" by Hella Wuolijoki and Bertolt Brecht. An introductory note stresses this aspect:

> Iso-Heikkilä's intoxication is in the nature of a divine dionysiac drunkenness. As a steadfast man of Tavastland, he never falters—an inner radiance like the brightness of early morning and an always human kindness and strength shine forth from his face. Alcohol is only the magic potion which releases all the sources of kindness in the man, the landowner, Iso-Heikkilä.

"The structure," she wrote, "is entirely Brecht's. The idea of including epic tales in the scenes with the women was Brecht's. The stories themselves are entirely mine." The change of name apart, this version is very close to Brecht's own first typescript dated "2.9.40—19.9.40 (Marlebäck)," though the latter also seems to include some later amendments. Then entitled simply *Puntila*, it was retyped by Margarete Steffin and given its final title; duplicated copies were thereafter made and sent out by Reiss of Basel. Up to this point there were no songs embodied in the play, though those of Red Surkkala and Emma have been appended to the retyped copy, the former as an alternative to "The wolf asked the rooster" (p. 443 below). Then it was revised again after the Zurich première in 1948, when changes were made for Brecht's own production with Erich Engel for the Berliner Ensemble, the Puntila Song being written as late as 1949. Around that time the Munich publisher Kurt Desch acquired the stage rights, but at first he too simply duplicated the nine-scene version, which was described as "after Hella Wuolijoki's stories" with no mention of her play; she is not named as co-author on any of the German texts, though Brecht in 1949 told Desch that she was to get half the royalties.

By 1950, when Suhrkamp first published the text (as *Versuche 10*), the play had expanded from the nine scenes of the early versions—or ten in those scripts where the epilogue was counted separately—to the present twelve. From the first, however, it included the scene with the hiring market which had only figured in the last of the plans. The character of Surkkala introduced there was subsequently built up, being alluded to at various points and making a notable appearance also in scene 11. Like the village women's accounts of their lives in scene 3, their "Finnish tales" in scene 8 were an evident afterthought on Brecht's first script, those now given to Emma being omitted from the 1946 Finnish version, possibly because of the censorship. As Aunt Hanna's rôle diminished from landowner to housekeeper (shedding the "Aunt") and finally to nothing at all, around the end of the 1940s the shadowy Mrs. Klinckmann was introduced to perform some of her original functions, and various references to Puntila's marrying her or selling the forest worked in. Meanwhile in the joint Finnish version Hella Wuolijoki had given the attaché an uncle to be the owner of Kurgela and speak some of the lines now given to the lawyer. The Kurgela location still survives in the play, even though without the aunt or uncle most of its raison d'être disappeared, its main bath-hut episode being shifted to Puntila Farms and run together with the sobering-up operation to form the present scene 5. Finally there was a change of balance in the relationship between Eva and Matti (Kalle), which Wuolijoki seems to have wanted still to treat as a conventional love story destined for a happy ending (see the last scene of the 1946 Finnish version). Something of her interpretation can be detected even in the first Brecht scripts (as in the detailed account of scene 9 below), a greater element of ambiguity and coolness being introduced later. Throughout, the unchanging pillars of the play were the first half of scene 1, scene 3, the bath-hut episode in scene 5, Matti's dialogue with Eva in scene 6, scenes 7 and 9, and the mountain-climbing episode in scene 11.

The detailed notes which follow are based on comparison of Brecht's first script (1940), the fair copy (1940–41), the joint Wuolijoki-Brecht version (published 1946), the *Versuche* text (1950), and the final text as we have it. Changes made for the Zurich production of 1948 are separately dealt with in Brecht's own note on pp. 404 ff.

2. Scene-by-Scene Account

CAST

The first script includes the housekeeper Hanna and a doctor, has a peasant woman in lieu of Emma, and omits Surkkala and his children. The chauffeur is still Kalle, but becomes Matti on the fair copy. In the Wuolijoki-Brecht version of 1946 (or W-B version) Puntila is Johannes Iso-Heikkilä and his housekeeper is called Alina. There is an "Agronomist Kurgela, a relative of Iso-Heikkilä's, owner of the Kurgela estate," while the attaché is "Ilmari Silakkala, Kurgela's nephew, a foreign ministry official." A note to the W-B version says: "This all took place when Tavastland was still a cheerful place without a single war refugee."

Prologue

In the first script this is spoken by Kalle and omits eight lines in the middle. The W-B version has it delivered before the curtain by the whole cast and considerably alters the general sense. This is to the effect that a bad time can be expected in Finland, but one has to be able to laugh all the same. So the audience is invited to appreciate human character and take part in the wild excursions of master and man: never mind if the humor is broad and the element of mockery strong; the actors' work is only play. "This drama was written in praise of Tavast-land and its people."

In the 1950 text the opening couplet went "Ladies and gentlemen, the times are bad / When worry's sane and not to worry mad." The present version first appeared in 1952.

Scene 1

Brecht's original idea, which he amended on the first script, was to set the scene in a village tavern, with a landlord rather than a waiter. In the W-B version Iso-Heikkilä (whom we will call Puntila for simplicity's sake) is discovered drinking with Mr. Kurgela, at whose house Eva has been awaiting them for the past three days. It is he rather than the judge whom Puntila harangues and tells to "Wake up, weakling" (p. 109), continuing "I realize you're only drinking with me because I've got a mortgage on your estate." The judge, by his own account, is more abstemious because of his job. The passage about walking on the aquavit is not in the first script or the W-B version; the latter, incidentally, has them drinking cognac.

After Puntila has described his attacks, ending "Take my thoughtless treatment of a fine man like you" (p. 112), Kalle asks what sort of state he is in when signing his highly profitable timber contracts. A state of senseless sobriety, answers Puntila:

> When I'm a human being and having a drink then I only discuss art. If a timber merchant came along asking "Can't you bring the price down?" I'd say "No, you rascal, today I'm only discussing art. Today I like nice people, whoever they are."

Matti's long speech about seeing ghosts, which ensues, underwent some reworking, while after "Mr. Pappmann yelled and screamed at me" (p. 112) it originally went on:

> —saying he'd tell the police about me, and that I should go to the Pferdeberg and have a good look at the piles of

Reds who were shot there because it was what they asked
for.

PUNTILA I've got nothing against socialists [originally:
Marxists] so long as they drive my tractor . . .

and so on as on p. 112.

In the fair copy the speech ends with a much longer excursion about the Reds before going on to Puntila's "I see, you
only lost your job" (p. 112) as at present. In the W-B version
much of the speech is like a paraphrase of the present text,
relating not to Mr. Pappmann's estate but to "the agronomist's
at Kortesoja" where the trouble was not so much the food as
the clock-watching and general stinginess. Probably the whole
speech derived from one of Hella Wuolijoki's stories.

In Puntila's speech the reference to Mrs. Klinckmann (p.
113) is not in the three early versions, which have him saying
"and I've got woods" rather than "I'll keep my forest." The
first script made him allude to the day when he "married a
papermill and a sawmill" in explanation of his evident prosperity. All three early versions then cut straight from Matti's
"No gulf" (p. 113) to Puntila's instruction "There, take my
wallet" (p. 114), the intervening dialogue about Mrs. Klinckmann and the sale of the forest only being introduced in the
1950 text. At the end of the scene the W-B version has the two
men wake the comatose Kurgela, who says he won't drive
home as he is frightened of Hanna. Puntila responds "Down
with all Hannas" and gets Kalle to echo this.

Scene 2

The title of this scene on the first script, followed by W-B,
was "Puntila and his daughter Eva," on the fair copy "Puntila
is ill-treated," and in the 1950 text "Eva" as now. Originally
Eva was discovered reading, not munching chocolates, and the
attaché entered left, not from an upper level.

The opening allusions to Mrs. Klinckmann were added to
the first script, which originally started with the attaché's "I

just phoned again." His next speech, after "it was my father"
(p. 115) was

ATTACHÉ   Regrettable, yes.
EVA   Aunt Hanna is in such a bad mood. Imagine Father
leading Uncle Kurgela astray.
ATTACHÉ   Aunt Hanna will forgive him. What disturbs me
is the scandal.

—suggesting that, despite her changed rôle, Hanna is still being
seen as part of the attachés family. Then on as on p. 115, up to
Puntila's entrance. In all except the final text the latter "bursts
through the door in his Studebaker [or Buick in the W-B
version] with a great crash and drives into the hall"; he also
gets into the car again when preparing to leave. The allusions
to Mrs. Klinckmann on p. 117 were to Aunt Hanna in the W-B
version, where after "And telling me I won't get a woman" (p.
118) Puntila tells Eva "I'm going, and Kalle's going to be
your fiancé!"

After Eva's "That's no way to talk about your employer. I
don't like it" (p. 119) both the first script and W-B have Kalle
saying that he is on the contrary sticking up for Puntila against
Eva. He then asks Eva if she wants to get away, and is told he
is being inquisitive. This leads him to discuss inquisitiveness,
saying "it was pure inquisitiveness that led to the invention of
electricity. The Russians were inquisitive too." Eva continues
"And don't take what he said" etc., as now, up to the present
end of the scene. The W-B version prolongs this by making
Eva reply to Kalle's last remark, "You forget you're a servant."

KALLE   After midnight I'm not a servant, I'm a man. (*Eva
runs off*) Don't be afraid.
ATTACHÉ (*entering*)   Who are you, fellow?
KALLE   Mr. Iso-Heikkilä's chauffeur, sir.

The attaché takes a dislike to him and threatens to check up
on his past record. Kalle replies that he has been talking to the
ghosts of departed ladies of Kurgela: "I'm a sort of substitute
bridegroom. Good night."

Scene 3

The fair copy specifies at the outset that "a tune like 'Valencia' is being played." In all three early versions Puntila starts by rousing a "fat woman at the window," then the pharmacist's helper, and has a bawling match with both before being sent on to the cow doctor and picking up (virtually) the present text from p. 121. Emma appears after he has been given his prescription; in the first script and W-B she has no song; in the fair copy it is tacked on at the end of the play. Otherwise the rest of the scene follows very much as now, though each woman's description of her life is an evident addition to the original script. These accounts could well originate in stories told by Hella Wuolijoki, though in the W-B version there are some differences: thus the dairymaid does get meat, while the telephone operator has "enough money for pork drippings, potatoes, and salt herring" and gets a box of chocolates from the doctor.

Scene 4

In the three early scripts this follows the bath-hut scene, the present scene 5. The first script and fair copy limit Puntila's opening speech to "I'm through with you," followed by the last sentence ("One little drink" etc., p. 126). In the W-B version the setting is a "hiring market at Hollolan Lahei, a small park with a café, right. Left, a coffee stall with table and benches. Men are standing in scattered groups, the farmers are selecting laborers. Two stable girls giggling, left. Enter a fat man, left." When the latter comments that there is not much doing, a laborer explains that people prefer to take forestry jobs, since the wages are going up there. Then Puntila enters, and the sense of what follows is much the same as in Brecht's script. In both, however, the proposed conditions of work are less bad than in the final version: the redhaired man is promised his meals and a potato patch, while the (first) worker is told that he will get wood delivered. In all three of these scripts Puntila's first speech after sitting down to coffee (p. 129) tells

Kalle/Matti that he must control himself with respect to Eva, and it is this that Matti answers by "Let's not talk about it," after which the scene continues as now for about half a page. However, Surkkala (p. 130 f.) is Salminen in the W-B version, and the reason why the parson wanted him thrown out was not because he was a Red but "because he has a wife he's not married to, and appears suspect to the defense corps in various other ways." All three versions of the scene end with Puntila's "for that kind of stupidity" (p. 132).

Scene 5

In all three early scripts this precedes the hiring market scene. All are headed "Puntila [or Iso-Heikkilä] betroths his daughter to an attaché," as in the plan. All omit the arrival of the laborers from the hiring market and place Puntila's sobering-up process in the bath at the beginning of scene 6. They set the present scene not on Puntila's estate but at Kurgela

> *with a bath-hut that can be seen into. Kalle sits whistling beneath some sunflowers as he cleans a carburetor. Beside him the housekeeper [or in W-B the maid Miina] with a basket. It is morning.*

HOUSEKEEPER Kindly have a look at the door. Last night when you drove the Studebaker into the hall you ripped off the hinges.

KALLE Can be managed; but don't blame that door business on me; it's him that was drunk.

HOUSEKEEPER But if he sees it today he'll be furious. He always inspects the whole estate and checks every corner of our barns, because he holds our mortgage.

KALLE Yes, he's fussy; he doesn't like things to be in a mess.

HOUSEKEEPER *(leaving)* The mistress is staying in bed with a headache because she'd just as soon not run into him. We're all nervous so long as he's here; he shouts so.

PUNTILA'S VOICE Tina! Tina! [or in W-B, "Miina!"]

KALLE *(to the housekeeper as she tries to go)* I'd stay where you are; he's amazingly quick on his feet and if you try to get away he'll spot you.

PUNTILA (*entering*) [accompanied by Kurgela in W-B]
There you are; I've been looking all over the house for
you. I'm tired of having showdowns with you people,
you're ruining yourselves in any case; but when I see
things like the way you preserve pork it sends me up the
wall. Come Christmas you chuck it away, and the same
goes for your forest and all the rest. You're a lazy crew,
and you figure I'll go on paying till kingdom come. Look
at the gardener going around with patched trousers; well,
I wouldn't complain if it was his knees that were patched
and not his bottom. If it's a gardener the knees of his
trousers ought to be patched. And the egg ledger has too
many inkblots over the figures. Why? Because you can't
imagine why there are so few eggs. Of course it has never
dawned on you that the dairymaid might be swiping the
eggs; you need me to tell you. And don't just hang around
here all day!
(*The housekeeper leaves in a hurry*)
PUNTILA (*in the doorway*) I've got you now, you crook.

—and so into the episode with the wallet (p. 137). Then after
Matti's third "Yes, Mr. Puntila" (p. 138) Puntila leaves and
Eva appears (out of the bath-hut in the first script and carrying
a towel) asking "Why don't you stick up for yourself?" etc.,
thus cutting out the exchange between Puntila and the two
workers. The Eva-Matti dialogue and the ensuing bath-hut
charade then follow very much as in our text, but with the
Kurgela housekeeper of course instead of Laina. In the W-B
version Kalle has gathered from Eva's father that the attaché
is to be got rid of, and so the six lines from Eva's "that I wish
he'd break it off" to "I am a brute" (p. 139) are missing, as is
Matti's ensuing speech "Well, when Mr. Puntila was drunk"
with its allusion to Tarzan. Otherwise there are only very slight
differences between all three versions and the final text.

Scene 6

The three early scripts have the title "What Kalle [Matti] is
and is not prepared to do." As later, the scene is set in the

Puntila kitchen, but begins with the sobering-up episode that was later shifted to scene 5 (pp. 134–37). Thus the first script:

> *Estate Kitchen at Puntila Farms. Kalle is trying to sober Puntila up by pouring cold water over his head. The sickly-looking worker is sitting in a corner. It is late evening.*

There is music. The scene starts with Matti's "You'll need another few bucketfuls" (p. 134); then after "I put that fat slob in his place this morning" and before Fina's entry Puntila goes on:

> . . . by the car, he was just going to collect the piglet and missed it. That's enough buckets, I never have more than eleven. (*Shouts*) Fina! Coffee!
> (*Enter Fina*)
> PUNTILA   Here comes our little treasure with the coffee!
> FINA   Miss Hanna says wouldn't you rather take your coffee in the drawing-room; Kalle can have his here.
> PUNTILA   I'm staying here. If Kalle isn't good enough for her I'm having my coffee in the kitchen. Where is it?
> FINA   (*goes and produces coffee from the stove*) Here you are, Mr. Puntila.
> PUNTILA   Is it good and strong? . . .

Then, after Kalle/Matti's "No liqueur," Puntila says to hell with his guests, Fina must hear the story of the fat slob, which he then recounts, starting from "There was this disagreeable, pimple-faced fat slob" (though "a regular capitalist" is not in the early scripts). The rest of the episode is virtually as in our text except that after Puntila's second coffee (p. 136) Matti's speech about love of animals, with its reference to Mrs. Klinckmann, is replaced by the exchange between him and the sickly-looking man which is now on pp. 133 ff. immediately after Puntila has gone into the bath-hut. Thereafter it is Kalle who asks Puntila if the coffee was strong enough, and the remainder down to "despise me when he's drunk" (p. 137) is as in our text.

The link between the sobering-up episode and the present beginning of the scene (p. 146) was simply a ring on the bell, leading Fina to say "I forgot to say Miss Eva wants a word with you." Then Hanna (or Alina) comes in—after the eighteen-line dialogue between Matti and Fina, ending with her sitting on his lap, which is all cut in W-B—and tell Fina to tidy the library and take the sickly-looking man to the room where he is to spend the night prior to leaving; he must also return his 100 marks earnest money (most such sums being divided by ten in the course of revision). On his complaining that he has lost two days' work Hanna blames Kalle. Then the judge and lawyer (replaced by Agronomist Kurgela in W-B) come in, after which the rest of the scene continues much as in our text. However, the first two stage directions (p. 148) describing Eva's would-be seductive walk were added later, while the third (on her reentering on p. 148) originally read "wearing sandals and pretty shorts."

Scene 7

With the exception of Emma's last speech with its snatch of song (p. 159) and her action in sitting on the ground, this scene has remained essentially as it was when Brecht first wrote it, as envisaged in the preliminary plans. Among the small modifications incorporated in the 1950 version (and thereafter in our text) are the conception of the two-level set, the Sunday atmosphere with its bells, Puntila's phrase about the wedding costing him a forest (p. 153), the women's straw garlands and Matti's haranguing of the broom. In all three early versions Puntila's remark about forming a labor union (p. 158) is answered by Matti: "Excuse me, Mr. Puntila, it's not a labor union because there are no dues. So nobody's interests are represented. It was just for a joke and maybe for a cup of coffee." Finally in lieu of Emma's last speech the telephone operator tells Puntila:

> But it's only a joke. You invited us yourself . . .
> EMMA   You have no right to say we wanted to blackmail you.
> PUNTILA   Get off my land!

End of scene.

Scene 8

This had no title before the 1950 version. In the first script it is unnumbered but inserted separately from scene 7, which suggests that it was added later; it is followed by a photograph of a peasant woman. In the fair copy it is numbered 7a, and in the W-B version "Scene 7, conclusion, to be played on the forestage." Emma's first tale (starting "the wife of the former police chief") is not in W-B; the telephone operator's tale ("Their heads are screwed on tight") is delivered by the dairy-maid; and the latter's ("So am I" p. 161) is spoken by the peasant woman in the first script and by Emma in W-B. This is then followed by a comment from the telephone operator "What fools we women are," which in W-B ends the scene. The first script adds Emma's long story (pp. 161–62) but gives it to the telephone operator.

Scene 9 [8 in the early scripts]

Again the title and general sense of the scene have remained unchanged ever since Brecht's first plans, though a long section was cut out of its middle (which somewhat alters the picture of Eva) while the ending with Red Surkkala's song was tacked on to the fair copy. Originally the opening conversation was among parson, judge, doctor and lawyer (or agronomist in W-B); there was a slight redistribution and cutting of lines once the doctor had been eliminated. At first too the attaché appeared accompanied not only by the parson's wife but also by Hanna/Alina, who delivered what are now the parson's wife's lines, sighed, and left.

The major change occurred after the parson's wife's reproachful cry of "Eva!" (p. 168), before Puntila reappears. Here there enter, not Puntila at first but

> *the cook and Fina the maid with a great basket full of bottles. They clear the dining table and place them on it)*

EVA   What are you doing, Fina?
FINA   Master told us to reset the table.

PARSON'S WIFE   Are you saying that he came to the kitchen?

THE COOK   Yes, he was in a hurry, looking for the chauffeur.

EVA   Has the attaché driven away?

FINA   I think so.

EVA   Why can't people say things for certain? I hate this awful uncertainty all around me.

FINA (*laughing*)   My guess is that you're not sorry, Miss Eva.

(*Enter Puntila and Kalle, followed by the doctor*)

PUNTILA   Hear that, Eva? There was I, sitting over my punch, thinking about nothing in particular, when suddenly I caught myself looking at the fellow and wondering how the devil anyone could have a face like that. I blinked and wondered if my eyesight had gone wrong, so I had another glass and looked again, and then of course I knew what I had to do. What are all you people on your feet for?

PARSON   Mr. Puntila, I thought that since the party's over we ought to take our leave. You must be tired, Anna.

PUNTILA   Rubbish. You're not going to resent one of old Puntila's jokes, not like that pettifogging lawyer Kallios who keeps picking holes in everything I do and just at the very instant when I've realized my mistake and want to put it right; yes, the attaché was a flop but I did a good job once I'd caught on, you'll bear me out there. Puntila may go off the rails, but not for long before he sees it and becomes quite human again. You found the wine? Take a glass and let's all sit down; I'll just tell the others there's been a mistake and the engagement party's going on. If that attaché—a grasshopper, that's what he is, and I'm amazed you didn't realize it right away, Eva,—as I was saying, if he imagines he can screw up my engagement after weeks of preparation then he can think again. The fact is I decided a long time ago to marry my daughter to a good man, Matti Altonen, a fine chauffeur and a good friend of mine. Fina, hurry up and tell whoever's dancing in the park that they're to come here as soon as the dance is over; there've been some interesting changes. I'll go get the foreign minister. (*Goes out*)

KALLE   Your father's going too far, even allowing for him being drunk.

EVA   [illegible]

KALLE   I'm amazed you let him treat you like that in public.

EVA   I like being an obedient daughter.

KALLE   He's going to be disappointed, though. Maybe he can give your hand to anyone he chooses, but he can't give mine, and that includes giving it to you.

Eva answers "Don't look at me like that" etc., as on p. 168, down to Matti's "it had nothing to do with getting married," after which she continues:

I don't believe you. That wasn't how you held me at Kurgela. You're like Hulda down in the village, who had five illegitimate children with a fellow and then when they asked why she didn't marry him she said "I don't like him."

KALLE   Stop laughing, and stop telling dirty stories. You're drunk. I can't afford to marry you.

EVA   With a sawmill you could.

KALLE   I already told you I'm not playing Viktor to you. If he wants to scatter sawmills around he can give them to you, not to me. He's human enough when he's stewed but when he's sober he's sharp. He'll spend a million on an attaché for you but not on a chauffeur.
(*Parson, judge, parson's wife and doctor have been standing as a group in the background and putting their heads together. Now the parson goes up to Eva*)

PARSON   Eva, my dear, I must speak to you like when I was preparing you for confirmation. [An illegible line is added.] Mr. Altonen is welcome to stay, in view of his unfortunate involvement. Eva my dear, it is your hard duty to tell your father in no uncertain terms that he cannot dispose of you like a heifer and that God has given you a will of your own.

EVA   That would conflict with my obedience to parental authority, Reverend.

PARSON   It is a higher form of obedience, an obedience that goes against accepted morality.

KALLE   That's just what I say.

PARSON   I am glad you have so much good sense. It makes the situation considerably easier for you, my child.

EVA   What's so hard about it? I shall say to my father in bell-like tones: I propose to do as you command. I am

going to marry Kalle. Even if it means risking his saying
in front of everybody that he doesn't want me.

KALLE   If you ask me, the problem's a lot simpler than that,
Reverend. I think he'll have forgotten all about it by the
time he comes back here. I'll be the sacrifice and go into
the kitchen with him, we'll have a bottle or two and I'll
tell him how I've been sacked from job after job, that's
something he likes hearing about.

EVA   If you do that I'll go into the kitchen too.

PARSON   I am sadly disappointed in you, Eva. (*He goes back
to the others*) It's unbelievable. She's determined to marry
the man.

DOCTOR   In that case it's time I went; I'd rather not be present; I know Puntila. (*Goes out*)

PARSON   All I can say is that I'd leave too if I didn't feel it
my duty to drain this cup to the dregs.

PARSON'S WIFE   Besides, Mr. Puntila would be displeased.
(*The dance music next door suddenly stops. A confused
sound of voices which likewise stops after a moment. The
ensuing silence allows one to hear the accordion playing
for the dancers in the park*)

KALLE   You're taking advantage of the situation.

EVA   I want my husband to be a man.

KALLE   What you want is a lively evening, never mind
what anyone else may think. You're your father's daughter all right.

(*Enter Puntila by himself, angry*)

PUNTILA   (*taking a bottle from the table and drinking from
it*)   I have just looked deep into the depravity . . .

and so on as on p. 168. Then there is a cut straight from his
"Fina, you sit next to me" (p. 168) straight to *All sit down
reluctantly* (p. 169).

Thereafter there are only small differences in the scene at
the table with Matti testing Eva. One is that Puntila's query
"Matti, can you fuck properly" (p. 170) down to Matti's
"Never mind" (p. 170) is not in the first script or the W-B
version but was an addition to the fair copy. Then when Matti
slaps Eva's behind both the first version and the fair copy have
her evading the slap; she simply says "How dare you," etc. In
the first version the scene ends with the exit of the cook and

the parson's wife (p. 178). In the fair copy, however, Matti's immediately preceding speech continues after "unforgiving":

> It's only that the kitchen staff will be here in a minute; the music has stopped. You made Fina call them to hear about some new development. What are you going to say when they get here, led by Miss Hanna with her sharp tongue?
>
> PUNTILA   I'll tell them that I've disowned my daughter for being a crime against Nature.
>
> MATTI   You might do better to tell them that tomorrow.

Then he turns "to the parson's wife and Laina" as on p. 177 down to their exit, after which one hears singing from the dance off:

> The wolf asked the rooster a question:
> "Shouldn't we get to know each other better
> Know and understand each other better?"
> The rooster thought that a good suggestion
> Must have responded to the question
> I'd say, seeing the field's full of feathers.
> Oh, oh.
>
> The match asked the can a question:
> "Shouldn't we get to know each other better
> Know and respect each other better?"
> The can thought that a good suggestion
> Must have responded to the question
> I'd say, seeing the sky's turning crimson.
>
> The boss asked the maid a question:
> Shouldn't we get to know each other better
> Know and respect each other better?
> The maid thought that a good suggestion
> Must have responded to the question
> I'd say, seeing her stays are convex.
> Oh, oh.   [Tr. by John Willett]

PUNTILA   That was a dig at me. Songs like that wound me to the quick.

The last stage direction first appears in the 1950 text. Red Surk-kala's song was added at the end of the fair copy, developing the theme of the first stanza of the above, then in the 1950 version supplanted it.

Scene 10

This is not in the W-B version but is included in the first script with no scene number or title. In the fair copy it is numbered 8a.

Scene 11 [9 in the early scripts]

In the first script the title is "Puntila and Kalle climb Mount Hatelma," in the fair copy "Puntila sits in judgment and climbs Mount Hatelma," in the W-B version "Iso-Heikkilä condemns Kalle." The setting in the first script is the

> *Library at Puntila Farms. Hanna, the old housekeeper, is writing out accounts, when Puntila sticks his head in, with a towel round it. He is about to draw back when he sees that Hanna has observed him, and walks across the room to the door. On her addressing him he is painfully affected and stops.*

HANNA Mr. Puntila, I have to talk to you. Now don't pretend you've got something important to do, and don't look so pained. For the past week I've said nothing because what with the engagement and the house guests I've had my hands so full I didn't know where I was. But now the time has come. Do you realize what you've done?

PUNTILA Hanna, I have a dreadful headache. I think if I had another cup of coffee and a bit of a nap it might help; what do you think?

HANNA I think you've needed something quite different and been needing it a long time. Do you realize that his honor the judge has left?

PUNTILA What, Frederick? That seems childish.

HANNA Do you expect him to stay in a place the foreign

minister's been thrown out of? Not to mention the attaché, who moves in the very best circles and will be telling everybody about you? You'll be left sitting at Puntila Farms like a lone rhinoceros. Society will shun you.

PUNTILA   I can't understand that minister. He sees I'm a bit high, and then goes and takes everything I say literally.

HANNA   You've always made a nuisance of yourself, but ever since that chauffeur came to the estate it's been too much. Twenty years I've been at Puntila Farms, but now you're going to have to make up your mind: it's the chauffeur or me.

PUNTILA   What are you talking about? You can't go. Who'd run the business? I've got such a headache, I think I'm getting pneumonia. Imagine attacking a man in such an inhuman way.

HANNA   I'll expect your answer. (*Turns towards the door*)

PUNTILA   You people grudge me even the smallest pleasure. Get me some milk, my head's bursting.

HANNA   There won't be any milk for you. The cook's passed out too, she was drunk. Here come the parson and the doctor.

PUNTILA   I don't feel like seeing them, my health isn't up to it. (*Hanna opens the door to the two gentlemen*)

PARSON   Good morning, Mr. Puntila, I trust you had a good night's rest. (*Puntila mumbles something*) I ran into the doctor on the road; we thought we'd drop by and see how you were.

PUNTILA   (*dubiously*)   I see.

DOCTOR   Rough night, what? I'd drink some milk if I were you.

PARSON   My wife asked to be remembered to you. She and Miss Laina had a most interesting talk.
(*Pause*)

PARSON   (*gingerly*)   I'm very much surprised to hear Miss Hanna is thinking of leaving.

PUNTILA   Where did you hear that?

PARSON   Where? Oh, I really couldn't say. You know how these rumors get around.

PUNTILA   By telephone, I suppose. I'd like to know who phoned you.

PARSON   I assure you, Mr. Puntila, there was no question of anybody phoning. What made me call was simply being upset that someone so universally respected as Miss Hanna should be forced to take such a step.

DOCTOR   I told you it was a misunderstanding.

PUNTILA   I'd just like to know who has been telephoning people from here behind my back. I know these coincidences.

DOCTOR   Don't be difficult, Puntila. Nothing's being done behind your back. We're not having this conversation behind your back, are we?

PUNTILA   If I find you've been intriguing against me, Finstrand, I'll put you on *your* back soon enough.

PARSON   Mr. Puntila, this is getting us nowhere. I must ask you to consider our words as words of friendship because we've heard you were losing the valuable services of Miss Hanna, and it's very hard to imagine what Puntila Farms would do without her.

DOCTOR   If you want to throw us out like yesterday, go right ahead. You can put up a barbed-wire fence around the estate and drink yourself to death behind it.

PUNTILA (*with hostility*)   So somebody did phone.

DOCTOR   Oh God, yes. Do you think everyone in Lammi just takes it for granted when you insult a cabinet minister under your own roof and drive your daughter's fiancé off the estate by stoning him?

PUNTILA   What's that about stoning? I'd like to know who's spreading that stoning story.

PARSON   Mr. Puntila, let's not waste time on details. I fear I have come to the conclusion that much of what happened yesterday is not at all clear in your memory. For instance, I doubt whether you are aware of the exact wording of the insults which you hurled after our foreign minister, Mr. Puntila.

DOCTOR   It may interest you to know that you called him a shit.

PUNTILA   That's an exaggeration.

PARSON   Alas, no. Perhaps that will make you realize that when you are in that deplorable condition you don't always act as you might think wise in retrospect. You risk incurring considerable damage.

PUNTILA   Any damage I incur is paid for by me, not you.

DOCTOR   True. But there is some damage which you can't pay.

PARSON   Which money cannot set right.

DOCTOR   Though it's the first time I've seen you take things so lightly when somebody like Miss Hanna gives notice in the middle of the harvest.

PARSON   We should overlook such material considerations, doctor. I've known Mr. Puntila to be just as understanding where purely moral considerations were concerned. It might not be unrewarding to take the matter of Surkkala as an example of the dangers of over-indulgence in alcohol, and discuss it with Mr. Puntila in a friendly, dignified spirit.

PUNTILA   What about Surkkala?

All this long introduction, which was replaced by the present text in the 1950 version, takes us only to p. 181, after which the scene continues as now as far as Puntila's shaking of the parson's hand on p. 182, apart of course from the giving of Laina's lines to Hanna.

Thereafter the parson, before leaving, begs Hanna not to abandon her employer but to go on acting as his guardian angel; to which she replies: "That depends on Mr. Puntila." The doctor advises him to drink less, and the two men go out. Puntila's ensuing speech about giving up drinking ("Laina, I'll never touch another drop," etc.) is addressed to Hanna, not Laina, and is somewhat shorter than now. In the W-B version it follows straight after Hanna's statement that the cook was drunk (p. 445 above), the whole episode with the parson and the doctor/lawyer being thus omitted. To return to the first script, Hanna then replies:

Liquor and low company are to blame. I'll send for that criminal chauffeur, you can deal with him for a starter. (*Calls through the doorway*) Kalle! Come into the library at once!

PUNTILA   That Surkkala business is a lesson to me; imagine my not throwing him out. That's what happens once you let the demon rum get a toe-hold.

Surkkala's appearance with his family is omitted, Kalle/Matti entering at this point with his "Good morning, Mr. Puntila," etc. as on p. 182. He then has to defend himself not to Puntila himself (and against the accusations of the latter's friends) but to Hanna, to whom he says that he was merely carrying out instructions and (as in the final text) could not confine himself to the sensible ones (p. 183).

HANNA   There's no need to top it all by being impertinent. They told me how you chased after your master's daughter at Kurgela and pestered her in the bath-hut.

KALLE   Only for the sake of appearances.

HANNA   You do everything for the sake of appearances. You put on a show of zeal and manage to get yourself ordered to force your lustful attentions on your employer's daughter and smoke Puntila's cigars. Who invited those Kurgela creatures over to Puntila Farms?

KALLE   Mr. Puntila, down in the village at half-past four a.m.

HANNA   Yes, but who worked them up and got them to come into the house where the foreign minister was being entertained? You.

PUNTILA   I caught him trying to make them ask me for money for breach of promise.

HANNA   And then the hiring market?

PUNTILA   He frightened off the redhaired man I was after and landed me with that sickly-looking fellow I had to send packing because he scared the cows.

KALLE   Yes, Mr. Puntila.

HANNA   As for the engagement party last night . . . You ought to have all Puntila Farms on your conscience. There's Miss Eva sitting upstairs with a headache and a broken heart for the rest of her life, when she could have been happily married in three or four months' time.

KALLE   All I can say, Miss Hanna, is that if I hadn't restrained myself something much worse would have happened.

HANNA   You and she were sitting in the kitchen on Saturday night, do you deny that?

KALLE   We had a perfectly harmless conversation which I am not going to describe to you in detail, Miss Hanna, you being a spinster, and I don't mean that as an insult but as my personal conclusion based on certain pieces of evidence that are not relevant to the present discussion.

HANNA So you're dropping your hypocritical mask, you Bolshevik. It all comes of your boozing with creatures like this, Mr. Puntila, and not keeping your distance. I'm leaving.

Puntila then tells Matti/Kalle, in much the same words as now used to Laina on p. 182, to bring out all the bottles containing liquor so that they may be smashed. He follows with a shorter version of his speech on p. 183 down to "That is too little known," after which Matti reappears with the bottles. The dialogue is close to that of our text, but with Hanna/Alina fulfilling Laina's rôle of trying to stop Puntila drinking, until he turns on her (p. 185) after his "I never want to see it again, you heard me." Then instead of going on as in our text he says:

And don't contradict me, woman; you're my evil genius. That gaunt face of yours makes me sick. I can't even get a drink of milk when I'm sick, and in my own house too. Because there you are, telephoning everyone behind my back and bringing in the parson to treat me like a schoolboy; I won't have it. Your pettiness has been poisoning my life for the last thirty years. I can't bear pettiness, you rusty old adding machine.

Then come four lines as in our text from "You people want me to sit here" to "figuring the cost of cow fodder," continuing:

I look across the table, and what do I see but you, you sleazy piece of black crape. I'm giving you notice, do you hear?

HANNA That beats everything. The two of you getting drunk before my very eyes!

PUNTILA Get out.

HANNA Are you trying to give *me* notice? Here's the man you promised you'd give notice to. You promised the parson himself. You were going to report him to the authorities. (*Puntila laughs, picks her up and carries her out, cursing him at the top of her voice*) Wastrel! Drunkard! Tramp!

PUNTILA (*returning*) That got rid of her.

Matti/Kalle's speech "I hope the stuff is all right," etc. follows as on p. 185, together with Puntila's next speech as far as "always a calamity." Then instead of the reference to Surkkala and the half-page of dialogue with him and his family Puntila runs straight on:

> I always said it takes a certain inner strength to keep on the right path.
>
> KALLE You always get more out of it if you wander off, Mr. Puntila. Practically everything that's at all pleasant lies off the right path, you'd almost think the right path had been thought up on purpose to discourage people.
>
> PUNTILA I say the pleasant path is the right one. And in my opinion you're a good guide. Just looking at you makes me thirsty.
>
> KALLE I'd like to say something about yesterday's engagement party, Mr. Puntila. There were one or two misunderstandings due to the impossibility of suppressing human nature, but if I may say so inhuman nature can't be suppressed either. You rather underrated the gulf between me and Miss Eva until I tickled her backside; I suppose it was because offhand you didn't see why I shouldn't go catching crayfish with Miss Eva just as well as the next man, which is an offhand way of looking at the sexes and one that doesn't get under the surface—as if only the intimate things mattered and not upbringing. As far as I know, though, nothing that happened at the party was so disastrous that you can't put it right, though all that came of it really was that the parson's wife now knows how to put up mushrooms.
>
> PUNTILA I can't take it tragically. Looking at it from the broad point of view, not from a petty one; devil take the woman, she's got a petty outlook, she's nothing. Eva will inherit the estate even if she makes a bad marriage.
>
> KALLE Even if. Because so long as she's got the estate, and the cows yield milk and there's someone to drive the milk cans to the cooperative and they keep an eye on the grain and so on, nothing else counts. Whether it's a good or bad marriage isn't going to prevent her from selling her trees. You can chop down a forest even with a broken heart.

Then Puntila asks what his pay is, as on p. 186 (though the amount varies from script to script) and goes on, as in our text, to propose climbing Mount Hatelma. After his "We can do it in spirit" (p. 186) Matti/Kalle interposes in the first script (not in W-B):

> In spirit is always much the simplest way. I once got sore at an Englishman for parking his car so stupidly that I had to shove it out of the way with my drunken boss sitting in the Ford cursing me. In spirit I declared war on England, I defeated them in spirit, brought them to their knees, and laid down stiff peace terms; it was all very simple, I remember.

Then Puntila finishes with "All we need is a few chairs," etc. (p. 186) and the dialogue continues virtually as we have it for some two pages, omitting only the stake direction on p. 187 with its mention of the billiard table. After Puntila's "Are you from Tavastland?" (p. 188), however, Kalle gave details, e.g., from the first script:

> Originally, yes. I was born the other side of those forests in a cabin by the lake, and I grew up on bare stony ground.
> PUNTILA Hold on, let's take it all in proper order. First and foremost, where is there such a sky?

—and so on as in our text to the end of the scene. In the W-B version there are some cuts, and Kalle adds after his present concluding line "Long live Tavastland and its Iso-Heikkilä!" after which the two men sing the lines about the Roina once again. (These come from the nineteenth-century poet Topelius, and the Roina is a lake in central Finland.)

Scene 12 [10 in the first script]

Laina's second speech and both Matti's first two were additions on the fair copy. In the first script, after Laina's "until Mr. Puntila gets up" (p. 190) Kalle continues:

> I'm glad I was able to straighten out that business with the housekeeper. It got me a settlement of two months'

pay, and she was so glad to be rid of me she gave me a decent reference.

COOK   I don't get it. When you're in so good with the master.

KALLE   That's just the problem. I couldn't have *him* writing a reference for me; I'd never get another job so long as I lived.

Then as in our text from Laina's "He'll be lost without you" to her exit, after which Kalle flings a stone at one of the balcony windows and Eva appears in night attire.

EVA   What's up? Why have you got your suitcase?

KALLE   I'm leaving.

EVA   (*after a pause*)   Why do you want to leave?

KALLE   I can't stay forever.

EVA   I'm sorry you're going, Kalle.

KALLE   I'll send you a crayfish for your birthday.

EVA   I'd sooner you came back yourself.

KALLE   Right. In a year from now.

EVA   I'll wait that long.

KALLE   By then I'll have my sawmill.

EVA   Fine. I'll have learned how to darn socks by then.

KALLE   Then it will work. Bye.

EVA   Bye. (*Goes back into her room*)

The epilogue follows with some very slight variations.

The W-B version tacks this scene on to the preceding one by having Eva enter and call Puntila down from his mountain, after which he goes off with Fina and Laina, leaving her and Kalle alone. She asks "Why have you got your suitcase?" as above, but the dialogue differs from that in the first script by having her press him to make it less than a year and suggesting that her father might give her a sawmill. Kalle says he will send her books, and she agrees to read them; then she comes close to him, forcing him to say "Go away and lead me not into temptation." He pushes her off, and the epilogue follows.

THE RESISTIBLE RISE
OF ARTURO UI

Texts by Brecht

Instructions for Performance

In order that the events may retain the significance unhappily
due to them, the play must be performed in the grand style,
and preferably with obvious harkbacks to the Elizabethan theater, i.e., with curtains and different levels. For instance, the
action could take place in front of curtains of whitewashed
sacking spattered the color of ox blood. At some points pano-
rama-like backdrops could be used, and organ, trumpet, and
drum effects are likewise permissible. Use should be made of
the masks, vocal characteristics, and gestures of the originals;
pure parody however must be avoided, and the comic element
must not preclude horror. What is needed is a three-dimensional
presentation which goes at top speed and is composed of clearly
defined groupings like those favored by historic tableaux at
fairs.

> ["Hinweis für die Aufführung," from GW *Stücke*, pp.
> 1837-38.]

Alternative Prologues

Friends, tonight we're going to show—
A little spirit, you in the back row!
And lady, your hat is in the way!—
The great historical gangster play!
Containing, for the first time, as you'll see

THE TRUTH ABOUT THE SCANDALOUS DOCK SUBSIDY.
Further, we give you for your betterment
DOGSBOROUGH'S CONFESSION AND TESTAMENT.
ARTURO UI'S RISE WHILE THE STOCK MARKET FELL
THE NOTORIOUS WAREHOUSE FIRE TRIAL, WHAT A SELL!
THE DULLFEET MURDER! JUSTICE IN A COMA!
GANG WARFARE: THE KILLING OF ERNESTO ROMA!
All culminating in our stunning last tableau:
GANGSTERS TAKE OVER THE TOWN OF CICERO!
Brilliant performers will portray
The most famous gangsters of our day
All the hanged and the shot
Disparaged but not
Wholly forgotten gangsters
Taken as models by our youngsters.
Ladies and gentlemen, the management knows
There are ticklish subjects which some of those
Who pay admission hardly love
To be reminded of.
Accordingly, we've decided to put on
A story in these parts little known
That took place in another hemisphere—
The kind of thing that's never happened here.
This way you're safe, no fear you'll see
The senior members of your family
In flesh and blood before your eyes
Doing things that aren't too nice.
So just relax, young lady. Don't run away.
You're sure to like our gangster play.

> ["Prolog (2)" from GW *Stücke*, pp. 1838–39. Written
> subsequently to the first version of the play, which in-
> cludes the prologue given in our text.]

Ladies and gentlemen, the management's aware
This is a controversial affair.
Though some can still take history as they find it
Most of you don't care to be reminded.

Now, ladies and gentlemen, surely what this shows is
Excrescences need proper diagnosis
Conveyed not in some polysyllabic word
But in plain speech that calls a turd a turd.
And if you're used to something more ethereal
The language of this play suits its material.
Down from your gallows, then! Up from your graves!
You murderous pack of filthy swindling knaves!
Let's see you in the flesh once more tonight
And hope that in our present sorry plight
Seeing the men from whom that plight first came
Moves us not just to anger but to shame.

> [BBA 174/131. Inserted at the end of the first version of
> the play, but evidently written for a German audience
> after the end of the Second World War.]

Notes

1. PREFACE

The Resistible Rise of Arturo Ui, written in Finland in 1941,
represents an attempt to make Hitler's rise intelligible to the
capitalist world by transposing it into a sphere thoroughly familiar to them. The blank verse is an aid in appraising the characters' heroism.

2. REMARKS

Nowadays ridiculing the great political criminals, alive or dead,
is generally said to be neither appropriate nor constructive.
Even the common people are said to be sensitive on this point,
not just because they too were implicated in the crimes in question but because it is not possible for those who survived among
the ruins to laugh about such things. Nor is it much good

charging at open doors (as there are too many of these among the ruins anyway): the lesson has been learned, so why go on dinning it into the poor creatures? If on the other hand the lesson has not been learned it is risky to encourage a people to laugh at a potentate after once failing to take him seriously enough; and so on and so forth.

It is relatively easy to dismiss the suggestion that art needs to treat brutality with kid gloves; that it should devote itself to watering the puny seedlings of awareness; that it ought to be explaining the garden hose to former wielders of the rubber truncheon, and so on. Likewise it is possible to object to the term "people," as used to signify something "higher" than population, and to show how the term conjures up the notorious concept of Volksgemeinschaft, or a "sense of being one people," that links executioner and victim, employer and employed. But this does not mean that the suggestion that satire should not meddle in serious matters is an acceptable one. Serious things are precisely its concern.

The great political criminals must be thoroughly stripped bare and exposed to ridicule. Because they are not great political criminals at all, but the perpetrators of great political crimes, which is something very different.

There is no need to be afraid of truisms so long as they are true. If the collapse of Hitler's enterprises is no evidence that he was a halfwit, neither is their scope any guarantee that he was a great man. In the main the classes that control the modern state use utterly average people for their enterprises. Not even in the highly important field of economic exploitation is any particular talent called for. A multimillion-mark trust like I. G. Farben makes use of exceptional intelligence only when it can exploit it; the exploiters proper, a handful of people most of whom acquired their power by birth, have a certain cunning and brutality as a group but see no commercial drawbacks in lack of education, nor even in the presence among them of the odd amiable individual. They get their political affairs dealt with by people often markedly stupider than themselves. Thus Hitler was no doubt a lot more stupid than Brüning and Brüning than Stresemann, while on the military plane Keitel and Hindenburg were pretty well matched. A military specialist like Ludendorff, who lost battles by his political immaturity, is no more to be thought of as an intellectual giant than is a lightning calculator from vaudeville. It is the scope of their enterprises that give such people their aura of greatness. But this aura does not necessarily make them all that effective, since it only means that there is a vast mass of intelligent people available, with the result that wars and crises become displays of the intelligence of the entire population.

On top of that it is a fact that crime itself frequently provokes admiration. I never heard the petty bourgeoisie of my home town speak with anything but respectful enthusiasm of a man called Kneisel who was a mass murderer, so that I have remembered his name to this day. It was not even thought necessary on his behalf to invent the usual acts of kindness towards poor old grannies: his murders were enough.

In the main the petty bourgeois conception of history (and the proletariat's too, so long as it has no other), is a romantic one. What fired these Germans' poverty-stricken imagination in the case of Napoleon I was of course not his Code Napoléon but his millions of victims. Bloodstains embellish these conquerors' faces like beauty spots. When a certain Dr. Pechel, writing in the aptly named *Deutsche Rundschau* in 1946, said of Genghis Khan that "the price of the Pax Mongolica was the death of several dozen million men and the destruction of twenty kingdoms," it made a great man of this "bloodstained conqueror, the demolisher of all values, though this must not cause us to forget the ruler who showed that his real nature was not destructive"—on the mere grounds that he was never petty in his dealings with people. It is this reverence for killers that has to be done away with. Plain everyday logic must never let itself be overawed once it goes strolling among the centuries; whatever applies to small situations must be made to apply to big ones too. The petty rogue whom the rulers permit to become a rogue on the grand scale can occupy a special position in roguery, but not in our attitude to history. Anyway there is truth in the principle that comedy is less likely than tragedy to fail to take human suffering seriously enough.

3. JOTTINGS

Kusche: ". . . but at the very point where the projections un-mistakably relate *Ui* to a specific phase of German history . . . the question arises: 'Where is the People?'"

"Brecht has written, apropos of Eisler's *Faustus*, that 'our starting point has to be the truth of the phrase "no conception can be valid that assumes German history to be unalloyed misère and fails to present the People as a creative force".'"

"What is lacking is something or other that would stand for this 'creative force of the People' . . . Was it all a mere internal affray between gangsters and merchants? Was Dimitroff (as it is simpler to give that force an individual name) a merchant?"

Ui is a *parable* play, written with the aim of destroying the dangerous respect commonly felt for great killers. The circle described has been deliberately restricted; it is confined to the plane of state, industrialists, Junkers, and petty bourgeois. This is enough to achieve the desired objective. The play does not pretend to give a complete account of the historical situation in the 1930s. The proletariat is not present, nor could it be taken into account more than it is, since anything *extra* in this complex would be *too much;* it would distract from the tricky problem posed. (How could more attention be paid to the proletariat without considering unemployment, and how could that be done without dealing with the [Nazi] employment program, also with the political parties and their abdication? One thing would entail another, and the result would be a gigantic work which would fail to do what was intended.)

The projected texts—which K. takes as a reason for expect-ing the play to give a general account of what happened—seem to me, if anything, to stress the element of selectivity, of a peep-show.

The industrialists all seem to have been hit by the crisis to the same extent, whereas the stronger ought to knock out the weaker. (But that may be another point which would involve us in too much detail and which a *parable* can legitimately skip.) The defense counsel in scene 9 [our scene 8], the warehouse fire trial, possibly needs another look. At present his protests seem designed merely to defend a kind of "honor of the profession." The audience will of course want to see him as Dimitroff, whether or not it was meant to.

As for the appearance of Röhm's ghost, I think Kusche is right. ("As the text now stands it makes a drunken Nazi slob look like a martyr.") [...]

The play was written in 1941 and conceived as a 1941 production. [...]

> [From GW *Schriften zum Theater*, pp. 1176–80. Written for a proposed volume of the *Versuche* whose preparation was interrupted by Brecht's death in 1956. Since the play was first published in *Sinn und Form* only after that date, the characteristic East German criticisms voiced by Lothar Kusche (and originally made at a meeting between Brecht and younger writers in late 1953) must have been based on a reading of the script.]

Later Texts

Notes by Manfred Wekwerth

1. LESSONS OF A PILOT PRODUCTION AT ANOTHER THEATER

Scene 1 [*1a*]

The members of the trust display those same gangsters' attitudes and costumes that we know from American films; two-tone suits, a variety of hats, scarves, and so on. This misses the point, essential to the story, that here we have old-established businessmen who have been in the trade "since Noah's ark." These trust members are too much like parvenus, profiteers, so that the element of solid respectability—the bourgeois element—is lost. As a result their subsequent alliance with Ui, far from being worthy of remark, seems natural. Gangsters seeking out their own kind: *not* the bourgeois state turning to something it had expressly branded as its own mortal enemy—organized crime.

For the same reasons the crisis too is ill-founded, since people who make such an impression are used to running into money troubles, because their business (profiteering) involves risks.

Scene 2 [1b]

Ui, Roma, and Ragg emerge on to the apron from below stage and hurry past Clark one by one. In this way they formally announce themselves as gangsters emerging from a sewer manhole and not, as the story demands, as gangsters offering their services to the trust in a particularly offhand and gentleman-like manner.

Scene 3 [2]. Dogsborough's Restaurant

Unless Dogsborough appears above all as an immovable, unchangeable, impregnable, rocklike fortress (i.e., solidly or immovably set in an attitude which, to judge from the text, Brecht took from Hindenburg), the great turning point where he crumbles will not be properly brought out. Instead of a "great personality" succumbing to an economic force we get an average personality doing what is only to be expected. The actor gave us a lively, forceful, decisive, far too young Dogsborough, with an agile mind and agile gestures. When he looks out of the window and succumbs to the house by the lake, he turns round at least two times in order to express his reservations, and in so doing destroys the great instant of succumbing.

Similarly with Dogsborough's treatment by the trust people. They should not address him as if he were one of their own sort—i.e., in business jargon—but ought to deploy considerable human resources in order to get him to listen to them at all. They should all the time be confirming his reputation as honest old Dogsborough.

As to the identification of the characters with the Nazi leaders: Dogsborough bore no kind of resemblance to Hindenburg, neither of attitude, gesture, tone of voice, nor mask. The necessary degree of likeness to Hindenburg could only be achieved once one had taken in the inscriptions and after the play had ended. The highly amusing way in which the course of the action instantly and directly alienates the gangsters into top Nazis was missed, or at any rate seemed vague and inexact.

The play was written against Hitler and the bigshots of those times. No general conclusions can be drawn until this story, transposed into terms of the gang world, can be concretely recognized so as to allow people in subsequent times to generalize from concrete knowledge and detect fascist trends. To start off by generalizing—i.e., by making the characters identifiable not merely with Hitler and Hindenburg—makes the events less concrete and prevents any true historical generalization. This is particularly true of our own time, where the historical events are barely remembered and the top Nazis virtually unknown except from photographs. Brecht himself rejects such a discreet approach inasmuch as he uses allusive names (Dogsborough, Giri, Roma, etc.), and calls for prescribed similarities of voice, gesture, and masks. Without this, the work degenerates into a *roman à clef*.

Scene 4 [3]. Bookmaker's office

In the bookmaker's office the group of leaders—Ui, Ragg, and Roma—associate with the other gangsters, with the result that their discussions degenerate into everyday conversation instead of being a crucial conversation between leading personalities; for the crisis would hardly be discussed before all and sundry. This is accentuated by the unrelievedly pliable, deflated, rubbery, unassertive attitude of Arturo Ui, who is in no way shown as a boss, but more as a passive plaything among strong men. Presented in such a wretched niggling light, his plans do not emerge as dangerous; what is being shown is not so much the large-scale planning of lunacy as the actual lunacy itself. This means that the Nazis' logical approach—which admittedly developed on a basis of lunacy and lack of logic—is never established, so that every subsequent action seems more or less accidental and not thought up with a vast expenditure of effort. Hence Nazism emerges as haphazard and individualistic instead of being a system: a system based on lunacy and lack of system.

Puny swindles ought to be mightily pondered, underhand actions conceived on a vast scale, instances of thoughtlessness realized by enormous thought.

Ui as a character

Ui is presented as a passive plaything in the hands of strong men (Goebbels, Göring, Papen). He has pathological features which run unchanged right through the play. All through he gives evidence of exhaustion and lack of enterprise, needing to be prompted and jogged by Givola even during his big speeches. In this way the character is emasculated and the main weight of responsibility shifted to the strong men, but without any explanation why they in particular should be strong.

One of the dangerous things about Hitler was his immensely stubborn logic, a logic based on absence of logic, lack of understanding, and half-baked ideas. (Even the concentration camps were no accidental creation, having been planned as early as 1923.) Precisely Hitler's languidness, his indecision, emptiness, feebleness, and freedom from ideas were the source of his usefulness and strength.

The impression given in this production is that Hitler's feebleness and malleability were a liability to the movement, and that given greater energy and intelligence fascism would have proved much easier to put up with, since its shortcomings are here attributed to human weakness. [...]
[...]

The investigation [Scene 5]

The legal process fails to come across. It is impossible to tell who has convened the inquiry, who is being accused, what part is being played by Dogsborough, how far an appearance of justice still matters, what official standing Ui has there. This scene accordingly comes across as a muddle, not as a bourgeois legal ritual that gangsters can use unchanged. Rituals and arrangements should therefore be portrayed with especial precision and care. Only the dignity of the traditional procedures can show the indignity of what is taking place.

The Warehouse Fire Trial [Scene 8]

This scene is not helped by the symbolic grouping which has the populace represented by Nazis who stand a few inches behind the centrally placed judges (pointing a pistol at their heads!).

The fact that the Nazis needed the seal of approval of the bourgeois court, along with its dignity and its traditions, is thereby made incomprehensible. Instead it becomes an unceremonious gang tribunal, and accordingly without any meaning as a court.

If all that is to appear is how the court's bourgeois traditions are flouted, then it becomes impossible to show how the bourgeois court, by the mere fact of its existence, flouts justice; how crime is an integral part of its traditional procedures; and how it is unnecessary for this tradition to be broken to make it criminal.

> [From Manfred Wekwerth: *Schriften*, Arbeit mit Brecht, East Berlin, Henschel-Verlag, 1973, pp. 144–7. The production in question was that of the world première at Stuttgart under Peter Palitzsch's direction in November 1958, a pilot for the subsequent Berliner Ensemble production directed by Palitzsch and Wekwerth together.]

2. TWO NOTES ON THE BERLINER ENSEMBLE PRODUCTION

(a) The historical references

After the third rehearsal we gave up trying to base the principal parts on their correspondences with the Nazi originals. The mistake became particularly evident in the case of Schall, who gave an extremely well-observed imitation of Hitler's vocal characteristics and gestures, such as we had seen a day or two before on film. The faithfulness of this imitation wholly swamped the story of the gangster play. What resulted was a highly amusing detailed parody, but of details from a play about Nazis. The more profoundly amusing point—the parallel between Nazis and gangsters—was lost, since it can only be made if the gangster story is sufficiently complete and independent to match the Nazi story. It is the distancing of the one story from the other that allows them to be connected up on a historical-philosophical, not a merely mechanical plane. We asked the actors to be guided by a strong sense of fun, free from all historical ideas, in exploiting their extensive knowledge of American gangster movies, then carefully on top of that to put recognizable quotations from the vocal characteristics and gestures of the Nazi originals, rather as one puts on a mask.

(b) About the music

The basic character of the music was dictated by setting the "great historical gangster play" of the prologue within the colorful shooting-gallery framework of a fairground. At the same time it was the music's job to stress the atmosphere of horror. It had to be garish and nasty.

This suggested using pieces of music which had been abused by the Nazis, e.g., the theme from Liszt's *Les Préludes* which they degraded into a signature tune for special announcements on the radio. The idea of playing Chopin's "Funeral March" at set intervals throughout the long-drawn-out warehouse fire trial was suggested by Brecht. Tempi and rhythms of these themes were of course radically altered to accord with the basic character established for the production.

The orchestra consisted of just a few instruments: trumpet, trombone, tuba, horn, piccolo, clarinet, electric guitar, saxophone, piano, harmonium, and percussion.

The sharpness and the fairground effect were furthered by technical effects in the course of recording on tape.

All music was on tape. For the first time the accompaniments to the three songs—Ted Ragg's song poking fun at the delay, Greenwool's soppy "Home Song" and Givola's "Whitewash Song"—were all reproduced from tape.

[Ibid., pp. 147–8, "Probennotat," and p. 150, "Die Musik." In this production Ekkehard Schall played Ui: an outstanding performance. The music was by the Ensemble's musical director Hans-Dieter Hosalla.]

Songs for the Berliner Ensemble Production

1. RAGG'S SONG

There was a little man
He had a little plan.
They told him to go easy
Just wait, my little man.
But waiting made him queasy.
  Heil Ui!
For he wants what he wants right now!

[Derived from the "Was-man-hat-hat-man Song" in scene 7 of *The Round Heads and the Pointed Heads*, GW *Stücke*, p. 993.]

2. GREENWOOL'S SONG

A cabin stands beside the meadow
It used to be my happy home.
Now strangers' eyes are looking out the window
Oh, why did I begin to roam?
Home, take me home
Back to my happy home!
Home, take me home
Back to my happy home!

[Origin uncertain. Not by Brecht.]

3. WHITEWASH SONG

When the rot sets in, when walls and roof start dripping
Something must be done at any price.
Now the mortar's crumbling, bricks are slipping.
If somebody comes it won't be nice.
But whitewash will do it, fresh whitewash will do it.
When the place caves in 'twill be too late.
Give us whitewash, boys, then we'll go to it
With our brushes till we fix things up first-rate.
Now, here's a fresh disaster
This damp patch on the plaster!
That isn't nice. (No, not nice.)
Look, the chimney's falling!
Really, it's appalling!
Something must be done at any price.
Oh, if only things would look up!
This abominable fuck-up
Isn't nice. (No, not nice.)
But whitewash will do it, lots of white will do it.
When the place caves in 'twill be too late.
Give us whitewash, boys, then we'll go to it
And we'll whitewash till we've got it all first-rate.
Here's the whitewash, let's not get upset!
Day and night we've got the stuff on hand.
This old shack will be a palace yet.
You'll get your New Order, just as planned.

> [GW *Stücke*, tr. by Ralph Manheim, p. 936. This song
> originated as an appendage to Brecht's treatment ("The
> Bruise") for *The Threepenny Opera* film, and was then
> taken into *The Round Heads and the Pointed Heads*,
> where it is sung to a setting by Hanns Eisler as an inter-
> lude between scenes 2 and 3.]

Editorial Note

Though *Ui* was among the most quickly written of all Brecht's plays we know little about its antecedents in his fertile mind. He himself spoke of it (in a journal entry for March 10, 1941) as inspired by thoughts of the American theater and harking back to his New York visit of 1935, when he no doubt was made particularly aware of the Chicago gangs of the prohibition era and the films made about them by such firms as Warner Brothers and First National. The highly un-American name *Ui*, however, and its application to a Hitler-type leader, evidently originated slightly earlier when he was planning his never-finished prose work about the Tui's or Tellect-Ual-Ins, upside-down intellectuals whose ineffectiveness allowed such leaders to come to power. Walter Benjamin, making one of his visits to Brecht in Denmark in September 1934, noted that in addition to this more ambitious work he was then writing a satire called *Ui* "on Hitler in the style of a Renaissance historian." This materialized in an unfinished and untitled short story set in classical Italy and describing an upstart city boss of Padua named Giacomo Ui, which can be found among Brecht's collected stories. Its style is deadpan, somewhat like that of the Julius Caesar novel which followed; its content is virtually the story of Hitler transposed into Roman terms. It resembles the eventual play in its depiction of his rages, his aggressive ambitions, his currying of popular favor and even the way in which

> he was taught how to speak and walk by an old actor who had once in his heyday been permitted to play the mighty Colleone, and accordingly also taught him the latter's famous way of standing with his arms folded across his chest.

But the eight short sections of this story hardly get beyond establishing the character, and nothing is said about Hindenburg, the Reichstag-fire trial and the murder of Ernst Röhm, let alone the territorial annexations which were still to come. There are, however, several allusions to that anti-Semitism which the play curiously ignores (as do the notes on it) but which formed a major theme of another play in mock-Elizabethan style dating from 1934–35, *The Round Heads and the Pointed Heads* (which had itself developed out of an adaptation of *Measure for Measure* begun before 1933).

For years the three threads of gang warfare, the Ui-Hitler satire, and the elevated Elizabethan style, seem to have lain loosely coiled at the back of Brecht's mind before finally coming together in the spring of 1941. A further element may have been the example of Chaplin's *The Great Dictator*, even though Brecht could hardly yet have seen the actual film. On March 10 he roughed out a plan for ten or eleven scenes; by March 29 the first typescript was complete; after which Margarete Steffin drove him to tighten up the blank verse, another fortnight's work (all this according to his journal). The complete play, virtually in its present form, was ready about a month before the Brechts set out on their trip to the United States, whose imminence had of course helped to prompt it. There is thus much less than usual in the way of alternative scripts and versions, most of the revisions, such as they were, having been made directly on the first typescript. Many of these are primarily concerned with the iambic meter of the verse.

However, it appears that the Cauliflower Trust originally contained another member called Reely, who appeared in lieu of Butcher in scene 2. Dogsborough's first appearance was to have been in his city office, not in the homely surroundings of his restaurant, an amendment on the first script. In scene 3 Ui's first speech was shorter, the present version only having been established since the play's appearance in *Stücke IX* in 1957, when not all Brecht's amendments were available. The first three lines were as now, down to "Is fame in such a place," after which the speech concluded

          Two months without a brawl
    And twenty shoot-outs are forgotten, even
    In our own ranks!

There were also differences in the wording of Roma's speech which follows, though its sense was similar. In scene 6, with the old actor, Ui's and Givola's prose speeches were broken into irregular verse lines, and it was an afterthought to have Ui take over the Mark Antony speech from the actor and deliver most of it solo. The name "Dockdaisy" too was an afterthought; to start with she was simply "Mrs. Bowl" or "the Person." Clark's speech in scene 7, showing the trust's solidarity with Ui and his gang, was added at some point after the first script, together with Ui's ensuing speech down to where Clark is heard to applaud it (pp. 247–48). Then in the trial scene the playing of Chopin's "Funeral March" on the organ was an afterthought on the first script, as were all references to Giri's habit of wearing his murdered victims' hats (which echoes an incident at the beginning of *Happy End*, written in 1929). The first script ends with the woman's speech later shifted to scene 9 (i.e., immediately prior to the interval in the Berliner Ensemble production), this shift having been made after the play's publication in 1957. The epilogue was not in the first script.

When the play was finally staged by Palitzsch and Wekwerth in 1959 further changes were made, which were not included in the published text but were meant to take account of the changed public understanding of the historical background. According to Wekwerth, Brecht himself was long chary of staging this play in view of "the German audience's lack of historical maturity"; he did not allow his younger collaborators to read it until the summer before he died. They had to treat it as confidential, nor was it to be produced until they had first staged *Fear and Misery of the Third Reich* as an introduction to the tragic circumstances which it satirized. Thus warned, and well aware of the type of criticism voiced by Lothar Kusche (p. 458), the two directors now set to work to implicate Dogsborough and the industrialists more closely with Ui and to discourage German audiences from sympathizing with Roma. Ui accordingly was not referred to in scene 1a, and only entered the play once Sheet had refused to sell his shipping business in 1b. Dogsborough's packet of shares was given to him, not sold, while in scene 7 instead of seeming merely passive he was seen actually to give Ui his backing. The episode with Goodwill and Gaffles was cut (pp. 228–30), to be replaced by a new section stressing the involvement of heavy industry. Roma was made to murder the journalist Ted Ragg, and scene 14 with his Banquoesque ghost was omitted; he still, however, emerged as a good deal less unpleasant than Giri and Givola. The name of Chicago was replaced by Capua or Capoha throughout. Finally an extra song was introduced, the "Whitewash Song" from *The Round Heads and the Pointed Heads*, which Givola sang after the interval.

The main interest of the scripts, however, lies rather in the evidence which they give of Brecht's intentions with regard to the play. The title varies: once or twice it is simply *The Rise of Arturo Ui*, while the copy formerly belonging to Elisabeth Hauptmann is headed "*Arturo Ui*. Dramatic Poem. By K. Keuner"—Mr. Keuner (or Mr. Naobody) being the alter ego who features in Brecht's prose aphorisms, as well as figuring as a character in two of the unfinished plays. Elsewhere Brecht referred to *Ui* as "the gangster play," a title which he also tried rendering into English as *The Gangster Play We Know* or again *That Well-known Racket*. There is a table too, giving what he calls "The Parallels," to wit:

Dogsborough = Hindenburg
Arturo Ui = Hitler
Giri = Göring
Roma = Röhm
Givola = Goebbels
Dullfeet = Dollfuss
Cauliflower Trust = Junkers (or East Prussian landowners)
Vegetable dealers = Petty bourgeoisie
Gangsters = Fascists
Dock aid scandal = "Osthilfe" [East Aid] scandal
Warehouse-fire trial = Reichstag-fire trial
Chicago = Germany
Cicero = Austria

—Röhm having been Captain Ernst Röhm, chief of staff of the brownshirted S.A. or main Nazi private army, who was murdered in the "Night of the Long Knives" in June 1934, while the Osthilfe scandal related to a controversial pre-1933 subsidy to the Junkers. There are also slightly varying versions of the historical analogies provided by the projected "inscriptions." Thus in the first script the inscription following scene 4 read:

In January 1933 President Hindenburg more than once refused to appoint Party Leader Hitler as Reich Chancellor. He was, however, nervous of the proposed investigation of the so-called "Osthilfe" scandal. Moreover he had accepted state money for the Neudeck estate that had been presented to him, and failed to use it for its intended objective.

After scene 8, the trial, there was a now-omitted inscription which read:

When Reich Chancellor Schleicher threatened to expose the tax evasions and misappropriation of "Osthilfe" money, Hindenburg on January 30, 1933, gave power to Hitler. The investigation was suppressed.

That after scene 13 read as follows:

The occupation of Austria was preceded by the murder of Engelbert Dollfuss, the Austrian Chancellor. Tirelessly the Nazis continued their efforts to win Austrian sympathies.

—and the final inscription simply:

Perhaps there is something else that could stop him?

Further light on the play's topical meaning is given by the photographs stuck into the pages of Brecht's first script. Scene 2, with Dogsborough, is followed by a portrait of Hindenburg, scene 3 by a drawing of gangsters captioned "Murder Inc." In scene 6, with the old actor, there are four pictures of Hitler in his characteristic attitude with the hands clasped before the private parts, followed by two more with the arms folded and one captioned "Hitler the Orator." A further picture of Hitler speaking precedes the trial scene (8). In scene 10, following Givola's forgery of Dogsborough's will, there is a photograph of Hitler and Goebbels going over a document together, then at the end one of Hitler and Göring shaking hands. Scene 11 (the garage) is preceded by a picture showing Göring and Goebbels in uniform, while in scene 13 (Dullfeet's funeral) there is a photograph of a gangster funeral in Chicago.

ONE-ACT PLAYS AND
PRACTICE PIECES

Text by Brecht

Note [for *How Much Is Your Iron?*]

This little play must be performed in slapstick style. The iron
dealer must have a wig with hair that can be made to stand on
end; the shoes and cigar are enormous. The backdrop should if
possible be plastered with quotations from Scandinavian states-
men.

> ["Anmerkung" to *Was kostet das Eisen*, GW *Stücke*, p.
> 2850.]

Editorial Notes

These two topical one-acters were written in the early summer
of 1939, while the Brechts were living on Lidingö near Stockholm, and are said to have been designed for a left-wing ama-
teur group organized by the actor Hermann Greid. Only the
second was actually performed, with Ruth Berlau as director.
Since Brecht himself was not supposed to take any part in
political activities while living in Sweden, he gave the author's
name as John Kent, an echo of his early "Ballad of Hannah
Cash." The first script, entitled *Little Deals in Iron* (*Kleine*

Geschäfte mit Eisen) was dated by Margarete Steffin "Lidingö
2 vi 1939."

A fragmentary scene suggests that there was to have been a
third playlet, set in the house of Norsen the Norwegian. Dansen and Svendson call to see him, to the sound of thunder and
the glow of a distant fire. He reproaches them with giving in
so easily and failing to make a threefold alliance against the
stranger/customer which would certainly have kept him out.
The stranger/customer then appears wearing a steel helmet,
takes over the meeting and forces them to make an alliance,
but under his protection and in order to carry out his wishes.
The three thereupon shake hands.

Presumably history intervened. The Norsen piece was not
finished, *Dansen* (so far as we know) not performed. None the
less he rounded off the latter with three brief dialogues that
seem to have been designed as a framework for it, introducing
each of the three successive scenes. They go thus:

Two Scandinavians sitting over breakfast.

1

THE OPTIMIST   You are an incorrigible pessimist.

THE PESSIMIST   And you are an incorrigible optimist.

THE OPTIMIST   If only you wouldn't always turn up here
    with your prophecies just as I am sitting having a meal!

THE PESSIMIST   When else am I to turn up? You're always
    sitting having a meal.

THE OPTIMIST   But every time I listen to you I lose my ap-
    petite.

THE PESSIMIST   Mine goes every time I see you.

THE OPTIMIST (*gives an irritated grunt*)

THE PESSIMIST   It's bound to end badly. Look at what has
    happened.

THE OPTIMIST   What has happened?

THE PESSIMIST   Shall I tell you a little story to remind
    you? Eh?

THE OPTIMIST   All right.

2

THE PESSIMIST Was that, or was that not how it was?

THE OPTIMIST An extremely pessimistic view. And a very uncharitable picture of Dansen. Not a word about his undisputed love of freedom, etc., etc.

THE PESSIMIST My dear fellow! I was positively flattering Dansen. Now comes his big moment.

THE OPTIMIST Really? That sounds promising.

THE PESSIMIST Let me just go on with the story.

3

THE OPTIMIST Well?

THE PESSIMIST Well what?

THE OPTIMIST Well, what's wrong with that pact? Suppose I go on with the story this time? I'll show you how the pact is going to work out. You'll be amazed.

THE PESSIMIST I certainly will. Just watch out!

The practice pieces for actors were written the following winter for a class which Helene Weigel was conducting in the Stockholm acting school run by Naima Wifstrand, the actress cast as Mother Courage in the planned Swedish production of that play. Brecht's journal for January 14, 1940, mentions their use of the Macbeth scene as training in the fresh study of Shakespeare. An introductory note in *Versuche 11* (1951), where they were first published, allocated them to the *Messingkauf*, and they were subsequently included in the first German publication of that work. Appended to them were also the catch "A dog went to the kitchen" from *Drums in the Night* (volume 1 of the present edition, pp. 96–7) and the "Contest between Homer and Hesiod," a dialogue in hexameters adapted after the Second World War from a book by Wolfgang Schadewaldt. The pieces themselves however have a quite distinct origin and character, casting fresh light on Brecht's unceasing concern with the Elizabethans.

VINTAGE CRITICISM,
LITERATURE, MUSIC, AND ART

VINTAGE BIOGRAPHY AND AUTOBIOGRAPHY